THE PREHISTORY OF EAST AFRICA

THE PREHISTORY OF EAST AFRICA

by Sonia Cole

Introduction by Richard Carrington

ILLUSTRATED WITH PHOTOGRAPHS, MAPS,
DIAGRAMS, AND DRAWINGS

The Macmillan Company, New York

First Printing

Library of Congress catalog card number: 63-11790

The Macmillan Company, New York
Collier-Macmillan Canada, Ltd., Toronto, Ontario

Printed in the United States of America

DESIGN BY RICHARD A. KASELER

Acknowledgments

For help and advice in writing certain sections of this book, I am most grateful to Dr. A. J. Arkell, Dr. W. W. Bishop, Mr. E. C. Lanning, Dr. M. Posnansky, and Dr. J. S. Weiner.

I should like to thank the following for permission to reproduce their photographs: Dr. L. S. B. Leakey (Plates 2, 3, 4, and 7); Professor J. D. Clark (Plate 5a); Mr. Peter Young (Plate 10).

The following are reproduced by kind permission: Table 2 (Royal Meteorological Society, after G. C. Simpson); Figs. 4 and 12 *Sunday Times*, London); Fig. 8 (British Museum [Natural History]); Fig. 33 (a) and (b) (Editor of the *Proceedings of the Prehistoric Society* after R. Wright); Map 4 (Trustees of the British Museum).

The following figures have been redrawn from photographs: Figs. 1, 33 (c) (A. J. Arkell); Figs. 3, 9, 13 (L. S. B. Leakey); Fig. 54 (G. Smolla); Fig. 58 (E. C. Lanning); Fig. 60 (H. J. Braunholtz); Fig. 6 (adapted from W. W. Bishop and R. Pickering); Map 15 (adapted from M. Posnansky).

Maurice Wilson drew Figs. 4, 8, 12, 14, and 34; Rosemary Powers, Figs. 3, 9, 13, 54, 58, 59, 60; J. A. Hodges, Figs. 6 and 7 and Maps 1, 2, 3, 5, 6, 7, 8, 10, 15.

The plates, figures, and maps not mentioned above are from *The Prehistory of East Africa*, Baltimore, Md., Penguin Books, 1954.

CONTENTS

List of Figures

List of Plates

17

List of Tables

List of Maps

INTRODUCTION

Introduction

The science of prehistory, which attempts to decipher the story of the human family before the appearance of written documents, has now so captured the imagination of the public that it is difficult to realize how recently it has come into being. According to the Oxford English Dictionary, the very word "prehistory" was not coined until 1871—the date of the publication of *The Descent of Man* by Charles Darwin. Even at this time, when the principles of evolution had already been established and accepted by thoughtful men for more than a decade, the great majority of people in the Western world still believed that man was the end product of a six-day creative process. Historians and scholars of high repute fervently maintained the orthodox view, set out in 1658 in Archbishop Ussher's *Annals of the World*, that the earth had been created on Saturday, October 22, 4004 B.C., at eight o'clock in the evening, and that the whole development of man and his works had occurred since that time. It was not until the twentieth century was well advanced that it was even considered by most people that this view might be wrong and that the story of mankind was not represented by an inbuilt hierarchy of perfection with heathens and savages at the bottom and archbishops at the top.

The basic heresy of *The Descent of Man* in the minds of the conventional was, of course, that our species was not a unique product of special creation, but had evolved over vast aeons of time in accordance with the same fundamental principles that had governed the development of the rest of the living world. Man, in fact, was not a fallen angel but a promoted ape. He was simply an exceptionally intelligent member of an order of mammals known as the Primates, which included such humble creatures as lemurs and tarsiers, and the monkeys that our Victorian grandparents were wont to observe with supercilious interest at the zoo.

Between 1871 and today the change in human attitudes toward evolution has been swift and spectacular, and the science of prehistory has been recognized as of vital importance in interpreting the early history of man and his relationship to the universe at large. The fossils of apelike primates and of the ancestors and relations of *Homo sapiens* himself have been discovered in many parts of the world. Similar remains, which had been found before Darwin and Wallace had worked out their evolutionary theory in coherent form, were seen to be not isolated phenomena but pieces in a jigsaw puzzle that, taken in conjunction with later finds, could be fitted into the over-all pattern of human development. At the same time the tools and other material objects used by pre-*sapiens* primates, long known from the researches of antiquarians, took on a new significance. These bones and tools became recognized as essential clues in deciphering the course of human history before the invention of writing.

During the ninety-odd years in which prehistory has grown as a serious science, the focus of interest has moved from one part of the world to another, according to the various discoveries that have been made. The Neanderthaloids of Europe and the Pithecanthropoids of Asia have at different periods mainly occupied the attention of prehistorians. More recently the discovery by Professor Raymond Dart of the man-apes of South Africa, known as Australopithecines, gave a new impetus to our thinking; here at last, it seemed, a group of primates had come to light that might be intermediate between the apes of several million years ago and the sub-men and true men of later times. In the last decade, however, the emphasis has again switched to a new area. East rather than South Africa has come to be regarded as the region in which man went through the earliest stages of his evolutionary development. Largely through the dedicated work of Dr. L. S. B. Leakey of the Coryndon Museum in Nairobi, new fossils and implements have been discovered in Kenya and Tanganyika which support the view that this region was the cradle of mankind. Some of the fossils discovered have been of Australopithecine type, and are still regarded by several authorities as being merely a local variant of the family originally discovered by Dart. But others are more equivocal and, moreover, push the story back far farther in time.

The ferment of intellectual activity which has resulted from these new discoveries makes the appearance of the present book particularly timely. The first edition of Mrs. Cole's *Prehistory of East Africa* appeared in 1954, and was immediately hailed as a remarkably succinct, scholarly, and lively survey of the state of our knowledge of human evolution in East Africa at that time. Since then, however, the new discoveries made in the region have caused radical reassessments to be made concerning the interpretation of the evidence. Moreover, the development of absolute-dating techniques, based on the potassium-argon method for the early part of the story and the carbon-14 method for the later part, have revolutionized our concepts of the time scale in which developments in the region took place. For the first time we have sufficient data to give at least some details of the story based on solid scientific evidence rather than intelligent guesswork.

These exciting developments, which have taken place in such a remarkably short period, mean that Mrs. Cole's book is now much more than a revised reissue of her former work. It has, in fact, been almost totally rewritten and gives the latest picture of our present state of knowledge. Experts will immediately recognize the competence and thoroughness with which the author has reorganized the basic material in the light of the new finds, but, for the sake of those who may be introducing themselves for the first time to this fascinating subject, it may be helpful to give a brief summary of the main discoveries that have led to the radical reorientation of the book.

Of the actual fossils found in the region, four are of major importance. Three of these belong to creatures with very close human affinities, the fourth to a fourteen-million-year-old ape which is very probably close to the true human line of evolution. All the discoveries were made either by Dr. Leakey or members of his family, to whom prehistorians owe an immeasurable debt.

The two most important finds were made, respectively, by his wife and by his son Jonathan. The first occurred in 1959, when Mrs. Leakey noticed a piece of bone being eroded out of a deposit in Olduvai Gorge in Tanganyika, where her husband was conducting excavations. This proved to be the skull of a young male hominid, which was later designated *"Zinjanthropus,"* or, more popularly, "Nutcracker Man," from its formidable teeth. Its status is still in doubt, and many authorities regard it simply as an East African *Australopithecus*. Leakey, however, has maintained that the skull is sufficiently different from that of other Australopithecines to give it generic distinction. This question is still being debated.

The second discovery occurred in 1961, when Jonathan Leakey found the mandible and two parietal bones, also at Olduvai, of a child that seemed to be related to *Zinjanthropus*, although the fossils dated from an earlier period. Again, it has been suggested that this fossil can be ascribed to an existing species of *Australopithecus*, but Leakey believes that it could belong to a quite distinct type of early hominid.

The third fossil with human affinities was discovered by Leakey himself in 1960 at the same site. This was a skull that he believes to have a number of resemblances to the Pithecanthropoids of Asia, but in other respects is more like the Steinheim skull, which itself may be intermediate between the Neanderthalers and *Homo sapiens*.

More recent than any of the above has been the discovery by Leakey in 1962 of two fragments of the upper jaw of an ape at Fort Ternan, in western Kenya. This he has named *"Kenyapithecus wickeri,"* after Mr. F. Wicker, a farmer on whose land the bones were found. It seems possible that this animal was in the direct line of human ancestry, although the fact that it has been dated to a period some fourteen million years ago makes all such assumptions extremely speculative. The significance of the fragments is now being argued out by paleontologists.

The full significance of these finds, and their relevance to the course of human evolution as a whole, is discussed by Mrs. Cole in the pages that follow. Her new material also includes a critical assessment of the dating techniques recently developed by Drs. J. F. Evernden and G. H. Curtis, physicists at the University of California, and a discussion of the recent revolution of ideas on climatic interpretations. Evidence of past climatic changes in East Africa has been subjected to much healthy criticism, and Mrs. Cole ably explains the new techniques which are revising our interpretation of the climatic environment of early man.

In conclusion, a word should be said about the approach to prehistory that has characterized writings in the field in the postwar period. The new emphasis on mass education has tended to produce a spate of books which seem based on the idea that the general reader is still a semi-moronic being who needs to be captivated by purple prose, face-tious academic asides, and a general "jollying along" before he is prepared to absorb any kind of information. It is a privilege to be able to introduce a book that makes no concessions to this essentially old-fashioned approach. The reader with a genuine interest in prehistory will find to his relief that in the following pages the author has treated him as an adult. He will have much hard work to do, but if he pursues the matter to the end he will certainly come to realize that an intelligent articulateness can be far more rewarding than journalistic clichés. I warmly recommend this book to anyone, be he professional student or intelligent layman, who wishes to scent the authentic excitement that prehistorians feel in unraveling the story of man and his origins.

RICHARD CARRINGTON
London, 1962

THE PREHISTORY OF EAST AFRICA

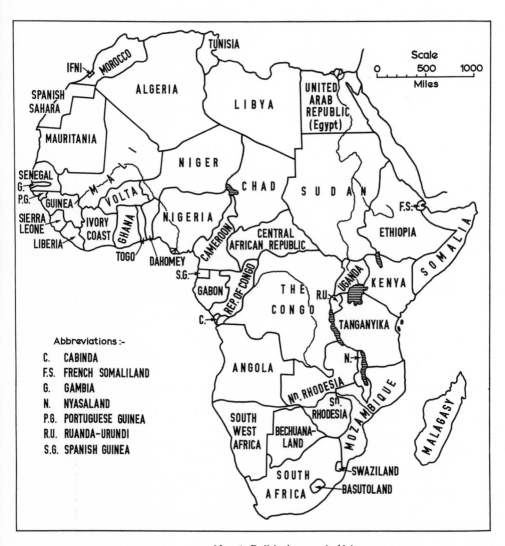

Map 1. Political map of Africa.

Chapter One

INTRODUCING EAST AFRICA

East Africa has been called a land of contrasts. These contrasts are due largely to variations in altitude caused by tremendous upheavals of the earth's crust and intense volcanic activity that affected the distribution of rainfall, soils, plants, and animals, including man.

On a journey westward along the equator from the east coast of Kenya to Uganda, for example, we would encounter an astonishing variety of landscapes. The warm waters of the Indian Ocean lap against coral reefs and mangrove swamps. The narrow coastal plain, leased from the Sultan of Zanzibar, has a climate tolerable to Europeans since it is tempered by sea breezes; here sisal and pineapple plantations are interspersed with coconut palms and gnarled baobab trees. Beyond this belt is hot bush country, much of it uninhabited because of lack of water and the presence of the tsetse fly, which makes cattle-keeping impossible. Farther west again, the equator cuts through the climatically favorable volcanic highlands above 5,000 feet, which support a flourishing population, both black and white. Here stock can be grazed

33

on the plains and agriculture practiced on the rich soils of hillsides.

The eastern branch of the great rift valley cuts a slice through the country from north to south, and west of it the altitude decreases again. Western Kenya is connected more with Uganda, not only in the nature of its modern inhabitants, but also in its cultural connections in pre-historic times. The political boundary between the two countries runs through Mt. Elgon and Victoria Nyanza, a huge, shallow inland sea the size of Ireland and the source of the Nile. The intensely cultivated land typical of western Kenya continues over most of Uganda, though some of the drier steppe country leading to the western rift valley and the Ruwenzori Range is uninhabited. In the southwestern part of Uganda, dense forests, the home of chimpanzees and gorillas, stretch as far as the western branch of the rift valley and on into the Congo.

South of the Kenya highlands and continuing into Tanganyika, vast plains dotted with acacia thorns and euphorbia trees are the home of

Map 2. Main vegetation zones of Africa.

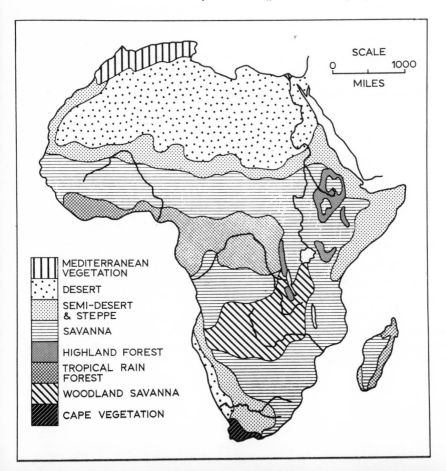

SCALE
0   1000
MILES

MEDITERRANEAN
VEGETATION

DESERT

SEMI-DESERT
& STEPPE

SAVANNA

HIGHLAND FOREST

TROPICAL RAIN
FOREST

WOODLAND SAVANNA

CAPE VEGETATION

all kinds of game. Elephants and rhinos, lions and zebra, wildebeest and gazelles, roam over game reserves secure from the rifle, though unfortunately not by any means secure from the poacher's traps and arrows. This open savanna country must be very much the same as it was over a million years ago, when the earliest hominids* graduated from apelike creatures to humans in this very area. North of the highlands, the low-lying country is again very different; the Northern Province of Kenya, by far the largest part of the country, Somalia, and the Sudan are desert or semidesert. Between the White and the Blue Niles is the Gezira, much of which has been brought under cultivation by extensive irrigation channels. The semidesert country is not always sandy; often it consists of salty or alkaline earth strewn with lava boulders. In places it supports sparse scrub and succulent plants that are able to store up moisture in their fleshy stems. Here nomadic pastoralists herd camels and goats from one water hole to the next, in the same way that their forebears did thousands of years ago.

As a complete contrast to the semidesert country of the rest of the Horn, the highlands of Ethiopia are forested and cultivated, enjoying a plentiful summer monsoon rainfall. The volcanic highlands of Ethiopia and Kenya were thrown up comparatively recently, geologically speaking. Early in the Pleistocene period, when man was already inhabiting the area, East Africa was the scene of tremendous volcanic eruptions and earth movements. These events were responsible for the most spectacular scenery of East Africa today.

The highest mountains are themselves the results of fairly recent volcanic activity. The snow-capped peaks on the equator, which caused such incredulity when they were first described by explorers and missionaries during the middle of the last century, are extinct volcanoes. Kilimanjaro, nearly 20,000 feet high, is the highest mountain in Africa; its highest peak, Kibo, consists of a huge, snow-covered dome, while the lower peak, Mawenzi, is rocky and rugged. Mt. Kenya, which gives its name to the country, was called after the native name for the cock ostrich, whose black and white plumage was thought to resemble the contrasting volcanic rocks and glaciers on the twin

---

* Hominids are members of the family Hominidae, which includes modern and extinct forms of men. Together with apes, they are included in the superfamily Hominoidea (suborder, Anthropoidea, order, Primates).

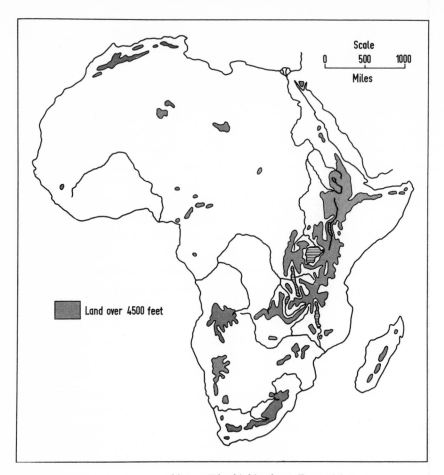

Map 3. The highlands of East Africa.

peaks. The mysterious Ruwenzori Range, on the borders of Uganda and the Congo, is thought to be the "Mountains of the Moon" mentioned by ancient geographers. The slopes of all these mountains are clothed in valuable forests; above the forest belt are moorlands, on which grow fantastic giant groundsels and lobelias up to 20 feet in height. Here live endemic bird species separated from others of their kind by hundreds of miles. This must mean that in former times, when the climate was colder and wetter, moorlands and forests extended farther down the slopes and once covered lower mountains in between.

Apart from the mountains, the most spectacular feature of East Africa is the Great Rift Valley. This immense gash in the earth's crust was formed along a line of weakness stretching from the Jordan to the Zambezi, including the Red Sea and the Gulf of Aden. Most of its course is marked by a chain of lakes, where Stone Age man camped to hunt animals as they came down to drink. A series of small lakes lines the floor of the Danakil Rift in Ethiopia; farther south, the Omo River continues along the rift into the largest lake of the eastern branch of the rift, Lake Rudolf. In Kenya, most of the lakes are saline and shallow, often pink with flamingos, though Naivasha is a fresh-water lake. Lake Magadi, in southern Kenya, has extensive deposits of soda, which form one of the most valuable mineral assets of the country. North of Lake Nyasa, the eastern branch of the rift is joined by the western branch, marked by Lakes Albert, Edward, Kivu, and Tanganyika.

The rift valley averages 40 miles across and its floor lies about 1,500 feet below the general level of the surrounding country. It is an area of internal drainage, with intermittent streams flowing from the escarpments into the shallow lakes. Many of the lake basins are separated from one another by extinct volcanoes. As a reminder that volcanic activity has not yet ceased, steam jets and hot springs issue from the sides of these mountains and from the walls of the rift valley in a number of places.

The People of East Africa

The native inhabitants of East Africa fall into three main groups: Nilotic, Hamitic, and Bantu (Map 4). Strictly speaking, the last two terms are linguistic, but there are also great differences in the appearance and cultures of the Hamitic-speakers and Bantu-speakers. The Nilotic Negroes of the Sudan, Uganda, and western Kenya, such as the Dinka, Nuer, and Luo, have mixed to a certain extent with the Hamites, so that they differ from the Negroes of West Africa. The Dinka and Nuer, who are among the tallest people in the world, live on the swampy plains of the southern Sudan, but the Luo tribes are scattered over a wide area in Uganda and along the eastern shores of Lake Victoria in Kenya.

Between the Nilotes to the west and the Hamites to the east are certain Nilo-Hamitic tribes who have a great deal of Hamitic blood and look very different from true Negroes. They are generally lighter in color, with finer features and an aristocratic demeanor. In the north, to the east of the Nile, are the Bari; a central group between Lakes Kioga and Rudolf includes the Lango, Karamojong, and Turkana; farther south, in the highlands of Kenya and northern Tanganyika, are

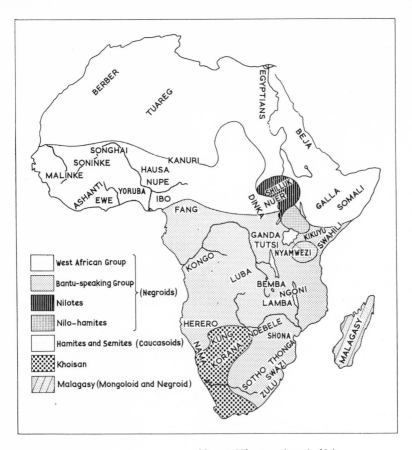

Map 4. The peoples of Africa.

the Suk, Nandi, and Masai. They are pastoral and semi-nomadic and in the past were much feared for their warlike tendencies; the Masai and Nandi especially were the terror of Bantu tribes, Arabs, and Europeans alike.

The Eastern Hamites of the Horn, belonging to the Ethiopian branch of the Caucasoid race, include among many others the Kushitic-speaking Somali of Somaliland, eastern Ethiopia, and northeastern Kenya; and the Galla of southwestern Ethiopia. The Somali are nomadic, keeping camels, cattle, goats, and sheep, while the Galla are agricultural as well. The tribes of Ethiopia are legion; they are said to speak over 70 languages, including Amharic, the Semitic language of the emperor.

The most numerous group in eastern Africa are the Bantu, a word which means simply, "people." These Negroids extend from Uganda and southern Kenya down to the south of the continent, and speak a great many dialects, all of which are connected. It is thought that the spread of knowledge of food production and ironworking may both be connected with the expansion of the Bantu. The tribal origins of these people may stretch back no farther than 2,000 years; but many of the present tribes were organized only during the sixteenth century, after the Galla invasions. The Bantu are essentially agriculturalists, though most of them also own stock. The tribes are too numerous to enumerate, but among the best known are the Ganda and the Kikuyu.

When Europeans first ventured inland, just over a hundred years ago, they found the indigenous population of East Africa using crude iron tools and practicing a very primitive economy. Some cultivated cereals and other plants, which quickly ripened in rich soil under the tropical sun, at the cost of very little effort on the part of the planters. Others grazed stock in drier, tsetse-free areas, or combined pastoral and agricultural activities. A hoe, or more often a digging stick (for iron hoes were the subject of many taboos), served very well for breaking up the soil, so that the plow was unnecessary. Only the Galla of the Horn used the plow before the coming of Europeans (Pliny mentions the "Ploughmen Aethiopians"). While agriculture was essentially women's work, stock was the concern of the male and the apple of his eye. Domestic animals were seldom used for food except on ceremonial occasions, though they were of course milked, and some tribes drained blood from a vein in the neck for food. They were never used as beasts of burden, for the human back (generally female) was all that was required in the way of transport. Wheeled transport, probably introduced into Egypt by the Hyksos or Shepherd Kings about 1600 B.C., never penetrated south of the Sudan. Rock engravings all over the Sahara depict carts, but they were unknown in Black Africa.

Apart from its geographical isolation, caused by the Sahara and the Nile swamps, the mental stagnation of most of Africa may be largely due to climatic and biological causes. A hot climate tends to discourage much effort, though obviously this is not an insuperable obstacle to progress—one has only to think of Egypt or India. The energies of the inhabitants of East Africa were absorbed by endless internecine warfare and by intense preoccupation with witchcraft and superstition. The natives were also busy contending with big game and fighting the ravages of insect-borne diseases. Diseases must certainly have sapped the vitality of East African peoples in the remote past, just as the present-day tribes are affected profoundly by them, in spite of modern drugs. The lethargy of the inhabitants of East Africa after Stone Age times, then, may be accounted for, paradoxically, by a climate that made the satisfaction of elementary needs too easy, insect pests that made anything more too difficult, and geographical isolation that prevented the stimulus of fresh ideas from penetrating, whether by competition or invasion.

The Importance of East African Prehistory

In the earliest times, East Africa was by no means the cultural back-water that it became later. It seems, on the other hand, to have been a center of evolutionary progress and an area of movement; later it became a passageway for migrants to Europe and Asia. As the ice retreated at various times during the Pleistocene period, people of African origin may have penetrated into Europe and then moved back into the more hospitable tropics as the climate again began to deteriorate.

Long before anything was known of man's ancestors in Africa, Darwin shrewdly remarked, "It is somewhat more probable that our early progenitors lived on the African continent than elsewhere." It has now been shown that his words, as a prophecy of facts collected very recently, were remarkably true. Twenty million years ago there was a great variety of apes living in western Kenya and eastern Uganda, which makes it seem probable that this area was their main evolutionary center. Kenya has, in fact, yielded the earliest ape skull known from anywhere in the world, which has shed considerable light on problems of man's remote ancestry.

This period of tremendous radiation of the apes began during the Miocene period, from about 25 million to 12 million years ago. The succeeding Pilocene period in almost the whole of Africa is a complete blank; this is most unfortunate, as it seems certain that it was during this time that our ancestors left the forests, probably because of increasing desiccation, and took to moving about on their hind legs in more open country. By the time we meet them next, during the early part of the Pleistocene, over a million years ago, they were making good use of their hands.

Within the last few years, East Africa has become the focus of attention for all students of human evolution. Dr. Leakey's famous "Zinjanthropus," and the somewhat earlier "pre-Zinjanthropus" from

Olduvai Gorge in northern Tanganyika, are among the first toolmaking hominids, the most ancient members of our own family. Geological evidence leaves little doubt that they are older than the well-known Australopithecines of South Africa (though a specimen from the Lake Chad area is probably somewhat earlier).

Olduvai Gorge, in the Serengeti Plains just to the west of the eastern branch of the rift valley, is unrivaled in importance anywhere in the world for evidence of man's early development. Its sides are stratified in layers like a slice of cake; and, to change the metaphor, the story told in those layers can be read almost as clearly as the pages of a history book by those who know how. The deposits contain quantities of fossil mammals and stone tools, unfolding in a gradual evolutionary sequence from bottom to top. Olduvai, in fact, is an essential framework not only to early East African prehistory but to world prehistory.

In the lowest bed of the gorge, Bed I, recent excavations have exposed the actual spots where *Zinjanthropus* and his predecessors squatted to eat their meals, scattering around them a circle of rubbish in the form of chipped pebbles and bones cracked with these crude but quite efficacious tools. At this stage, the hominids could not manage to kill the huge herbivores that shared their environment. Their way of life must have been little different from that of a troop of baboons, constantly foraging for vegetable food and seldom enjoying the luxury of meat. But they had one enormous advantage over baboons: their forelimbs and hands were not tied to the ground.

After Bed I times at Olduvai, a large proportion of mammals became extinct, just as they did at the end of the Lower Pleistocene in other continents. A few continued almost or entirely unchanged right through to the end of the Middle Pleistocene, represented by Bed IV; these included both close relations of modern forms and also many gigantic and fantastic beasts that died out after this time. Some of them are new to science and were first described at Olduvai. Not only are they of tremendous interest in themselves, but they also enable us to picture early man's environment and give new insight into his skill as a hunter.

By the time of formation of Bed II at Olduvai, man the scavenger had become man the hunter. He had learned to work in groups, and presumably this implies that he communicated with his fellows in some form of language more advanced than grunts. Packs of wolves, of course, had learned the principles of cooperation millions of years before, and group hunting in itself is nothing new; but whereas it is an essential in the way of life of carnivores, it was something that had to be learned by the predominantly vegetarian primates. Although primates could never compete with the carnivores in swiftness, they relied on something far more significant: intelligence.

Plate 1. Skull of Chellean Man found in 1960 at Bed II, Olduvai.

A skull from Bed II, Olduvai, generally known as "Chellean Man,"* has a sizable braincase rather more advanced than that of *Pithecanthropus* from Peking, but still a long way from that of the modern *Homo sapiens*. The gap between the Australopithecines of Bed I and the Pithecanthropines of Bed II seems to be of the order of about a million years—if potassium-argon dating can be relied upon, which, at present, is anything but certain—and, at first sight, progress during this long period appears to have been relatively small. This apparent stagnation seems astonishing compared with the extraordinary strides made by man later on, an acceleration due to culture, which is, of course, unique in the animal world. In the evolution of other vertebrates, however, a million years is a very short space of time, and regarded in this context—the purely anatomical rather than the cultural—the expansion of man's brain between Bed I and Bed II times is phenomenal.

* Named from the earlier Chellean stage of the Lower Paleolithic Chelles-Acheul culture, which is characterized by crude hand axes and was originally found at Chelles and St. Acheul, France.

The *"Zinjanthropus"* level in Bed I was dated recently, at the University of California, by the new potassium-argon method to 1.7 million years. Conflicting results have been obtained for lava *underlying* Bed I, one of them younger than the date for the bed itself. The differences are not so grave as they might seem and will no doubt be resolved when the technique overcomes its teething troubles. At least they make it probable that *"Zinjanthropus"* is more than a million years old rather than a mere 600,000 years, as had been allotted to him previously on the basis of informed guesswork. A potassium-argon date of 360,000 years for the Chellean skull from Bed II is quite satisfactory, because it agrees with the presumed age of Peking Man and of Europe's oldest human remains, a jaw from Mauer, near Heidelberg, both attributed to the time of the Second or Mindel Glaciation, which has been dated by potassium-argon at a number of different localities to around 400,000 years.

The implications of the potassium-argon dating of Bed I are enormous. Previous results obtained by this method from samples of volcanic rocks in North America and elsewhere had already suggested that the length of the Pleistocene, which had usually been quoted as a million years, must be at least doubled. The Olduvai dates not only support this conclusion, but they also make it likely that the age of the hominids themselves must be doubled, perhaps even trebled. This is a great relief, for the age hitherto alloted to man was embarrassingly short for such a precocious creature.

At Olduvai, the Chelles-Acheul hand-ax culture can be seen to evolve out of the simple pebble tools of Bed I and continues to develop through various evolutionary stages until the end of Bed IV. Although named after classic sites in France, Western Europe was apparently a mere outpost of the Chelles-Acheul, whose makers roamed over the whole of Africa, southwestern Asia, and parts of India. Eastern Africa, in fact, seems to have been the center of this culture.

Greater concentrations of hand axes—which continued for about 300,000 years with only minor changes in technique and design—have been found in East Africa than anywhere else in the world, not excluding the famous sites of the Somme Valley. Acheulian hand axes and cleavers, probably used mainly for chopping meat and skinning game, are the most spectacular and best-known implements of these times, but they were by no means the only ones. In fact, they formed quite a small proportion of the tool kit, which included also various kinds of scrapers,

knives, and other flake tools, as well as picks and stone balls. Little can
be learned from mere concentrations of one kind of implement, but a
good deal can be learned from the distribution of different kinds of
tools, evidently related to specialized activities. From recent excavations
of actual occupation floors at such sites as Olorgesailie in the Kenya Rift
Valley, Isimila, in the southern highlands of Tanganyika, and Kalambo
Falls, on the border between Tanganyika and Northern Rhodesia, we
are beginning to get this kind of evidence.

Man's choice of lake shores for his camps has meant that his equipment has been preserved in exactly the same position, where it was
discarded many thousands of years ago. Instead of being transported

Plate 2. Olorgesailie, an Acheulian site in the Kenya Rift Valley.

and scattered by rivers, as generally happened at early Paleolithic sites in Europe, the tools and bones were gently covered with sediments as increased rainfall brought a rise in lake level. When the lake receded once more, as a result of desiccation, later bands of hunters occupied the newly exposed shore; and so in East Africa we often find a succession of living floors of different ages, something that is very rare in the study of early prehistory.

Kalambo Falls is a particularly exciting site, for its waterlogged deposits have preserved quantities of vegetable material, including a number of wooden tools; fruits and nuts eaten by the hand-ax makers; and pollen grains, which give a good idea of the nature of the vegetation and hence climate of the time. A carbon-14 date of about 55,000 B.C. has been obtained for the final Acheulian at Kalambo. As in the case of potassium-argon, carbon-14 dates of this magnitude—near the backward limit of the method—must be treated with reservation. But even if this date is only very approximately correct, it is still of immense significance.

The Acheulian of Africa had been thought to be contemporary with its counterpart in Europe, which coincides approximately with the Third or Riss Glaciation and the preceding Great Interglacial. From the Kalambo date, however, it seems that the Acheulian of Africa continued into the early part of the Last or Würm Glaciation. The fact that hand-ax industries should have survived so long in Africa compared with Europe is almost as astonishing as the knowledge that they started so early. It is no exaggeration to say that the Olduvai and Kalambo dates are the cornerstones around which is built the whole structure of the early prehistory of Africa south of the Sahara.

In the future, we may expect a succession of absolute dates based on potassium-argon for the early part of the Pleistocene (the principles of this method are mentioned on p. 123), and on carbon-14 for the later part, though there is an unfortunate gap in the middle not yet adequately covered by any of the present techniques. Mention must be made, however, of a little-known method with strict limitations but which may prove useful under the special circumstances of the rift valley. This is the obsidian method, which can be used to date artifacts made of this volcanic glass, a material much used by Stone Age peoples of East Africa and traded over long distances. Obsidian is an unstable mineral that solidifies very rapidly before crystallization has had time to take place. In order to reach stability, it absorbs water on all newly fractured or flaked surfaces. A "layer of hydration" is formed, which contains ten times as much water as the interior of the rock. This layer has a higher refractive index and a greater density and can be seen through the microscope under polarized light as a luminescent band. The rate of hydration differs according to the temperature of the surroundings, but this can be worked out for different areas. After approximately a hundred years, the layer will be one micron (0.001 mm.) thick. When the layer reaches a certain thickness, it is spalled off, thus limiting the effective dating range to about 200,000 years.[1] Artifacts of an evolved stage of the Middle Stone Age Stillbay culture in Kenya have been dated by the obsidian method to about

33,000 years, but the archaeological evidence suggests that this may be too old (see p. 204).

As yet there are pitifully few absolute dates for East African prehistory, still fewer that have been confirmed independently by other results. In the meantime, older methods of relative dating cannot be neglected, and Olduvai more than any other site can supply answers to the vexed questions of correlation that have plagued geologists and archaeologists in Africa for so long. Its abundance of fauna and artifacts will provide material for detailed studies and comparisons for many years to come.

Early attempts to build a chronology on climatic changes during the Pleistocene served their purpose quite well in the absence of anything better; but it is now realized that the situation is far more complex than was thought. The suggested equivalents of pluvial periods in the tropics with glacials in higher latitudes, and of interpluvials and interglacials, may be broadly true, but much work remains to be done on the details.

Apart from the hominid remains from Bed I, Olduvai, and the Pithecanthropine skull from Bed II, East Africa has produced few early human remains. The only skeletal material believed to be associated with an Acheulian industry are skull fragments from Kanjera, in western Kenya. They are still one of the greatest puzzles in the story of fossil man, owing to their completely modern appearance. This goes against all other evidence, which shows that before the appearance of *Homo sapiens* some 30,000 to 40,000 years ago, man had robust, projecting brow ridges, whereas the Kanjera foreheads are quite smooth. The Kalambo date has done something toward making the suggested age of the Kanjera skulls and their associated Acheulian industry more acceptable; but even if we regard them as no more than about 55,000 years old, they would still be the earliest true *Homo sapiens* in the world.

A quite new interpretation of an even more controversial fossil, a jaw from Kanam, close to Kanjera, makes it probable that this individual was not an impossibly early *Homo sapiens* from the Lower Pleistocene, as had been supposed, but fairly close to Rhodesian Man and the comparable Neanderthalers of the Upper Pleistocene.

Although the bones of early man are rare in East Africa—as indeed they are anywhere—his tools are ubiquitous. Up till the end of Acheulian times, the industries of East Africa are almost exactly like their counterparts elsewhere; but afterward there were distinctive local variations, with specialized equipment to suit different environments such as forest and savanna. Man spread into new areas and expanded both geographically and technologically.

In order to avoid confusion with implications attached to the terms Lower, Middle, and Upper Paleolithic, African cultures are grouped as Earlier, Middle, and Later Stone Age, abbreviated to E.S.A., M.S.A., and L.S.A. The Lower Paleolithic, up to the end of the Acheulian, is comparable with the E.S.A., though apparently the latter survived in Africa considerably later than the Lower Paleolithic of Europe. The Middle Paleolithic is associated mainly with the Mousterian flake culture of Neanderthal Man; and in Africa the rather similar early M.S.A. industries were made by the type represented by Rhodesian Man. A few of the later M.S.A. cultures of Africa, such as the Stillbay, are more like the Upper Paleolithic cultures of Europe. The L.S.A. began only a few thousand years B.C.—by which time the Upper Paleolithic had been succeeded by the Mesolithic in Europe and the Middle East—and continued until quite recent times in many areas.

The Mesolithic stage implies a more settled way of life, often based on fishing. In eastern Africa a few examples of typically "Mesolithic" communities are known, such as the Nile fishermen of Khartoum, those of Ishango on Lake Edward, and the Upper Kenya Capsians of the eastern rift-valley lakes. Unlike their predecessors, these latter people buried their dead carefully instead of throwing them to hyenas. This praiseworthy custom has meant that entire skeletons have been found— for the first time in East African prehistory—and we know very well what these people looked like. They were tall and longheaded, almost indistinguishable skeletally from Mediterranean Caucasoids and from the Hamitic peoples of the Horn. The Khartoum fishermen, on the other hand, are among the earliest recognizable Negroids in Africa. Their other claim to fame is that they may have been the inventors of pottery. The Ishangian fishers of Lake Edward, described by their discoverer as Proto-Bushmanoid with Negroid affinities, may have invented the bone harpoon, presumably quite independently from the Magdalenians of Europe. Unfortunately there are no firm dates for these interesting "Mesolithic" cultures as yet, though it seems likely that they flourished about 8000–6000 B.C.

From this rapid survey of some of the main trends, it will be apparent that the importance of East Africa in the study of world prehistory lies essentially in the Earlier Stone Age. This certainly does not imply that all the later prehistory of East Africa is unimportant or dull, but merely that we have not yet found the means of interpreting the evidence. When we have a solid foundation of absolute dates, we may expect some surprises. We may find that inventions credited to peoples in other parts of the world in fact originated in Africa, as seems more than likely in the case of pottery.

If we are to be completely honest, however, it must be admitted that such surprises are not likely to be very numerous. It is rather the fashion nowadays to make excuses for the negligible contributions to civilization made by the inhabitants of Africa other than Egypt; to take a different view and concede their backwardness compared with the rest of the world is to invite being labeled a racist or an imperialist. One writer at least has recently had the courage to express such an opinion; the theme of his article is conservation, and he describes some very successful experiments in ranching antelopes and other wild ungulates in Southern Rhodesia and South Africa. "It is much to the discredit of the African native that he has not long ago domesticated this splendid animal [the eland]. . . . No contribution to the arts of civilization has come out of Africa south of the Sahara, which has produced nothing but destruction and ruinous exploitation of its natural resources."[2]

The Egyptians, of course, made various attempts to tame many kinds of wild animals, as we know from tomb paintings such as the delightful one from Beni Hasan showing oryxes being fed. But apart from not absolutely certain evidence of domesticated goats in the Sudan during the fourth millennium B.C., there are few indications of stockkeeping in sub-Saharan Africa before the Iron Age, which started at various times during the first millennium A.D. in different areas; and the evidence for agriculture is equally nebulous. A Neolithic stage, in fact, is generally absent (or at least cannot be distinguished), and there was also no Bronze Age in Africa, apart from Egypt.

Tremendous strides have been made in unraveling East African prehistory during the past few years, but the number of problems as yet unresolved presents a fascinating challenge for the future. In the meantime, it now seems certain that for the interpretation of the first million years of man's existence, East Africa is unique.

Pioneer Prehistorians

The study of East Africa's prehistory has been undertaken only comparatively recently and there is certainly a very great deal awaiting discovery. When it is remembered that the problem has been tackled sporadically only during the past 40 years, and that large-scale excavations have been launched over only the past 5 years or so, the amount of facts already at our disposal is really remarkable. This is due to the untiring efforts of a mere handful of men who have gradually collected evidence and undertaken excavations, initially in their spare time and without financial aid.

Fred Hoyle, reviewing the work of two other great astronomers, wrote, "Science has scope within its terms of reference not only for the vital details of Eddington but also for the broad perspective of Jeans." In Africa there have been a few notable historians who have not only supplied the details but have attempted the broad perspective. Elsewhere in the same article Hoyle asks, "Should we be content to work out each detail separately in the hope that all the details will eventually combine together into a coherent whole? Or should we boldly construct a general theory in spite of the admitted imperfections of present-day knowledge?"[3] Surely the second is as important as the first, and the two should be tackled simultaneously. Eventually the mass of incoherent detail has to be sifted if we are to gain anything from it. Therefore, while admitting that more detailed evidence is badly needed, no apology is made for advancing theories concerning East Africa's past. Even if future research proves some of them to be wrong, they will be of interest historically in presenting a picture of what is still only the pioneer stage of East African prehistory.

The first East African territory to receive archaeological attention was Uganda, where E. J. Wayland worked on the cultural succession and past climatic changes during spare time from his duties as the Director of the Geological Survey soon after the First World War. He recognized several distinct cultures, including the "Kafuan" pebble culture (now no longer accepted as being of human workmanship), the Sangoan, and the Magosian, which he named after type sites on the Kafu River, Sango Bay, on the shores of Lake Victoria, and a water hole known as Magosi, in Karamoja. In the absence of fossil fauna as a means of dating cultures, Wayland suggested using the evidence which he found of changes of climate during the Pleistocene period for correlation with other areas. Alternating periods of pluvial and arid conditions in Uganda might eventually, he hoped, be linked with European glacial and interglacial phases, though this theory was put forward very cautiously and with repeated warnings against drawing premature conclusions. The earliest "pluvial" he named the Kageran, after the Kagera River, and attributed it to the Lower Pleistocene.

Accounts of Wayland's discoveries have been published in his *Annual Reports of the Geological Survey of Uganda* and other journals. T. P. O'Brien (1939) attempted the first summary of the prehistory of Uganda; and the South African archaeologist, Professor C. van Riet Lowe (1952), published the first detailed account of the cultural sequence. It was concerned especially with Nsongezi, on the Kagera River, Uganda's most important prehistoric site, discovered by Wayland in 1930. Unfortunately Part I of this memoir (*Geology*, by Wayland) has not yet appeared, but much progress in the interpretation of Uganda's past has been made in the last few years by the geologist W. W. Bishop and the archaeologist M. Posnansky.

In 1926, L. S. B. Leakey first began the systematic investigation of the Stone Age cultures of Kenya. He was born and brought up in Kenya and returned there soon after graduating from Cambridge University. Eventually he became curator of the Coryndon Museum, Nairobi, a post which he held until 1961. During his first East African archaeological expedition in 1926, he started work in the Naivasha-Nakuru lake basins of the rift valley and soon realized that the problem of past climatic changes was going to be of fundamental importance to his archaeological study. In this work he was helped by Wayland and later by E. Nilsson, a Swedish geologist who was investigating the Kenya Rift Valley independently. They noticed traces of ancient terraces high above the levels of the present lakes, and came to the conclusion that these were left, not by a gradually dwindling lake, but by lakes that fluctuated as a result of a series of climatic oscillations.

During his pioneer trek across Masai country in 1893, that great geologist J. W. Gregory had observed that a large lake must have existed in the rift valley to account for the vast deposits of diatomite which had accumulated in the area of the Kamasian escarpment west of Lake Baringo and elsewhere. He dated this Kamasian lake to the Miocene period, but Leakey found hand axes actually embedded in these lake deposits and so realized that they were in fact of Pleistocene age. Thus it was that Gregory's name "Kamasian" was adopted to denote a so-called pluvial period in the Kenya Rift Valley; the second in the series, following Wayland's "Kageran." Later, Leakey subdivided this pluvial into two, calling the later one Kanjeran after lake deposits at Kanjera, near the Kavirondo Gulf of Lake Victoria. The latest pluvial period, called the Gamblian, was attributed on the evidence of the fauna that it contained to the Upper Pleistocene, and two postpluvial wet phases, the Makalian and Nakuran, were also distinguished. As a result of the recognition of these pluvial periods in East Africa, the idea of a climatic sequence for the Pleistocene was developed and elaborated; on this framework a means of dating human cultures was built up which became standard throughout the whole of Africa. Recent work has shown, however, that at any rate the earlier part of this climatic scheme is of limited value for correlation purposes, and criticisms of the evidence are discussed in the next chapter.

In 1931 Leakey's book *The Stone Age Cultures of Kenya Colony* was published. In this he recognized the existence in Kenya of the hand-ax culture, a flake culture, a blade-and-burin culture, as well as so-called "Mesolithic" and "Neolithic" industries. Clearly much had been achieved within the space of five years. He had unearthed skeletal remains not only of "Upper Paleolithic," "Mesolithic," and "Neolithic" peoples, but soon he was to discover early human remains at Kanam and Kanjera, in western Kenya, which he believed dated from the Lower and Middle Pleistocene; these finds Leakey described in *The Stone Age Races of Kenya*, published in 1935.

The study of prehistory in Tanganyika was not properly begun until 1931, although as early as 1913 the late Dr. Hans Reck, a German geologist, discovered a skeleton at Olduvai Gorge which he believed to be contemporary with Middle Pleistocene deposits. He later found burial mounds in Ngorongoro Crater that contained skeletons as well as stone bowls and beads. Although Reck had collected fossil fauna from Olduvai, he had found no Stone Age implements there. In 1931 and 1932 Leakey visited the gorge, one of the objects being to settle the age of the Olduvai skeleton. During this expedition he collected the first hand axes from this remarkable site, which proved to be the richest and most important in the whole of East Africa. Between 1932 and 1935, Leakey made several other expeditions to Olduvai and collected a wealth of archaeological and fossil material.

He also settled the question of the age of the Olduvai skeleton (it was "Upper" Pleistocene and had been buried into earlier deposits). Within the last few years he has been able to excavate at Olduvai on a huge scale, thanks mainly to grants from America, and his finds have revolutionized our knowledge of early man.

In 1935, the German L. Kohl-Larsen found fragments of a highly specialized human skull near the shores of Lake Eyasi, not far from Olduvai. Its peculiarities led H. Weinert to create a new genus for this fossil—*Africanthropus*—though this name was soon abandoned. There seems little doubt that Eyasi Man should be regarded as a near relation of Rhodesian Man, whose skull had been turned up by a mining company at Broken Hill in 1921.

It was not until some time after the discovery of Rhodesian Man that much attention was paid to the question of his dating by means of associated fauna and industries. It now seems that his remains are roughly contemporary with the Eyasi skull, dating from the early part of the Later (Upper) Pleistocene.

Although the Rhodesias are not treated in this book, they cannot be neglected entirely, since it is essential to link up evidence from East Africa with adjacent areas. The important region of Northern Rhodesia, connecting South Africa—the prehistory of which has been fairly well known for many years—with East Africa proper, was practically unknown from the archaeological point of view until the outbreak of the Second World War. Although some pioneer work had been done both in Northern and Southern Rhodesia, by Neville Jones and A. L. Armstrong, the relative ages of the cultures they discovered were unknown. During 1939 and 1940, however, the archaeologist J. D. Clark, curator of the Rhodes Livingstone Museum in Livingstone (and now at the University of California), H. B. S. Cooke, and F. Dixey, geologists from South Africa and London, respectively, managed to build up a climatic and cultural sequence for the Upper Zambezi Valley that was of the utmost importance, and was found to be applicable for the whole of the Rhodesias. For more than 50 years the Zambezi Gorge near Victoria Falls had been noted for the profusion of Paleolithic implements found in its gravels, yet until 1939 no proper sequence had been established. Just as in East Africa past climatic changes were found to be helpful in dating archaeological material, so in the Rhodesias the correlation of prehistoric cultures hinged largely on successive advances and retreats of Kalahari sands, as a result of climatic fluctuations; these phases have been interpreted largely through the work of the geologist G. Bond of the National Museum of Bulawayo, in Southern Rhodesia.

Both in Northern Rhodesia, where his important excavations at Kalambo Falls have already been mentioned, and in the Horn of Africa, J. D. Clark was responsible for filling in the immense gaps in our knowledge of the prehistory of the peripheral areas of East Africa proper. During two and a half years of war service in Ethiopia and Somalia, he succeeded in collecting an amazing amount of new detailed evidence and also furnished a "broad perspective" of the climatic and cultural succession in this area. Surface finds had been collected in the Horn over many years, including much material found by Seton-Karr from 1897 onward, in British Somaliland. At Issutugan, 90 miles southwest of Berbera, Seton-Karr found "Acheulio-Levalloisian" artifacts which are still the most ancient known from the Horn. Other collections in British Somaliland were made by C. Barrington-Brown (1929–30), in the northeast, and by A. T. Curle (1931), on the plateau around Hargeisa.

The de Bourg de Bozas expedition to Italian Somaliland (1901) brought back a very large collection of implements, from about 40 surface sites, which were eventually described by the late Abbé Breuil and Harper Kelley in 1936. The late Father Teilhard de Chardin investigated sites in French Somaliland and also in Abyssinia, near Dire Dawa and Harar, in 1928–29. He found important sites between Obok, on the French Somaliland coast, and Mt. Mabla. He also excavated a trial trench in a painted rock shelter known as Porc Epic near Dire Dawa; this work was continued in 1930 by Breuil and P. Wernert.

Owing to the wealth of later archaeological material in the Sudan, few interested themselves in the early prehistory of this area; but during his time as Commissioner for Archaeology and Anthropology to the Sudan Government from 1938 to 1948 (excluding four years of war service), A. J. Arkell discovered many Paleolithic sites that had remained unnoticed until then. He also excavated an interesting Mesolithic site at Khartoum and a Neolithic site at Esh Shaheinab.

The western boundaries of our area are with the Congo, so that this area too is of importance in tracing cultural influences. Collections of stone implements from the surface were made in very early days in the Belgian Congo, starting in 1891. In 1901, V. Jacques described the "Haas Collection," and two years later he published a comparative study of the relative ages of material discovered up to that time. It was not until 1926, however, that the first excavations were undertaken in the country, by Jean Colette at Kalina, near Leopold-ville. From material found at Kalina he recognized "Middle" and "Upper" Paleolithic stages, as well as "Mesolithic" and "Neolithic". Although some of the terms he used to describe these cultures have been abandoned, Colette established a framework for the prehistory of the Congo, based on implements found *in situ* in stratified deposits. Previously (1925), the German O. Menghin had classified the whole of material of various ages collected from the surface at Tumba and other areas in the western Congo as "Tumbian." This term was abandoned at last and replaced by "Sangoan" (after Wayland's site in Uganda), as the result of collections made by F. Cabu in the Belgian Congo, sorted with the help of the Abbé Breuil and Professor C. van Riet Lowe in South Africa. More recently, the work of three geologists —L. Cahen, J. Lepersonne, and G. Mortelmans—made possible an interpretation of the Pleistocene stratigraphy and climatic phases in the Congo; these were linked up with archaeological finds, many of which have been made lately by another Belgian geologist, J. de Heinzelin de Braucourt. In Ruanda Urundi, J. Hiernaux, a physical anthropologist, has recently made important advances in knowledge of the later prehistory of East Africa, in particular the beginnings of the Iron Age.

Chapter Two

THE GEOLOGICAL BACKGROUND

Man is so dependent on his environment that we cannot begin to understand his habits and mode of life without studying the many factors that affected, and indeed created it. Environment depends basically on climate and geology, which together determine the nature of the soil and vegetation and hence the animals that live in each particular area.

The direct effects of climate on man are seen most clearly during the Pleistocene period in Europe, when successive advances and retreats of the ice had a profound influence over his movements. Although man is the most adaptable of all animals, if it had not been for his discovery of the use of fire he could not have survived in parts of Europe where he is known to have lived during the severe climate of the Last Glaciation. It was obviously no easy task to make fire and to keep it going in early times, and probably it was used only when altitude and climate made it essential. If he had not made this revolutionary discovery, man would have been forced to move, along with

56

most of his fellow animals, away from the advancing ice. After he had learned to control fire, however, he could take shelter in caves and cook such cold-loving beasts as remained, particularly those that nature had provided with woolly coats. So in Europe for nearly a million years, glacial periods and interglacials modified the soil, vegetation, and fauna, and inevitably affected the habits and distribution of man himself.

To a certain extent, though far less profoundly, man in East Africa was affected by successive pluvial and interpluvial periods during the Pleistocene. That there were times when the climate was wetter than it is today, and other times when it was drier, is not disputed; it is the intensity of these changes that is questionable. It has been suggested that "the cumulative effects of either of these conditions [pluvial and arid phases] could have done no more than decrease the human population without destroying it or driving it away";[4] on the evidence available, this seems a very reasonable comment. The general pattern of rainfall distribution in Africa probably remained largely unchanged throughout the Pleistocene, though minor increases and decreases of precipitation could have had quite important local effects: a rise of ten inches in the annual rainfall, providing that it was suitably distributed, could change desert into scrub, though a similar increase in the equatorial forest zone would make little if any difference to the vegetation.

Not only is it important to know something of the climatic background because of its direct effects on man and his environment, but also because of its historical associations. Leakey's climatic sequence, already outlined, is shown in Table 1, with presumed equivalents in Europe according to the most recent evidence. Briefly, the main pluvial periods and postpluvial wetter phases are as follows (each separated from the next by an interpluvial or drier phase):

Nakuran wet phase ⎫	Post Pleistocene
Makalian wet phase ⎭	
Gamblian pluvial	Later Pleistocene
Kanjeran pluvial	Early part of Later Pleistocene and perhaps also later part of Mid Pleistocene
Kamasian pluvial	Mid Pleistocene
Kageran pluvial (?)	Earlier Pleistocene

Table 1. The East African Climatic Sequence and Presumed Equivalents in Europe.

Years B.C.	European climatic phases	East African climatic phases	Olduvai	Other East African sites
800	Present	Nakuran		Lake Nakuru
2,500	Sub Boreal	Drier		145 ft.
5,500	Atlantic	Makalian		L. Nakuru 335 ft.
7,500	Boreal	Drier		
8,000	Pre Boreal	Makalian 1?		L. Nakuru 375 ft.? Gamble's Cave?
8,850	Younger Dryas	Drier	Bed V	Deighton's Cliff
10,000	Alleröd			
10,500	Older Dryas			
11,000	Bölling			
12,500	Late Würm	Gamblian 3		L. Nakuru 375 ft.
18,000	Brandenburg	Drier		
24,000	Middle Würm (main phase)	Gamblian 2		L. Nakuru 510 ft.
25,000	Paudorf	Drier		
30,000	Middle Würm (early phase)	Gamblian 1		L. Nakuru 720 ft.
45,000	Göttweig	Drier		MN horizon, Kagera
54,000	Early Würm			Kalambo Isimila Semliki series Olorgesailie Kanjera?
		Kanjeran	Bed IV	
60,000	Interstadial			
65,000	Cold oscillation			
100,000	Third interglacial (Eemian)			
200,000	Riss	Wetter?	Bed III?	
250,000	Second interglacial (Great)			
400,000	Mindel	Kamasian	Bed II	Rawi
500,000	First interglacial (Cromerian)		Non-sequence	
1,000,000	Günz		Bed I	Laetolil
2,000,000	Pre-Günz			Omo Kanam Kaiso

It is unfortunate that the names of the first three "pluvials" all begin with the letters Ka. An easy way to remember which comes first is to think of the *third* letter in each case; these are in alphabetical order, *g*, *m*, and *n*—Ka-*g*eran, Ka-*m*asian, and Ka-*n*jeran. Students have long adopted such a method of remembering the order of the glacial periods in Europe: G, M, R, W, for Günz, Mindel, Riss, and Würm.*

The East African climatic sequence provided the first means, however nebulous, of correlating human remains and industries with those of other areas. Such relative dating was achieved by piecing together clues of many different kinds: climatic fluctuations revealed by high strand lines above lakes; high river terraces; raised sea beaches; ancient soils showing chemical alterations due to changes in temperature and rainfall; and so on. We shall discuss some of these lines of evidence later and see how useful they can be for interpretations of climate and correlations, but first we must try to discover how such climatic changes came about at all during the Pleistocene.

World Changes of Climate

Climatic fluctuations that took place in tropical zones during the Pleistocene must obviously bear some relationship to glacial and interglacial periods in Europe, Asia, North America, and, to a more limited extent, parts of the Southern Hemisphere. Both glacial and pluvial periods, interglacials and interpluvials, must have been caused by worldwide changes of climate. Although many attempts have been made to correlate pluvials in low latitudes with glacials in high lati-

---

* Since there is no space to list the American equivalents of the European glacial and interglacial phases in Table 1, it may be helpful to mention some of the main corresponding phases here:

Europe	North America
Younger Dryas	Valders readvance
Alleröd Interstadial	Two Creeks phase
Older Dryas	Port Huron-Mankato readvance
Bölling Interstadial	Lake Arkona recession
Middle Würm main phase	Wisconsin glacial maximum
Eemian Interglacial	Sangamon Interglacial
Riss Glacial	Illinoian Glacial
Great (Hoxnian) Interglacial	Yarmouth Interglacial
Mindel Glacial	Kansan Glacial
Cromerian Interglacial	Aftonian Interglacial
Günz Glacial	Nebraskan Glacial

tudes, agreement has by no means been reached. It does appear probable, however, that pluvial periods in the tropics were broadly contemporary with glacial periods elsewhere, though it seems most unlikely that they fit exactly. In Europe there were four main glaciations, and until quite recently it was generally accepted that there were four major pluvials in East Africa during the Pleistocene.

Many theories have been put forward to account for the Ice Age as a whole and for the fluctuations within that period. There are two main schools of thought on the subject. One is based on astronomical considerations, depending on the inclination of the earth's axis, the eccentricity of the earth's orbit, and the longitude of the perihelion (precession of the equinoxes). This is known as the Milankovitch theory, and it has been championed particularly by F. E. Zeuner, whose book *Dating the Past* is based on it. It is claimed that absolute dating can be calculated from curves representing changes of solar radiation on various latitudes during the past 650,000 years (unless one is mathematically inclined, however, these "curves" look like the temperature chart of a patient suffering from a virulent tropical fever). Some of the dates for the later part of the Pleistocene do not seem to agree at all well with radiocarbon dates.

The other school of thought follows G. C. Simpson's theory (see pp. 62–63), which accounts for climatic changes by rhythmical variations in the sun's radiation. R. F. Flint elaborated on this in his Solar-Topographic hypothesis, which is based on two essential principles: (1) the fluctuation of solar radiation is the cause of worldwide temperature changes; (2) the presence of highlands is the prime factor in determining the accumulation of snow and the distribution of glaciers. As Flint put it, "The fluctuation of solar energy was able to cause extensive glaciation only at those times when the upheaval of highlands reached up, as it were, to meet the falling temperature."[5] Although this theory fits well with the Pleistocene Ice Age, it is more difficult to reconcile with earlier glacial periods, such as that which took place in Carboniferous times in South Africa, where there is no evidence of contemporary uplift.

Worldwide earth movements causing uplift of mountains immediately before and during the Pleistocene epoch were very pronounced. The Himalayas, for example, were formed during the late Tertiary and early Quaternary. In many parts of Africa there is abundant evidence of tectonic movements and volcanic activity at this time. These movements were especially intense in East Africa and resulted not only in the formation of the rift valley but also in the uplift of many volcanic cones. Very high mountains like Kilimanjaro, Mt. Kenya, and the Ruwenzori Range disturb the atmospheric circulation and increase precipitation around them.

Once an ice sheet has formed, high-pressure conditions are established over it and the cyclonic belt is shifted toward the equator, probably through as much as 15 degrees of latitude. The effects of this displacement of climatic zones would be felt right down to the equator, resulting in increased rainfall, while cloudiness would reduce evaporation. Pluvial periods in low latitudes must obviously be controlled by atmospheric circulation, which in turn would depend on the extent of ice sheets in high latitudes.

H. B. S. Cooke[6] pointed out that regions of semi-arid climate related to the subtropical anticyclonic belt are likely to be particularly sensitive to latitudinal shifting of pressure systems. He visualized conditions involving changes in rainfall in some parts of Africa which might be in the opposite sense to those taking place in periglacial regions and in the equatorial rainfall belt. This might explain certain anomalies between the Pleistocene climatic sequence worked out in East Africa and in South Africa. In general, Cooke concluded that precise equivalence of glacial and pluvial periods is highly improbable.

The late Professor A. du Toit gave these words of warning, which have not always been heeded: "The chief source of error [in interpreting past climates] lies in the general assumption that the conditions deduced from one or two spots must prove representative of the country, or even be applicable to half a continent."[7] He might have added also, to different continents, for many workers happily tried to link pluvials in the rift area of tropical Africa with glacial periods in Europe, even though the two are separated by thousands of miles of desert and the winter rainfall area of the Mediterranean. In fact it is more likely that pluvial conditions in low latitudes may coincide with arid periods in the winter rainfall belts of the Northern and Southern Hemispheres, and vice versa.

To add to the confusion, Bernard maintains that *interpluvials* in the tropics coincide broadly with the glacial periods of higher latitudes. A strong supporter of Milankovitch's astronomical theory, he believes that at certain times the equator (that is, the parallel with the least seasonal variation in insolation) was displaced by a maximum of 10°

N. and 10° S. and that the whole climatic system shifted accordingly. At the time of pluvial periods with a tropical regime in the Northern Hemisphere there was heavy summer rainfall and dry winters; this he calls a displuvial. At the same time, equatorial regions and low southern latitudes had regular rainfall the whole year round, which he calls an isopluvial. When, on the other hand, the displuvial was located in the Southern Hemisphere, northern latitudes had an isopluvial.[8] Dates calculated by Bernard on the basis of this theory, at least for the later parts of the Pleistocene, do not fit with radiocarbon dates any more than do Milankovitch's dates. The beginning of the Last Glaciation, Würm, is given as 116,000 years, and the beginning of Würm II, or Middle Würm, as 71,000 years. Radiocarbon points to only about half this time, around 60,000 years for Early Würm and 30,000 years for Middle Würm. Much work remains to be done before it can be seen whether Bernard's interpretation fits the field evidence, but his concept of displuvials and isopluvials seems useful.

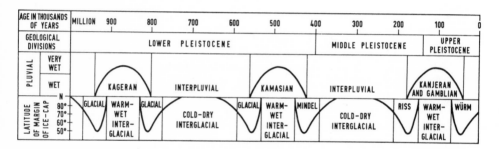

Table 2. Pluvial and glacial phases (from climatic curve). After Simpson.

Sir George Simpson made a bold attempt at correlation between East Africa and Europe, and, in view of his high reputation as a meteorologist, his scheme deserves serious consideration. On his theory of variations in the sun's radiation, exact correlation of pluvials with glacials is impossible. Instead, he drew a curve (Table 2) showing each pluvial embracing the latter half of a glacial, a warm, wet interglacial, and the first half of the succeeding glacial.[9] In bracketing the Kanjeran and Gamblian pluvials together, he seemed at first sight to refute the evidence from East Africa, where there is a great difference between most of the "Kanjeran" fauna of Bed IV, Olduvai, which had always been correlated with Riss, and the modern fauna of Gamblian times.

On the Kalambo evidence, however, a wetter climate associated with Late Acheulian hand-ax industries about 55,000 B.C. must be correlated with Early Würm (see Table 1), rather than with the Riss Glaciation, which had previously been thought to mark the end of Acheulian times. The Gamblian pluvial, with its Middle Stone Age industries and modern fauna, would then be correlated with Middle Würm and Late Würm. Once again, as happened so often during the earlier parts of the Pleistocene, archaic mammals probably survived later in Africa, in this case into the Early Würm, whereas elsewhere they became extinct before this period. By revising ideas on the age of the Kanjeran pluvial and making it contemporary with Early Würm rather than with Riss, the apparent difficulties in Simpson's scheme are overcome.

A point emphasized by Simpson in making his theoretical pluvial-glacial and interpluvial-interglacial correlations is that there are two very different kinds of interglacial: one is warm and wet, the other cold and dry; this is shown in diagram. A warm, wet interglacial such as the Eemian (Riss-Würm) should correspond with a tropical *pluvial;* while a cold, dry interglacial would correspond with an *interpluvial.* But so far, pollen analysis has not confirmed that the Great interglacial was cold and dry, according to Oakley.

One of the main difficulties in achieving correlation between different parts of Africa, and still more so with other continents, lies in deciding just what constitutes a "pluvial" of general significance and what is a wetter oscillation in the local climate. In Africa today, the distribution of rainfall varies enormously within quite short distances as the result of altitude. Farmers on the floor of the rift valley gaze wistfully at rain clouds discharging themselves on their neighbors' land only a few miles distant horizontally but several thousand feet vertically above them.

This brings us to one of the main problems in assessing climatic evidence in East Africa. Such tremendous tectonic movements and volcanic flows took place in this unstable area throughout the Pleistocene that the geologist's task is often a formidable one. He sees a fine strand line that he would like to attribute to a large lake fed by plentiful rain; but has the whole area been downthrown by faulting in the meantime, or was the former lake ponded by a lava flow blocking its outlet?

Climatic Evidence in East Africa

The interpretation of past changes of climate in East Africa has been based mainly on the following lines of evidence: (1) raised lake and river terraces, denoting rainfall higher than that of the present time (*if* the effects of earth movements can be ruled out); (2) greater extension of glaciers on high mountains in the past, suggesting wetter and cooler conditions than those prevailing today; (3) the study of fossil soils and chemical alterations such as ferruginization and calcification, which indicate different climatic conditions at the time of their formation, as well as the presence of wind-blown sands, denoting arid conditions. These factors are studied mainly in the interior of the continent, but useful correlations between different areas can be achieved also by linking the heights of raised sea beaches at the coast. High beach levels are caused either by worldwide climatic changes— such as a rise of sea level caused by melting ice following a glacial period—or, in some cases, by relative movements of the land that have nothing to do with climate.

The study of fossil fauna in East Africa has so far given few indications of climatic changes, since most of the work has been done on the larger mammals, which are very adaptable. When the enormous collections of micro-fauna—small creatures such as insectivories and rodents—from Olduvai have been studied in detail, these should provide plenty of evidence of climatic conditions. The fauna as a whole throughout the Olduvai sequence suggest that climatic changes were not at all extreme during the Pleistocene. Far more useful information may be expected from the study of pollen grains, which has only been attempted in East Africa within the past few years. At Kalambo Falls, on the border of Northern Rhodesia and Tanganyika, very useful results have been obtained by palynology and by identifying fruits and other vegetable remains preserved in waterlogged deposits. More recently still, pollen diagrams have been made from peat samples from a bog near the tree line in the Cherangani Hills of western Kenya. One of the horizons, at a depth of about three meters, represents a cold, treeless phase that has been dated by carbon-14 to 12,650 ± 100 years, or about 10,700 B.C. This is probably contemporary with the Oldest Dryas of Europe. In addition, other temperature fluctuations revealed by the pollen diagram appear to be identical and contemporaneous with those in Europe and in the Andes.[10] This is one of the most important and encouraging results ever to come out of work on past climates in East Africa, and whether interpretations of earlier periods are right or wrong, it seems that for the later part of the Pleistocene at least, we are on firm ground.

LAKE AND RIVER TERRACES

All workers in East Africa are agreed that fluctuations in the levels of lakes and rivers took place during the Pleistocene, though their interpretation of the causes of these oscillations is not always the same. O'Brien and Solomon maintained that raised lake and river terraces in Uganda were to be attributed largely to earth movements resulting in tilting. Certainly in some cases tilting produced changes in levels of lakes and rivers *locally*, though it hardly seems plausible to credit all the very widespread and constant raised terraces found throughout Africa to tectonic events. Not only are raised terraces found in the unstable rift area, but also in such places as the Vaal River in South Africa, where there is no evidence of earth movements during the Pleistocene. Wayland in Uganda, Nilsson and Leakey in Kenya, and many other workers in other parts of Africa attributed raised terraces to lakes and rivers enlarged by pluvial conditions of varying degrees of intensity. In part, this could have been caused by less evaporation if the temperature were lower; but the difference in heights between past and present lakes is so enormous that this cannot be the main explanation.

Correlations over great distances between river and lake evidence are often unreliable, for the deposits of one may be out of phase with the other. Thus at times when lakes were high, during a wet period, probably little erosion took place in river valleys, owing to the protective covering of vegetation. Then, as the rainfall diminished, a gap would be left in the lake evidence, but there would be active downcutting by rivers; this period of downcutting would be followed by aggradation—that is, the building up of deposits of gravels and alluvium. This main period of downcutting and aggradation takes place during the *intermediate* periods between extremes of wetter and drier conditions.

During arid phases, when lake levels were very low or lakes dried up altogether, wind-blown deposits formed in river valleys. As rainfall

gradually increased once more, probably some erosion took place in
river valleys until the vegetation became re-established, while in lake
basins there may be no evidence until the lakes reached a high level
once again. Thus it is easier to correlate drier phases than wet ones;
during arid periods, evidence of low lake levels and wind-blown deposits in river valleys is often well marked, whereas although lakes will
leave high strand lines as a result of wetter periods, there is no geological evidence from rivers.

In tropical climates the conditions of formation of river deposits are
very imperfectly known. It is difficult to distinguish between material
brought down during rare torrential floods and material deposited as
the result of a long period of increased rainfall. Although in East
Africa evidence of former climatic conditions is sometimes masked by
the effects of earth movements and volcanic activity, in the more stable
area of South Africa it is possible to make climatic interpretations
from the cutting and filling of river valleys and the distribution of
wind-blown sands. These matters have been gone into at some length,
since the pitfalls that exist in interpreting past climates in Africa are
not always appreciated.

GLACIERS ON HIGH MOUNTAINS

As well as doing detailed work on ancient lake levels in the rift
valleys of Kenya and Ethiopia, Nilsson calculated the former extent
of glaciers on many East African mountains. He found, not only that
existing glaciers on such mountains as Kilimanjaro and Mt. Kenya came
down much lower than they do today during certain periods of the
Pleistocene, but also that certain other mountains which now have no
glaciers (such as Elgon and the Aberdare Range) were glaciated in
the past. On Kilimanjaro, Mt. Kenya, and in the Semien highlands of
Ethiopia, Nilsson found traces of a series of moraines along the sides
and in front of valleys; the most conspicuous are those which he
attributed to the time of the Gamblian pluvial, but below these are
older, consolidated morainic material that was dissected by melt-water
streams during the later Pleistocene Gamblian pluvial. The lowest altitude reached by glaciers is calculated to have been about 10,000 feet;
today, glaciers on Kilimanjaro and Mt. Kenya do not come down
lower than 15,000 feet.

The height of the snow line depends essentially on summer temperature; it has been estimated that at times when glaciers extended 5,000 feet lower than they do now, the climate may have been 10-12°F. colder than it is today. Although a lower snow line also suggests more precipitation, these conditions could have been largely local and need not have affected the whole country to any great extent. But since the evidence from glaciated areas fits in so well with evidence of enlarged lakes in the rift valley during the later part of the Pleistocene, it does strengthen the case for attributing raised lake terraces to pluvial conditions rather than solely to tectonic movements.

SOILS AND CHEMICAL ALTERATIONS

The study of fossil soils can be very helpful in interpreting past climates. Soil formation is dependent not only on the nature of the bedrock but also, to a great extent, on temperature and rainfall. These two factors are intimately connected in tropical regions, where heat causes much evaporation. An annual rainfall that would be adequate to support vegetation in a cooler climate is offset in the tropics by the amount lost in evaporation before the moisture can sink into the ground far enough to reach the roots of trees or grass.

Formerly it was assumed that reddened land surfaces implied arid conditions, but this is not necessarily so; very often, in fact, red soils result from a wetter climate. Red deposits may be laid down in deserts, but they are generally derived from a source region where the climate is much wetter. The leaching factor, which depends on both temperature and rainfall, is very important in the formation of soils. Red earths, for example, are known to form where the mean annual temperature is between 50° and 65°F. and the rainfall is over 40 inches per annum. When the mean annual temperature is greater than 65°F., crusts of ferricrete or laterite may form (ferricrete is rich in iron and aluminium, but poor in calcium, magnesium, potassium, and sodium salts). The formation of red earths is usually associated with moderate to rather great annual rainfall with occasional torrential showers, while ferricrete crusts imply strongly seasonal distribution of the rainfall. In general, red soils do not mean that the rainfall was small, as was supposed in early work on the climatic sequence in East Africa, but rather that there was considerable seasonal variation in its distribution.

This increased knowledge of the conditions under which red soils
and ferricrete crusts form at the present time has affected the interpretation of Pleistocene climates considerably. The red bed at Olduvai,
Bed III, need not necessarily represent an interpluvial, as had always
been assumed; on the contrary, recent work suggests that it implies
rather wet conditions in the volcanic highlands from which the material was derived.

Evidence of drier phases is generally more reliable than evidence for
wetter phases, since they were often relatively short and clearly defined. The deposition of wind-blown sands, in, for example, the Vaal
and Zambezi valleys and parts of the Horn, indicates conditions of
great aridity. Chemical alterations resulting in siliceous or calcareous
crusts also suggests a rather dry, hot climate.

Much valuable information about climatic conditions in the past
might be obtained from bore holes in closed lake basins in the rift
valley, where alternating fresh-water deposits and saline precipitates
often occur. This subject has been little studied, though in the Kitui
District in western Kenya, for example, gypsum indicating arid conditions was found alternating with fluviatile deposits.

RAISED SEA BEACHES

During glacial periods, much moisture was locked up in the form
of ice and snow, and the sea level, consequently, stood much lower
than it does today; it has been estimated that if glacial conditions
reached their maximum in all the known glaciated areas at the same
time, the sea level would have been lowered by as much as 305 feet.
Unfortunately it is not always possible to distinguish the effects of
changes in sea level from the effects of earth movements. If the earth
had always been stable, then raised beaches would represent interglacials, when the ice melted and returned its moisture to the oceans
and the sea level was high as a consequence.

Africa in particular was affected by severe earth movements during
the Pleistocene, so that correlations between raised beaches in different
areas are not easy to make. Raised beaches are found right around
Africa, from the Mediterranean to the Cape; as well as affording evidence of changes in sea level, they indicate that there was a progressive
rising of the continent during the Pleistocene—especially marked
toward the end of this period. Heights of ancient sea levels have been

studied very thoroughly along the coasts of the Mediterranean; perhaps in the future it may be possible to link these up with raised beaches farther south so that the effects of relative movements of land and sea can be distinguished. When this has been done, it will be of inestimable value to prehistory, for it will help to date industries contained in and between the beaches.

On the east coast of Somalia, river terraces in the Nogal Valley have been linked with coastal formations at its mouth. Gravel terraces containing industries on Mt. Mabla, French Somaliland, were also connected with coral formations at the coast near Obok, where evidence of two periods of marine transgression was obtained.

As early as 1908, it was pointed out that tidal creeks along the Kenya coast were originally land valleys, drowned at times of marine transgression; at these times, coral reefs extended 3 or 4 miles inland of the present shore line and at least 75 feet above present sea level. The great variations in height of raised coral reefs led Gregory to suppose that land movements rather than changes in sea level were largely responsible. An interesting discovery was made in 1962, when survey ships found that the eastward-tilted continent of Africa continues beneath the Indian Ocean as a zone of sedimentary rocks two hundred miles wide, extending from Madagascar to Socotra in the Arabian Sea. Probably the land subsided in early Tertiary times, showing that Africa has not been so stable as had been supposed. Along the Kenya coast, raised beaches at heights of about 300 feet, 250 feet, 120 feet, 30–40 feet, and 15 feet have been found.[11] Beach lines in the region of Dar-es-Salaam have been traced at heights of 100 feet, 80 feet, 50 feet, 35 to 40 feet, and 15 feet.[12] Eventually it may be possible to equate some of these ancient beaches with levels of the Mediterranean with their associated and fairly well dated fauna and industries, as has been done brilliantly on the Atlantic coast of Morocco by P. Biberson.[13] Here the study of mollusks has given a good idea of climatic conditions during various periods of the Pleistocene. Broadly, it has been found that periods of marine transgression correspond with drier phases, periods of regression with wetter phases, supporting the correlation of pluvials with glacials and interpluvials with interglacials. Needless to say, conditions on the Atlantic coast cannot be compared with those of the Indian Ocean; but the work done recently in Morocco shows what can be achieved through detailed studies of beach levels, fauna, and associated industries.

Criticisms of the Climatic Evidence

At the Third Pan-African Congress on Prehistory, held at Living-stone in 1955, several geologists, climatologists, and archaeologists, while recognizing the value of the *stratigraphic* sequence in East Africa, admitted that they were worried at the way *climatic* implications of this sequence had been applied over almost the whole of Africa. A resolution was passed recommending that the terms "Kageran," "Kamasian," "Kanjeran," "Gamblian," "Makalian," and "Nakuran" should be recognized as stratigraphic climatic divisions only in the East African region and that they should not be applied in other parts of the continent except where correlation is firmly attested by at least two of three lines of evidence: paleontological, archaeological, or the geological setting. It was also recommended that the terms, "Lower," "Middle," and "Upper Pleistocene," as applied in other continents, should not be used in Africa until correlations were less uncertain.

At the Livingstone conference, H. B. S. Cooke, a geologist from South Africa, questioned the climatic evidence in East Africa itself. Both Cooke[14] and Flint[15] went into the whole problem in some detail, and it is largely due to their criticisms that the overworked climatic sequence is gradually being abandoned in favor of stratigraphic units. For example, if we speak of "Olduvai, Bed II" times we immediately associate it with the period of Chellean Man and his culture and with a particular fauna, whereas to speak of "Kamasian" times implies a pluvial climate that may not have existed. Now that we are beginning to get potassium-argon dates for the early part of the Pleistocene, the value of inferred pluvials and interpluvials as a means of correlation is less than it was. The same, of course, applies to the last 60,000 years, which are gradually being covered by radiocarbon dates. At present, however, very few absolute dates are available, and until such time as they are, climatic correlations may still be useful, if they are used with caution. As Clark put it, it is a pity to throw out the baby with the bath water.

Flint doubted whether any pluvials or interpluvials earlier than the Gamblian could be inferred from the field evidence except at one locality, Olorgesailie, in the Kenya Rift Valley. Here he recognized that a lake in pre-Gamblian times, implying wetter conditions than those prevailing in this very arid area today, must have been responsible for the extensive deposits of diatomite, clays, and marls containing hand axes and fauna. We must now look at the evidence for the East African climatic sequence in detail and see whether such criticisms are valid.

THE KAGERAN "PLUVIAL"

Wayland, as well as Lowe, attributed the 270-foot and 200-foot terraces of the Kagera River in Uganda to an early Pleistocene pluvial named after this river. Flint pointed out that the river has recently been moving rock particles not greatly different from the coarsest alluvium exposed in its ancient terraces and that therefore their presence does not necessarily imply conditions more "pluvial" than those of the present time. He also doubts whether the Kagera gravels can be correlated with sediments elsewhere, since they contain no fossils and, as Bishop discovered, their so-called "pebble tools" are probably not artifacts at all. If the "pebble tools" are set aside, there is in fact nothing to prevent the 270-foot terrace from being older than the Lower Pleistocene. There is undoubted evidence of tilting of the Kagera area, which eventually resulted in the reversal of the river. With respect to Uganda in general, Bishop concluded, "These tectonic influences have so dominated the stratigraphic record that it is seldom possible to infer the type of climate prevailing at any particular period. . . . However, local evidence [in the Western Volcanic series of the Lake Edward basin] indicates that the climate of Uganda has varied during the Pleistocene."[16]

Other deposits which have been attributed to the "Kageran pluvial" are clays and tuffs at Kanam, on the Kavirondo Gulf in western Kenya, which contain fauna comparable with that of the Lower Pleistocene Villafranchian stage of Europe and Asia. A somewhat later fauna, probably Upper Villafranchian and mainly contemporary with Olduvai, Bed I, exists in the Omo Valley, north of Lake Rudolf. Also partly contemporary, but extending backward for an unknown length of time —possibly into the Pliocene—is fauna from the Kaiso series of the western rift, known particularly from the shores of Lake Albert, as well as on the Kazinga Channel and along the eastern shore of Lake Edward.

There is little evidence of "pluvial" conditions at any of these localities at the time of formation of the deposits, though conditions at Olduvai during Bed I times were probably rather wetter than at present. Clark pointed out that bone at the *"Zinjanthropus"* living floor in Bed I is completely unweathered, and mineralization must have begun at once, the land surface having been covered over immediately as a result of a fluctuation in the lake. At the present time, bone lying on the ground splits up and disintegrates rapidly. If in Bed I times the temperature had been somewhat lower and the rainfall more evenly distributed, the rate of destruction of the bone would have been slowed down. He also pointed out that, although most of the fauna of Bed I is of the savanna type (lion, zebra, hartebeest, gazelle), ancestors of the forest- and swamp-living okapi and sitatunga were also present, suggesting wetter conditions than those of today.[17]

Whether Bed I represents the "Kageran pluvial" in the old sense of the word is another matter. The "Kageran" as originally defined embraced an earlier period than Olduvai. But since it now seems that there is a very long time interval between Beds I and II, they cannot both be bracketed together in one "pluvial period," the "Kamasian." These names have lost much of their meaning and may eventually be dropped altogether. But we can at least say that the climate of Bed I times was relatively wetter than it is at present.

THE KAGERAN-KAMASIAN "INTERPLUVIAL"

In general, the so-called "interpluvials" might better be called "nonpluvials," or, simply, drier periods. Evidence of the first "interpluvial," the Kageran-Kamasian, was claimed by Wayland for ironstones in the Kaiso bone bed; these he interpreted as bog iron ore deposited in drying pools of a former lake. The presence of gypsum in the sediments also suggested drier conditions. Flint, however, considers that these phenomena could equally well be attributed to the emergence of the area resulting from earth movements.

There is good evidence of a dry climate at the end of the period represented by Bed I at Olduvai, where Leakey has recently recognized a desert surface containing remains of desert-living mammals such as the jerboa, as well as "desert roses," curious crystals that form in parts of the Sahara and other arid regions at the present time. In Bed I times, a shallow lake existed at Olduvai into which were ejected volcanic tuffs from the volcanoes of Ngorongoro and Lemargut, to the southeast. The lake does not necessarily imply "pluvial" conditions, but clearly it dried up completely at the time of the desert surface near the top of

Bed I. We can therefore confidently describe this time as a drier period, though it cannot be ascribed to the "Kageran-Kamasian interpluvial" when there is no clear definition of the Kageran pluvial itself.

THE KAMASIAN "PLUVIAL"

The name "Kamasian" is, as we have already noted, particularly unfortunate; most of the diatomites in the Kenya Rift attributed to Gregory's "Lake Kamasia" should more properly be called Kanjeran, since they contain Acheulian hand axes of the same stage as those of Kanjera and of Bed IV, Olduvai.

Bed II at Olduvai is attributed to the "Kamasian pluvial" since it consists of clays and marls laid down in a Mid Pleistocene lake. In fact, the climate at the time of the shallow and fluctuating Bed II lake may have been not very much wetter than it is today. It has been pointed out that in the Ol Balbal Depression east of Olduvai Gorge a seasonal lake forms annually at the present time, which, no doubt like the lake in the area of the gorge in Mid Pleistocene times, is very susceptible to minor changes in rainfall.[18] The Olduvai Pleistocene fauna, however, includes crocodiles and hippopotamuses, which are not found in the area today. This suggests that the climate in Bed II times was relatively wetter than at present.

THE KAMASIAN-KANJERAN "INTERPLUVIAL"

The concept of a Kamasian-Kanjeran "interpluvial" was based mainly on the evidence of a major faunal break at the end of Bed II times at Olduvai, and on the presence of Bed III, a red terrestrial deposit intervening between two lake beds. It is now generally agreed that this red bed suggests a wetter rather than a drier climate, and the red material, derived from the volcanic highlands to the east, was probably already colored before it was carried to its present position by streams. If the red soil was forming contemporaneously in the source region, the climate could not have been arid. The Olduvai lake might well have retreated farther to the west at that time, having been blocked on its eastern side by volcanic material.

The Upper Rawi beds near Kanjera were also thought at one time to have been laid down during this "interpluvial." They contain numerous remains of fish, presumed to have died as the lake in the present Lake

Victoria basin diminished. Flint, however, considers that the evidence does not warrant an interpluvial interpretation.

THE KANJERAN PLUVIAL

Once we get to the Kanjeran pluvial we are on firmer ground. Even Flint admits that at Olorgesailie, in the rift southwest of Nairobi, there is evidence of a pre-Gamblian pluvial, at the time when the Acheulian hand-ax makers camped beside the shores of a fluctuating lake.

Lake deposits at Kanjera associated with hand axes, fossil mammals, and human skull fragments are also attributed to this period, which, of course, derived its name from the site. Both the fauna and the Acheulian industry make it clear that Kanjera and Olorgesailie are broadly contemporary with Bed IV, Olduvai. At Kariandusi, in the Kenya Rift Valley, diatomites and other lake deposits also contain a similar hand-ax industry, showing that at least some of the rift diatomites are of Kanjeran rather than Kamasian age.

Near the top of the Semliki series of lake and river deposits in the Lake Edward and Lake Albert basins of the Congo and Uganda, Acheulian hand axes have been found. Overlying these deposits are dark, humic fossil soils covered by volcanic ash. These dark soils suggest heavier rainfall, which must probably be attributed to the Kanjeran pluvial.

The Kanjeran pluvial has always been correlated with the Riss Glaciation by Leakey and most other workers. The question of dating this period, however, may need revision as a result of the carbon-14 date from Kalambo Falls. Although this has already been mentioned, it is so important that it must be repeated. An evolved Acheulian industry with evidence of a wetter climate was dated to about 57,300 years ago. This suggests that at least the later part of the Kanjeran may be contemporary with the Early Würm Glaciation rather than Riss.[19] It would, of course, be possible to say that the wetter climate at the time of the Kalambo Acheulian represents the Gamblian pluvial and not the Kanjeran. But there is a strong argument in favor of correlating the Kanjeran with the Early Würm. The Kanjera skull fragments, mentioned already, have a very modern appearance, and anthropologists have been distinctly worried in attempting to reconcile the appearance of the skulls with their presumed antiquity. If, however, they are dated to about 55,000 years ago or less—contemporary with the early part of the Last Glaciation in Europe—these difficulties are not nearly so great. A suggested correlation on this basis is shown in Table 4.

The former extent of the Kanjeran lake in the Kenya Rift Valley presents an interesting problem. Because of the almost continuous lake deposits over long distances, this hypothetical lake was at one time thought to have stretched most of the way from Rudolf in the north to Magadi in the south. Its ends at Rudolf and Magadi, however, are some 3,000 feet lower than the middle part of the area around Naivasha and Nakuru. Obviously no lake could exist under these circumstances, and the only way to account for it was to postulate an upward thrust in the Naivasha-Nakuru region after Kanjeran times. This is not impossible, but 3,000 feet is, nevertheless, rather a tall order. The present rift-valley lakes are divided into separate basins by volcanoes, lava flows, and faults in the floor of the rift. The floor thus consists of a series of steps of different heights, formed during the Later Pleistocene. It seems far more probable that the lake basins were similarly separated during Kanjeran times, rather than that the whole area was occupied by a huge, single lake. It is more likely that the elevation of the Naivasha-Nakuru region was due to the piling up of a considerable thickness of volcanic material, in which case an extensive lake could not have existed.

One way to solve this problem of the existence of Middle Pleistocene lake deposits almost the whole way along the rift-valley area would be to make a detailed study of the diatomite. Diatomite looks rather like chalk, only it is lighter and of quite different chemical composition, being almost pure silica. It is made up of billions of skeletons of diatoms, minute organisms that live in lakes and form one of the chief items in the flamingos' diet.

Specimens of diatoms were collected from below the Acheulian beach at Kariandusi and from between land surfaces 5 and 6 at Olorgesailie. In each case genera of diatoms were present that are epiphytic on submerged vegetation; there were others that are free-swimming on the bottoms of lakes. At Kariandusi, most of the diatoms were a planktonic species whose depth range is 2-4 meters, which suggests that the diatomite was laid down not closer than 100 meters from the shore of the lake. At Olorgesailie, a very few planktonic diatoms were present, suggesting that the deposit was formed in shallow water, near the mouth of a stream.

Other specimens were collected from above a fish band in Kanjeran deposits in the Nasagum Valley, northwest of Marigat, near Lake Baringo. They consist entirely of planktonic species, indicating that the depth was sufficient to prevent growth on the bottom, owing to lack of light. The samples from Lake Baringo are therefore central, while the Kariandusi and Olorgesailie specimens are marginal, as would indeed be expected, since hand-ax man had lived beside the lake shores at both these latter localities. If more samples were collected from different areas of the rift valley, and analyzed, then it might be possible to arrive at some conclusions about the extent and depth of the Kanjeran lakes.

THE KANJERAN-GAMBLIAN INTERPLUVIAL

After the end of Kanjeran times, there is evidence that the lakes dried up; this still happens today in the case of shallow, alkaline lakes such as Nakuru when the rains fail, and it does not necessarily imply a regime very different from that of the present. In contrast with the succeeding Gamblian pluvial, however, the climate was certainly drier during this interval. In the Kagera Valley in Uganda, the so-called MN horizon associated with an early Sangoan industry marks a major and probably climatic break in lacustrine and estuarine sediments at the head of a former embayment of Lake Victoria.[20] The Kenya Fauresmith culture of this period is found at high altitudes beside permanent streams which would not have dried up during this drier phase.

The deposits in a small basin at Isimila, near Iringa, Southern Tanganyika (see p. 161), may also have been laid down during this drier pre-Gamblian period. There is evidence of a prolonged wet climate in Mid Pleistocene times, followed by a period when the forested cover on hill slopes changed to a bushland vegetation with largely barren slopes. The deposition of clays with bands of coarser sands containing Late Acheulian industries started under still drying climatic conditions.[21]

Great earth movements and volcanic activity took place at this time, resulting in the rift valley's attaining its present form. Faults associated with its formation cut through Kanjeran deposits in the Naivasha-Nakuru area, while downthrows of over a thousand feet took place on the Kinangop Plateau above Naivasha. Near Olduvai, the country between the Serengeti Plains and the Balbal Depression is marked by a series of four steps caused by faulting at this time.

All workers seem to be in agreement that the climate of Gamblian times may fairly be described as pluvial. This applies to most of Africa, in fact; to mention but one example of the evidence, there is a well-marked ferricrete horizon associated with Sangoan industries throughout Central Africa.[22] Strand lines above the rift-valley lakes show that they stood very much higher than they do at present and, since some of them are horizontal over long distances, the causes are probably climatic rather than tectonic. These strand lines in the Naivasha, Elmenteita, and Nakuru basins were leveled at many points by Nilsson and Leakey; the former also extended this work into the Hannington and Baringo basins in Kenya, as well as into the Zwai Shala and Tana basins in Ethiopia. There is remarkable similarity in the curves joining the heights of old lake levels in these widely separated areas.

During the Gamblian pluvial, Lake Nakuru stood 720 feet and 510 feet above its present level; there is, for example, a beach sediment 510 feet above Lake Nakuru at Gamble's Cave II near Elmenteita, where skeletons of the Upper Kenya Capsian people were found (p. 260). On this evidence it was thought that the Gamblian pluvial had two maxima, but later Leakey considered that it had three, owing to a strand line at 375 feet at 'Nderit Drift, near Elmenteita (see Plate 3). This is at the same height as the first strand line attributed to the Makalian wet phase, so that it is not easy to distinguish the two.

A strong unconformity divides Kanjeran and Gamblian deposits, which, if the Kanjeran is correlated with Early Würm, might represent the time of the Göttweig Interstadial in Europe. The three Gamblian maxima would then correspond well with the early and main phases of Middle Würm, beginning about 30,000 and 24,000 B.C., respectively, and with the Late Würm, which lasted from 12,000 to 8000 B.C. (see Table 1).

Earth movements continued in the rift valley throughout Gamblian times and many of the lake terraces have been affected by tilting. Tilting may result in the deviation of drainage, as well as causing leakage into the underlying rocks; these factors can account for falls in lake levels just as much as drier climatic conditions. It is known, for example, that a considerable drop in the level of Lake Naivasha in Later

Plate 3. 'Nderit Drift in the Kenya Rift Valley, where Makalian beds overlie Gamblian deposits unconformably. (The photograph shows delegates to the first Pan-African Congress on Prehistory in 1947.)

Pleistocene times was caused by an overflow of water through Njorowa Gorge, to the south. There is, however, a visible break between Gamblian and Makalian deposits that suggests a change of climate at this time. This is further confirmed by the presence of wind-blown sand in Gamble's Cave II, attributed to the time of the Gamblian-Makalian interval.

The Makalian Wet Phase was named after an intermittent stream flowing into Lake Nakuru, and is said to have had two peaks when the lake stood 375 feet and 335 feet above its present level. It may perhaps be correlated broadly with the wet Atlantic climatic phase in Europe,

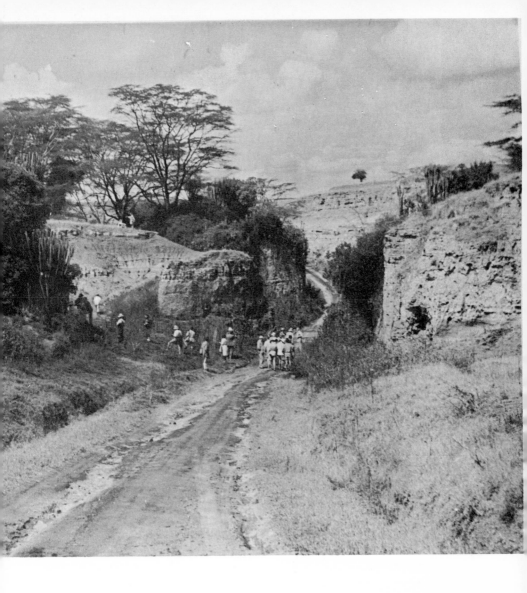

lasting from about 5500 B.C. to 2500 B.C. It was followed by a drier period, represented by more wind-blown sand in Gamble's Cave. The final high strand line in the Kenya Rift Valley, at 145 feet, represents the *Nakuran wet phase*, presumed to have started about 800 B.C., which marks the beginning of the present climatic regime in Europe.

Since that time, the rift-valley lakes have been receding gradually, with minor oscillations. Lake Nakuru has a mean annual rainfall of about 35 inches at the present time, but very often there are years of drought, and soda from the desiccated lake blows in unpleasant white clouds for miles around. During more arid periods in the past, when the lakes dried up, the rainfall may have been not less than about 25 inches per annum; but the cumulative effects of many years of rainfall 10 or even only 5 inches less than that of the present time would be seen clearly in the geological record.

Correlations with Other Parts of Africa

Whether there were the same number of wetter periods during the Pleistocene in all parts of Africa, and how many fluctuations there were within each, are questions that have not been settled. As is the case with glacial deposits in Europe, it is impossible to find exposures in any one area covering the whole of the Pleistocene period. In other cases, there are beautiful exposures (such as the diatomite in the rift valley) but not a fossil is to be found in them, so that dating remains uncertain. Since there are as yet very few absolute dates for East Africa, relative dating is often dependent on human artifacts used as "zone fossils," based on the typology of the implements. But this is not what we are looking for; we want the evidence to work the other way around, so that stratigraphy, including detailed studies of the fauna contained in the deposits, can help us to date the artifacts.

The African climatic puzzle is gradually being solved, but a great deal remains to be done. Evidence has been collected from Northern Rhodesia, the Congo, and the Horn, which fits in fairly well with the picture in Kenya, Tanganyika, and Uganda. In all these areas, three main wetter periods during the Pleistocene have been distinguished ("Kamasian," Kanjeran, and Gamblian).

In the Victoria Falls area there seems to be a fairly satisfactory connection between climatic conditions there and those of Kenya, 1,600 miles to the north, as well as with the Vaal Valley, 800 miles to the south. A further link between the Zambezi and the Vaal was provided by evidence from the Lochard area, 30 miles northeast of Bulawayo, in Southern Rhodesia.

In the Zambezi Valley, three major wetter phases seem to be followed, as in Kenya, by two minor wet phases. During intervening drier periods, successive deposits of Kalahari sands accumulated.

Turning to the area north of Kenya, the Horn: while Clark was not able during the limited time he could spare from war duties to work out a detailed climatic sequence over the whole area, the evidence he found is not incompatible with events farther south. Unfortunately there is little paleontological evidence in the Horn, and the cultural succession starts only with "Acheulio-Levalloisian" industries, probably rather later than the final Acheulian of Kalambo Falls.

The Ethiopian and Somali plateaus are separated from one another by regions of faulting and rifting. The Ethiopian and Danakil rifts trend from northeast to southwest, in line with the Kenya Rift Valley. The Somali Plateau slopes from the northwest toward the Indian Ocean and was probably tilted during the Kanjeran-Gamblian interpluvial. The plateau is drained by three main rivers flowing toward the southeast: the Nogal, Webi Shebeli, and Juba. Their tributaries consist of deep watercourses or "tugs," which are dry except during limited periods just after the rains.

Except in the Ethiopian high plateau, Clark considered that the "pluvial" periods which occurred during the Pleistocene, while wetter than conditions today, did not cause the climate of the Horn to pass out of the "arid" or "semi-arid" category.

In western Somalia, in the Nogal and Webi Shebeli valleys, and in the Danakil Rift (between Dire Dawa and the former territory of French Somaliland) it was found that a long period of valley cutting occurred during the earlier part of the Pleistocene, followed by calcification of deposits. During Kanjeran times, coarse gravels were laid down in the Webi Shebeli and Nogal valleys, indicating conditions considerably wetter than those of today. Diatomaceous lake beds in the Danakil area in Somalia are similar to those in the Ethiopian Rift and the Kenya Rift Valley; these sediments were affected by earth movements, rifting and faulting in Later Pleistocene times, as they were in Kenya. Calcification and ferruginization followed, denoting somewhat drier conditions. In Gamblian times, a series of lakes formed in the Danakil Rift, again closely comparable with events in Kenya. In western Somalia, two phases of Older Tug Gravels and alluvium were deposited during the early part of the Gamblian pluvial, followed by two phases of Younger Tug Gravels and alluvium. "Lower" and "Upper" Tug Gravels were laid down also in the Webi Shebeli and Nogal valleys. Land rubble and red sands indicating arid conditions were deposited at the end of this phase. Two minor wet phases followed, separated from each other by red, wind-blown sand.

NORTH AFRICA

The main sequence of events in the vast area between East Africa and the Mediterranean can be pieced together from evidence collected along the Nile Valley and at two depressions on the edge of the Libyan Desert, the Kharga Oasis, and the Fayum. The Nile terraces should have great potentialities as a means of linking up climatic events in Ethiopia and the Mediterranean, since the river derives most of its water from the highlands of Ethiopia via the Blue Nile, Atbara, and Sobat, and carries gravels and silts along with it. It should therefore be possible to correlate more "pluvial" conditions in the Upper Nile Basin with glacial regressions or interglacial transgressions of the ocean, as reflected in the Mediterranean. There are indications of a period of high rainfall in early Chelles-Acheul times followed by arid conditions and a further wetter period in late Chelles-Acheul times, revealed in high terraces above the Nile. From the Sudan border to Asyut, Nile and wadi gravels at 25 to 30 meters are attributed to Lower Acheulian times; at 12 to 15 meters to the Middle Acheulian; and at 8 to 10 meters to the Acheulio-Levalloisian.[23]

At Kharga Oasis, Miss Caton-Thompson concluded that although the term "pluvial epoch" is justified on the scarp, this was not the case within the Kharga Depression, where Paleolithic man was dependent on mound springs for his water supply (these were subartesian and independent of local rainfall). Plateau and wadi tufas on the scarp show that there was an early Pleistocene wetter period followed by a prolonged dry period associated with the formation of breccias and red sands, succeeded, in turn, by a second but less intense wetter period. At this time, presumably broadly equivalent to the early Gamblian of East Africa, man moved into the depression and the favorable climate lasted into Levalloisian-Khargan and Khargan times, or the end of the Middle Paleolithic, in European terminology; from the succeeding Aterian stage onward, no more tufas formed and precipitation decreased. The Khargan is thought to be the equivalent of the Sebilian of the Nile Valley, during which time there were high floods associated with terraces at various heights (depending on the topography) along the Atbara. Aeolian sands in the later silts associated with Sebilian industries near Luxor suggest that the Sahara climate at this time for once was out of phase with the wetter climate of Ethiopia.[24]

In Middle Paleolithic times, the Nile had access to the Fayum Depression and the lake stood 278 feet above its present level; this corresponds with 131 feet, O.D. (Ordnance Datum), for the Fayum lake is now 147 feet below sea level. The lake then dried up completely, but rose again to several progressively lower levels, ending with 206 feet or 59 feet, O.D., just before the Neolithic settlement. As it tapped the Libyan water table, the lake was not entirely dependent on local rainfall. After supplies of Nile water were cut off, however, two well-marked beaches at 180 and 140 feet (33 feet and −7 feet, O.D.) mark pauses in the progressive fall of the lake and indicate two periods of increased rainfall, the second occurring from late Neolithic to Old Kingdom times. There is evidence of a decline in the Nile floods and advance of dunes from about 2400 B.C. to the beginning of Middle Kingdom times, about 2000 B.C.

In the western Sahara, Chelles-Acheul hand axes have been found far from present water supplies, showing that much of the desert was habitable at that time. This was followed by a long, dry interval during which deposits of gypsum formed in various places. Again in Aterian times, the climate must have been wetter, for evidently man moved freely across what is now desert. A second wetter epoch is marked by formations of laterite at Tibesti and Hoggar. A rock engraving of an elk at Tibesti (Fig. 1) shows that the climate of the Sahara in Late Pleistocene times was considerably wetter and colder. There is also strong evidence of a much wetter climate at the time of Mesolithic Khartoum (about 7000 B.C.), and pottery of the type found there was diffused westward over the Sahara, implying that communications were relatively easy. All over the western desert rock paintings and engravings show that hunters and Neolithic pastoralists were living near springs and wadis that are now dry. In historical times, Libya fed the Roman Empire and provided its timber, but since the Arab invaded with his flocks of goats, the cover of vegetation has been slowly eaten away, accelerating soil erosion and precipitating desert conditions. This has been happening all over Africa; man and the goat between them are changing the face of the continent.

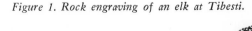

Figure 1. Rock engraving of an elk at Tibesti.

At the cave of Haua Fteah Cyrenaica, in eastern Libya, McBurney excavated an important sequence of deposits covering the whole period from the time of the Last Interglacial onward. During the Early Würm, the climate was wet; a Neanderthal jaw associated with a Levalloiso-Mousterian industry at this level was dated by carbon-14 to about 43,000 years ago. A drier period followed, ending with an abrupt change in the fauna about 28,500 B.C.[25] The succeeding cold, wet period correlated with Middle Würm fits well with the suggested age of the Gamblian pluvial in East Africa.

Climatic Changes and Man

Having examined some of the evidence for climatic changes during the Pleistocene, and discussed the desirability of building up a climatic framework, however tentative, in order to try to correlate human remains and cultures, we must now see what direct effects these events had on man himself and on other fauna. In theory it seems obvious that man would have moved to lower altitudes during cold, wet periods and up into the highlands during drier intervals. These assumptions are borne out to a certain extent by archaeological evidence.

During times when the icecap on the East African mountains came down to about 10,000 feet above sea level instead of 15,000 feet, as it does today, much of the present highlands of Kenya and Ethiopia would have been too cold for human habitation. No hand-ax industries have, in fact, been found above 6,000 feet, and man lived mainly beside lakes in the area of the present rift valley, or on the shores of other lakes, such as Olduvai.

In Later Pleistocene times, after the main rift-valley faulting had taken place, volcanic eruptions in the floor of the trough divided it up into the present series of lake basins. Again man made his home beside the lakes, which were deeper and more extensive than they are today. Not only did he live beside lakes to obtain his water supply, but animals would also concentrate around lakes and water holes and man followed them there to obtain his food.

During the drier periods, covered by the First and Second Intermediate Periods (between the Earlier Stone Age and the M.S.A. and between the M.S.A. and the L.S.A., respectively), there is evidence that man moved up to higher altitudes as the lakes dried up. Industries of these periods are found beside permanent rivers, which flowed from diminished glaciers on the highest mountains; others are concentrated around tectonic springs or rock cisterns, as, for example, in the case of the Magosian (p. 206).

In the Horn, climate evidently had a profound influence over the distribution of industries. During drier phases, settlement was restricted to the larger valleys, or was centered around springs issuing from escarpments on the plateau (the distribution of the Somaliland Stillbay culture illustrates this). During the two postpluvial wet phases, however, water must have flowed in the tugs, for Mesolithic and so-called "Neolithic" industries were spread all over the plateau.

Other mammals are usually affected by climatic changes more than man, who is generally more adaptable. Thus fossil fauna sometimes provides a helpful guide to climate, since desert-living types, animals that prefer bush country, or wet forests can be distinguished. Although it is useful to supplement deductions made by other means, too much reliance should not be placed on this kind of evidence, since some animals are nearly as adaptable in their choice of habitat as is man himself. In the next chapter we shall meet some of the Pleistocene mammals that played an important part in the lives of Paleolithic hunters.

Chapter Three

MAN AND EXTINCT BEASTS

Apart from the value of fossil fauna as a means of dating prehistoric cultures, no account of Stone Age man would be complete—or even intelligible—without a description of some of the animals that lived beside him. Even today, when their numbers have been so sadly reduced, Africa would be unthinkable without its wild animals. In the days when the human population consisted only of scattered bands of hunters, the whole continent must have been teeming with game, just as it is in the very few protected areas such as the Serengeti Plains today.

With the exception of those whose principles prevent them from eating meat, most people prefer a mixed diet. Even the predominantly vegetarian apes, and also baboons, enjoy an occasional taste of flesh. Man is far more carnivorously inclined than the apes, and when the supply of game is low, he will sometimes take to cannibalism to satisfy his craving for meat. Two German geologists who lived in the Namib Desert in southwest Africa during the war to avoid being put in a concentration camp described how their obsession with hunting made

86

them see visions of animals throughout the hours of wakefulness as well as in their dreams. They could well understand why Stone Age men covered their rock shelters with pictures of animals they had killed and hoped to kill.[26]

But before meeting some of the curious extinct beasts which lived with man during the Pleistocene, we must go back some 20 million years earlier, to the Miocene period, to evaluate East Africa's contribution toward understanding the evolution of apes and humans themselves.

The Earliest Apes

Long before man appeared on the scene at all, apes lived in East Africa that have thrown considerable light on his ancestry. The earliest known fossil apes come from Oligocene beds in the Fayum, Egypt, about 40 million years old; their remains are, however, extremely fragmentary. In 1923, a site at Koru in western Kenya, near the Kavirondo Gulf of Lake Victoria yielded the first fossil apes from East Africa. They are believed to be of early Miocene age, some 20 million years old.

From 1931 onward, Dr. Leakey and his colleagues started working at this and neighboring sites, especially at Songhor and on Rusinga Island near the mouth of the Kavirondo Gulf. They were rewarded by finding many ape remains, consisting mostly of fragmentary jaws, embedded in old lake deposits. In 1934, Dr. A. T. Hopwood described three new genera of apes from East Africa: *Proconsul, Xenopithecus* (later named *Sivapithecus*), and *Limnopithecus*, all of Lower Miocene age.

An almost complete jaw of *Proconsul africanus* was found in 1942, and it was seen that the creature was less like a chimpanzee than had been supposed from the appearance of the smaller fragments found up till then. From that moment, Leakey was determined to go on searching until he found a complete skull of *Proconsul*. This his wife managed to do in 1948, and the precious skull (Plate 4), insured for £5,000, was flown to England clutched in Mrs. Leakey's lap, for Professor W. E. Le Gros Clark to study at Oxford.

Inevitably an important find such as this, the earliest ape skull known from any part of the world, is a matter of luck. It was also the reward

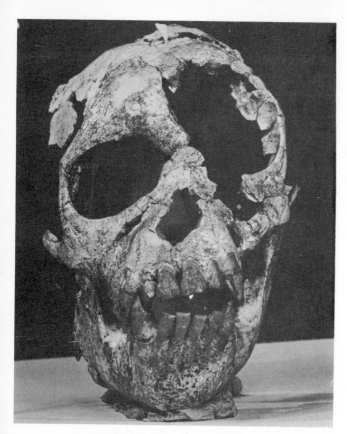

Plate 4. Skull of Proconsul africanus *found on Rusinga Island in 1948.*

for many years of backbreaking work among the eroded, sun-scorched gullies of Rusinga Island. The Miocene lake beds in which the fossils are found are whitish, and the glare from the equatorial sun is terrific. The ground is strewn with fossil tortoise scutes and crocodile verte-brae, so that it is not easy to pick out worthwhile fossils. Most of the bones have been chewed by Miocene crocodiles or by *Hyenodon,* an unpleasant early carnivore of the group known as Creodonts; together these predators have ruined many a good fossil. In spite of these diffi-culties, identifiable ape fossils found since 1947 number several hun-dreds, from eight different sites, and include at least three genera and six species, ranging in size from a gibbon to a gorilla. Enormous quan-tities of fossils of all kinds have been discovered in these Miocene de-posits, including not only mammals, reptiles, fish, birds, and mollusks, but also insects such as grasshoppers and caterpillars, with the soft parts of their bodies beautifully preserved, as well as fruits and seeds.

The concentration of apes in this area (Rusinga Island is only about nine miles long and five miles wide) must, therefore, have been enormous, allowing for the hazards of preservation and discovery of the fossils. The Miocene seems to have been a period during which apes produced new genera and species at a tremendous rate; this sudden exuberance is noticed over and over again in the evolution of many forms of life and has been called "explosive evolution."

Recent work has shown that there are three species of *Proconsul*: *africanus*, *nyanzae*, and *major* (the latter is thought to have been as large as a gorilla). The other genera found at Miocene sites in western Kenya are *Sivapithecus* (also known from Upper Miocene or Lower Pliocene deposits of the Siwalik Hills in India), *Limnopithecus*, represented by two species and probably ancestral to the gibbon, as well as jaws of an unidentified small pongid. As well as apes, other primate remains include those of monkeys, lemurs, and galagos. These Miocene fossils range from the Kavirondo Gulf in the south to Lake Rudolf in the north. Teeth of *Proconsul nyanzae* and *major*, as well as remains of *Sivapithecus*, *Limnopithecus*, and a new galago genus have also been found recently at the volcanic mountains of Napak, in Karamoja, eastern Uganda.[27]

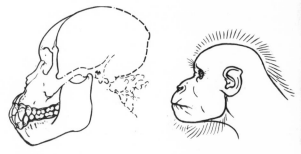

Figure 2. (Left) Proconsul africanus, *with conjectural restoration of back of skull in broken line; (right) reconstruction of* Proconsul africanus.

After studying *Proconsul* (Fig. 2) and the other Kenya Miocene apes, Professor Le Gros Clark came to several interesting conclusions that throw considerable light on man's early ancestors. One of the most important facts to emerge is that these apes were essentially unspecialized and in many ways monkey-like; exaggerated features such as the pronounced brow ridges seen in modern anthropoids had not yet appeared. Among the many characters different from those of the modern great apes, the following are the most striking: (1) the absence of a continuous bar or torus across the brow; (2) the absence of a simian shelf; (3) the shape of the dental arch, which is almost horseshoe-shaped, as in man, instead of having the parallel sides characteristic of apes; (4) the condyles joining the lower jaw with the upper are small and rounded, as in man.

The first feature, the absence of a torus, is characteristic of monkeys and also of modern man; the two superciliary arches are continued outward away from the nose as the supraorbital ridges, which are only slightly pronounced in modern man, still less in woman. In the case of modern anthropoids and also in some forms of fossil man, such as the *Pithecanthropus* group from Java and Peking, Neanderthal Man, and Rhodesian Man, the supraorbital ridges are exaggerated and fused into a single bar or bony ridge which gives attachment to the chief muscles of mastication, the temporal muscles. A pronounced torus, therefore, goes as a rule with a massive jaw and large teeth, and means that the individual had to contend with a diet that required strong chewing. The tusklike canines of most apes (including *Proconsul*) are more developed in males than in females and probably served mainly for purposes of defense. It would be expected that the enlargement of man's brain would be accompanied by a reduction in the size of jaws and teeth; as his brain developed, man presumably became more selective in his diet, and eventually he discovered fire and cooked his meat. He also relied for defense less on his teeth and more on his hands and the weapons that he made to put in them. From the study of *Proconsul*, however, it is seen that the smooth brow ridges of modern man are a very primitive or generalized character, and a heavy torus associated with powerful jaw development is a late specialization.

The second feature of *Proconsul* mentioned above is the absence of a simian shelf; this feature must also be considered as a late specialization of the great apes. The two sides of the lower jaw or mandible are joined at the symphysis, in the middle of the chin region; at the back of the symphysis, in the case of apes, is a bony projection known as the "simian shelf," which serves as an extra reinforcement for the mandible. Man and monkeys never evolved this specialization of modern apes, which is also apparently absent in the earliest apes.

Apart from some characteristics that are essentially apelike, such as the large canine teeth, *Proconsul* has a great many features that are typical of the Cercopithecoid, or monkey stage of development. The pattern of the brain shows that it had evolved little beyond the monkey stage, and the constriction of the nasal aperture is monkey-like.

As well as the skull, several limb bones and a complete hand of *Proconsul* have been found which are of extreme interest. Among the essential physical differences between man and apes are the superior development of the brain and the change in function of the forelimbs from locomotion to that of handling objects. These two characters are mutually interdependent: without adequate brain space, the freedom of the arms and hands would have little value; a developed brain is essential to control the complicated muscles that have to be coordinated for the maintenance of an erect posture. Similarly, the human brain would never have reached its full development without the accompanying development of efficient hands for the making and handling of tools. Locomotion by means of the hind limbs alone necessitates a modification of the vertebral column. The foramen magnum (the hole through which the spinal column passes into the brain through the base of the occipital bone) is shifted so that the head can be held erect; the direction of sight then lies at right angles to the spine. Evidence that an erect posture was assumed long before maximum development of the brain is seen in such fossils as *Pithecanthropus erectus* of Java, whose limb bones are similar to those of *Homo sapiens*, while the braincase is still relatively small.

Recent work makes it clear that the hand and limb bones of *Proconsul africanus* would have been most suited to the type of arboreal locomotion practiced by the modern langurs, particularly the proboscis monkey of Borneo. This "semi-brachiation" is intermediate between quadrupedal walking in the trees and proper brachiation, or arm swinging. It was also found that the thumb was not yet opposable—that is, capable of rotating on its own axis.[28]

Le Gros Clark pointed out that the tarsal pattern of the modern human foot could have been derived more readily from a foot like that of *Proconsul* than from the type of foot seen in the modern great apes. The straight slender shaft of the femur implies agility and lightness of build. Taking all the features of *Proconsul* together, and adding the generally accepted evidence that the Hominidae and Pongidae separated from a common ancestral stock not later than Miocene times, Le Gros Clark concluded that man's ancestors of 20 million years ago must have been very similar to *Proconsul*.

At a press conference in Washington in March, 1962, Leakey announced the discovery of two fragments of the upper jaw of a hominid from Fort Ternan in western Kenya (Plate 5), which he named *Kenyapithecus wickeri*, after Mr. F. Wicker, a farmer on whose land the site lies.[29] The deposits contain two fossiliferous strata with a very

Plate 5. Fragment of upper jaw of Kenyapithecus wickeri, found at Fort Ternan in 1961.

plentiful fauna, including a hitherto unknown diminutive giraffe. Presumably they are a continuation of the *Proconsul* beds and they have been dated by potassium-argon to about 14 million years ago, probably late Upper Miocene or perhaps early Pliocene. Potassium-argon dates obtained for the *Proconsul* beds range from 15 to 22 million years, so the new jaw may not be very much later than *Proconsul*.

One of the most significant features is the canine tooth, which is very much smaller than that of *Proconsul* and of the smallest known Dryopithecine female canines (*Dryopithecus* is an ape whose remains are fairly well known from Miocene and Pliocene deposits in Europe and Asia; while it shows great variety in the teeth, the cusp pattern of the molars is similar to those of early fossil man). It has been suggested that the earliest known hominid may be represented by a jaw of *Ramapithecus brevirostris* from the Nagri Zone of the Siwaliks of India, dated to the Middle or Upper Pliocene of about five to seven million years ago.[30] The Fort Ternan jaw and teeth seem to be very similar, although at least twice the age of *Ramapithecus*. It strongly reinforces the suggestion, previously based only on hints in such forms as *Sivapithecus*, that the hominids branched off from the general hominoid stem far earlier than has been generally supposed.

Pleistocene Mammals

The study of East African fauna began in 1911, when Dr. F. Oswald went out to Kenya to examine Miocene beds at Karungu, on the eastern shores of Lake Victoria, on behalf of the British Museum (Natural History). He also collected some Later Pleistocene fossils from Kanjera. In 1931, Leakey started work at Olduvai, where Dietrich had collected fossils in 1916; he found that the lowest bed contained the remains of *Dinotherium*, a primitive relation of the elephants, associated with pebble tools. *Dinotherium* had previously been regarded as a Miocene and Pliocene form, which had become extinct before the appearance of man. Leakey therefore went to the Kanjera area to attempt to check the Olduvai evidence.

At Kanam, a few miles west of Kanjera, he found a human jaw, as well as the teeth of a *Dinotherium* similar to those of Olduvai, Bed I, and the remains of other primitive elephants. At Kanjera, he found human skull fragments and fossil fauna, including "*Palaeoloxodon recki*," an elephant apparently very similar to the well known straight-tusked elephant of Europe and Asia, *Palaeoloxodon antiquus*.

It is characteristic of Africa that archaic types of fauna tend to persist longer there than in other continents, and the appearance of new forms is always a more reliable guide to geological age than the extinction of old forms. Archaic fauna probably survived longer in Africa than elsewhere because the climatic changes were not so severe as they were in parts of Europe, Asia, and North America during the Ice Age; thus the food supply was more stable and fewer adaptations had to be made to new conditions.

Dr. A. T. Hopwood recognized three faunal stages in East Africa, just as there are in Europe and Asia, corresponding roughly with the three major divisions of the Pleistocene, Early, Middle, and Late. From evidence at Olduvai, Leakey later came to the conclusion that there were not three faunal stages in East Africa but four. He called them Kageran, Kamasian, Kanjeran, and Gamblian, and differentiated them on the grounds that, during the dry periods between each, a number of genera and species became extinct. Hopwood, on the other hand, maintained that there was insufficient distinction between the Kamasian and Kanjeran stages (he called both the Olduvai stage) to justify their separation, although no less than 40 per cent of the known fauna from the second (Kamasian) stage became extinct before the third (Kanjeran) stage.

At the Third Pan-African Congress on Prehistory at Livingstone, in 1955, four faunal stages were recognized and were named as follows: (1) Omo-Kanam; (2) Lower Olduvai (Beds I and II); (3) Upper

Map 5. East African Pleistocene sites with fossil fauna.

Olduvai (Beds III and IV), (4) Post-Olduvai. As Leakey's recent work at Olduvai has shown that the fauna of Beds I and II are very different, and as Omo appears to be later than Kanam, it will certainly be necessary to revise these stage names yet again. Eventually it will no doubt be possible to distinguish three major divisions as in Europe and Asia; in the meantime, five subdivisions of the Pleistocene may be suggested, which for convenience might be referred to as (1) Kanam; (2) Lower Olduvai; (3) Middle Olduvai; (4) Upper Olduvai; (5) Post-Olduvai, or Gamblian.

The main Pleistocene fossiliferous sites of East Africa are shown on Map 5. The first faunal stage, equivalent to the Lower or Middle Villafranchian of Europe and Asia, is represented at Kanam and in part of the series in the western rift named after Kaiso, a fishing village on Lake Albert. The second faunal stage, equivalent to the Upper Villafranchian, is known from Olduvai, Bed I; from a later part of the Kaiso series; in the Omo Valley, north of Lake Rudolf; and at Laetolil, near Olduvai. The third stage is Mid Pleistocene and perhaps equivalent in part at least to the Cromerian Interglacial of Europe; it is represented at Olduvai, Bed II, and perhaps also at Rawi, near Kanam. The fourth stage may span both the late Mid and early Later Pleistocene (late Middle and early Upper Pleistocene in European terminology); as well as at Olduvai, Beds III and IV, this stage is known from a good many sites, including Olorgesailie in the Kenya Rift Valley; Kanjera in western Kenya; and the Semliki series of the western rift in Uganda and the Congo. The fifth stage of the time of the Gamblian pluvial (which, it is suggested, should be correlated with Main and Late Würm) consists almost entirely of living species, though sometimes the assemblages are rather different from those of the same area at the present time and suggest a wetter climate.

The fauna of Olduvai as a whole from Beds I to IV, as we have seen, gives little indication of major changes of climate during the Pleistocene; it suggests a savanna environment similar to that of today, though generally slightly wetter than at present. In 1951 it was calculated that 57 per cent of the fauna of Bed I became extinct at the end of that period, and 41 per cent of the fauna of Bed II became extinct before Beds III and IV times.[31] At the time of writing, the Olduvai fauna is being revised, so it would be misleading to give details of the lists published so far. Leakey, however, now estimates that over 90 per cent of the larger mammals of Bed I became extinct before the formation of Bed II.[32] There appears to be a far greater difference between the second and third faunal stages than there is between the third and fourth: Bed I, Olduvai, is apparently separated from Bed II by a very long time interval, whereas there is relatively little difference between the fauna of Beds II, III, and IV.

We shall now look at a few of the Pleistocene mammals represented in the five faunal subdivisions. The first and second faunal stages are correlated with the Lower Pleistocene or Villafranchian, named after Villafranca d'Asti in Italy, where *Elephas*, *Equus*, and *Bos* appear with an otherwise characteristically Tertiary fauna. The beginning of the Pleistocene in Africa, as elsewhere, is characterized by the first appearance of true elephants, the one-toed horse, and modern cattle. But there are, in addition, many archaic types which survived into the Pleistocene of Africa long after they became extinct in other parts of the Old World; examples are mastodonts, chalicotheres (clawed ungulates), three-toed horses (*Stylohipparion*), and antlered giraffids (*Sivatherium*). Many of these continued even later than the Villafranchian.

Most fascinating of all the Pleistocene mammals of East Africa, perhaps, are the ancestral elephants and the giant pigs; such a variety of both these animals existed that it seems extraordinary that they were able to compete with one another, though each genus must have occupied its own particular environment and had its own individual food preferences.

Strangest of all the elephant's distant relations was *Dinotherium*, a beast with downward and backward curving tusks in the lower jaw; in Asia and Europe it died out before the beginning of the Pleistocene, but in East Africa it continued as late as the Mid Pleistocene, into Olduvai, Bed II. A long-jawed trilophodont (distinct from the shorter-jawed mastodonts) known as *Anancus*, which had tremendously long, straight tusks, lived during the Kanam, Bed I, and Bed II, Olduvai, stages. These were side branches of the line leading to the true elephants, among whose ancestors is *Stegodon*; this form is well known from Pliocene and Pleistocene deposits in the Siwalik Hills of India and is represented at Kaiso and Kanam, but apparently not later than the first faunal stage in East Africa.

The earliest true elephant of Villafranchian times is "*Archidiskodon*," now generally classed as *Elephas* (the same genus as the modern Indian elephant). The most primitive species is *subplanifrons*, represented at Kanam. Cooke has revised the complicated nomenclature of the African elephants and considers that there were only two main branches stemming from "*Archidiskodon*" *planifrons*, one consisting of extinct archidiskodonts, the other including species of *Loxodonta* leading to the modern African elephant of that name.[33] In East Africa, the next stage after "*Archidiskodon*" *subplanifrons* is *A. exoptatus*, described by various names in the past and represented at Kanam, Omo, Laetolil, and Olduvai, I. Stages in elephant evolution are judged mainly by the height of the crown of the molars and by the increasing com-

plexity of the plates of these teeth. The final archidiskodont stage
in East Africa is represented by *A. recki*, particularly characteristic
of Olduvai, Bed IV, but also found much earlier, at Omo and from
Bed I onward at Olduvai. This animal is usually referred to as
"*Palaeoloxodon recki*," since it was thought to be very similar to the
well-known straight-tusked elephant *Palaeoloxodon antiquus* of Asia
and Europe. From his work at Omo, however, Arambourg considered
this resemblance to be superficial. But since it is usually described in
the literature as *P. recki*, it will be less confusing if we stick to this
name here.

Pigs were even more varied than the elephants, and Leakey listed
no less than 11 genera (including three still living) and 23
species; probably their nomenclature will also be revised and simplified
in the future. *Notochoerus euilus* is the earliest and was present at
Kaiso, Omo, and Bed I, Olduvai; other species of *Notochoerus* continue
throughout Beds I to IV. *Mesochoerus olduvaiensis* appears in Beds I
and II, but an earlier species of this genus is present at Kaiso and Omo.
The formidable *Afrochoerus nicoli*, as large as a modern rhino and
with tusks a yard long, occurs in Beds II to IV (Fig. 3).

As far as the hippos are concerned, the earliest is *Hippopotamus
imaguncula* of Kaiso and Kanam. *H. gorgops* whose projecting brow
ridges suggest that he had periscopic eyes, existed from Bed I to Bed
IV times. The modern hippo, *H. amphibius*, was already present in the
Kaiso series. Other mammals with a long time range are the modern
giraffe and its distant relative *Sivatherium*, a short-necked antlered
giraffid that survived into Bed IV and later still in various other parts of
Africa. The three-toed horse *Stylohipparion* and the large one-toed
Equus olduvaiensis both survived from the Kanam and Kaiso stage
right through into Bed IV. A huge baboon, *Simopithecus*, lived from
the time of Omo up to Bed IV; and in Bed II times there was an even
bigger baboon whose jaw is larger than a gorilla's.

The fantastic *Pelorovis olduvaiensis* (Fig. 4 and Plate 6) is a new genus
first described from Olduvia (Beds II to IV). It has been described as
a sheep, but recent studies suggest it may not have been a sheep at all.

Figure 3. Upper tusk of Afrochoerus nicoli,
*Bed II, Olduvai, compared with corresponding
tusk of a modern warthog (top).*

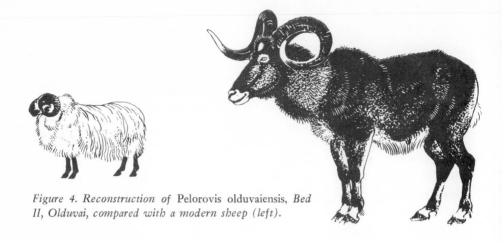

Figure 4. Reconstruction of Pelorovis olduvaiensis, Bed II, Olduvai, compared with a modern sheep (left).

It was larger than a modern buffalo, with horn cores measuring up to 7 feet tip to tip; judging by the proportion of core to horn in modern sheep, this implies that the horn span of *Pelorovis* may have been as much as 12 feet! A giant buffalo, *Bularchus arok*, was also discovered at Olduvai (Beds II to IV). The long-horned buffalo *Homoioceras nilssoni*, which resembles the Indian water buffalo *Bubalus*, first appears in Bed IV, Olduvai; another species was found at Singa, on the Blue Nile, and others occur in South Africa; it is one of the few extinct mammals that persists into Gamblian times.

It seems strange to find side by side with their curious extinct relatives modern forms that have continued unchanged since the Early Pleistocene up to the present; examples are the hippopotamus, white rhino, giraffe, and various kinds of antelopes. Probably it was their bulk that caused many of the huge forms to die out. The trend toward gigantism happens frequently in the course of evolution and no really convincing reason for it has yet been suggested. Giants are particularly characteristic of the Pleistocene of Africa; were minerals and trace elements in the volcanic soils responsible for increased glandular activity? But of course there were also gigantic mammals in non-volcanic parts of the world. The smaller size of most modern mammals compared with their forerunners during the Pleistocene is much easier to account for; it is a disadvantage to be conspicuous and cursed with a big appetite in a world overrun by man.

The huge herbivorous animals of Pleistocene times must have provided a stimulus to the ingenuity of early man, and we know that hunters from the time of Bed II, Olduvai, onward met this challenge successfully. We may imagine that group cooperation in the chase led to the communication of ideas and hence to some form of speech. As well as stimulating man's social life and culture, the taste for meat must have modified his physical appearance. Natural selection favors hunters with strong legs and a wiry frame able to endure long hours of following up a wounded animal. This applies in open country where the game is plentiful—for example, in the case of the Upper Paleolithic reindeer and mammoth hunters of Europe, or the Plains Indians who lived almost entirely on bison. For creeping through forests, on the other hand, it is advantageous to be a pygmy, and, since game is scarce and elusive in the forests and the pygmy's diet is perforce low in protein, he is in any case unlikely to be as large as the more fortunate hunters of the plains.

Plate 6. Skull and horn cores of Pelorovis olduvaiensis, *in the course of excavation at Olduvai.*

During the greater part of the Pleistocene, the fauna was more or less the same all over the African continent. Fossils from sites in East Africa are similar to those from South Africa or from Algeria and Morocco. At various times during the Pleistocene, the Sahara was apparently well watered, and primitive elephants, giraffids, white rhinos, and hippopotamuses were ubiquitous from the Cape to the Mediterranean. During the time of the Last Glaciation, however, European migrants such as "Merck's rhinoceros," deer, and bears moved into North Africa, while typically African forms such as elephants, lions, and antelopes made a counter-movement into Europe. European forms very rarely penetrated south of the Atlas, though the discovery of a rock engraving depicting an elk in the Tibesti region shows that there may have been exceptions (see p. 83). Soon after the wetter and colder climate that tempted elks to Tibesti, the Sahara effectively separated the truly African or "Ethiopian" fauna from that of the Mediterranean region.

If such movements were possible for animals during the time of the Last Glaciation, it seems even more probable that man migrated from one continent to the other. He may have made use of skin boats or rafts from very early times, long before they are known from the archaeological record, to cross the shallow seas over parts of the Mediterranean. It seems probable that the hand-ax culture was carried by land from its original home in eastern or central Africa to Western Europe and Asia, and it makers may have returned to Africa as the ice advanced.

Africa may have been connected with Asia across the southern part of the Red Sea during the early part of the Pleistocene; the faunas of these two continents are even more closely connected than those of Africa and Europe. Land communications across the Red Sea may have existed up to Later Pleistocene times, enabling the hand-ax culture to spread from Africa across Arabia and Persia to India. As in the case of the Sahara, the Arabian Desert was not always such a formidable barrier as it is today, and movements of men and other animals across it were sometimes possible.

Chapter Four

THE EARLIEST HOMINIDS

Before beginning a study of man, it is important to define what is, in fact, meant by "man." This sounds obvious and simple enough, yet when we try to arrive at such a definition we find ourselves up against considerable difficulties. Classification of a fossil skull is made after a detailed consideration of its morphological features, yet even after all the features have been studied exhaustively, it often happens that experts are in profound disagreement over the status of the find. It must first be decided whether an individual is "man" or "ape," and, if man, to which of the groups of mankind he belongs. The line dividing man and apes is so arbitrary that considerations other than the anatomical features have to be taken into account; we are forced to fall back on defining man as a toolmaker, or as having the power of speech. We depend on his mental attributes more than on the shape of his bones. Since it is difficult to assess these qualities in a fossil many thousands of years old, the subjective element creeps in unavoidably; the first physical anthropologist to describe a fossil names it according to the resemblances or differences he sees in it with regard to known forms. Another equally eminent scientist may see it in quite a different light.

Classification of Man

Man has been classed in the order of Primates, which also includes apes, monkeys, lemurs, tarsiers, and tree shrews. Along with apes and monkeys, he is grouped in the suborder Anthropoidea. Man and apes belong to the superfamily Hominoidea, which is further subdivided into two families; the Hominidae, comprising modern and extinct forms of man, and the Pongidae, or anthropoid apes. Very broadly, the Hominidae may be defined as walking unsupported on two legs, while the Pongidae are dependent also on their arms for locomotion.

Many theories have been held during the present century regarding the classification of the Hominidae. Nowadays the Hominidae are generally divided into two sub-families: the Australopithecinae and the Homininae. In the past some authorities held that the line of evolution of the Homininae was a straight one, beginning with *Pithecanthropus* and continuing through Neanderthal Man to *Homo sapiens*. This theory of straight-line evolution has now been rejected; it is accepted that the general trend has been in this direction, but with Neanderthal Man as a side branch of the main stem.

The main trouble about the classification of fossil man is, of course, his rarity. Too few specimens are known to attempt a proper classification, and such specimens as exist are often fragmentary, sometimes represented by nothing more than part of a mandible. There is always a danger, therefore, that an aberrant individual may be fixed as a type from lack of comparative material.

In the past, the "splitters" have been more numerous than the "lumpers." The excitement over each fresh fossil find led to the creation of many genera and species that, in the light of subsequent work, appear unjustified. It is difficult to be objective over man; certainly he has been unduly "split" when compared with the classification of the rest of the animal kingdom. Recently the trend has gone in the opposite direction and an effort has been made toward simplification. A few taxonomists nowadays would like to see all hominids, extinct and recent, including the Australopithecines, classified in a single genus *Homo*. The vast majority, however, distinguish at least two genera: *Australopithecus* and *Homo*. Some also recognize a second genus of the

Australopithecines, *Paranthropus;* and many also accept *Pithecanthropus,* though others prefer to call the latter *Homo erectus. Homo neanderthalensis, Homo soloensis,* and *Homo rhodesiensis* are regarded by some authorities as species distinct from *Homo sapiens,* while others consider them to be only sub-species of *Homo sapiens.* In many ways, Solo Man and Rhodesian Man are the Asiatic and African equivalents of the Neanderthalers, yet they appear to be rather closer to *Homo sapiens* than are the Neanderthalers.

Ashley Montagu defined a species as being "reproductively isolated from other species, being either actually unable to exchange genes with other similar groups or capable of doing so under conditions which do not effect the specific integrity of the group.[34] Fertile crossings have been made not only of species but also of genera of mammals under "artificial" conditions—that is, conditions promoted by man, for example, in the case of cattle and buffalo. Such crosses would occur very rarely, if ever, under natural conditions and would not affect the "specific integrity" of the group. A genetical definition of species, by Mayr, is "Actually or potentially interbreeding natural populations which are reproductively isolated from other such groups."[35] In the past, of course, populations were far more isolated geographically and hence genetically than they are today.

A solution to the old question of whether the Neanderthalers of Mt. Carmel in Palestine crossed with modern *Homo sapiens* may now be nearer. As a result of studies of fauna and climate, supported by carbon-14 dates, it has been suggested that the "classic" Neanderthalers of the Tabun Cave may be 11,000 years earlier than the "hybrid"-like forms from the Skhūl Cave.[36] * This does not, of course, rule out the possibility that crossings did occur; but it is perhaps more likely to have been at an earlier stage, between more generalized types and before the end product "classic" Neanderthalers became so specialized.

Probably the range of variation in man was far more marked during the Pleistocene than it was later; the wide variety of types known from the fossil record—and presumably there were many others still unknown to us—is less surprising than the fact that natural selection has eliminated all save *Homo sapiens* in his modern form. Following the *Pithecanthropus* stage, about 200,000 years ago, there was probably a "spectrum" of varieties of early *Homo,* ranging from generalized pre-Neanderthal and pre-Rhodesian to more *sapiens*-like forms; the

* While this book was on press, however, Dr. Dorothy Garrod announced that she considers the people of Tabun and Skhūl to have been contemporaries after all.

Steinheim and Swanscombe skulls perhaps occupy an intermediary
position in the "spectrum" (see Table 3).[37] Some of these populations
would have mixed, while others may have remained relatively isolated
and turned into end products such as the classic Neanderthalers and the
Rhodesioids.

Almost certainly, too, there was far greater sexual dimorphism in the
past than there is today, since there was greater need for the males to
defend the females. Sexual dimorphism, as well as a great range of
individual and geographic variations, must account for many of the
distinctive features of the various Australopithecines, and the recognition of this fact helps to clear up some of the confusion in terminology
caused by "splitters."

*Table 3. Sites of fossil man and time ranges of the Australopithecines, Pithecan-
thropines, and Homo. The heavy lines divide these three main groups and also
the Neanderthalers and similar forms in Asia (Solo Man) and Africa (the
Rhodesioids). The horizontal scale gives an approximate indication of the range
in space of the various hominids. For example, there were no hominids other
than the Australopithecines, so far as is known, up till about 500,000 years ago,
when the Pithecanthropines began to overlap with them. By about 250,000
years ago, the Australopithecines were extinct and Homo began to overlap with
the Pithecanthropines, which themselves became extinct about 100,000 years ago.*

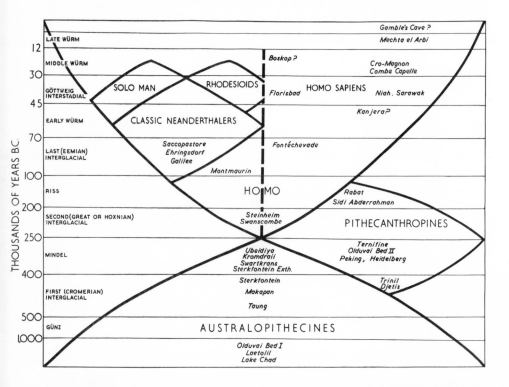

Briefly, present views on the classification of man may be summarized as follows:

First Stage: *Australopithecus* (including "*Paranthropus*," "*Meganthropus*," and "*Zinjanthropus*"), with two species, *A. africanus* and *A. robustus*. At least one and three-quarter million years to *c.* 400,000 years ago. Lower Pleistocene in Sahara and East Africa, early Middle Pleistocene in South Africa, Java, and Palestine.

Second Stage: *Pithecanthropus* (sometimes known as *Homo erectus*), *P. modjokertensis*, and *P. erectus, c.* 500,000 years in Java. In Germany (Heidelberg jaw); Peking (*Pithecanthropus pekinensis*), East Africa (Olduvai Bed, II), and Algeria ("*Atlanthropus*"), *c.* 350,000 years (Mindel Glaciation). In Morocco, persisting up to *c.* 200,000 years (Early Riss).

Third Stage: *Homo.* Generalized "*sapiens*-Neanderthaloid" ancestors in England and Germany (Swanscombe and Steinheim), *c.* 250,000 years (Second Interglacial).
Homo neanderthalensis in Europe, Asia, and North Africa, *c.* 70,000 to 35,000 years.
"Rhodesioids" (*Homo rhodesiensis* and *Homo soloensis*), in Africa and Java, *c.* 35,000 years.
Homo sapiens, Combe Capelle, Europe, *c.* 30,000 years. Florisbad, South Africa, *c.* 35,000 years; Niah, Sarawak, *c.* 40,000; Kanjera, East Africa, *c.* 55,000(?).

Hominid Anatomy

The adaptation primarily responsible for the origin of man, or the hominids as distinct from the other hominoids, is concerned with the pelvis and feet; the expansion of the brain came later. The pelvis had to make radical changes to fit the body for the bipedal position. There are indications in the fossil record (for example, in the Australopithecinae) that this adaptation took place before any significant modifications in the skull or brain. The pelvic region is but rarely preserved; fossil remains most commonly found are jaws or parts of the cranium, so that it is generally necessary to base classifications on features that evolved in a human direction *after* man had adopted an erect posture.

In assessing the status of a fossil skull, the absolute size of the brain is important, but as a diagnostic feature it should be used with caution unless details are known about the body size of extinct forms and their rate of growth. Relative to the size of the body, the brains of some small monkeys can equal or even surpass those of man. In man, the brain continues to grow for a longer period and at a more intense rate than in the case of apes; in the same way, the brain size of apes surpasses that of monkeys by continuation and intensification of growth.

The complexity of the brain is more important than its absolute volume; and the relative proportions of different centers, when they can be assessed from brain impressions in fossil skulls, often reveal interesting facts about the progress of evolution. The last part to become fully developed, apparently, was the frontal association area, the most important and highest center of the brain.

Early hominids such as *Pithecanthropus* from Java clearly had smaller brains than modern man; yet the average Neanderthal brain was larger than the modern mean. Within the *Pithecanthropus* group from Java and Peking, however, although the average cranial capacity is estimated as 950 c.c., individual variation apparently ranged from about 780 c.c. in Java to 1300 c.c. in a specimen from Peking, thus overlapping the range of variation of both modern apes and modern man. It can be seen, therefore, that brain size by itself is no absolute criterion of intelligence. Considering their size, the Australopithecines had brains slightly above the average of modern apes (chimpanzees average 400 c.c.), yet they fall a long way short of the modern human brain. Cranial capacities of the three main stages of hominid evolution are as follows: Australopithecines, 450-550 c.c.; Pithecanthropines of Java, 775-900 c.c. and of Peking, 1000-1300 c.c.; *Homo sapiens*, 1100-1500 c.c.

A comparison between cranial capacity and the area of the palate is also significant. The highest ratio of brain to palate occurs in infancy, after which jaw development gains rapidly on brain expansion. As man's brain increased in size, the area of the palate has tended to decrease. In *Homo sapiens* the ratio of palate to cranial capacity may be of the order of 1:60, while in the chimpanzee the ratio may be as low as 1:8. In the Australopithecines, the ratio is intermediate, averaging 1:26; but it must be considerably lower in the case of "*Zinjanthropus*" from Olduvai.

These few examples are enough to show that the Australopithecines are in many ways intermediate between apes and men, though in most essentials they are nearer to men.

The Australopithecines of South Africa

We cannot study the Australopithecines of East Africa without first looking at their better-known cousins from South Africa. The Australopithecinae, a long word that means simply, "southern apes," were first discovered by Professor Raymond Dart in Bechuanaland and later by the late Dr. Robert Broom in the limestone caves of the Transvaal. Dart was cautious when he named them apes, though far from cautious in other respects. From the time of his first description of the infant *Australopithecus* from Taung in 1924 until Broom began finding adult specimens in the late thirties, Dart was practically alone in the scientific world in his insistence that his baby was no mere ape.

Eventually he was backed up by Le Gros Clark, who said that on the basis of dental morphology alone it was impossible to exclude these small-brained, prognathous creatures from the family Hominidae. The molars are large, certainly, but the shape and form is essentially the same as in our own and quite unlike those of the apes. Teeth are more durable than bone and are often preserved when little else remains; it was only natural, therefore, that the shape, size, and pattern of the teeth were thought to be among the most diagnostic features, and, for want of anything else, classifications of a good many fossil forms have been made on the basis of teeth alone. The Australopithecines have shown that there is an overlap rather than a hard-and-fast boundary between pongids and hominids.

Some of the South African fossils are very finely preserved, so that a detailed study of features other than teeth is possible. It has revealed a combination of characters not previously known either in the Pongidae or Hominidae. In the proportions of their brains and in the facial bones they resemble the modern great apes; but in the size, shape, and pattern of their teeth and in their limb bones they must be classed with the Hominidae, and today they are regarded as members of this family.

The limb bones and pelves indicate that they were able to stand and run on two legs, though probably the heavier forms would have been able only to shuffle along rather than walk in the human fashion.[38] The poise of the head must have approached that of man. The evenly curved horseshoe-shaped dental arch differs little from that of *Pithe-*

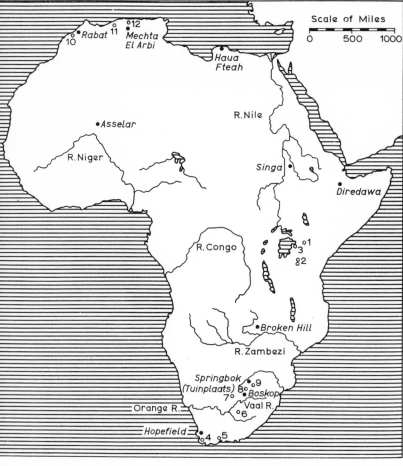

Map 6. *Main sites of fossil man in Africa. Key: (1) Gamble's Cave, (2) Olduvai and Eyasi, (3) Kanam and Kanjera, (4) Cape Flats and Fish Hoek, (5) Matjes River and Tzitzikama, (6) Floris- bad, (7) Taung, (8) Sterkfontein, (9) Makapansgat, (10) Sidi Ab- derrahman, (11) Ternifine, (12) Afalou-bou-Rhummel.*

canthropus and is typically hominid. The canine teeth are small and do not interlock as in the case of modern apes, while the molars and pre- molars are worn flat, characteristic of a human way of chewing. The large first lower premolar has two cusps, as in man, instead of the sectorial type of cusps seen in apes.

The "splitters" divided the Australopithecinae into a number of genera and species, but they seem to fall into two main groups. The earlier ones are less specialized (*Australopithecus africanus* from Taung, "*Australopithecus prometheus*" from Makapan, and "*Pleisianthropus transvaalensis*" from Sterkfontein) (see Map 6). The later group (*Paranthropus robustus* from Kromdraai and "*P. crassidens*" from

Swartkrans) have more exaggerated features and are more robust and apelike. Another specimen from Swartkrans, represented only by a fragmentary jaw, was named *Telanthropus*.

The first group is now classed as *Australopithecus africanus*, the second usually as *Australopithecus robustus*, rather than as a distinct genus, *Paranthropus*. With regard to *Telanthropus*, J. T. Robinson, who succeeded the late Dr. Robert Broom in his great work on the Transvaal Australopithecines, recently proposed that the name "*Telanthropus*" should be dropped and that this solitary and controversial jaw should be regarded as *Homo erectus*. This is the name adopted by some taxonomists for *Pithecanthropus erectus* of Java.

The teeth suggest that the *Australopithecus africanus* group (Fig. 5) was omnivorous, while the *A. robustus* group, with their huge molars (see Plate 10), were largely vegetarian. The former, which were far more lightly built, are more adapted to life in open country, the latter more suited to a forest environment. Much progress has been made on dating these creatures lately, by means of comparisons of the accompanying fauna, and as the result of C. K. Brain's work on sand grains in the Australopithecine deposits. This has shown that the earlier *A. africanus* group lived during an arid period, the *robustus* group during a succeeding wetter phase (see Table 3). The former, in fact, may have been already occupying the Sterkfontein Valley when the latter moved in, during the early part of the Mid Pleistocene.

From time to time, various reports appeared suggesting that the Australopithecines made tools, both of bone and stone. Dart ardently championed the cause of what he called the osteodontokeratic culture of the Australopithecines and to try to prove his point made extremely

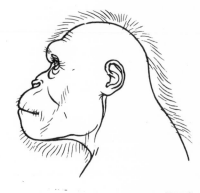

Figure 5. Reconstruction of Australopithecus africanus, *from Sterkfontein.*

detailed statistical analyses of broken bone, teeth, and horns in the Limeworks Cave at Makapansgat. He maintained that many of these fragments had been not only used but also worked into tools and weapons. Others believe that the bones represent a midden of food refuse, accumulated as the result of scavenging from the kills of carnivores. Owing to their lack of effective cutting tools, the Australopithecines would tear off only certain parts of the carcass—hence the preponderance of heads and limb bones of antelopes in the cave. Having brought their booty back to the rock shelter, they would then break open the skulls for brains and the long bones for marrow. Oakley does not accept any of the bones he has examined from Limeworks Cave as showing undoubted signs of having been used as tools or weapons, though he agrees that broken bones and teeth were no doubt used sometimes in ways such as Dart so imaginatively envisaged.[39]

In spite of diligent search, no stone tools were found in the gray breccia containing Australopithecine bones at Makapansgat, nor in fact at any of the sites dating from the earlier arid period. The only tools associated with *Australopithecus* come from the Sterkfontein Extension Site, near the type site, and from Swartkrans, where stone tools have been found in the pink breccia containing remains of *A. robustus* and *"Telanthropus."* The tools are probably early Chellean rather than pre-Chellean or Oldowan, as at first supposed.

The question now arises: Which of the hominids, *Australopithecus africanus*, *A. robustus*, or *"Telanthropus"* was the toolmaker? Or were all three toolmakers? It seems unlikely that *Australopithecus* made tools in his early stages, during the drier climatic phase, or some would surely have been discovered in the Limeworks Cave midden. By the time of the succeeding wetter phase represented at Sterkfontein Extension Site he may have learned this art; or of course there is the possibility that the pebble tools there were made by another kind of hominid, although their remains have not been found at this site. It seems very likely that the Pithecanthropine *"Telanthropus"* was the maker of the Chellean-type tools at Swartkrans, for we would expect *Australopithecus*, if he made tools at all, to make Oldowan pebble tools only.

As a result of studies of the Australopithecine limb bones, Napier has concluded that the hand of *Australopithecus africanus* would be more suited to shaping pebbles than the hand of *A. robustus*, who in general is heavier and clumsier. This question of the identity of the toolmaker arises again in connection with the East African Australo-pithecines, with which we are more concerned in this book but which cannot be appreciated properly without this preliminary glance at their relations. ¶

More Australopithecines

In the very natural excitement over Leakey's *"Zinjanthropus"* and "pre-*Zinjanthropus*" finds at Olduvai, it is sometimes forgotten that these were not the first Australopithecines to come from East Africa. The first, in fact, was discovered by Kohl-Larsen as long ago as 1939. It came from the Laetolil beds near Lake Eyasi, 50 miles south of Olduvai. The lower part of these deposits is thought to be somewhat earlier than Bed I, Olduvai, though the upper part almost certainly overlaps in time with Bed I. The find consists of a fragmentary upper jaw with two premolars. It was named *"Meganthropus africanus"* by Weinert, who thus included it in the same genus as *Meganthropus paleojavanicus*, from the Djetis beds of Java. Robinson, with his great knowledge of the South African Australopithecines, considers that these forms are similar to *Australopithecus robustus*, though earlier than *A. robustus* of the Transvaal.

Nor are the Australopithecines confined to South and East Africa. The Java fossil is one example from Asia; another may be a specimen found by M. Stekelis at Ubeidiya, near Afikim in the Jordan Valley in 1960 which is being studied at the time of writing. It consists of only two fragments of a cranium, said to be four times as thick as that of modern man, accompanied by fossil mammals and pebble tools.

In 1961, a French paleontologist, Y. Coppens, discovered a frag-mentary Australopithecine skull at Koro Toro, northeast of Lake Chad, in the Sahara. It was apparently associated with Lower, or possibly Middle, Villafranchian fauna, including *Anancus osiris* and *Archi-diskodon africanavus*, a mammoth very similar to, if not identical with, one from Kanam. If this dating is confirmed, the Lake Chad Australo-pithecine (which may perhaps be *A. robustus*) would be by far the earliest yet known (see Table 3).

Before looking at *"Zinjanthropus"* from Olduvai, it may be useful to recapitulate the known distribution and relative dating of the

Australopithecines. With the earliest at the bottom, the sequence seems to be as follows:

MIDDLE PLEISTOCENE

A. robustus(?)	Ubeidiya, Jordan Valley	c. 400,000 years(?)
A. robustus	Kromdraai Swartkrans	
A. africanus	Sterkfontein Extension Sterkfontein Makapan Taung	
A. robustus	Djetis beds, Java	c. 500,000 years

LOWER PLEISTOCENE

A. robustus ("Zinjanthropus")	Olduvai	1,700,000 years (?) (potassium-argon date)
"Pre-Zinjanthropus"	Olduvai	
A. robustus ("Meganthropus")	Laetolil	
A. robustus(?)	Lake Chad	c. 2,000,000 years (?)

From the evidence available so far, the Australopithecines seem to have evolved somewhere to the north and east of the forest belt of equatorial Africa. Perhaps their ancestors lived on the edges of these forests and gradually spread into the open country, where they adopted the erect posture and began experimenting with their hands. From this region, they spread during the early Middle Pleistocene into South Africa and Asia. There is always the possibility of independent parallel evolution in Asia, but so far no Australopithecine remains dating from the Lower Pleistocene have been found anywhere outside the Sahara and East Africa.

By the time of the first known *A. robustus* in Java, the first Pithecanthropine, *Pithecanthropus modjokertensis*, had already appeared and remains of both are found in the same Djetis beds (see Table 3). The overlying Trinil beds in Java containing *Pithecanthropus erectus* have been dated by potassium-argon to less than 500,000 years. These first Pithecanthropines are almost certainly contemporary with the later Australopithecines of South Africa, the *A. robustus* group, and with the creature first called *"Telanthropus"* but now considered to be a Pithecanthropine.

So far there is no very conclusive evidence as to whether *Australopithecus africanus* or *robustus* was earlier; in fact they seem to overlap in time; in South Africa, however, *A. africanus* appears to be consistently earlier than *A. robustus*.

Olduvai Gorge

Olduvai Gorge, (Plate 7), certainly one of the most imposing Paleolithic sites in the world, was first seen by a German entomologist, Professor Kattwinkel, in 1911. His delight can well be imagined when he suddenly came upon this great gash in the country, about 300 feet deep, looking like the Grand Canyon on a smaller scale. Rhinos and lions are a common sight in and around it, but the chief difficulty in excavating the site is the absence of water. Daily expeditions to fetch it are necessary, and Leakey once estimated that this precious liquid cost him three shillings for each gallon brought to the gorge, only a little less than a gallon of gasoline at that time. Only the toughest vehicles can approach Olduvai over the boulder-strewn tracks; often they break down a hundred miles or so from the nearest spare part.

Although it is usually one of the driest places in East Africa, Olduvai sometimes cannot be approached at all during the rainy season, as the track becomes impassable, the dust turning into a sea of mud. In 1962, a raging torrent flowed through the gorge such as had not been seen for thirty years, and its erosive force must have been tremendous. After the First Pan-African Congress of Prehistory, held in Nairobi in 1947, delegates from all over Africa and other continents had an opportunity of visiting the gorge; few of them will ever forget their adventures over flooded roads on the return journey. On the outward trip they were taken via Ngorongoro, the largest caldera in the world, some twelve miles across, formed by the subsidence of a volcanic cone. From what appears to be the roof of the world, on the rim of this caldera, the vast Serengeti Plains stretch out to the horizon, dotted with herds of zebra and wildebeest. In the foreground are the mountains of Oldeani and Lemagrut, hiding Lake Eyasi to the southwest; the gorge itself is reached after crossing the Balbal Depression. It assumed its present form, with narrow floor and steep sides, in Post-

Plate 7. Olduvai Gorge, Tanganyika.

Pleistocene times, when erosion cut right down into the Pleistocene deposits, thereby exposing the great series of sediments seen today.

Olduvai is unique as a prehistoric site, for not only have eleven distinct stages of the Chelles-Acheul hand-ax culture been distinguished (by far the longest evolutionary sequence of this culture known), but they overlie the pre-Chellean Oldowan pebble culture, named after this site.

As we have seen earlier, there are four Pleistocene beds at Olduvai, as well as the Post-Pleistocene Bed V. They have been repeatedly faulted, so that nowhere in the gorge is the complete succession ex-

posed one above the other (Fig. 6). Overlying the uneven surface of the lava is Bed I; it consists of volcanic tuffs, up to more than 100 feet thick in hollows of the lava, but reduced to as little as 12 feet where the lava rises. The tuffs were laid down into an Early Pleistocene lake of maximum length 20 miles and a width of from 7 to 10 miles.[40] The lake was probably initiated as a result of ponding of water on an uneven surface of Basement Complex quartzites and gneisses by a flow of lava (on whose uneven surface Bed I rests) from Ngorongoro and Lemagrut to the east.

Bed I, as we have seen, contains Villafranchian fauna, as well as

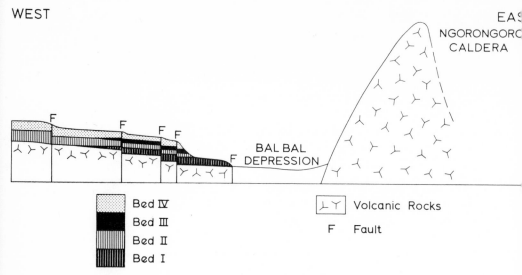

WEST

EAS
NGORONGORO
CALDERA

BAL BAL
DEPRESSION

Bed IV
Bed III
Bed II
Bed I

Volcanic Rocks

F   Fault

Figure 6. Diagrammatic section of Olduvai Gorge (vertical scale exaggerated 18 times).

Australopithecines and the pebble culture which they made. Near the base of Bed I, Leakey has recently found a semicircular arrangement of rocks which he believes may represent some form of structure made by hominids. Two living sites in this bed have yielded "pre-*Zinjanthropus*" and *Zinjanthropus*, while a third, just below the top of the bed, is associated with an industry transitional between the Oldowan and Chellean stage 1 (see Fig. 7).

Near the top of Bed I there is evidence of desert conditions, with crystals known as "desert roses" and remains of animals such as the jerboa which live in the Sahara today. Between it and Bed II there is an unconformity which may cover several hundred thousand years, according to potassium-argon dating. This period, not represented at all at Olduvai, probably spans the time of the Australopithecines of the Transvaal, though Mrs. R. F. Ewer of Rhodes University, South Africa, who has made a detailed study of the fauna, has said that on faunal grounds there is not the least justification for suggesting that Olduvai, Bed I, is any older than the South African deposits at Makapan and Sterkfontein.

The Olduvai Australopithecines

On July 17, 1959, Dr. Leakey was unwell and remained in camp while his wife searched the slopes of Bed I, Olduvai, at a site known as FLK. I. Tired and thirsty after several hours in the hot sun, she was about to return to camp when her keen eyes noticed a piece of bone in the process of being eroded out of the deposit. She recognized the texture of a skull, and closer inspection revealed the tops of some teeth. Excitedly she rushed back to fetch her husband, whose sickness vanished at once. Restraining their impatience to begin excavations, they waited until photographs of the find had been taken before it was disturbed.

It proved to be the skull of a young male hominid, broken up into tiny fragments that had to be pieced together like a jigsaw puzzle (Plate 9). It had been broken by expansion and contraction of the

Figure 7. Diagram to show position of hominid remains, living sites, industries, and potassium-argon dates in Beds I to IV, Olduvai.

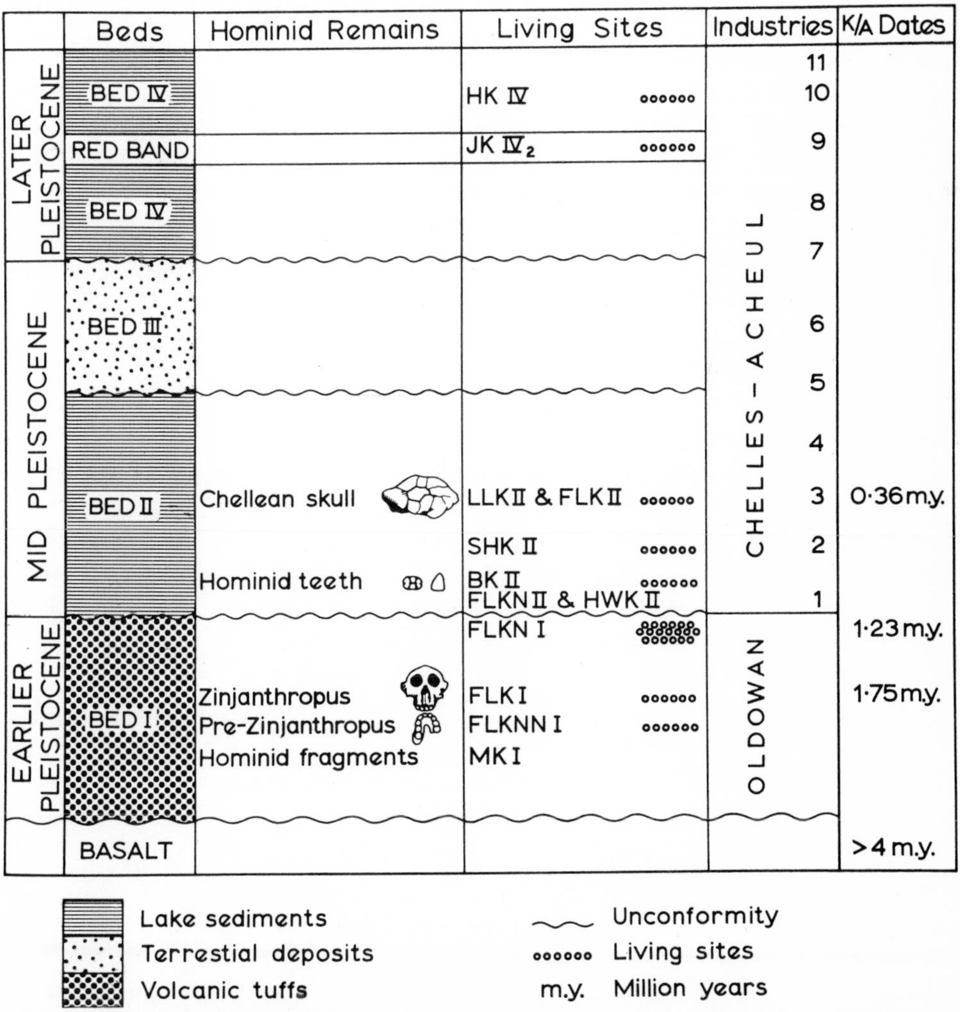

	Beds	Hominid Remains	Living Sites	Industries	K/A Dates
LATER PLEISTOCENE	BED IV		HK IV ᴏᴏᴏᴏᴏᴏ	11 10	
	RED BAND		JK IV₂ ᴏᴏᴏᴏᴏᴏ	9	
	BED IV			8 7	
MID PLEISTOCENE	BED III			6 5	CHELLES–ACHEUL
	BED II	Chellean skull	LLK II & FLK II ᴏᴏᴏᴏᴏᴏ	3	0·36 m.y.
			SHK II ᴏᴏᴏᴏᴏᴏ	2	
		Hominid teeth	BK II ᴏᴏᴏᴏᴏᴏ FLKN II & HWK II	1	
EARLIER PLEISTOCENE	BED I		FLKN I ᴏᴏᴏᴏᴏᴏ	OLDOWAN	1·23 m.y.
		Zinjanthropus	FLK I ᴏᴏᴏᴏᴏᴏ		1·75 m.y.
		Pre-Zinjanthropus	FLKNN I ᴏᴏᴏᴏᴏᴏ		
		Hominid fragments	MK I		
	BASALT				>4 m.y.

Lake sediments — Unconformity
Terrestial deposits ᴏᴏᴏᴏᴏᴏ Living sites
Volcanic tuffs m.y. Million years

Plate 8. Living floor at the "Zinjanthropus" site, with broken bones representing the remains of his meals. The horn cores are those of Parmularius altidens, a type of hartebeest.

bentonitic clay in which it lay, 22 feet below the top of Bed I, which at this point is about 40 feet thick; but the bones had not been distorted in any way, and even such fragile pieces as the nasals were recovered.

The skull was associated with a living floor containing Oldowan pebble tools and waste flakes, as well as broken animal bones (Plate 8). These included remains of birds, amphibians, snakes, lizards, rodents, and immature pigs and antelopes. Evidently they represented the debris from the hominid's meals, for the bones were smashed and scattered, unlike the fragments of the skull, which were all found together within the space of a square foot. This strongly suggests that the hominid occupied the living site, made and used the tools, and ate the animals. Since the skull is almost complete, it seems unlikely that its owner was the victim of cannibalism, or of some hypothetical more advanced type of man. Since his later find of "pre-*Zinjanthropus*," however, Leakey has expressed the view that it was this larger-brained type that made the tools, rather than "*Zinjanthropus*."

Leakey exhibited the skull soon after its discovery at the Fourth Pan-African Congress of Prehistory at Leopoldville, where it caused tremendous excitement and was affectionately referred to as "Dear

Figure 8. "Zinjanthropus boisei" ex-
poses his "nutcracker" molars.

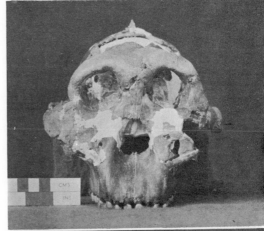

Plate 9. Front and side view of skull
of "Zinjanthropus boisei" from Bed
I, Olduvai.

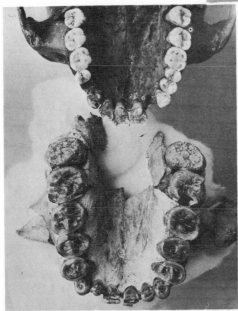

Plate 10. Palate and teeth of
"Zinjanthropus" (below), compared with those of an Australian aborigine.

boy." Its other nickname, "Nutcracker Man," refers to the enormous size of the molars and premolars (Fig. 8), larger than those of any other known hominid except for *Gigantopithecus* of China, which in any case is almost certainly an ape rather than a hominid, as has sometimes been claimed.

Officially the new skull was referred to a new genus and species, "*Zinjanthropus*" *boisei*; "*Zinj*" is the ancient name for East Africa; the specific name is in honor of Mr. Charles Boise, whose substantial financial aid had made excavations at Olduvai possible. Leakey regarded it as a member of the sub-family Australopithecinae, but considered that it differed from both *Australopithecus africanus* and *A. robustus* even more than they differed from each other and hence warranted the creation of a new genus.

Characters that Leakey believed distinguish "*Zinjanthropus*" from the other Australopithecines concern the architecture of the face, the horizontal position of the foramen magnum (the hole through which the spinal column passes into the skull), and the size and shape of the mastoid processes, which he considers resemble those of modern man. Statistical work on the teeth, he says, showed that those of "*Zinjanthropus*" far exceed the highest extreme point of variation in the South African groups.[41]

Among the most striking features, apart from the size of the molars and premolars, is the great depth of palate, which in *A. robustus* is relatively shallow. The canines are very small compared with the premolars and molars, even more so than in the case of *A. robustus*, where this is a marked character and there is no diastema, or gap, between the canines and the small incisors.

The skull itself is notable for the massive ridges above the eye sockets, above the mastoids, and across the occipital bone at the back of the skull, where the ridge forms a nuchal crest for the attachment of the neck muscles. There is also a pronounced sagittal crest running along the top of the skull from front to back, as in male gorillas (see Plate 9). These features were necessary for attachment of the strong muscles needed for chewing—which, judging by the size of the molars, must have been hard work. The frontal bone is curiously shaped, so that the top of the forehead is concave rather than domed. The thick bones of the skull are "pneumatized"—that is, lightened by air spaces—and the over-all impression of heaviness is in fact largely superficial. A straight and slender tibia and fibula were found at the same site later and are presumed to belong to "*Zinjanthropus*." If so, it is clear

Figure 9. Bone tool, worked and polished at one end, from Bed I, Olduvai.

that "*Zinjanthropus*" was by no means large and was fairly lightly built.

Leakey announced the discovery of the limb bones in December, 1960; he also reported a small piece of pelvic girdle, additional teeth, and parts of the skull of a second individual, all from the same spot, FLK. I.[42] He also found teeth and parts of a skull of a hominid at a site known as MK, four miles away and certainly below the "*Zinjanthropus*" level. At the same time he announced new finds from a site called FLKNN. I, about 250 yards from the main site, but at a slightly lower level. These hominid fossils consist of fragments of a skull and teeth, two clavicles, most of the bones of a foot, finger bones, and ribs. The foot bones are the earliest ones of a hominid yet known; after the Australopithecines the next are those of Neanderthal Man. Associated with them was a bone tool, worked and polished at one end (Fig. 9)—an incredible achievement for these early hominids and one that revolutionizes our ideas of their capabilities. The main diet of the hominids at this site seems to consist of tortoise and catfish, which are easy to catch, as they often come into shallow water.

The next announcement from Olduvai, in February, 1961, was almost as exciting as the one that heralded the original "*Zinjanthropus*" skull. It described the discovery of a mandible and parts of two parietal bones by Leakey's son Jonathan at FLKNN. I, where he had already

Plate 11. Parietal bone of "pre-Zinjanthropus" from Bed I, Olduvai, showing fracture lines said to have been caused by a blow on the head.

found the jaw of a saber-toothed tiger, not previously confirmed among the Olduvai fauna. Apparently the mandible and parietals belong to the same individual as the foot and hand bones and one of the clavicles reported previously. The juvenile clavicle is said to be as large as that of a modern male adult. Judging by the rate of present-day tooth eruption, Leakey judged this hominid to be about twelve years of age at the time of death, though in early Pleistocene times growth might well have been more rapid and the child might have been even younger than twelve. The thin parietals (Plate 11), although they belong to a child, are said to be larger than those of "*Zinjanthropus*," who is estimated as being about eighteen years old at the time of death. Apparently "pre-*Zinjanthropus*," as he is generally called, had a bigger brain capacity than his successor.

The dental pattern is said to be different to that of "*Zinjanthropus*" or of any other Australopithecine: the length of the premolars, for example, is greater than the width. "It seems," wrote Leakey, "that we are dealing with a quite distinct type of early hominid."[43]

Many authorities, however, would prefer to see both "*Zinjanthropus*" and "pre-*Zinj.*" grouped within existing genera. Referring to the Olduvai finds, Le Gros Clark wrote: "Probably nothing has tended to obscure or discredit the undoubted importance of these (and other) discoveries so much as premature claims that they represent hitherto unknown genera or species of the Hominidae."[44] Evidence from South Africa shows that there was tremendous individual variation within the Australopithecinae and even greater variation between them and the East African forms must be expected. Possibly they may represent distinct species, perhaps only local races or subspecies. Unless a good many fossils are found, so that detailed comparisons between the sexes and between individuals can be made, this question cannot be answered. In the meantime many authorities regard "*Zinjanthropus*" as a subspecies of *A. robustus*, while "pre-*Zinjanthropus*" may perhaps be a more advanced form—possibly similar to "*Telanthropus*."

A statement of quite a different kind also caused some stir at the time. At a press conference in Washington, Leakey claimed that the "pre-*Zinj.*" child had been murdered. He based this theory on the fact that fracture lines radiating from a central point on the larger of the two parietal bones could only have been caused by a blow on the head (Plate 11). Very likely the Australopithecines did attack each other in this way—Dart has collected much evidence suggesting homicide in the Transvaal caves—but it is difficult to be certain whether the blow was inflicted before death or *post mortem*, in order to get at the brains.

As a result of his examination of the "*Zinjanthropus*" living site, Clark was of the opinion that some of the long bones have fractures on the interior surface that could have been caused only by a blunt, rounded instrument. Most of the bones consist of broken splinters, articulated ends of long bones, and broken mandibles. This debris, as well as stone tools and waste flakes, lies in a circular area of about 15 square feet, with the larger pieces on the outside. Since no complete animal skeletons were found, the meat was presumably carried to the mud flats beside the lake shore to be eaten. Very likely it was collected by scavenging from the prey of carnivores. Only at a later living floor at the very top of Bed I did Leakey find evidence to suggest that the hominids had become rather more accomplished hunters, killing adult animals as well as immature ones such as were associated with "*Zinjanthropus*." By Bed II times, there is no doubt that they were capable of hunting as a group, probably surrounding large animals and driving them into swamps. This progress was probably due to two main developments: one in mental powers, resulting in group coordination; the other in refinement of the limb bones, making it possible to run swiftly rather than shamble along in a slow and clumsy way.

The Dating Evidence

In July, 1961, J. F. Evernden and G. H. Curtis, physicists at the University of California, announced the eagerly awaited results of dating samples from Bed I by the potassium-argon method.[45] The average of 1.7 million years for the "*Zinjanthropus*" level, which nearly trebled most previous estimates, at first sight seemed very startling. But, as we shall see later, other dates obtained for early Pleistocene deposits had been consistently pointing to the fact that the duration of the Pleistocene must be considered to be at least two million years rather than one million.

The potassium-argon method can be applied to any rocks containing minerals such as feldspars and biotite, which are rich in potassium. It depends on the distinegration at a constant rate of the radioactive istotope potassium-40 which occurs with ordinary potassium in rocks in the proportion of 0.01 per cent. Potassium-40, which has a half life of 1.3 x 10⁹ years, decays into calcium-40 and argon-40. One of the main difficulties is getting rid of atmospheric argon adsorbed on the surface of the crystal samples; this problem has been largely overcome by preheating the sample and taking great precautions to lose none of the radiogenic argon during the preheating.

The importance of the potassium-argon method in the study of the early development of the hominids is unique. It is the *only* method known so far for calculating absolute ages within the time range of a few hundred thousand years back to many millions of years, where it overlaps with other methods used for dating older geological formations. It can cover periods much earlier than those spanned by the obsidian method (p. 46), and of course is far beyond the range of carbon-14 dating. At first the method was applied mainly to Tertiary formations, but since 1957 Evernden and Curtis have been working also on minerals from Lower Pleistocene volcanic ashes and tuffs.

Potassium-argon dates for minerals of the Blanco Formation of North America, regarded by many paleontologists as the equivalent of the Villafranchian, exceed 2 million years. Of course it is possible that part of the Blanco Formation is Upper Pliocene. But dates for a number of unquestionably Lower Pleistocene deposits exceed a million years; for example, biotites in volcanic ashes overlying a very early till of the Sierran glaciation of California have given dates of about 1.6 million years. And yet the middle of Bed I, Olduvai, where the fauna is *Upper* Villafranchian, has worked out even older—1.7 million years.

This figure represents the mean from a cluster of dates ranging from 1.57 to 1.89 million years for the *"Zinjanthropus"* level and levels immediately above and below it. The top of Bed I, 22 feet farther up, gave results ranging from 1 million to 1.3 million, which is about what one might expect for the Upper Villafranchian. The latter dates are based on determinations of the radiogenic argon in two different minerals, oligoclase and biotite (of which the latter, giving 1.0 and 1.1 million years is believed to be the more reliable). The difference between the two clusters of dates implies that Bed I took about three-quarters of a million years to form, an incredibly slow rate of accumulation.

In November, 1961, four months after Evernden and Curtis's dates were published, W. Gentner and H. J. Lippolt of Heidelberg announced the results of independent potassium-argon determinations of samples from Olduvai. Two basalt pebble tools from Bed I were dated to 2.25 and 1.4 million years. Basalt underlying Bed I was found to be 1.3 million years old, about the same age as Evernden and Curtis obtained for the top of the bed.[46] Which of the two results is more likely to be right? Leakey has expressed the view that the sample used by Gentner and Lippolt must have been taken from near the exposed surface of the lava flow and might give an inaccurate result owing to weathering. Oakley, on the other hand, considers that potassium-argon dating of a lava originally as homogeneous and fluid as basalt is likely to be nearer the truth than the dating of crystals from tuffs. There is a chance that the tuffs of Bed I might contain traces of older generations of argon-40, either as occlusions formed in contemporaneous crystals before their eruption, or as invisibly fine detritus from much older basement rocks. Gentner and Lippolt do not think the discrepancy in dates is due to measuring techniques, for they were in close agreement with a determination of half a million years obtained by Evernden and Curtis for basalt associated with *Pithecanthropus erectus* in the Trinil beds of Java. The difficulty, they say, comes from the sample itself. In connection with another problem, they worked on samples of biotite and sanidine from tuffs and found that their ages may be too high because of inherited argon. The argument, obviously, can be settled only by testing many more samples, from both basalt and tuffs.

In May, 1962, after this chapter was written, Curtis and Evernden announced two widely different dates they had obtained for basalt underlying Bed I: 4 million years and 1.7 million years. The proportions and types of minerals are different in the two samples, making it unlikely that they came from the same flow, and both appear to be altered as a result of weathering. The two physicists come to the conclusion that "the basalts at Olduvai are at least 4 million years old but they are unreliable for dating purposes."[47]

At the same time, W. L. Straus and C. B. Hunt criticized the Olduvai dates on the grounds that they were obtained from different minerals and from crystals of various sizes. The escape of argon is believed to be controlled less by the internal structure of minerals than by their size, the loss being greater from small crystals than from larger ones. Confidence in the results, therefore, would be felt only if a series were obtained for different levels from the same minerals in each case, and from crystals of the *same size*. They also point out that, although the use of weathered basalt for dating purposes has been condemned, the permeable volcanic tuffs of Bed I are just as likely to be weathered and in fact some layers obviously are. They conclude that the age of "*Zinjanthropus*" is *sub judice*.[48] Curtis and Evernden, on the other hand, say that "all data so far available agree that there is no alternative to accepting an age for "*Zinjanthropus*" and for the Lower Pleistocene of approximately 2 million years."

The Earliest Tools

Although the bones of early men are scarce, evidence of their activities is abundant in the tools that they scattered so lavishly over the country. Pebble tools made by the first hominids, however, are very rare, and it takes a trained prehistorian to recognize them as artifacts at all. It has been said that "the earliest stone tools may have been no better than the hand that made them."[49] It seems likely that once habitual tool using and toolmaking was established, the hand would have undergone rather rapid modifications as the result of natural selection. Now that hand bones of the Australopithecines are known, it will at last be possible to judge just how primitive they were; this may well explain the incredibly slow progress of tool technology.

Early man camped beside lakes and rivers and in such places most of the material available for toolmaking is in the form of rounded, water-worn pebbles and boulders. In order to produce a cutting edge, it was generally necessary to go to the trouble of splitting the pebbles or removing a few chips from one end. Pebble tools from Olduvai, Bed I, have been described as follows: "The commonest tool type of the Oldowan culture is a crude chopper, varying in size from about the dimensions of a ping-pong ball to that of a croquet ball. The chopping edge is made by the removal of flakes in two directions along one side of the pebble . . . the intersection of the flake scars resulting in an irregular jagged cutting edge."[50] (Fig. 10.)

Figure 10. Pebble tool or chopper of Oldowan culture, Bed I, Olduvai.

Such pebble tools have been found notably at Olduvai, Bed I; at Ain Hanech, in Algeria; and at several sites in Morocco. They have been reported from many other parts of Africa, but in most cases they probably form part of later assemblages, for pebble tools continued to be made long after the Oldowan culture had been superseded. Oldowan industries were said to occur on the surface of the Basal Older Gravels of the Vaal and at the Australopithecine Sterkfontein Extension Site; but the latter industry is almost certainly Chellean, and Mason considers that no stage earlier than what he calls the "Earlier Acheulian" (the equivalent of the Chellean) has yet been found anywhere in South Africa. He believes that the earliest artifacts in the Union are those of the "Earlier Acheulian" of Klipplaatdrif, which consist mostly of irregular flakes but include also a very few hand axes.[51] In the Congo, de Heinzelin discovered chopping tools, polyhedral stones and flakes at Kanyatsi which may perhaps come from the Kaiso series, though it is possible that they may have fallen into fissures in these deposits from higher levels; he compares these artifacts with the Oldowan of Olduvai, Bed I, and of Ain Hanech.

The pebble tools of Africa are very similar to the chopping tools of southeastern Asia first described by Movius. The Soan industry of Choukoutien (the site of Peking Man) is now thought to date from the time of the Second Glaciation, the period of the first known artifacts in Europe. Here the oldest certain artifacts are those of the Abbevillean, comparable with the Chellean of Africa, and probably dating from an interstadial in the Second Glaciation.

The controversial "eoliths" of East Anglia were formerly thought to be of Pliocene age, though under the new definition of the Pleistocene, some of them now come within the Lower Pleistocene. Although many strongly suggest human workmanship, it is now considered that they are all of natural origin. The flaking has been produced by pressure from rocks during landslides, or during transport by glaciers, or as a result of buffeting by rivers. Flaked and faceted pebbles in river terraces and gorges from many different parts of Africa have often been attributed to human workmanship in the past, but are now recognized as being due to natural agencies. In assessing whether an object is really an artifact, the context is all-important.

Until quite recently, the "Kafuan" was believed to be the earliest human culture in the world, preceding the Oldowan. It was named after the Kafu Valley in Uganda, where Wayland first found "pebble tools" in 1919. The two highest terraces yielded no "artifacts," but he found split and chipped pebbles in the 175-foot and 50-foot terraces and in the Flats Gravels. In 1959, Bishop made detailed investigations in the Kafu Valley, including mapping and leveling, and concluded that the pebbles were not artifacts at all and that their age was not proven. No 175-foot terrace could be distinguished, and debris up to 6 feet thick at the foot of the slope, derived from an older and higher conglomerate, is the result of recent creep. Some of the pebbles at present eroding out of this conglomerate have been fractured recently and resemble "Kafuan" artifacts. The profusion of fractured pebbles in the extensive gravel spreads suggests, he said, a natural origin rather than a dense pebble-toolmaking population at all levels and throughout the area.

Lowe extended the "Kafuan culture" to the Kagera Valley. He recognized a still earlier stage than the oldest from the Kafu; this was in an ironstone band at the base of the "270-foot terrace" at Nsongezi, and he called it "Earliest Kafuan." The 200-foot terrace he associated with "Early, Later, and Developed Kafuan." The "Earliest Kafuan" was said to contain pebbles split in three main directions; the "Early Kafuan" included "pebble points" and primitive "scrapers"; the "Later Kafuan" showed the introduction of "wedge points," evolving into "rostrocarinates" of the "Developed Kafuan."

Bishop investigated the 270-foot and 200-foot terraces of the Kagera at the one locality where they are known to exist, 16 miles downstream from Nsongezi, over the Tanganyika border. Again he considers that the rolled pebbles show natural fractures and that in such a setting it is impossible to recognize artifacts. The base of the lake deposits underlying the 100-foot terrace at Nsongezi, from which Lowe recorded "Developed Kafuan," Bishop assigns to a river terrace of Later Pleistocene age, postdating the "100-foot" lake deposits and containing derived and rolled material from the horizons within the earlier lacustrine series.[52]

The earliest certain artifacts, then, are the Oldowan pebble tools (though in Morocco, Biberson considers that there are two stages of the pebble culture earlier than that of Olduvai, Bed I). Presumably these crude implements were used for skinning game and for cutting off pieces of meat into hunks small enough to be tackled with teeth and hands. For other purposes, such as digging up roots, a pointed stick would have been quite effective: even chimpanzees have been found to use a stick for digging. After lying on the ground, or being embedded in it, for a million years, it is only to be expected that today we find only the more enduring of man's tools; but before experimenting with stone at all, he must have used bone and wood to a very great extent. Wood can be worked with a naturally sharp rock, and crude scrapers associated with early industries were presumably used for shaping wood or scraping hides, or both.

Before they got to the stage of shaping stones for a specific purpose, hominids must have used any rock or boulder that was handy, selecting those of suitable size, shape, and sharpness. These first "tools," though they have not perished like the wooden ones, cannot of course be recognized as having been used as artifacts.

Although so far there is no proof of man's existence during the Pliocene, it would have been impossible for him to have evolved into the many different forms in which we find him during the Pleistocene unless he had already adopted an erect posture and thus freed his hands long before the time of the earliest hominids discovered so far. We may imagine him during the Pliocene in a form similar to the Australopithecines of South Africa, with his brain still at a primitive, apelike stage, yet with his hands free to handle and experiment with any object that aroused his curiosity. It seems likely that at least some of the Australopithecines were cannibals, a practice that is by no means uncommon among true humans. They must have handled weapons of some sort, particularly bones, to smash the skulls. It is certainly not beyond the bounds of possibility that, having acquired the taste for marrow and brains and finding their not very large canines and their nails inadequate, they also utilized natural boulders as weapons long before they reached the stage of actual toolmaking.

Chimpanzees in captivity use sticks to reach objects they cannot get at in any other way, but this they will do only to fulfill an immediate need, and their brains are not developed enough to allow them to plan ahead or to construct tools for specific purposes. Miss Jane Goodall has recently observed chimpanzees in the wild using "tools" in the form of straws, which they poke into termites' nests; they then lick off the insects clinging to the straw. The earliest stone tools, split and flaked pebbles, have obviously been constructed in order to obtain a cutting edge for a specific purpose. We cannot learn very much from these earliest pebble tools, but in this, as in every stage, we can deduce something about the level of man's intelligence and his mode of life by the kind of implements he made. Making tools in a regular pattern, and perhaps storing them for future use, implies conceptual thought transcending the ape mentality.

The most extraordinary thing about early man is his astonishing slowness in cultural development. Although we know almost nothing about his perishable equipment, except by indirect evidence (for example, stone scrapers must have been used for working wood or leather), we do know that for a million years or so man evolved nothing more elaborate in the way of stone tools than flaked pebbles, hand axes, cleavers, rough scrapers, points, and blades. It is not until later Pleistocene times that there were any marked improvements in workmanship or more elaborate inventions.

This lack of inventiveness on the part of early men can probably be explained by the fact that the males must have spent almost their whole time hunting and scavenging, while the women were no doubt fully occupied in food collecting and gathering and protecting their young from savage beasts. The mortality rate must have been extremely high and the expectation of life very low. Probably many of the most enterprising men, the daring hunters, were killed off at an early age. The elderly and infirm would certainly not have been supported, and those that could not keep up with the rest would have been abandoned. In such a struggle for existence, there would have been little time for experiment.

Chapter Five

THE HAND-AX MAKERS

The Pithecanthropines

In the last chapter we looked at the Australopithecinae, the first stage of hominid evolution; we now move on to the second stage, which begins with the first members of the sub-family Homininae, or true men. These are the Pithecanthropines of Mid Pleistocene times, which evolve gradually into *Homo*.* In Africa, both Pithecanthropines and early *Homo* seem to have been the makers of the long-lasting Chelles-Acheul hand-ax culture.

Crude though his implements were, we cannot but feel the greatest respect for early man. Life must have been far from easy, and his brain must have been alert for him to have survived at all, unprotected by tooth and claw and inefficiently armed as he was. He had to defend himself against large and savage beasts, which roamed the country in great numbers. In East Africa he probably did not live above about 6,000 feet, since the highlands were relatively wet and

* Many authorities now classify *Pithecanthropus* as *Homo erectus;* but as this type is better known by its old name, it will be less confusing if we stick to it in this book.

131

cold, as they are today. He would also have avoided the dark forests and camped beside lake shores or rivers, hunting in savanna country.

In other parts of the world too, hand-ax man seems to have lived in open country and is known as a cave dweller only late in Acheulian times, after he had learned to control fire. The apparent fire-making capabilities of Peking Man seem to be exceptional at such an early date. In Africa, the earliest evidence of the use of fire comes at the very end of the Acheulian stage at Kalambo Falls, in Northern Rhodesia, and at the Cave of Hearths, in the Transvaal. As von Koenigswald put it: "In a permanent tropical climate, there was no need to retire into dark and wet caves, inhabited by bats, snakes, evil spirits, and scorpions." Thus it is that the remains of cave dwellers like Neanderthal Man are quite often found, but the bones of those who lived out in the open were no doubt left to be devoured by scavengers. Although hand axes have been found in millions, in many parts of Western Europe, southern Asia, and all over Africa, the individuals known to us who made them can be counted on the fingers of one hand. Notably, there are the Steinheim and Swanscombe skulls, both dating from the Second or Great Interglacial.

In Western Europe, the first *bifaces* of the Chellean stage of the hand-ax culture appear early in the preceding Mindel Glaciation. It seems probable that this is roughly contemporary with Bed II at Olduvai, where the skull of one of the makers of Chellean artifacts has recently been found. In Europe there seems to be no gradual transition from Chellean to Acheulian as we find at Olduvai, but rather there appears to be a sudden break. Was this perhaps due to the arrival of immigrants, from Africa or Asia, bringing knowledge of new techniques with them? Or is it simply that the intervening stages have not yet been found?

As far as human remains in East Africa are concerned, there is an immense gap between the Chellean skull, dated by potassium-argon to 360,000 years ago, the Kanam jaw, and skulls from Kanjera in western Kenya, all of which are uncertainly dated, but which are probably no more than about 55,000 years old and possibly younger still.

The Manufacture of Early Tools

A distinction used to be made between "core" industries with hand axes and "flake" industries typified by those of the Levalloisian and

Mousterian cultures. It is now recognized that such a distinction is worthless, since both cores and flakes were used for the manufacture of implements in nearly all industries.

Three main techniques were used to make implements during the Lower and Middle Paleolithic. The simplest of all is to remove flakes from a nodule or pebble with the aid of a hammerstone; this technique was used in the manufacture of pebble tools, and continued throughout the Chellean stage of the hand-ax culture. Another technique was to swing the lump of rock against a stone anvil; this is known as the "block-on-block" technique, formerly called the "Clacton" technique since it was used in the Clactonian industry, but it is also an essential part of the Chelles-Acheul culture in Africa. The Acheulian stage was heralded by the invention of the "cylinder-hammer" technique, which first appeared in Europe during the Mindel-Riss Interglacial and in East Africa after the end of Bed II times at Olduvai. Experiments have shown that by using the *side* of a cylindrical hammer, preferably made of bone or hardwood, it is possible to remove flatter flakes from a core or a large flake, resulting in the more perfect implements with shallow-flake scars seen in the Acheulian stage. The whole tool is not, of course, shaped by using the side of the cylinder hammer; it was first roughly blocked out with the point of an ordinary hammerstone, or else by the block-on-block technique, and was afterward trimmed with the cylinder hammer.

Another method of producing flakes is by the "prepared-core" technique, which is described in Chapter Six. Prepared "tortoise" cores with faceted striking platforms are characteristic of the Levalloisian culture, but various forms of prepared core were also made in the Acheulian of Africa. The so-called Victoria West industries, which are part of the Acheulian sequence of South Africa, are characterized by particular kinds of flakes struck from cores that have been specially prepared.

The term "hand ax" is misleading, since, whatever else they were used for, it is doubtful whether these ubiquitous implements served as axes; the French term *coup-de-poing* is preferable (*biface* is often used to describe hand axes, but a *biface* may be any implement worked over both surfaces). It has been suggested that hand axes were used for digging up roots, constructing game pits, and so forth, but it is unlikely that this was their only use. It is probable that hand axes, as well as cleavers, were used mainly for skinning game and chopping the meat up into manageable portions (Fig. 11 and Plate 12).

It seems unlikely that such heavy tools were hafted, yet at Isimila, Tanganyika, hand axes were found with very thin butts, almost as if deliberately prepared for hafting.

In many cases the implements show little signs of use; in certain areas they are found in such incredible numbers that, remembering that the Stone Age population was small, it would be inconceivable that they had all been used. The perfect finish of some of the later specimens makes it seem that craftsmen took an artistic pride in their work beyond the needs of pure utility. When they were displeased with a tool, they discarded it and started afresh. Just as any modern boy will whittle away at a stick until it is smooth, for sheer pleasure, so toolmaking was probably a hobby to Acheulian Man: the urge to create something well is one of man's basic instincts.

The best-known artifacts of the Acheulian culture are, of course, hand axes; in Africa, cleavers and stone balls are also quite common, as well as a great variety of less spectacular tools. Unfortunately the latter have not always been collected and described in the past, though nowadays it is realized that they are very important in forming a complete picture of the equipment. In some of the Acheulian industries of South Africa, hand axes and cleavers are found in extremely small proportions; hand axes with the Late Acheulian of the Cave of Hearths form only 3 per cent of the total assemblage, while at the Late Acheulian site of Wonderboom only one hand ax was found. At such sites as Kalambo Falls in Northern Rhodesia and Isimila in Tanganyika, statistical analyses of the various tool types have been made. Miss M. Kleindienst subdivided the artifacts according to whether they have a long, sharp cutting edge; a steep scraping edge; a sinuous chopping edge; and various other kinds of working edge. Di-

Figure 11. Acheulian Man skinning Sivatherium with a hand ax.

Plate 12. Dr. L. S. B. Leakey skinning an antelope with a cleaver that he had made himself.

viding them into large (over 10 cm. long), and small (less than 10 cm.), she recognized the following types among others:

Large	cutting-edged tools:	hand axes, pointed flakes, cleavers, knives.
	scraping-edged tools:	side scrapers, end scrapers, combined side and end scrapers.
	various-edged tools:	chisels, push planes, discoids.
	heavy-duty tools:	picks, core scrapers, trimmed pebbles or chunks, choppers.
	stone balls:	missiles, polyhedral, "bolas" (smooth-surfaced spheres).
Small	scraping-edged tools:	side scrapers, end scrapers, combined.
	various-edged tools:	proto-burins, burins, points, chisel-ended tools, etc.

Almost all these types occur at all Late Acheulian occupation sites in East Africa. At different areas at Isimila, it was found that the concentration of large cutting-edged tools decreases as that of the small, scraping-edged tools increases, suggesting different functions at various parts of the site. Probably this will be found to be the case elsewhere when sites are studied in detail in this way, which should enable us to get a very good idea of what actually went on at the time of occupation. While there is an extreme range of frequency for all classes of implements, the average percentage of hand axes, cleavers, and knives at Isimila and Olorgesailie is 40 to 60 per cent while that of small tools is 20 to 45 per cent.[53]

Olduvai: Bed II

When we last looked at Olduvai it was at Bed I, with its Australopithecines and their pebble tools. This site also affords the most complete evolutionary sequence of the Chelles-Acheul hand-ax culture, which followed the Oldowan pebble culture but in which pebble tools continued to be used extensively.

Bed I is separated from Bed II by an unconformity that probably represents a long period of time, and the fauna of the two beds, according to Leakey, is quite distinctive. The lists given in his *Olduvai Gorge* (1951) will certainly need much revision; in many cases the species are not identified; in other cases, the provisional identifications were made on very fragmentary material. A great many new discoveries have been made in the meantime, not only of fossil mammals but also of the various stone industries. As the result of a substantial grant from the National Geographic Society of Washington and other sources, excavations at Olduvai have speeded up tremendously. During the year 1960-61, 92,000 man hours were spent at Olduvai, compared with 40,000 over the previous 30 years.

While Bed I is composed of volcanic tuffs ejected into the lake, Bed II consists of marls and other lake sediments up to 90 feet thick in places. It contains industries of the first five stages of the Chelles-Acheul hand-ax culture.

CHELLES-ACHEUL: STAGE 1

In Leakey's book on Olduvai he described a small excavation in the lowest level of Bed II which yielded only 47 artifacts; of these, approximately half were said to represent a distinct evolutionary advance over the Oldowan tool types of Bed I. This very small sample obviously gave a false impression of the technical advance; for at the living floor at site BK. II, excavated between 1952 and 1955, Leakey states that out of thousands of artifacts—which include numerous waste flakes, used flakes, and small flake tools—there were only 22 hand axes compared with 575 pebble choppers.[54]

The hand axes are crude and simple, comparable with those of the Chellean stage of France. Some are made from large pebbles, others from lumps of quartz or lava. All are flaked in three or four directions, and the intersection of the jagged cutting edges makes a good chopping surface. Although the vast majority of artifacts are indistinguishable from those of the Oldowan stage, it is by the appearance of *new* forms that a cultural stage is recognized; no hand axes at all appear with the Oldowan of Bed I. As well as pebble tools and hand axes, there were rough stone spheres, small flake tools, hammerstones, utilized flakes, and a vast quantity of waste flakes, and also imported lumps of rock, obviously raw material for toolmaking. Two lumps of red ocher had also been brought to the site; it is difficult to imagine the early hominids of the time adorning themselves with coloring matter, still harder to think of any utilitarian use for the red ocher.

The living floor at BK. II is at the lowest level of the bed, where it rests unconformably on the eroded surface of Bed I. The fauna includes the giant baboon *Simopithecus*, several species of giant pigs, the huge "sheep" *Pelorovis*, two species of hippopotamus, a rhinoceros, the three-toed horse *Stylohipparion* as well as the large one-toed *Equus olduvaiensis, Sivatherium,* numerous species of antelopes and gazelles, also carnivores such as a hyena and members of the cat tribe. There were also a number of rodents, many bird bones, fragments of ostrich eggshells, and some crocodile and other reptile remains. Most of the bones on the living floor had been broken open to extract the marrow, and skulls had been smashed to obtain the brains. In a small, clay-filled gully adjoining the living floor, lower limb bones of *Pelorovis, Sivatherium,* and *Bularchus* were found articulated and standing upright. There were also vertebral columns and skulls with horns—that is, the

Figure 12. Chellean hunters driving Sivatherium *and* Pelorovis *into a swamp, Bed II, Olduvai.*

heavier parts of large animals. This suggests that these animals had been driven into a swamp by the Chellean hunters, who then presumably pelted them to death with rocks and stones (also found in the clay) or perhaps attacked them with wooden spears from the edge of the swamp (Fig. 12). The protruding and lighter parts of the carcasses were then presumably hacked off and dragged to the nearby butchering site, where the meat was cut up and devoured and the numerous implements were abandoned after the feast.

In 1955, Leakey found two hominid teeth associated with the BK. II living floor. They were a canine and a huge molar, both of which he considered to be milk teeth belonging to a child of about three to five years of age. The cusp pattern of the molar, he said, differed considerably from that of the Australopithecines and had affinities with some modern human teeth, but particularly with those of Peking Man and the Heidelberg jaw.

Robinson, however, considered that it is not a lower deciduous molar, as Leakey supposed, but a permanent upper molar; in this case, it would be well within the range of adult Australopithecine molars.[55] He agrees that the canine is a milk tooth, however, in which case it would obviously belong to another individual. Leakey argues that the two teeth were found within a few inches of each other and it is therefore much more likely that they belong to the same individual. This argument is by no means conclusive—at the "pre-*Zinj*." level the bones of a child and an adult were discovered close together—though it is certainly suggestive. Dahlberg agrees with Robinson that it is an upper molar, within the range of the Australopithecines, but lists several features which suggest it is a milk tooth rather than a permanent one.[59]

CHELLES-ACHEUL: STAGE 2

The second stage of the cultural sequence was poorly known at the time of the 1951 Olduvai book. Hand axes are described as large, with thick, massive butts and a marked flattening on the lower face. Along the upper face, a steep ridge is prominent, running centrally along the anterior part and curving from about the center of the implement to the butt end. This type is known as a rostrocarinate, or beak-shaped, implement. Tools of this type were recovered from a level about 10 to 15 feet above the base of Bed II, some 7 to 12 feet above those of stage 1.

Since that description was written, a living floor of stage 2 has been excavated at the site SHK. II. Pebble tools were still dominant—792,

Figure 13. Flake tool of hippopotamus ivory from Chellean 2 living site, Bed II, Olduvai.

compared with 142 hand axes—and other artifacts were similar to those of the stage 1 level at BK. II. A flake tool made of hippopotamus ivory, with a marked bulb of percussion and secondary trimming at the end opposite the butt, was also found (Fig. 13). The fauna differs in no way from that of the earlier level, though the antlered giraffid *Sivatherium* is scarcer and pieces of tooth of the strange archaic "elephant" *Dinotherium* occur at this site. A tusk of the gigantic pig *Afrochoerus nicoli* measures 785 millimeters (about a yard) on the curve. A jaw of an enormous baboon, which may be a new genus, was also found. Unfortunately no hominid remains of this stage were recovered.

Stage 2 at Olduvai may perhaps be comparable with stage 1 in the Vaal sequence, known from the 45-foot terrace at Vereeniging, and with stage 1 or "*Acheuléen ancien*" of Morocco.

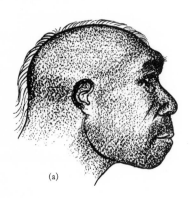

(a)

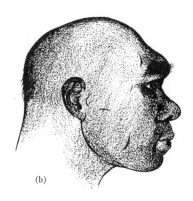

(b)

Figure 14. (a) Java Man; (b) Chellean Man, Olduvai; (c) Steinheim Man; (d) Rhodesian Man.

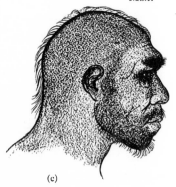

(c)

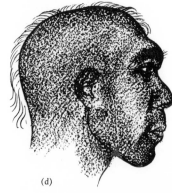

(d)

Chelles-Acheul stage 3 is found approximately halfway up Bed II, about 20 feet above stage 2. The tools appear to be direct derivatives from the rostrocarinates of stage 2, but have certain new characters. The hand axes are large and thick, "more or less triangular but sometimes roughly oval in outline when viewed from above. The lower face is remarkably flat . . . due to careful flaking which usually extends over the whole inferior face."[57]

A living floor of this stage at the site known as LLK. II yielded a very rich industry, including thickset hand axes and stone balls, as well as fauna.

In 1960, Leakey discovered a human skull washing out of the slopes at this site (see Plate 1, p. 42). The skull is very large, 209 millimeters long and 150 millimeters wide. The vault is lower than that of the Steinheim skull, though higher than that of Peking Man. Its most striking feature is an enormous supraorbital torus, or brow ridge, more projecting than in any other known human skull. The cranium is wide in the frontal region, with no constriction as in the case of Peking Man.

Leakey said that it has a number of resemblances to *Pithecanthropus* but that in other respects it is more like the Steinheim skull (which is probably intermediate between and perhaps ancestral to the Neanderthalers, and modern man). He also points out that the Chellean skull resembles Rhodesian Man and may be ancestral to this group. The situation, in fact, seems to be very similar to that of Java, where *Pithecanthropus* evolves into Solo Man; in Africa, we have the Olduvai skull evolving into Rhodesian Man (Fig. 14).

Leakey claimed that, apart from the two teeth associated with the Chellean 1 stage at Olduvai, the skull is the first remains of Chellean Man ever to be found. The *"Atlanthropus"* (*Pithecanthropus*) mandibles from Ternifine, Algeria, he considers to be later because the hand-ax industry is more evolved and "Acheulian" rather than "Chellean." Biberson, however, classifies the associated industry as *"Acheuléen ancien,"* which would be comparable with the Chellean of Olduvai, Bed II.[58] The shores of the lake at Ternifine were occupied over a very long period of time, and probably several industrial stages are present in the deposits. The human mandibles came from sandy levels at the base, and here the industry is *"Acheuléen ancien"* or Chellean.

Biberson tells me that he considers the Olduvai skull goes admirably with the parietal and three mandibles from Ternifine, which are probably roughly contemporary with it.

Evernden and Curtis dated a tuff from about the same level as the Chellean skull to 360,000 years (this was announced at the same time as their potassium-argon results on the "*Zinjanthropus*" levels of Bed I).[59] This would fit well with the suggested Mindel age of the Ternifine remains, and also with the presumed date of the Heidelberg jaw and of Peking Man. Thus we have four Pithecanthropines from the three continents of the Old World of approximately the same age. It is unfortunate that the Olduvai skull has no jaw for comparison with those of Ternifine and Heidelberg. It seems that Olduvai and Ternifine may be somewhat later than Heidelberg and Peking; the Olduvai skull has a higher cranial vault than Peking, and is well on the road to *Homo*.

"*Atlanthropus*" is also represented by a jaw from the Littorina Cave at the quarries of Sidi Abderrahman, on the coast about 4 miles south of Casablanca (see Map 6), which Biberson associates with stage 6 of the Chelles-Acheul culture "*Acheuléen moyen*," correlated with the early part of the Riss Glaciation. Another jaw from Rabat, which has been called "Neanderthaloid," is probably of the same general age and affinities.

This may give a clue to the status of what is probably the most controversial mandible of all time, variously described as *Homo kanamensis;* by far the earliest *Homo sapiens;* an Australopithecine of the "*Zinjanthropus*" type; and—the latest and most likely hypothesis—a creature of "Neanderthaloid" affinities, perhaps rather similar to the Rabat jaw and intermediate between the Pithecanthropine "*Atlanthropus*" and Rhodesian Man. This rather embarrassing find is described in Chapter Six.

CHELLES-ACHEUL: STAGES 4 AND 5

Stages 4 and 5 of the hand-ax sequence are said to be transitional between Chellean and Acheulian in typology. Biberson in Morocco and Mason in South Africa do not recognize separate Chellean and Acheulian stages, but classify the sequence as Early or Earlier, Middle, and Evolved or Later Acheulian. Mason has criticized Leakey's division between Chellean and Acheulian on the basis of the introduction of the cylinder-hammer technique in the latter stage, for, he says, a small proportion of artifacts in the "Earlier Acheulian" (Chellean) already show this technique. He also disputes that an increased proportion of hand axes in an industry indicates an advance in the evolutionary scale.[60] Leakey's published evidence suggests that this criterion does apply to Olduvai, although it may not be valid elsewhere, for example, at the Transvaal sites.

Of the 36 specimens recorded by Leakey as obtained from a level 10 feet below the top of Bed II, 17 are said to be of a new type. The hand ax considered typical of stage 4 has a cutting edge all around instead of only at the anterior end. The lower face is much flatter than the upper, so that, when viewed from the side, the cutting edge is nearer to the lower than the upper face. Stage 5 comes from the junction of Bed II with Bed III. The main difference between it and the preceding stage is that it includes a few implements made by the cylinder-hammer technique, which is generally taken to be characteristic of the Acheulian stage; none of the hand axes from previous stages show signs of this improved workmanship.

Olduvai: Bed III

Bed III is a red bed consisting of earths and torrential gravels up to 40 feet thick in places; unlike the other lake beds at Olduvai, Bed III consists only of terrestrial or river-borne deposits. It is unconformable on Bed II and wedges out toward the west (see Fig. 6). Leakey reported 87 isolated artifacts collected from different levels in Bed III, classed as stage 6 in the Chelles-Acheul sequence. They reveal, he says, a considerable advance over those of the preceding stage at the top of Bed II. The cleaver now makes its first appearance, as well as stone balls of the "bolas" type (see p. 155). Among the hand axes are specimens which display "a very developed form of the cylinder-hammer technique comparable to some of the finest Acheulian flaking in Europe."[61]

This stage 6 industry has been compared typologically with stage 5 or 6 of the Acheulian sequence in Morocco, which Biberson correlates with the Mindel Glaciation of Europe. He points out, however, the lack of published description of the cores (that is, the stage at which prepared cores first appear), and waste material from this and other stages at Olduvai, which makes exact comparisons difficult. He also compares stage 6, Olduvai, with stage 4 in the Chelles-Acheul of the Vaal in South Africa. The Vaal stages 3 and 4 are known as Victoria West I and II, both characterized by extensive use of prepared side-struck cores. These two stages are both attributed to the "Kanjeran pluvial" and hence correlated with Bed IV at Olduvai and—by inference—with Riss.

Where, then, should Bed III, Olduvai, be placed? With Mindel, according to the evidence from Morocco? The unconformity between Beds II and III suggests that Bed III should be later than Mindel and a Mindel-Riss or a Riss age seems more acceptable. The Moroccan correlations with European glacial stages are based on very detailed stratigraphical work, including studies of past sea levels. The deposits attributed to the Amirian stage (Mindel) in Morocco are very thick and obviously represent an extremely long period of time. The Upper Amirian, with its stage 5 of the Middle Acheulian, comes just before the slow transgression of the sea during the Mindel-Riss Interglacial. But Biberson has shown that the "cold" forest fauna of the time, with the first appearance of bears, must be associated with pluvial conditions that can only belong to the final phase of Mindel. If these correlations are correct, and Biberson's comparisons of the industries are correct, the only conclusion to draw is that the industries of Morocco developed rather earlier than those of South and East Africa. After his book was written, Biberson tells me that he saw artifacts from Olduvai stage 6 which makes him think that it may be closer to the Moroccan stage 6 rather than 5. This would suggest a Mindel-Riss age for both, though the comparable industry in South Africa may be later.

Most of the stages in the hand-ax sequence at Olduvai, which so far we have traced up to the end of Bed III times, have not been recognized elsewhere in East Africa. The industries most often found are an advanced Acheulian, corresponding with stage 9 in Bed IV. Before describing these other sites, we may finish the Olduvai story that has taken up so much of our attention so far.

Olduvai: Bed IV

The earliest industry of Bed IV, stage 7 in the sequence, comes from the base of the bed in a deposit of sand that apparently represents a temporary beach level at a time when the lake was rising. This stage is said to be distinguished from previous ones by the high proportion of large, very well-made hand axes that are usually wider in proportion to their length than earlier ones. Cleavers are fairly common and are slightly narrower at the cutting edge than in the middle—that is, they are of convergent rather than parallel type. The nature of the raw material seems to have had little influence on technology, for many of the most perfect specimens are made from a coarse-grained quartzite. "Here at Olduvai," wrote Leakey, "we have a people . . . who, in part at least, were using materials quite as intractable as those used by *Sinanthropus* [*Pithecanthropus*] at Choukoutien, yet they achieved as high a perfection in their workmanship as did hand-axe men in those areas of England and France where flint of the finest quality was available."[62]

The first hand axes ever to be found at Olduvai were a small series from the lower part of Bed IV near the camp made by Leakey's 1931 expedition (Reck had found no implements at all at the time of his discovery of the Olduvai skeleton in 1913). These were subsequently attributed to stage 8; altogether 145 specimens were found *in situ* at this level, about 15 feet above the junction of Beds III and IV. The whole assemblage is said to reveal many differences from those of preceding stages, among which the most important are the addition of characteristic "S-twist" ovates, the size of the implements (which is much smaller than those of stage 7), and the shape of the cleavers, which are in the form of a V rather than a U, with their widest point at the cutting edge. There are also fewer traces of survival elements. It appears that stage 8 is not a direct derivative from stage 7; in fact, the implements of the succeeding stage 9 seem to be the direct and logical derivatives of stage 7. The stratigraphical evidence is, however, unmistakable, and stage 8 clearly belongs in time between stages 7 and 9. Leakey believed that the makers of stage 8 represent an intrusive element at Olduvai.

Biberson compares Olduvai, stage 8, with the evolved Acheulian stage 7 of Morocco, correlated with Riss, and with stage 5 in the Chelles-Acheul sequence of the Vaal attributed to the end of "Kanjeran" times. Here is another interesting conundrum in correlation. If stage 8 at Olduvai is really comparable with the Latest Acheulian of the Vaal, generally considered to be transitional to the Fauresmith of the First Intermediate Period, could it be taken to represent the end of Riss time? We would then have stages 9 to 11 of Olduvai extending into Würm I, as tentatively suggested here (see Table 1).

Within Bed IV is a reddened band, in which 96 artifacts were obtained *in situ*. These implements of stage 9 compare much more closely with those of stage 7, though a few hand axes with "S twists" characteristic of stage 8 are also present. The variation in size and shape of the hand axes of stage 9 is very great. Long, asymmetrical, but beautifully made implements occur side by side with symmetrical specimens only a few inches in length. Cleavers are relatively common and are U-shaped. Stage 9 may possibly represent more than one stage in the evolutionary sequence, and the reddening of the bed may indicate a fairly long period during which it was exposed as a land surface.

The upper parts of Bed IV are often missing at Olduvai, having been removed by erosion. At a very rich site known as HK, however, the upper parts of this bed are exposed. There is no trace of the red band in this area, but the exposures at HK seem to be at a higher level than the horizon yielding stage 9 elsewhere. Only a small part of the HK site had been excavated by 1951 when the Olduvai book was published, but 459 implements were recovered *in situ;* they were strewn thickly upon and within a thin band of beach sand. Many animal bones were also recovered from the same level, including a dismembered hippopotamus skeleton. The hand axes and cleavers nearly all had the cutting edges blunted and abraded through use—probably as the result of cutting up the hippopotamus carcass—and were apparently discarded on the spot when they became unserviceable. A plentiful supply of the white quartzite from which the implements were made is obtainable close at hand, so the making of new tools would have presented no difficulty.

It is in the western part of the southern branch of the gorge that the rare higher deposits of Bed IV are preserved. Scattered finds have been made in these topmost beds, all stratigraphically higher than the HK site. The hand axes are mostly rather small and degenerate, although a few magnificent specimens were also recovered. Some, in their flatness and outline, strongly recall those of the Fauresmith culture (pp. 184–185). One cleaver was as beautifully made as many Neolithic axes, and, if it had been hafted, it would have been quite capable of cutting down small trees; the edge is very straight and sharp.

Kanjera

At Kanjera, on the Kavirondo Gulf of Lake Victoria, a few miles from Kanam, Leakey found, in 1932, several human skull fragments

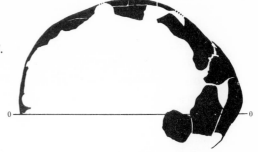

Figure 15. Fragments of Kanjera 1 skull.

and a femur. Some of the bones were picked up on the surface, others were *in situ* in the ancient lake beds, apparently associated with extinct fauna such as "*Palaeoloxodon recki*," *Simopithecus*, and *Pelorovis*.

The first fragments of the Kanjera skulls were collected from the surface, and, with the exception of two small pieces, all belong to the skull known as Kanjera 1 (Fig. 15). The fragments of Kanjera skulls 2 and 4 are so small that they can be left out of account here. Kanjera 3 is important, since some of the pieces were found *in situ*. About a hundred yards away from the spot where Kanjera 1 was found, excavations were made into the side of the slope where the surface fragments were collected. The middle layer, which yielded two skull fragments *in situ*, is composed of clays with limestone. One Acheulian hand ax was also found *in situ* here, and the same horizon elsewhere had already yielded other Acheulian tools (at first described as Chellean) as well as fauna. Near the site of Kanjera 3 skull a piece of a human femur was also collected.

The clays with limestone, at the base of which the fragments of Kanjera 3 were found, extend over a wide area and yield a large number of fossils, while the underlying and overlying beds are also fossiliferous. There was no trace of disturbance of the overlying beds, and it was apparent that the skull fragments had been broken before they became incorporated in the beds. All the bones in these beds consist, in fact, of broken and scattered material that had been washed into the lake from the surrounding land in Late Pleistocene times.

Kanjera 3 consists of seven fragments, two of which were found *in situ;* they include part of the occipital bone, two pieces of the left parietal, the left part of the frontal bone, another fragment of the left frontal that is significant, since it has part of the upper rim of the left orbit preserved, and a small piece of the right parietal.

Some skeptics doubt the ability of the anatomist to reconstruct an entire skull from a few broken fragments; it is important to emphasize that this is not done by guesswork. Reconstructions are, in fact, built on a solid framework of measurements and formulas. As long as some of the more diagnostic pieces of the skull are present, the shape and size of the whole can be computed with a fair degree of accuracy. In order to measure and compare different skulls, they must be oriented in a uniform way along some chosen plane, such as the subcerebral plane (0-0 in Fig. 15) or the Frankfurt plane (0-0 in Fig. 44). (This is the plane most commonly used when the skull is complete: it passes through the lower margin of the orbit or eye socket and the upper margin of the ear passage.)

The chief purpose of taking measurements is to determine *relative* proportions—for example, the length of the head compared with the breadth; on the living head, this is known as the cephalic index; on the skull, it is known as the cranial index. It is obtained by dividing the width into the length and obtaining the percentage. According to their cranial indices (c.i.), skulls are distinguished as follows:

Dolichocephalic (long and narrow)   c.i. less than 75.9 per cent
Mesocephalic (medium)   c.i. between 76 and 80.9 per cent
Brachycephalic (short and broad)   c.i. greater than 81 per cent

Most early human skulls are dolichocephalic; brachycephalization seems to be a late development that may have some adaptive significance. In the case of the Kanjera skulls, the finds are so fragmentary that it was possible to take only approximate measurements, but Kanjera 3 was apparently ultra-dolichocephalic.

The fragments of Kanjera 1 (Fig. 15) collected from the surface, are all very small, and some had been broken not long before they were found. They include a large part of the frontal bone, with the nasion and glabella region, part of the left parietal bone, a large part of the occipital, a small piece of the temporal bone, and a portion of the left malar and maxilla. This fragment affords the only clue as to the facial proportions of the Kanjera people and suggests that the facial skeleton was small.

Summarizing the characters of the Kanjera crania, they appear to be ultra-dolichocephalic (even allowing for possible errors in reconstruction and for *post-mortem* distortion, they are certainly long); the walls are very thick, with the exception of small fragments of Kanjera 4 that are considerably thinner. The very poor development of the superciliary and supraorbital ridges is a pedomorphic character, which, with other features, led some anatomists to consider the Kanjera crania to be of "Proto-Bushmanoid" type. If the individuals were not fully adult, this poor development of supraorbital ridges would be ex-

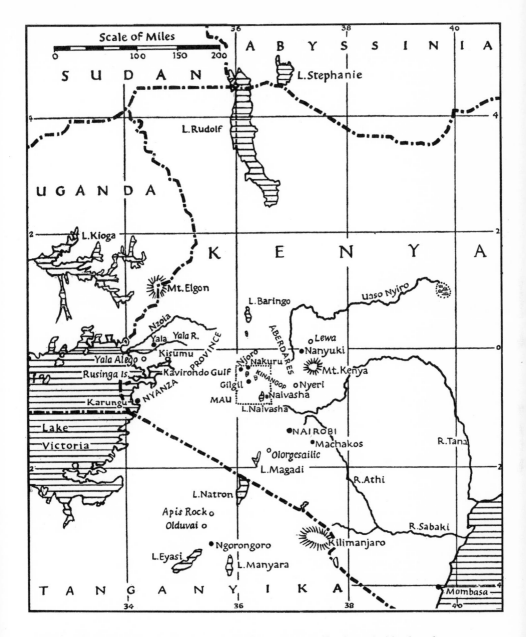

Map 7. *Stone Age sites in Kenya and northern Tanganyika (area inside dotted square is shown in Map 14).*

pected; the fragmentary nature of the finds makes it difficult to assess whether the sutures were fully closed and hence to determine the age of the individuals. From the length of the Kanjera 3 skull (according to the reconstruction), this individual would appear to be adult. A fragment of femur indicates that he was very muscular.

The fauna and artifacts suggest an age broadly equivalent to Bed IV, Olduvai. Oakley found that uranium tests on the Kanam mandible (described in the next chapter) did not support its presumed antiquity, but applied to the Kanjera bones there was no discrepancy in the radioactivity of the human skulls and the associated extinct fauna.[63]

Olorgesailie

While it is only at Olduvai that a complete evolutionary sequence of the Chelles-Acheul culture can be traced, several sites in East Africa have yielded magnificent series of Acheulian implements of stage 9 in the sequence at Olduvai, when the peak of the hand-ax makers' technique was reached. The most notable of these sites is Olorgesailie (Plate 2), which has been turned into a "museum on the spot."

Olorgesailie is situated some 40 miles southwest of Nairobi (Map 7) on the road to the Magadi soda lake, in the middle of the game reserve; and the site has now been made a national park. The drive there in the early morning or evening, when clouds or the Ngong Hills throw immense purple shadows over the plains, is surely one of the most lovely in the world. In the dry season, the plains are brown and the road dusty, but after the rains, fresh green grass springs up and all manner of lovely flowers appear, such as pink *Crinum* lilies and *Adenium*, the desert rose. The plains are dotted with round evergreen bushes (*Acokanthera*, from which various East African tribes obtained poison for their arrows) looking like toys out of a child's farmyard, with here and there tall candelabra *Euphorbia* trees. Against this scattered background of dark green are the ubiquitous brown "whistling thorns," armed with wicked spines and bobbles about the size of a horse chestnut. Each of these is the home of myriads of ants: the wind whistles through the holes they make in each bobble, giving the bush its popular name. The tender young shoots at the top are a favorite food of giraffes and gerenuk, a graceful little antelope with a long neck, which rises up on its hind legs to reach the shoots. Many other

Plate 13. Hand axes and cleavers at Olorgesailie.

kinds of antelope and gazelle are abundant on the road to Olorgesailie, as well as rhinos and buffaloes on the slopes of the Ngong Hills.

Suddenly, as one approaches Olorgesailie Mountain, the soil changes to white. Acres of diatomite, clays, and marls laid down in an ancient lake bear witness to the fact that this now very arid area once enjoyed a wetter regime (the average annual rainfall at the present time is about 20 inches). The stillness and isolation of this strange place seem to belong to some other planet, completely detached from man; it is difficult to believe that the capital of Kenya is only 40 miles away. Descending from your car (hot and sticky, for Olorgesailie is 3,000 feet lower than Nairobi), you find pleasant-looking rondavels, or grass-roofed huts, where the visitor can stay the night and explore this wonderful site in the cool of the early morning.

Gregory figured hand axes from this area in his book of 1921, but the chief site of Olorgesailie was discovered by Mrs. Leakey in 1942, and the main excavations at it were undertaken the following year. During and after the Second World War, three Italian prisoners and a few Africans lived and worked there for many months under the guidance of the Leakeys, fencing the area in, making paths through the hand axes, erecting shelters over places where implements and animal bones were thickest, and constructing the rondavels.

These Italians seldom saw another human being, save for an occasional Masai herd. Their water supply had to be brought 20 miles by truck, and food was sent twice a week from Nairobi. They had no milk, since it is too dry to keep a cow there permanently, and, although game abounds, shooting is forbidden in the game reserve. One would have thought that work under these conditions beneath a relentless sun would have made them discontented—not a bit; they sang and laughed all day long, and when the time came for them to be repatriated, one of them begged to be allowed to stay on. Their huts were full of ingenious devices to make themselves comfortable, and somehow they managed to rear hens and rabbits. The camp was a veritable tower of Babel: voluble Italian was interrupted to address Dr. Leakey in French; the latter spoke perfect Kikuyu to the African workmen; while the less-well-educated Europeans addressed them in Swahili, the *lingua franca* of the country.

In paying tribute to Europeans and Africans, a short account of conditions at Olorgesailie in the early days may be of interest to readers who can have little idea of what it is like to work a prehistoric site on the equator. One would arise with the sun, soon after six, when the air was fresh and invigorating, and work with boundless energy for about three hours, uncovering hand axes or fossil bones, sticking in posts where paths were to be made or huts to be built. Until some of the shelters had been made, it was hard to do much work between ten and four o'clock, as the heat nearly knocked one over. Once some of the shelters had been constructed, one could squat under them and work carefully away with dental picks and camel-hair brushes, uncovering some of the more fragile implements and fossils.

In the comparative cool of the evening, it was pleasant to explore for miles over the white earth and parched grass, prospecting for other sites. Just before the sun set, men and beasts shook off their stupor. Birds and animals of all kinds came down to a valley where a few damp patches of mud could be sucked up, in lieu of water. Frogs croaked and cicadas sang while later on, lions could be heard roaring and hyenas howling. Formerly the whole site was surrounded by an electric fence, which deterred rhinos most effectively, since their horns are very sensitive and if they touched the wire with their snouts, they knew all about it. But they became cunning and learned to avoid it, so the electric fence has gone and the site is now protected by thorns and wire. Giraffes never paid any attention to the electric fence, as they just walked over it.

It was very necessary to protect the site in some way, for a wandering rhino can do much damage to implements and fossils. Prehistorians get excited when they find a few dozen hand axes, but at Olorgesailie there are tens of thousands of them scattered over the surface of the ground (Plates 2 and 13), undisturbed since Paleolithic Man discarded them.

Acheulian Man lived near the fluctuating shores of a lake about 7 miles by 6 miles in extent, and surfaces marking temporary breaks in the sequence of lake deposits are marked by occupation sites, containing unrolled implements and bones. Evidence of periodic rises in lake level can be seen in thick deposits of silts, diatomites, and sands rich in pumice, which contain no artifacts. The deposits are up to 175 feet thick in places and have been heavily faulted and tilted. Sometimes they are covered over by lava or by unconformable lake beds of Late Pleistocene (Gamblian) age.

Within an area of a few square miles, 17 distinct horizons yielding fossil mammal remains and implements were at first distinguished. Posnansky, however, recognized only 14 such horizons.[64] All except for land surfaces 4, 5, and 8 were living sites of Acheulian Man, though it has been estimated that any one land surface was occupied for not more than tens to hundreds of years. The horizons 1 through 5 are separated from 6 through 9 by thick accumulations of fine sediments, which may represent hundreds to thousands of years, while levels 10 through 13 are higher again. The duration of the whole Acheulian occupation of the site may have been not more than a few tens of thousands of years.[65]

An industry that has been compared with the so-called Hope Fountain of Rhodesia, in which the implements were made by the block-on-block technique, was found unrolled on land surface 2 and rolled (derived) on land surface 6. Posnansky later excavated living floors of what he called the Hope Fountain culture at land surfaces 12 and 13 in the upper part of the series of lake beds. The tools consist of bifacial implements, and six different kinds of scrapers, as well as cores and flakes.

Clark first suggested that the Hope Fountain flake-chopper industry is in fact "a manifestation of a phase of culture rather than a separate culture in itself," since it has been found associated with pebble tools in the Vaal Valley, with the Acheulian—for example, at Broken Hill, in Northern Rhodesia—and perhaps also with early M. S. A. forms.[66] Later he suggested that the Hope Fountain was an activity variant, and this seems the most likely explanation. The large number of scrapers with abraded edges suggest that they were associated with working a hard substance, presumably wood or bone.

The late Archdeacon Owen discovered a peculiar "culture" at several sites in Nyanza Province, western Kenya, which he described as the Kombewa culture (Kombewa itself is eight miles north of the Kavirondo Gulf). Unfortunately it has not been possible to date it, though at one site it was found in a horizon with rolled and unrolled tools that may be Acheulian. Most of the artifacts of the Kombewa culture are made of close-grained basalt and are heavily rolled. They consist for the most part of struck cores, from which one (sometimes two, three, or four) shallow flake has been removed. The cores sometimes have rounded butts, but often they are faceted. The flakes are rounded in outline; most of them are too rolled to show retouching or signs of use. In nearly all cases the upper surface was left as plain as the lower. Presumably these simple flakes were used as knives or scrapers. The cores show that the flaking was well controlled, for in cases where two or three flakes are removed, the scars never overlap. Van Riet Lowe found a similar series of "Kombewa flakes" in the MN horizon at Nsongezi with a Sangoan industry.

It seems probable that the "Kombewa," like the Hope Fountain, is a particular technique or activity variant, rather than a culture. It has been suggested that the Tayacian of Europe, which has also been recognized in Morocco, may also represent some particular occupation rather than a distinct culture.

No detailed account of Olorgesailie has yet been published, and it may well be that more than one stage of the Chelles-Acheul sequence is represented; so far, however, all the material has been assigned to stage 9 of the Olduvai sequence. Artifacts are usually made from lava, occasionally from imported obsidian. Hand axes and cleavers are fairly common at all levels (see Plate 13)—particularly at land surfaces 7, 8 and 9—except those associated with the Hope Fountain variant. A high percentage of small implements (with a correspondingly lower proportion of hand axes, cleavers, and knives) occurs at land surfaces 1, 2, 3, 11, 12, and 13, and, to a lesser degree, at surfaces 6 and 10.[71] Some of the hand axes of surface 10 are very small, like those of stage 11 at Olduvai and also like those of the Fauresmith culture.

As well as many isolated stone balls, at least twelve sets in distinct groups of three were found in levels 6, 7, and 10. Leakey suggested that these stones in groups of three may be "bolas," a hunting weapon which at present is confined to South America and the Arctic. American Indians of Patagonia used a three-ball bolas; the balls are of different sizes, held in bags made of hide and tied together with twisted thongs of different lengths, while certain Eskimos use a much lighter bolas, for hunting birds. The weapon of the Patagonians is hurled at the legs of running animals, becomes entwined in them, and brings the animal down. Apart from the suggestive finds of stones in groups of three at a few Stone Age sites, there is no evidence that this weapon was ever used in Africa. A modern bolas-and-hoop game has been described from near Lake Tanganyika, and there are also records of this game's being played in Uganda; while the hoop is rolled along, the player throws a small, light bolas to entangle it and bring it down. Possibly this is a variation of the spear-and-hoop game played by many African tribes as training for throwing spears; the bolas-and-hoop game may therefore be a survival of a time when the bolas was used as a weapon.

Stone balls are common from many Paleolithic sites both in Africa and Europe, and many suggestions have been made as to their probable uses. Absolon, in his account of the finds at Vistonice in Czechoslovakia, gave a particularly full list of evidence collected from ethnographical sources. The *bola perida*, also used by South American Indians, consists of a single stone attached to a short thong and is thrown at animals in order to strike them (not to entangle the legs), or it may be used to kill a wounded animal. There are innumerable ways of attaching a stone ball to a wooden handle to form an effective club. On Beni Hasan tombs in Egypt there are pictures of cattle being caught with a cord weighted with one stone. Apart from Olorgesailie, the only report of stones in groups of threes comes from La Quina and Les Rebières (Dordogne), associated with Mousterian industries. These balls were pecked, not faceted like the Olorgosailie specimens, and the sharp surfaces of the Olorgesailie stone balls might conceivably mean that they were protected from bruising by a skin covering.

Modern usage of stone balls is common in most parts of Bantu Africa.

Native women pound the surface of their grindstones to roughen them when they become too smooth, using naturally shaped round boulders for the purpose. The same practice has been noted in northern and central Tanganyika among Hamitic groups and also among the click-speaking Sandawe. A spherical stone is also used by the latter for grinding or pounding tobacco (for snuff) and vegetables. While not suggesting that Acheulian Man had proper grindstones, it may not be too improbable to suppose that he pounded roots of edible plants on a horizontal rock surface with stone balls. In fact, innumerable uses for balls suggest themselves, such as anvils for toolmaking; but the main use of polyhedral stones must have been as hammerstones, and the smoothly rounded ball must have developed out of these. Stone balls have been found at Olduvai and at nearly all Fauresmith sites, but never in groups of three as at Olorgesailie. These groups were not only found on the surface, but also *in situ*; this led Leakey to form the theory that early Paleolithic Man may be credited with the ingenious invention of a true bolas, though the apparent grouping may well be fortuitous.

The gigantic size of most of the mammals in Middle Pleistocene times makes it probable that man relied largely on game pits to catch them. He probably also surrounded them and drove them into swamps where they could easily be dispatched as they struggled to free themselves; a concentration of animal bones in swamp deposits at Olduvai makes it likely that this is what happened in this case. Relics of man's prey are plentiful at Olorgesailie; bones were split to extract the marrow and skulls smashed to remove the brains. There are no traces of fire, so presumably the meat was eaten raw (it is, however, doubtful whether traces of fire would remain at early sites in East Africa, except in the case of cave deposits, as in the Cave of Hearths in the Transvaal, or in waterlogged sediments, as at Kalambo Falls). At horizon 7, the main diet seems to have been the giant baboon *Simopithecus* (who must have tasted very nasty); at level 8 it was the large horse *Equus olduvaiensis*, while at level 10, Acheulian Man mainly hunted the giant pig *Notochoerus*, which was almost as big as a modern rhino. In sands between occupation levels 5 and 6, many fossil remains were found, including the hippopotamus with periscopic eyes, *Hippopotamus gorgops*. An irregular line of stones on one of the temporary land surfaces by the shore of the former lake has been compared with the small fish weirs and dams commonly built in Africa today around the margins of lakes and rivers, where fish can be trapped as the water recedes at the end of the rainy season.[67] We know now that even hominids of the "pre-Zinj." stage ate catfish, and fishing—or at least scooping fish out of shallow water—may well have been nearly as important as hunting in early times.

Kariandusi and Other Kenya Sites

Another "museum on the spot" is Kariandusi, between Gilgil and Nakuru, in the Kenya Rift Valley. Here, as at Olorgesailie, the implements have been left *in situ*, exactly as they were found, and the area has been fenced off and a guard is in charge. Although by no means so impressive as Olorgesailie, Kariandusi is one of the most accessible of Kenya's Paleolithic sites; hundreds of motorists speeding along what was until the 1950s the only stretch of tarmac in the country, part of the Cape to Cairo route, stop to walk the few hundred yards that are necessary to inspect this hand-ax site. On one side of the road the land rises in an escarpment, clothed in *leleshua* bushes, while on the other side the grassy plains drop down to the little soda lake of Elmenteita, which in the soft light of morning or evening appears pink with flamingos. Below the hand-ax site, diatomite is worked commercially; the deposits are over 150 feet thick.

The artifacts are found in gravel beds laid down by a seasonal torrent at the edge of the Pleistocene lake. A few fragments of fossil mammals were recovered that show correspondence with Olduvai, Bed IV. The earlier implements were heavily rolled by the waters of the lake, while later tools are completely fresh. Some of the hand axes and cleavers, as well as the stone balls and picks, are made from lava; but the majority of cutting-edged tools are of obsidian, a black volcanic glass that lends itself readily to the manufacture of well-finished implements. Its homogeneous structure makes it as easy to work as flint. Only two groups of obsidian mines have been discovered in Kenya, one on Eburru Mountain, which divides the Elmenteita Basin from that of Naivasha; the other mines are on the steep side of Njorowa Gorge, south of Lake Naivasha, which formed an outlet for the lake in Gamblian times. From chemical analyses, it has been found that the obsidian used to make the implements at Kariandusi came from neither of these sources. Since both "mines" are fairly close to the site, one

Figure 16. (left) Acheulian hand ax, (right) cleaver, Lewa.

can only imagine that this obsidian had not yet been exposed in early Later Pleistocene times, for during the Gamblian phase, both Eburru and Njorowa obsidian was extensively used. Implements made from this material are found as far apart as Mombasa and Kampala, so evidently it was highly prized and a considerable trade in it went on. The source of the Kariandusi obsidian remains a mystery; possibly it has been buried beneath later volcanic eruptions.

The industry at Kariandusi is, like Olorgesailie, comparable with stage 9 in the Olduvai sequence. Another site where exceptionally well-made hand axes and cleavers of this stage occur is at Lewa, below the northern slopes of Mt. Kenya (Fig. 16). Some of these implements are of enormous size; they lie thick on the ground, as at Olorgesailie. Large flake knives with thick, battered backs and the opposite side trimmed have also been found at Lewa. It has not been possible to protect this site as has been done at Kariandusi and Olorgesailie; happily, it is at some distance from the road, in rather inaccessible country, so that, although some of the specimens get trampled on by cattle and sheep, they are in no imminent danger from souvenir hunters.

Hand axes have been collected from Mombasa Island, showing that the makers of the Chelles-Acheul culture reached the Indian Ocean. Many others were discovered by the late Archdeacon Owen in the area of the Yala River, western Kenya.

Hand-Ax Sites in Uganda

In Uganda, no living floors of Acheulian Man have yet been found, though many artifacts from the surface and some *in situ* leave no doubt that he lived beside lakes in the area of the western rift and possibly in the Kagera Valley. Recent discoveries in the western rift are associated with the Semliki series. This series consists of sandy deposits, coarser than the much older Kaiso series (mentioned earlier in connection with faunal stages), and divided from it by a major movement of the rift-valley faults.

At Paraa Lodge in the Murchison Falls National Park, near where the Victoria Nile emerges from Lake Albert, Bishop and de Heinzelin found artifacts in a gully formed by erosion of the Semliki series gravels and sands. They include hand axes, waste flakes, and worked quartz pebbles, and are compared with assemblages from Ruindi, south of Lake Edward in the Congo. The Ruindi industry is characterized by chopping tools made on flakes worked on one side and with a few short flakes removed from the opposite face.[68]

An industry that may be somewhat later was discovered by amateurs at Mweya Lodge, in the Queen Elizabeth National Park, on the Kazinga Channel. In 1958, Bishop excavated a small area of gravels containing hand axes, hammerstones, cores, flakes, and stone balls. The gravel here is only a few feet thick, and the artifacts lie at the base of the deposit, some 90 feet above the Kazinga Channel. They have been rolled by their inclusion in river gravel immediately postdating the underlying Semliki beds. The assemblage is compared with that of the Upper Terrace at Ishango (p. 248), on the Congo side of Lake Edward, which also overlies the Semliki series.

Both at Paraa and at Mweya, Acheulian Man lived beside the shores of the Semliki lake. Unfortunately no fauna has been found at these sites, though fossils that include "*Palaeoloxodon recki*" occur in the upper part of the Semliki series in the Congo.

The evidence for Acheulian industries in the Kagera Valley is less certain. Lowe distinguished stage 6 of the Chelles-Acheul sequence at the "M" horizon at Nsongezi, as well as stages 7 and 9 at the "N" horizon (and possibly pre-Acheulian antedating the "M" horizon), in addition to Sangoan industries. Recent excavations by Bishop and

Posnansky showed that there is only one rubble containing artifacts, the MN horizon, and that the industry is probaby Sangoan. A Lupemban industry occurs at the higher "O" horizon. The evidence is discussed in the next chapter, but, while recognizing that the industry of the MN horizon itself is Sangoan, Acheulian-type artifacts also occur scattered through the lake beds between the basal boulder bed (30 feet above present river level) and the MN horizon (about 65 feet above the river).

Hand-Ax Industries of the Sudan

The richest Paleolithic site in the Sudan is Khor Abu Anga, situated on a tributary one mile below the confluence of the Blue and White Niles. From this site, over 1,000 hand axes and other tools were recovered and transferred to the Khartoum Museum. Above the bedrock of Nubian sandstone at Khor Abu Anga is a narrow band of coarse, water-worn gravels and boulders overlain by fine gravel, both containing artifacts *in situ*. A few of the hand axes are similar to those of stage 9 of the Olduvai sequence, but only one cleaver was found; there were several polyhedral hammerstones and sandstone balls. It is not yet clear whether a true Acheulian is represented at this site, or whether —as may be more likely—the earliest industry there is Sangoan (see p. 192).

The most southerly Paleolithic site in the Sudan is Wadi Afu, where the earliest stage represented may be Acheulian, probably Chelles-Acheul stage 9. From here to the Uganda border, as well as west of the Nile, in Kordofan and Darfur, no Paleolithic cultures at all have been discovered. The Chelles-Acheul culture is found *in situ* north of the Sixth Cataract at Khor Hudi, a tributary of the Atbara River. Near Sarsareib, on the left bank of the Atbara, a series of old terraces may be seen above the river. Associated with the highest (33-foot) terrace, fossil mammal bones were found in the limestone, as well as split pebbles and Chellean-type hand axes and primitive cleavers, made by detaching two flakes from a pebble of chert, the first of which was struck off by the block-on-block technique. Rolled Chellean-type artifacts were also discovered in the coarse gravels of the lowest (14-foot) terrace and in the modern river bed, but no Acheulian-type implements were found at Sarsareib. Because of the presence here of primitive cleavers and the high proportion of tools made by the block-on-block technique, Arkell believes that early cultural influences connecting the Lower Paleolithic of Egypt with that of East Africa may have penetrated along the Atbara Valley rather than along the Nile itself.

Below the Fourth Cataract at Nuri, pebble tools were found *in situ* in gravel 160 feet above the present flood level of the Nile. Pebble tools and Chellean-type hand axes were recovered from gravel between the 100-foot and 50-foot terraces. About 175 miles downstream, at Lagiya, northwest of Dongola, hand axes made of ferricrete sandstone apparently of Chelles-Acheul stage 9 were found on the surface. A farther 70 miles downstream, at Wawa, Chellean-type tools and pebble tools were recovered from the surface of the 15-foot gravel, as well as cores and flakes made by the faceted-platform technique. At Sai Island, 15 miles north of Wawa, pebble tools and Chellean-type implements were made from large pebbles of quartz; again, part of the assemblage (which includes ovates) may be Sangoan.

Isimila

The site of Isimila, 13 miles southwest of Iringa, in the southern highlands of Tanganyika, was discovered in 1951 by D. A. Maclennan and was at first known as "Maclennan's *donga*" (*donga* means a small valley filled by a stream only during the rainy season). He collected "two rucksacks' full" of implements from the floor of the gully. They included 17 hand axes, 7 cleavers, a small prepared core, and a large backed blade. As well as normal-sized hand axes 5 to 6 inches long, there were two splendid specimens measuring 15½ inches in length, each weighing 9 pounds. They were made of quartzite and fashioned from side-struck flakes, which must obviously have been huge before they were reduced by trimming. It is difficult to imagine how enough force could have been applied to the block to detach these enormous flakes.

In 1957–58, the site was excavated by F. C. Howell of the University of Chicago. The deposits, which have been exposed by erosion, fill a small basin to a depth of over 60 feet. They suggest the presence of a large pond fluctuating to a marsh and consist of clays and silts, alternating with coarser sandy material. Occupation floors of Late Acheulian Man occur in these coarser deposits.

There are five main sands, up to one meter or more in thickness in the lower series (5, 4, and 3), and less in the upper series (2 and 1). As there are few exposures of sands 5 and the overburden is very thick, few implements were found at this level, though a number of small quartz artifacts were obtained from a deep pit into underlying sediments. The only horizon to yield fauna (apart from a hippopotamus tooth in the upper sands) was in sands 4. The bones are fragmentary and often soft, but they include part of a skeleton of *Hippopotamus gorgops*, probable remains of *Equus olduvaiensis* and of "*Paleoloxodon recki*" as well as tusks of the giant pigs *Mesochoerus* and *Afrochoerus*. Most of the artifacts consist of small quartz specimens, but there are also a few large ones.

In sands 3, four occupation floors were excavated. Hand axes and cleavers are scarce except at the floor K19, where there are more cleavers than at any other place in the site. K18 has the highest frequency of small flake tools in sands 3, but has no picks, few scrapers, cleavers, and choppers. At H15 there are many core scrapers and an extensive use of large granite chunks for heavy-duty implements.

Sands 2 seems to represent a period of sparse occupation, and there are few artifacts. Sands 1, on the other hand, contains very rich concentrations, exposed by erosion. In the lower band, 1b, two floors were excavated; as well as differing considerably from each other, these two floors are very different from those in the upper band, 1a. At K6 in 1b, 80 per cent of the shaped tools are large cutting-edged implements; few of these are cleavers, but there is a very high frequency of hand axes (54 per cent). At the other floor in 1b, J6-J7, there are only about half as many cutting-edged tools, but cleavers are more numerous; there are also many small flake tools. The character of all three occupation areas in the upper band, 1a, is similar. There are many large, well-fashioned cutting-edged implements; few knives, picks, and small flake tools; but a higher proportion of flake scrapers and stone spheres.

Isimila thus gives considerable insight into the distribution pattern of various assemblages. There is great lateral variation both in the occurrence of the main classes of implements and of types within those classes; the association of various raw materials with certain classes is also interesting. Detailed studies of this kind, which have been undertaken also at Kalambo Falls, are at last making it possible to attempt interpretations of the activities that went on at Acheulian sites. A number of fascinating questions are raised by the evidence. Was K19 in sands 3, with its many cleavers, a butchering site where the men chopped up the carcasses they brought in? What went on at K6 in sands 1b, with its high proportion of hand axes—perhaps skinning? And H15, with its many heavy tools, such as picks, was probably where heavy woodworking took place. Were the floors with a high proportion of smaller scrapers where men shaped their wooden spears? Or those with heavier scrapers where the women worked skins?

The site would obviously have been an excellent one for Stone Age man, with its good water supply in an otherwise arid area, and particularly because of the availability of suitable raw material for toolmaking. Mylonite, a fine-grained metamorphic rock, was used extensively, as well as quartz, quartzite, and granite (mainly for the heavy-duty tools). An interesting suggestion is that the time interval taken up by the deposition of the 60-foot-thick sediments, and hence the period of occupation of the site, may have been no longer than a few thousand years. This is based on comparisons with the rate at which water-storage reservoirs at Dodoma are silting up at the present time; it takes only a few hundred years of constant seasonal deposition to build up an equivalent thickness.[69]

Kalambo Falls

Kalambo Falls, one of the highest falls in Africa, lies at the southeastern end of Lake Tanganyika. Above the falls the Kalambo River, which forms the boundary between Northern Rhodesia and Tanganyika, meanders sluggishly through a wide valley. It then plunges 726 feet into a dark, narrow gorge and eventually flows into Lake Tanganyika. The area immediately above the falls was formerly occupied by a small lake, whose deposits contain industries from Late Acheulian up to historic times. This very important site was discovered in 1953 by Clark, who also excavated it and described it.[70] His detailed reports are not yet available and only a very brief account of Kalambo is given here, in spite of its great significance for the prehistory of East Africa.

The site is unique because its earliest deposits have always been waterlogged; thus vegetable material such as wood, seeds, fruits and nuts, as well as fossil pollen, is very well preserved, and charcoal has been obtained from most of the living floors for carbon-14 dating. Unfortunately the peaty acids that preserved the vegetable material must have destroyed every scrap of bone.

The three lowest floors, only just above water level today and extending also beneath the river, contain Late Acheulian industries; wood from floor 6 was dated by carbon-14 to 57,300 ± 300 B.P., or about 55,300 B.C. They are temporary surfaces, occupied when the lake level was abnormally low, and considered to represent probably not more than a season. There has been little or no movement of the material since the camps were deserted, and everything has been plotted in position, giving a clear pattern of tool concentrations. A number of fruits were found, including those of the Borassus palm, which presumably formed a major part of man's diet. Charred wood, charcoal, and ash occurred around a burned-clay area taken to be a hearth, while a circle of stones suggests a shelter of some kind. Concentrations of burned grass may have been bedding. Unique for this period in Africa are wooden tools; pieces of wood obliquely truncated at one or both ends were probably digging sticks; one with fine grooving may have formed part of a throwing stick; while another may have been the pointed end of a spear.

The vegetable remains and fossil pollen from the site indicate a climate somewhat cooler and wetter than the present one during the Late Acheulian phase. There was apparently forest around the water, fringed by savanna vegetation; the conditions may have been approximately the same as those found today at an altitude of 4,000-5,000 feet (Kalambo is at 3,500 feet).

Dating and Conclusions

How far can we get with the relative dating of the East African hand-ax sites? The only firm dates we have are 360,000 years for Chellean stage 3 and 57,300 years for the very late Acheulian of Kalambo Falls. To try to guess the date when Chellean evolved into Acheulian during the period represented by Olduvai, Bed III, would be meaningless—there is simply no evidence—and in any case this rather arbitrary division in the sequence is not very important. Bed IV, containing stages 7 to 11 and including the red band indicating exposure as a land surface, must span a fairly considerable length of time. Possibly part of it is of Riss age, perhaps part is equivalent to the Third Interglacial, probably the upper levels extend into the time of Early Würm; as yet, no correlations with Europe are firmly established.

The Kanjera artifacts are few and have not been described in detail, but both they and the fauna suggest a Bed IV age. The industries of Olorgesailie, which clearly have minor subdivisions, and of Kariandusi, have been compared with stage 9 in the red band of Bed IV, Olduvai. The age of the Uganda industries at Paraa and Mweya is uncertain, but since they come from the Semliki series, which in the Congo includes fauna such as "*Palaeoloxodon recki*," a correlation of part of the series with Bed IV seems justified. Too little is known about the Sudan sites to attempt to link them up with those of East Africa proper. The "Acheulio-Levalloisian" of the Horn (described in the next chapter) is very likely broadly contemporary with the Late Acheulian of Kalambo Falls, or perhaps somewhat later.

The problem of Isimila is rather difficult. Howell and Kleindienst consider the industries to be "broadly of an age comparable to, or slightly later than, that represented on Olorgesailie surfaces 9 and 10, and also stage 9 in Olduvai Gorge, Bed IV. It appears to be somewhat older than the Late Acheulian, represented in floors 5 and 6, at Kalambo Falls."[71] They also draw attention to the many artifact types characteristic of the Later Sangoan, such as picks, push planes, core scrapers, chisel-ended tools and discoids, many of which are present at the MN horizon of the Kagera River, thought to be later than Kalambo.

It seems unlikely that Isimila could be later than the Kalambo Acheulian because of the presence in sands 4 of extinct fauna such as giant pigs, "*Palaeoloxodon recki*," and *Equus olduvaiensis*. The climate at the time of both the Isimila deposits and the MN horizon seems to have been relatively dry, while at the time of the Kalambo Acheulian it seems to have been wetter. Since the Isimila occupation is believed to have lasted only a few thousand years, and the Kalambo Acheulian may represent only a few seasons, it would be useless to try to draw inferences from the climatic evidence.

A far more interesting problem than the relative dating of Late Acheulian sites, however, is the nature of the people who made these industries. The only human remains known from this important period in East Africa are the Kanjera skull fragments, and it is not even certain whether they are contemporary with the hand axes and extinct fauna. If they are, as the radioactivity tests suggest, they would presumably be the earliest representatives of modern *Homo sapiens* known (see Table 3).

The earliest hand-ax industries were made by Pithecanthropines, as at Olduvai, Bed II, and in Algeria and Morocco, and possibly in the

Transvaal ("*Telanthropus*" of Swartkrans). They were followed by a generalized *Homo*, represented by the Swanscombe skull of the time of the Great Interglacial, which could be ancestral to both Neanderthalers and modern man. Very likely this was the case also in Africa, and we may imagine generalized *Homo* descendants of Chellean Man giving rise both to the extreme form represented by Rhodesian Man and to *Homo sapiens*. Apart from Kanjera, the oldest *Homo sapiens* in Africa (using this name in a restricted sense, excluding the Rhodesioids) has generally been taken to be the peculiar skull from Florisbad in the Orange Free State. It has been dated by carbon-14 to between 28,000 and 35,000 years old, the age obtained for two layers of peat between which the skull was found. But there is a distinct possibility that the peat was contaminated by older carbon from coal deposits and the skull may well be considerably younger than this. The Florisbad skull has fairly heavy brow ridges, though not nearly so large as in Rhodesian Man, and a relatively small face. We might have expected the earliest *sapiens* in Africa to look something like the Florisbad skull, but the very modern-looking Kanjera skulls are certainly a surprise. On the other hand, skull fragments from Fontechevade in France, probably dating from the Last Interglacial, have only very slight traces of brow ridges. A skull from Niah Cave in Sarawak, dated by carbon-14 to about 40,000 years, is of completely modern appearance. So it may be possible to fit Kanjera into the *Homo sapiens* lineage without too much difficulty. Early Würm in Europe ended about 40,000 years ago; the Kanjeran pluvial with its hand-ax industries may have continued equally late, and the Kanjera skulls might date from the very end of this period, up to 15,000 years later than the Kalambo Acheulian. At present, of course, all this is pure speculation, but at least it offers some sort of solution to a very awkward problem.

Chapter Six

MAN BEGINS TO SPECIALIZE

For nearly half a million years, the hand ax had continued to serve a great many different purposes in hunting, food collecting, and domestic life. All over the African continent, parts of western and southwestern Asia, and Western Europe, this tool was so standardized that, given an isolated specimen, it would often be quite impossible to name even the continent of its origin. During the later stages of the Chelles-Acheul culture, this standard tool was beautifully finished, and its makers had complete mastery over their craft. While they used a great many different rocks for the purpose, and, in some cases, evidently obtained these rocks from considerable distances, they were perfectly able to fashion a well-flaked hand ax out of almost any material. Apparently they well understood cleavage and the granular structure of rocks. They had high standards, for the amount of waste material and discards found at most sites shows that they were satisfied only with the best. As well as hand axes, they made cleavers, picks, crude scrapers, knives, and other tools, but these wonderful, if limited, craftsmen never

167

seem to have evolved truly specialized tools throughout their long history. With a small population and a plentiful supply of game, simple tools sufficed; man usually only exerts himself toward inventiveness when forced to by competition.

While hand axes continued to be used in certain later industries, the end of Earlier Stone Age times ushered in a profound, if gradual, change of fashion. Cores, which had already been prepared in Acheulian times, now became more elaborate and were used to yield flakes that served many different purposes. The age of specialization had dawned.

Although in the past, flakes left over from the manufacture of hand axes had presumably been used for woodworking and skin scraping, in Later Pleistocene times flakes were specially prepared as carpenters' tools or as weapons of the chase and perhaps also of war. Chisels, gouges, and awls became more efficient; knife blades undoubtedly had as many uses then as they have today; hollow scrapers were used as spoke shaves, while end and side scrapers were more finely finished for dressing leather for bags or clothing. Many different kinds of points were almost certainly hafted to form daggers, spears, and, eventually, arrows.

Since we find only the stone tips of weapons and tools, it is easy to forget that most of them were probably gummed into bone or wooden handles, or bound onto them with sinews. Thus a clumsy-looking stone point would become an effective implement. When we study the tools made by modern peoples such as the Bushmen, Eskimos, and aboriginal Australians, we find that not only arrowheads, spears, and daggers but also scrapers, knife blades, and gravers are hafted into handles, held in place by natural gums or resin and sometimes bound as well, to give additional security. Rawhide thong twisted around the shaft shrinks considerably on drying and binds the parts together very securely. The Tasmanians, however, who became extinct at the end of the last century, used only crude scraping and cutting tools that apparently were never hafted.

John Smith, writing of the Indians of Virginia in 1606, said: "His arrow-head he maketh quickly with a little bone . . . of any splint of stone or glasse in the form of a heart, and these they glew to the end of their arrowes. With the sinews of deer and the tops of deer's horns boiled to a jelly they make a glew which will not dissolve in water."

Apart from glue made from boiled horns, natural pitch or resin found in many trees and plants would insure that primitive man had a plentiful supply of gum. The chief source of resin used by Bushmen in ancient times was said to be the roots of *Pterocelastrus variabilis*; this resin is very brittle and had to be mixed with other substances for cementing.

We can imagine, during the Middle Stone Age and Later Stone Age, various kinds of scrapers, chisels, and knife blades mounted in a mass of hard gum, as in Australia or the Admiralty Islands in modern times, or inserted into a handle of bone or wood and then glued, as with the *ulu*, or Eskimo woman's knife (side and end scrapers are hafted in much the same way). Some most interesting speculations have been made on the way of life of Middle Stone Age hunters, which envisage the use of traps and fire, more permanent dwellings in rock shelters, and group cohesion that seems to imply a common language, perhaps of the "click" variety as spoken by Bushmen and Hottentots.[72]

The First Intermediate Period

After the end of the Chelles-Acheul, a number of local industries arose during what is known as the First Intermediate Period. It is a rather tiresome term, for although in a sense intermediate between the Earlier Stone Age and the Middle Stone Age, there are no hard-and-fast boundaries, and the industries merge gradually into one another. In fact, it would be far more convenient to regard everything between the end of the Acheulian and the beginning of the L. S. A. as Middle Stone Age.

The only culture confined to the First Intermediate that seems to leave no direct descendants is the *Fauresmith*, which flourished during the drier period preceding the Gamblian pluvial. It is widespread in South Africa, but otherwise is known mainly from the highlands of Kenya and Ethiopia. Its Acheulian ancestry is obvious and it includes many similar artifacts, though on a smaller scale. The *Sangoan* is probably contemporary with the Fauresmith, but develops into various stages of the Lupemban culture during the M. S. A.; both Sangoan and Lupemban occur in the wetter forested zones of central Africa, centered on the Congo Basin but found also in Uganda, western Kenya, parts of the Sudan, the Rhodesias, and parts of South Africa (see Map 10).

The *Acheulio-Levalloisian* of the Horn, officially included in the First Intermediate, may be contemporary with M. S. A. industries farther south. The question of whether the earlier "*Levalloisian*" of Kenya and Tanganyika is a distinct culture or merely a particular technique is discussed later. It is succeeded by the *Proto-Stillbay*, which in turn evolves into the Stillbay; these industries are ubiquitous over the drier steppe and savanna country from the Horn to the Cape. The two most important and long-lasting cultures of different areas in East Africa during the M. S. A., the Stillbay and the Lupemban, are discussed in the next chapter (see Table 4).

The First Intermediate industries started soon after the Kalambo Acheulian, 55,300 B.C., and continued until the time of the Kalambo Sangoan, about 38,000 B.C. During this period, bifacial implements on the hand-ax pattern continued to be made, but flake tools from prepared cores became increasingly important. Stoneworking generally did not reach such a high standard as it did during the Acheulian, but this may have been mainly due to the increased use of other materials, particularly wood.

These rather dull and indeterminate industries are significant in our story, since they are associated with the Rhodesioids, the African equivalents of the Neanderthalers. No human remains have ever been found associated with the Sangoan, but skulls of the Rhodesioid type

Table 4. East African Stone Age cultures compared with those of Europe.

WESTERN EUROPE			EASTERN AND CENTRAL AFRICA		
Years B.C.	Cultures	Cultural divisions	Cultures not dated by Carbon 14	Industries dated by Carbon 14	Years B.C.
	Iron Age Bronze Age Neolithic	Neolithic	Hyrax Hill? Wilton Elmenteitan?	Njoro River Cave	950
4000		LATER STONE AGE		Shaheinab Neolithic	3300
	Mesolithic			Nachikufan I (Chifubwa)	4370
8000			Magosian Ishangian?	Magosian (Kalambo)	7600
	Azilian	SECOND INTERMEDIATE	Upper Kenya Capsian? Khartoum Mesolithic?	Lupembo-Tshitolian (Mufo)	9240
10,500					
	Magdalenian	UPPER PALEOLITHIC		Final Lumpemban (Mufo)	12,50(0)
15,000	Solutrean		Lower Kenya Capsian?		
18,000	Proto-Magdalenian	MIDDLE STONE AGE	Stillbay		
	Aurignacian Perigordian			Upper Lupemban (Kalambo)	25,00(0) 27,00(0)
30,000			Proto-Stillbay		
40,000	Mousterian	MIDDLE PALEOLITHIC FIRST INTERMEDIATE	Fauresmith	Sangoan – Later Lupemban (Kalambo?)	38,00(0) 41,00(0)
		EARLIER STONE AGE		Final Acheulian (Kalambo)	55,30(0)

have been accompanied by Fauresmith, "Developed Levalloisian," and Proto-Stillbay industries, which are all basically rather similar and broadly of the same age.

The Rhodesioids

Contemporary with the Neanderthalers of Europe, Asia, and North Africa were the Rhodesioids of Africa south of the Sahara. At one time they were known as "Proto-Australoids," not because any direct relationship with the Australian aborigines was implied, but because certain features such as heavy brow ridges were characteristic of both. It has been proposed that the term "Rhodesioid" should be used instead, a name that is obviously preferable in Africa since it conveys immediately what is meant.[73]

The Rhodesioids are represented by skulls from Broken Hill, Northern Rhodesia; Saldanha Bay, in Cape Province; and Lake Eyasi, northern Tanganyika. A skull from Singa, in the Sudan, and jaws from Kanam, in Kenya, and from Dire Dawa, in Ethiopia, may perhaps also be included in this general category. It seems to be only north of the Sahara—for example, at Rabat and at Haua Fteah, in Cyrenaica—that true Neanderthalers are known in Africa.

The Rhodesioids are gerontomorphic, which means very briefly that they had rather exaggerated or "masculine" features, such as heavy brow ridges needed for the attachment of powerful chewing muscles. Pedomorphism, on the other hand, results in more "feminine"-looking features, or the retention of infantile characters in the adult. Modern man as a whole, particularly in the case of the Mongol race and the Bushmen, is pedomorphic compared with his ancestors; and women are invariably more pedomorphic than men.

Although the original Rhodesian Man from Broken Hill does not come within the area covered by this book, he must be described as a typical representative of the Rhodesioid stock, since the very similar Eyasi finds from East Africa are rather fragmentary.

BROKEN HILL

During open-cast mining of lead and zinc ores, an extraordinary human skull was found in a cave in one of the kopjes at Broken Hill in 1921. This skull lay 60 feet beneath the ground, within a mass of soft lead ore; down to 40 feet only, the deposits were associated with zinc ore. According to the official account of the find, the skull was accompanied by other human bones; but four years after the discovery, when Hrdlicka interviewed the Swiss miner who found the skull, he told him that it was not associated with other bones except for a tibia, which was lying 3 feet away. Leakey, who visited the site in 1929, gathered that only lead was being smelted in 1921 and that when a search was made later and other human bones were found, these really came from the higher zinc levels.

In order to clear up this question, Oakley caused estimations to be made of the lead, zinc, and vanadium content of the human and animal bones found in association, as well as of the matrix containing humanly worked implements in the same cave. Contrary to expectations, it was found that the original cranium alone contained more zinc than lead. Since it is definitely known to have come from the lower lead levels, it was concluded that it probably lay in a pocket of zinc ore within the mass of lead carbonate. The other human bones contained as much lead as zinc, some much more, and the matrix of the implements was also rich in lead, suggesting that they all came from the lower levels. A fragmentary maxilla belonging to a second individual and a parietal were also found, and these too showed a relatively high lead content. Oakley reported that the spectrographic evidence favors the association of the maxilla with a left femur, a sacrum, and a male os innominatum, and that the new data do not contradict the reported association of the type cranium with the tibia.

L. H. Wells studied the differences between the isolated maxilla and that of the type skull. The maxilla of the original skull shows various features that are more "Neanderthaloid" than those of the fragmentary maxilla; the latter, for example, has a canine fossa (a hollow beneath the orbits or eye sockets found in modern *Homo sapiens* but not in the Neanderthalers).

In spite of these differences, the two individuals probably fall within the range of variation of a single type; possibly the maxilla may have belonged to a female. If this is so, then the differences between Rhodesian Man and modern man is less than would be supposed from a consideration of the type of skull alone. In many ways, too, Rhodesian Man is very like *Homo soloensis* from Java, who also worked bone tools and used stone balls.

Regarding the dating of the Broken Hill skull, Clark concluded that the associated industry is early M. S. A. The upper, yellow cave earth contained Stillbay implements, while the lower, black cave earth in which the skull was found contained a Proto-Stillbay industry. His later excavations at a nearby site, containing both Acheulian and M. S. A. industries, confirmed these conclusions. The accompanying fauna, although mainly of modern type, includes a few extinct forms such as *Homoioceras*, which suggest an early Gamblian date for the first human occupation of the cave.

Although Rhodesian Man's skull shows some Neanderthaloid features, the limb bones and pelvis are completely modern in appearance. In the same way, the skull of *Pithecanthropus erectus*—as his specific name implies—was associated with a modern type of femur, confirming that the pelvic region and limbs evolved in the direction of *Homo sapiens* much earlier than the brain and shape of the skull.

The most remarkable feature of Rhodesian Man is his supraorbital torus, or brow ridge, which reaches the immense width of 139 millimeters. The skull is dolichocephalic and the cranial capacity has been estimated by different authorities as 1280 c.c. and 1400 c.c. The brain was smaller than those of most of the Neanderthalers, but the walls of the skull are so thick that the space for the brain is only 81.4 per cent of the total length (the corresponding percentages for *Pithecanthropus* and modern man are 84 and 92, respectively).

The face is extremely long from eye socket to chin, but is not wide from orbits to ear holes as in Neanderthal Man. As would be expected with a heavy torus, the palate is huge; the palato-cranial ratio is 1:37 (in modern man it averages 1:50). All the teeth are greatly worn, and most of them show evidence of decay. On the left side of the skull are two small holes; from the appearance of grooves that are taken to have been caused by pus, it is assumed that the holes may have been caused by injuries connected with abscessed teeth. One leg bone shows rheumatic growths around the joint that may also be connected with the condition of the teeth. A round perforation of the bone (seen also in the Florisbad skull) could have been caused by the point of a wooden spear.[74]

Rhodesian Man stood about 5 feet, 10 inches, and held his head erect (the position of the foramen magnum confirms this evidence obtained from the shape of the limb bones). Unfortunately the mandible is missing, but it was probably massive (see Fig. 17[2]), as suggested by a jaw fragment found with the very similar Saldanha skull.

In 1953, a cranium very like that of the Broken Hill specimen was found in sandy veld country at the farm of Elandsfontein, between Saldanha Bay and Hopefield, 90 miles north of Cape Town. Unfortunately it has no face or upper jaw like the Broken Hill Man, and it is slightly smaller, but it has the same characteristic heavy brow ridges. The bones are very thick, and the open sutures indicate that the cranium belonged to a young adult. Two industries seem to be present at Elandsfontein: Fauresmith and Stillbay. The fauna includes many extinct forms such as the giant pig *Mesochoerus*, which we have met at Olduvai, an antlered giraffid *Griquatherium*, which is similar to *Sivatherium*, and the buffalo *Homoioceras*, which is found also in early Gamblian deposits in the Kenya Rift Valley. Tests have shown that the human skull has the same high fluorine content as *Mesochoerus* and other extinct fauna, which suggests that it is contemporary with the earlier Fauresmith industry.

The Fauresmith seems to occur during a relatively dry period preceding the Gamblian. The Hopefield fauna also suggests a pre-Gamblian date, though of course events down at the Cape may have been slightly retarded as far as both fauna and industries are concerned. Possibly the Saldanha skull may be slightly earlier than the Broken Hill and Eyasi specimens, but they seem to be of the same general age.

EYASI

During expeditions to Lake Eyasi, in northern Tanganyika, in the years 1934–36 and again in 1939, Kohl-Larsen discovered parts of three

Figure 17. (Left) Eyasi skull (after Weinert); (right) Broken Hill skull (with conjectural restoration of lower jaw).

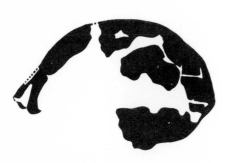

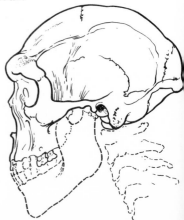

human crania. Two of these were represented by very small fragments, but the outline of the third could be reconstructed from a large number of pieces (Fig. 17).

The deposit containing the bones was exposed on the floor of the northeastern end of the present lake during the dry season. Associated mammal fossils fall into two groups, one rolled, the other unrolled and obviously later. The rolled fauna includes extinct species typical of the Mid Pleistocene. The human skull fragments are themselves unrolled and in the same state of mineralization as the later fauna, which is typically Later Pleistocene (early Gamblian). It consists entirely of living species, with the exception of one bovid; but it includes animals that do not live in the area today, such as the white rhino and the forest hog, implying wetter conditions at the time.

When Leakey and Reeve visited the site in 1937, they found flake tools of a type they called "Developed Levalloisian." In the Kenya Rift Valley, similar implements are found in Early Gamblian deposits. Both fauna and industry thus suggest a Later Pleistocene age.

The skull fragments include part of the left parietal, the greater part of the occipital and the left temporal bone, with the mastoid process. Several other pieces fit together to form part of the frontal, and it is clear that there was a very pronounced brow ridge. All the bones are very thick compared with those of a modern skull. The position of the foramen magnum is distinctive in being inclined backward at a considerable angle. A piece of left maxilla contains the broken sockets of two incisors, the canine, and the premolars; one loose upper molar was also found.

The Eyasi skull was named *Africanthropus njarensis* by Weinert in 1939, but this generic name had already been given to the Florisbad skull (subsequently called *"Homo helmei"* but eventually regarded as a most unusual *Homo sapiens.*) Eyasi Man is now recognized to be *Homo rhodesiensis*, or, as some prefer it, *Homo sapiens rhodesiensis*. The occipital region of the second Eyasi individual is more massive than the first and much closer to Broken Hill Man; possibly the former was male, while the more complete remains represent a female.

THE SINGA SKULL

In connection with a skull from Singa, in the Sudan, mention must be made of some of the numerous Later Pleistocene human remains from South Africa with which the Singa skull has been compared. At one time various skulls associated with M. S. A. and L. S. A. industries in South Africa were rather vaguely referred to as "Boskopoid," although by no means all of them were like the original Boskop skull. Tobias has done much to clarify a most complicated situation and proposed that the term "Boskopoid" should be restricted to pedomorphic skulls of ancestral Bushman type, such as those from Boskop, Fish Hoek, and the Matjes River. The term "Rhodesioid" is extended to include not only Rhodesian Man and his close relatives but also gerontomorphic skulls of the type known from Ingwavuma, Tuinplaats, Cape Flats, and various other sites.

In general, the Boskopoids are characterized by the pentagonal shape of the skull when viewed from above, caused by a bossing of the parietal bones (Plate 14). The face is short and rather flat, the forehead is smooth, with the brow ridges lightly marked, and the mastoid

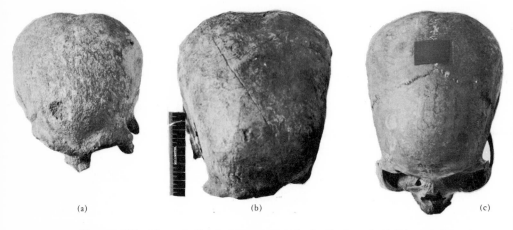

(a)   (b)   (c)

Plate 14. The Singa skull (a), compared with the Boskop skull (b), and that of a modern Bushman (c), viewed from above. The pentagonal shape is similar, but in the case of the Singa skull it may be due to an abnormality.

processes are small. With these characters in mind, we can now look at the Singa skull, which at one time was taken to be a far-flung representative of the Boskopoids, or a "Proto-Bushman."

Singa is on the Blue Nile (see Map 13) and the skull was associated with a rather indeterminate industry that may be Proto-Stillbay and hence similar to that of Broken Hill Man. This was somewhat embarrassing, owing to the apparently very different appearance of the two skulls. Recent studies, however, suggest that in fact the Singa individual may belong to the Rhodesioid group.

When viewed from above, the Singa skull is almost identical in shape with the uncertainly dated Boskop skull (Plate 14). The Boskop skull is very much larger and longer, though its transverse diameter is almost the same as that of the Singa skull. Both have the pentagonal shape and parietal bosses, as well as small mastoid processes. Owing to its different length and hence different cranial index, however, Wells pointed out that the Singa skull could not be included in the term "Boskopoid."

Recently, Brothwell found that statistically the Singa skull was quite abnormal. He believes that the growth from front to back was stunted and therefore there was a compensatory growth from side to side to accommodate the brain. Others of the Singa community, he suspects, would not have had such prominent parietal bosses (this feature is, in fact, not confined to Boskopoids and Bushmen but is also found in some predynastic skulls from Egypt). The small mastoid processes are also characteristic of Neanderthaloids, and the temple bone, which in the Singa skull Wells thought to be a pedomorphic feature, is also close to that of the Neanderthaloids. In its frontal contours, with rather prominent supraorbital ridges, Brothwell compares the Singa skull with Solo Man. In fact, it may be regarded as a modern-looking Rhodesioid.

We may compare the situation with the Neanderthalers, who varied from the earlier exaggerated "classic" types at Tabun to much more modern-looking individuals at Skhūl. The Rhodesioids of Broken Hill, Saldanha, and Eyasi would represent the "classic" Rhodesian Man. Unfortunately it is difficult to recognize their more modern-looking counterparts; possibly the Florisbad skull may represent the more advanced branch, and it would not be surprising if other variations ranging from "classic" to more modern were found in the future.

Figure 18. The Kanam mandible (left), compared with modern man.

THE KANAM MANDIBLE

In 1932, Leakey discovered a mandible at Kanam, in western Kenya, which he first described as *Homo kanamensis* but later considered to be *Homo sapiens*. It was reported to be associated with an Early Pleistocene fauna and pebble tools, and, since no remains of *Homo* from such a remote period had ever been found anywhere else—and never have been to this day—its dating was immediately questioned. A conference was convened at Cambridge in the year after its discovery to try to decide on the age of the mandible. It was agreed that it must be of high antiquity since it appeared to be in the same state of mineralization as the accompanying Early Pleistocene mammal remains. Fossils, however, often become heavily mineralized in a comparatively short time under tropical conditions, so this point was by no means conclusive evidence of age.

The Early Pleistocene lake beds at Kanam, consisting of light brown clays and volcanic tuffs, have been heavily affected by earth movements associated with the formation of the Kavirondo Rift Valley, and by eruptions from Homa Mountain, and the beds have been repeatedly tilted and faulted. The mandible was embedded in a very hard matrix and had been much damaged and weathered before it was washed into its resting place beside the lake shore. It lay in a gully running toward the lake, and the block of material in which it was embedded was detached from the side of the gully eight feet from the top. The whole region is one of heavy rainfall, and land surfaces are subject to considerable erosion, which, in fact, made the discovery of the jaw possible. In view of this rapid erosion, Leakey maintained that deposition of secondary material on the slopes of the gully would be well-nigh impossible and that therefore the block containing the mandible must be composed of undisturbed sediments of the same age.

The find (Fig. 18) consists of a small fragment of the area of the symphysis; the alveolar arch is preserved from the first molar root on the right-hand side to the root of the first premolar on the left. The only two teeth that have not been broken off are the two premolars, and neither of these is in perfect condition. The roots of the first right molar and those of the two canines and all incisors are preserved in their sockets. The jaw is exceptionally massive, and a crack indicates that the individual had received a fracture that had healed before death. The massiveness of the mandible, as well as certain features such as the absence of a "neck" in the premolars, led Leakey to think at first that a new specific name, *kanamensis*, was justified. But it was the presence of what appeared to be an incipient chin that made him class it as *Homo* and later as *Homo sapiens*.

There is, however, a bony growth from the symphysis toward the left of the jaw due to a sarcoma. Tobias came to the conclusion that the apparent "chin" was exaggerated owing to this pathological condition. He pointed out a number of primitive features, such as the great depth in the region of the symphysis and of the first molar, and considered that the fossil may be of Neanderthaloid affinities, perhaps intermediate between "*Atlanthropus*" (a Pithecanthropine from North Africa) and modern man. It is most similar, he says, to jaws from Rabat, Morocco (probably of Riss age), and from Dire Dawa, Ethiopia (Later Pleistocene).[75]

In 1948, Sir Arthur Keith concluded that the Kanam mandible was probably that of an Australopithecine. The combination of very small incisors and rather large canines is characteristic of the Australopithecines, and a few even have quite an impressive chin development like that of Kanam. In the Prologue of the 1960 edition of *Adam's Ancestors*, Leakey also expressed this view, calling it a female "*Zinjanthropus*."

Oakley made uranium tests on the Kanam jaw, and its radioactivity proved to be so low in comparison with that of the undoubtedly Early Pleistocene fossils from the site that he thought it most unlikely that it could be contemporary with them. This great difference in radioactivity strongly suggests that the time interval between the Early Pleistocene mammals and the Kanam jaw is a long one, which lends weight to Tobias's opinion that the individual is of "Neanderthaloid" (or more probably Rhodesioid) affinities rather than Australopithecine.

So the Kanam mandible, thirty years after its discovery, remains almost as enigmatical as ever. One thing now seems quite certain, however: it is not the most early *Homo sapiens*, as was claimed at one time.

THE DIRE DAWA MANDIBLE

Since Tobias compared the Kanam mandible with one from Dire Dawa, in Ethiopia, this is a convenient place to mention this find. Although it is generally classed as "Neanderthaloid" rather than Rhodesioid, it has not been studied in any great detail and may prove to be nearer to the Rhodesioids than to the Neanderthaloids.

The jaw came from the cave of Porc Epic, a few miles south of Dire Dawa, which was excavated by Wernert in 1933. The floor of the cave consists of ash containing disintegrated animal bones, forming a thick crust of calcium phosphate; firmly embedded in this crust, on an intrusion in the rock floor, was the fragment of heavily mineralized human mandible. In the lowest part of the ash was a Stillbay industry, and, while the jaw need not necessarily be contemporary with this industry, it may well be. In this case, it would be somewhat later than Broken Hill Man.

Having described the Rhodesioids, we must now look more closely at the industries they made.

The Problem of the "Levalloisian"

We have seen that the Eyasi skull fragments were associated with what was called a "Developed Levalloisian" industry. The technique employed in this industry was used also in other M. S. A. cultures, and it is important to understand what it involves. There was considerable confusion in the past because the term "Levallois" was used to describe both a technique and a particular culture. In the old definition of a pure "Levallois culture," hand-ax elements are absent; in many hand-ax industries, on the other hand (for example, in the Somme Valley, all over South Africa, and in parts of East Africa), the technique employed by the makers of the "Levalloisian culture" was used extensively. The side-struck cores of the Victoria West industries of the Vaal, recognized as stages in the Chelles-Acheul sequence (see p. 140), are the result of a technique that has sometimes been called "Proto-Levallois." At the First Pan-African Congress on Prehistory in Nairobi in 1947 it was decided to use the term "faceted platform" in place of the word "Levallois" to describe this technique. The "prepared-core" technique is not, strictly speaking, synonymous with the faceted-platform technique, since, although flakes with faceted platforms are necessarily obtained from cores prepared beforehand, a core can also be prepared with a flat striking platform as well as with a faceted one.

The faceted-platform technique is, briefly, as follows:

(1) A series of flakes is removed across the face of the core, as flat as possible, so as to leave the surface slightly convex; these flakes are struck off from different directions all around.

(2) At one end of the core, at right angles to the prepared convex face, another series of small flakes is removed, this time all in the same direction and roughly parallel to one another. In this way the striking platform is prepared.

(3) Finally, a sharp blow is struck on the prepared platform in such a way as to remove part of the convex face of the core. The core left after the removal of the final flake has a characteristic appearance and is known as a "tortoise core." The large flake obtained in this way was then made into the required tool. It retains part of the faceted striking platform at its butt end (at right angles to its long axis). The upper face of the flake shows a series of flake scars, mostly truncated, while the bulb of percussion is retained on the reverse face (Fig. 19).

This somewhat complicated process obviously involves considerable ingenuity on the part of the inventor. The faceted-platform technique in many parts of Africa is an integral part of the hand-ax culture and continues side by side with bifaced tools in many later industries, such as the Fauresmith, Sangoan, and Stillbay. "The progress of man's skill . . . [is measured] by an abandonment of old methods and by an improved technical skill revealed in the greater refinement and variety of his waste products in the form of smaller and more elaborately prepared cores and flakes,"[76] as he progressed from the Chelles-Achuel to the cultures of the First Intermediate period and the M. S. A.

The question now arises whether a pure Levalloisian culture exists at all, or whether it should be regarded merely as a basic flaking technique, employed by the makers of many different cultures.

A new appreciation of the nature of the Levalloisian resulted from statistical investigations made by Bordes on techniques employed in

Figure 19. Levalloisian flake.

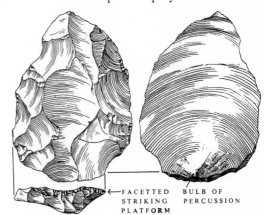

←FACETTED   BULB OF
STRIKING   PERCUSSION
PLATFORM

the Paleolithic of Europe. From the assessment of various assemblages, Bordes obtained four indices of fundamental significance: (1) the "Levalloisian" index; (2) the index of faceting; (3) the index of "Levalloisian" typology; (4) the bifacial (hand-ax) index. The results indicate the characteristics of the Mousterian complex statistically, but showed that there is probably no such thing as a "Levalloisian culture."

"By eliminating the Levalloisian in a cultural sense and defining it as one of two basic flaking techniques in use at one and the same time, Bordes has made a fundamental contribution to the methodology of Palaeolithic archaeology," wrote Movius.[77]

Bordes' statistical methods have, so far, been applied only to a limited extent in Africa, particularly in the Transvaal, by Mason. All that can be said at present is that there are many sites in northern and eastern Africa where tortoise cores and flake tools with faceted platforms exist unmixed with bifaced elements. It seems likely that in some cases they form part of other industries, such as Proto-Sangoan, Sangoan, Proto-Stillbay, and so on. But for the present, until these industries have been properly described, the name "Levalloisian" will have to be retained.

In Europe, "Levalloisian" industries with tortoise cores and faceted-platform flakes appear during the closing stages of the Third Glaciation (though such cores and flakes exist already in Chelles-Acheul industries in gravels of the Second Interglacial in the Somme Valley). In East Africa, "Levalloisian" elements appear toward the close of the Earlier Stone Age, continuing throughout the First Intermediate Period.

The "Levalloisian" has been described particularly from sites in the Nile Valley, where it was studied largely before the recognition of widespread "Levalloisian" techniques in other African cultures of the E. S. A. and M. S. A.

Leakey considered the early stages of the "Levalloisian culture" in East Africa to be contemporary with the Final Acheulian, at the very end of "Kanjeran" times and to continue in its "Developed" stage into the Gamblian pluvial. In Kenya, "pure Levalloisian" sites, he says, include Muguruk, twelve miles from Kisumu, where an industry of tortoise cores and flakes with faceted butts made of lava is found *in situ* between two Sangoan industries eroding out of beds beside the Muguruk River. A similar industry exists in the Kenya Rift Valley at Red Hillock in Melawa Gorge and also at the coast near Mombasa; other sites are known but have not been published. Characteristic implements include not only points made on flakes with faceted platforms but also side scrapers, occasional burins or gravers, and sometimes hand axes made by step flaking.

"Levalloisian" sites are known in many areas in northern Tanganyika, but none have been reported south of the central railway (Dar-es-Salaam-Dodoma-Tabora line). At Eyasi, Leakey and Reeve found no artifacts *in situ* in pits and trenches dug by the German expedition, but they found two implements by breaking open lumps of bone-bearing deposits on the dumps of the excavations. Some tools were also recovered from the surface of eroded slopes associated with fossil bone washed out of the bone bed. All these artifacts, as well as those in Kohl-Larsen's collection, are considered typical of a "Developed Levalloisian" assemblage.

The East African Fauresmith

Two cultures peculiar to Africa south of the Sahara that emerged as direct derivatives of the Acheulian are the Fauresmith and the Sangoan. They appear in distinct regions in East Africa, with little overlap between the two except on the eastern shores of Lake Victoria. The Sangoan is found near large rivers and lakes that did not dry up during the drier pre-Gamblian phase, while the Fauresmith seems to be confined to higher altitudes near permanent streams.

In South Africa, the Fauresmith also evolves directly out of the Final Acheulian, as seen clearly at the Cave of Hearths in the Transvaal. It is found mainly on the high veld and extends from Natal to the Cape, where it is associated with Saldanha Man, but it is absent in the Rhodesias (although Clark recognized Fauresmith affinities in the Kalambo Sangoan). The geographically remote, but typologically similar, East African Fauresmith is found in Kenya and in Ethiopia. Leakey believed that the Kenya Fauresmith might be the result of contact between Late Acheulian people and the makers of the "Levalloisian culture," who were contemporaneous in this area. This theory, however, seems less likely than an explanation in terms of various regional requirements. A combination of *biface* and faceted-platform techniques gave rise to the Sangoan in Uganda, while in Kenya this same combination resulted in the Fauresmith. The two cultures vary somewhat in the typology of the implements: the Sangoan, for example, includes picks that are unknown in the Fauresmith, while the little Fauresmith cleavers are not found in the Sangoan. These differences are, presumably, due to different environmental needs, the first having an emphasis on woodworking.

The Kenya Fauresmith was first named "Nanyukian," after the town and river of Nanyuki, where it was first found. Later, however, it was renamed East African Fauresmith, owing to its similarity to the South African Fauresmith. In the Nanyuki area, the implements are exposed in eroded gullies below the forested slopes of Mt. Kenya, at an altitude of about 7-8,000 feet. Similar industries are found in old swamp deposits on the Kinangop Plateau, at approximately the same altitude, as well as in many places on the slopes of the Aberdare Range. The Kinangop Fauresmith industries occur in laterite deposits unconformably overlying tuffs of the rift-valley escarpment.[78] The floor of the rift was apparently abandoned in favor of mountain slopes, where permanent streams insured a water supply at a time when the rift-valley lakes were dry. The East African Fauresmith seems to be confined entirely to the drier period preceding the Gam-

Figure 20. Fauresmith implements, Nanyuki.

blian pluvial, and in South Africa, too, it appears that the rainfall had started to decrease in Fauresmith times. It can be imagined also that the temperature was then higher than at present, for today the nights are very cold at an altitude of 8,000 feet and man could hardly have survived except in caves, which do not exist on these mountain slopes.

Typical Fauresmith implements (Fig. 20) include small hand axes and cleavers, numerous stone balls, and many tools made from flakes with faceted platforms, including scrapers and chisels. Examples of the more perfect types of Fauresmith implements have been well illustrated in Leakey's *Stone Age Africa* and *Adam's Ancestors*. The specimens in Fig. 20 are representative of the commoner, less well-made types. The Fauresmith is, in fact, a kind of crude miniature Acheulian.

The most northerly Fauresmith site found so far is in Ethiopia. War, apparently, is no deterrent to a keen prehistorian in new territory; though the latest missiles may be projected over his head, he keeps his nose firmly to the ground in search of weapons made many thousands of years ago. Clark has described his discovery of a surface Fauresmith site sixteen miles from Gondar as follows: "The time at my disposal . . . was cut to just under an hour between the time when our final military preparations had been made, and that at which we moved to our positions in the broken country below for the assault upon Gondar itself. . . . As representative a collection as possible was made, placed in a sack, thrown on one of the lorries and subsequently made its way to Gondar by another route after the town had fallen; this rather rough handling" [he adds apologetically] "has resulted in the chipping of several of the implements."[79]

Into the sack went no less than 96 implements and flakes. They included hand axes, mostly pointed, but a few almond-shaped and subtriangular cleavers, side scrapers, cores, flake tools, and stone balls, mostly made of fine-grained basalt that weathers badly. The hand axes included both very large and very small specimens, generally made from flakes rather than cores. Most of the flakes had been struck from unprepared cores, though some had been prepared by the faceted-platform technique. The cleavers were all made from end or side flakes and were commonly U-shaped. Tools classed as "choppers" may have been unfinished roughs for hand axes.

It is interesting that this industry was found at an altitude of 8,400 feet, comparable with that of the Nanyuki area and with sites on the Kinangop Plateau. The Gondar industry is presumed to be contemporary with the Kenya sites, at a time when arid conditions drove men up into the mountains to make their homes by permanent streams.

The Sangoan

The Sangoan is a forest-and-woodlands culture whose distribution seems to coincide rather closely with areas having over 40 inches' mean annual rainfall at the present time, with the exception of sites in the Sudan and the Sahara (see Map 10). It is found in the basins of great

rivers such as the Congo and Zambezi, as well as in lake basins such
as that of Lake Victoria. Possibly the first occupation of this more
wooded country was by the Sangoans, during the drier period preceding the Gamblian pluvial, when the forests retreated somewhat and
man advanced into new areas.

The Sangoan was split up into a number of subdivisions—for example, Proto-, Lower, Middle, Upper, and Final in Angola—and has
also been called by various names in the Congo, such as Tumbian,
Kalinian, and Djokocian (now abandoned). It is very doubtful whether
such subdivisions and local names are justifiable, and the scheme now
adopted by Mortelmans for the Congo and by Clark for the Rhodesias
restricts the name "Sangoan" to First Intermediate industries, with
Earlier and Later Lupemban to cover the M. S. A. In the L. S. A., the
Later Lupemban evolves into the Tshitolian. Carbon-14 dates for
Sangoan, Lupemban, Final Lupemban, and transitional Lupembo-
Tshitolian industries are given in Table 4. The Sangoan at Kalambo
Falls has been dated to 41,000–>38,000 B.C., and the Kalambo Lupemban
to 27,000–25,000 B.C. At Mufo, in northeastern Angola, an Upper
Lupemban industry is dated to 12,550 ± 560 B.C., a Lupembo-Tshitolian
industry to 9238 ± 490 B.C. In Lupemban industries, tools are mostly
smaller and better-made than they were in the Sangoan, while those
of the later Lupemban show a still finer finish, and pressure flaking is
common. Tanged points make their appearance, and there is an increasing use of blades, some of them backed.

For the sake of historic interest, it may be worth while to record
briefly how knowledge of the Sangoan, Lupemban, and Tshitolian has
gradually increased over the past forty years or so. The Sangoan culture was first discovered by Wayland in 1920, but it was not until
later that it was realized that both an "Early" and a "Developed" stage
were present in Uganda. The type site is in the hills above Sango
Bay, Uganda, on the western side of Lake Victoria. O'Brien first
pointed out that the Sangoan of Sango Bay was ancestral to the "Tumbian" of the Congo; he renamed the developed stage, "Proto-Tumbian,"
while the name "Sangoan" was retained to denote the early stage.

The name "Tumbian" was originated by Menghin, who, in 1925,
described a number of surface finds from the Congo, obviously of very
different ages but characterized by the persistent and typical "Tumbian
pick." He believed all the material was of the same culture and age:
"Das Kongomaterial ist als eine kulturelle und chronologische Einheit

zu betrachten." The name was taken from the type site Tumba, in the western Congo, where the Haas Collection was obtained (described by V. Jacques as early as 1900); it included points, scrapers, blades, arrowheads of many different sorts, flaked axes, polished axes, lanceheads, picks, and daggers—in fact, a wealth of beautiful but miscellaneous material.

Next came the work of J. Colette, who was the first to do any excavations in the Congo. From a site at Kalina, near Leopoldville, on the left bank of the Congo River, he obtained industries from stratified deposits in 1926 and 1927. He distinguished an early stage which he named the "Kalinian" and a later stage which he called the "Djokocian," as well as a "Neolithic" industry. The names "Kalinian" and "Djokocian" were formally adopted at the International Congress of Anthropology held in Brussels in 1936, to replace Menghin's "Tumbian." This name, however, persisted, and in a paper on the "Tumbian" culture of western Kenya, Leakey expressed reluctance to abandon the name, which by that time had become associated in the minds of prehistorians all over the world with the characteristic picks and lanceheads.[80]

In the meantime, Breuil and van Riet Lowe in South Africa had examined material collected by F. Cabu in the Belgian Congo and published a paper strongly urging that the term "Tumbian" be rejected in favor of Colette's names "Kalinian" and "Djokocian."[81] Van Riet Lowe, however, spoke of Cabu's collection from Mikalayi, in the Kasai Basin, as "A Congo variation of the Sangoan of Uganda with strong Fauresmith affinities or, it is equally true to say, a Congo variation of the Fauresmith culture with strong Sangoan affinities."[82] Moreover, he pointed out the connection between the later (Djokocian) stage and the Stillbay culture, particularly in the presence of laurel-leaf points. It is interesting that typical Stillbay points with a few Lupemban-like lanceheads have been found recently in Karamoja, eastern Uganda.

Further connections were suggested by Miss Caton-Thompson between tanged points found in derivatives of the "Tumbian" (that is, Lupemban and Tshitolian) and those of the Aterian of North Africa. She believed, "It may eventually be possible to discern ripples of 'Tumbian' dispersion from a mighty Congo reservoir, lapping against and revitalizing a pre-existent population in north-west Africa, with a resultant Aterian industry, owing its arrow-heads and foliate spears at least to Central Africa; and a similar, but perhaps at the start rather earlier, movement from the Equatorial reservoir east and south-east-wards, with a resultant Stillbay industry."[83] Connections between the Sangoan and Lupemban of the forests of Central Africa and the Aterian of the Sahara and North Africa now seem even more apparent than they were when these words were written nearly twenty years ago. Near Lake Wanyanga, Ounianga Kebir, in Chad Province, Arkell found Lupemban-like lanceheads similar to the one illustrated in Fig. 25, as well as hand axes and Aterian-type tanged points.

At the First Pan-African Congress on Prehistory in Nairobi in 1947, prehistorians finally decided to do away with both the names "Tumbian" and also "Kalinian" and "Djokocian"; since these industries evolved directly out of the early Sangoan of Uganda, they were all recognized as being stages and derivatives of this culture, and the prefixes Proto-, Lower, Middle, and Upper were added to the Sangoan. And so at last the confusing terminology of the cultures of the Congo seemed to be clarified, and after Leakey's work in Angola a whole Sangoan sequence was distinguished.[84] Congo workers, however, still clung to the terms "Kalinian" and "Djokocian" and only quite recently have they tended to drop them.

Janmart's paper on the Sangoan of northeast Angola made it clear that Sangoan industries first appear during the dry pre-Gamblian phase. Living sites are situated beside the larger rivers, which at that time flowed through semi-desert scrub country. Janmart did not believe that Leakey's "Proto-" and "Lower" Sangoan industries exist in northeast Angola; he found a typically "Middle" or "Upper" Sangoan assemblage at Musolexi at the *base* of Leakey's "Proto-Sangoan." He went on to say: "Does this mean that the kind of Sangoan found in our Redistributed Sands II is the oldest that exists in the Lunda? By no means. Though I think that the Proto- and Lower Sangoan as conceived by Leakey will not be found, I am sure that some sort of Proto- and Lower Sangoan, different from his, *does* exist."[85] The heavy, clumsy artifacts, such as picks, typical of the "Proto-" and "Lower" Sangoan, he regarded simply as a mining facies (or perhaps woodworking facies) of all Sangoan industries.

THE SANGOAN OF UGANDA

The Kagera Valley in southeastern Uganda (Map 8) was one of Wayland's great hunting grounds in the 1930s and again in the 1950s,

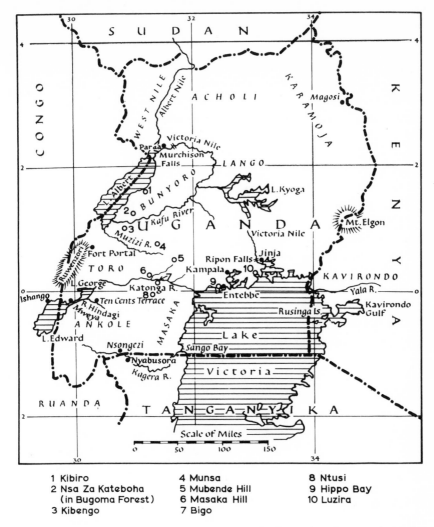

Map 8. *Stone Age and Iron Age sites in Uganda (Iron Age sites are shown by numbers).*

1 Kibiro	4 Munsa	8 Ntusi
2 Nsa Za Kateboha	5 Mubende Hill	9 Hippo Bay
(in Bugoma Forest)	6 Masaka Hill	10 Luzira
3 Kibengo	7 Bigo	

when he made extensive pits and trenches at Nsongezi. The industries of the 100-foot terrace at Nsongezi were described in detail by van Riet Lowe.[86] He recognized derived pebble tools in a basal boulder bed, as well as "Chellean" artifacts. At the so-called M and N horizons he distinguished Acheulian, "Lower" and "Middle" Sangoan industries; while at the O horizon he found an "Upper Sangoan" (Lupemban or Lupembo-Tshitolian). Surface material included tanged arrowheads, representing what would now be called a Tshitolian industry.

The rubble that makes up the old land surface of the so-called M and N horizons (now known to be a single horizon and referred to as MN) contains innumerable rounded boulders and pebbles that provided excellent raw material for toolmaking. This fact, together with a plentiful water supply, accounts for the long occupation of Nsongezi by Stone Age man. An incredible number of implements were found: from the numbers collected in 10 square feet of excavations, Lowe calculated that every acre of old land surface might be expected to contain nearly one and a quarter million artifacts!

The 100-foot or "Kafunzo" Terrace is not exposed naturally at Nsongezi, though it has been penetrated often enough by Wayland's pits. Above the basal boulder bed are sands and gravels, and a break in their deposition is represented by rubble; this rubble, the single MN horizon, was caused by down-slope creep during periods when the lake level fell temporarily. After the MN horizon was formed, tilting converted the area into a vast swamp, represented by clays above the lake sediments. In these swamp clays is a yellowish-red layer—the O horizon—containing a Lupemban industry, described in the next chapter.

Reinvestigations by Bishop and Posnansky have shown that during the Later Pleistocene the Kagera Valley was occupied by an arm of Lake Victoria, which extended some 70 miles west of its present shore. Tilting initiated, and eventually ended, the lake phase at Nsongezi, resulting in a reversal of the Kagera and causing it to flow in its present direction, eastward across the former lake deposits to Lake Victoria. These deposits now underlie "flats" on either side of the river, about 100 feet above its present level. Bishop and Posnansky distinguished only one industry at the MN horizon, an Early Sangoan only slightly more evolved than the Late Acheulian of Kalambo and Isimila. It contains hand axes, cleavers, picks, and large side-struck flakes or "knives" (Fig. 21), heavy scrapers and cores, but no stone balls.[87]

Another exposure of the 100-foot terrace was examined at Nyabusora, 25 miles east of Nsongezi (31 miles downstream) and over the Tanganyika border. Excavations into horizons probably equivalent to

Figure 21. Sangoan "flake knives," MN horizon, Nsongezi.

the MN horizon at Nsongezi exposed fossil fauna as well as artifacts in an upper gravel—also artifacts but no fossils at a lower horizon. Both occur within a series of clayey lake deposits, 77 to 65 feet above the Kagera River, and the upper artifact horizon is overlain by a further 40 feet of lake deposits. The upper gravel contains ashy material, charred bone, and other remains of fish and mammals that suggest a midden or heap of food refuse. The mammal remains consist mainly of teeth of small bovids, as well as hippopotamus bones and some teeth of rodents, carnivores, and monkeys.

The industry of the MN horizon, which obviously evolves directly out of the final Chelles-Acheul, may be slightly earlier than the Sangoan from the type site near Sango Bay, which does not contain Acheulian-like hand axes, but includes far more typically Sangoan forms, such as large picks. This site was discovered by Wayland in 1920. Most of the material was collected from the surface, but some of it is found in the soil above bedrock, which is reached 6 feet below the surface. The material used for the implements is flaggy or slabby quartzite that is not homogeneous in composition; this is also an open site and exposed to weathering, and these two factors make it of little value to sort the implements by the degree of patination. Thus they were all assigned to one stage at Sango Bay, the "Lower" Sangoan.

The tools include picks, rough hand axes and points, various kinds of prepared cores, and several kinds of scrapers made from flakes. Picks (see Fig. 22) are described as follows: "The typical Sangoan pick is an elongated, steep-sided, double-ended implement with small, flat dorsal and large ventral faces, rhomboidal in cross-section at the centre, segmental in cross-section near the blunter end and triangular or sub-triangular towards and near what appears to be the 'business' end. The most finely finished product is somewhat canoe-like in shape—sharp prow, blunt stem."[88] Some of these picks are a foot long; others are short and stubby, about six inches long. High-domed segmental scrapers, made from flakes by the block-on-block technique, are described as the most striking products of the industry.

In Kenya, the Sangoan is found mainly in the western part of the

Figure 22. Sangoan pick, Yala Alego.

country, near Lake Victoria; since it is overlain by Lupemban and later industries, it is described in the next chapter.

In Tanganyika, isolated surface finds of Sangoan-like artifacts have been made from time to time, although none have been recovered *in situ*. Collections from Tendaguru, northwest of Lindi (an area famous for its dinosaur remains), are housed at the British Museum in London and at Tübingen in Germany. They include choppers, various forms of scrapers and plane scrapers, a few "axlike" forms, tortoise cores, and flakes made by the faceted-platform technique. These assemblages are very similar to industries known as the "Kansenian" in Katanga and to those found on the island of Kilwa Kisiwani, off the Tanganyika coast.

One of the most northerly sites where the Sangoan may be represented is at Khor Abu Anga, near Omdurman and close to the confluence of the Blue and White Niles. Here Arkell found what may be a mixed assemblage, rather like that of Nsongezi; possibly it includes an Acheulian stage (mentioned on p. 160), probably a Sangoan, and almost certainly a Lupemban. While most of the tools were found on the surface, others were *in situ* in gravels which may have been relaid, while still others were contained in a white calcareous soil that overlies the gravel in places. As well as hand axes, cores, and flakes made by the faceted-platform technique, some fine picks and lanceheads were recovered. An interesting feature was the presence of incipient tangs on some of the points. At Lake Wanyanga in the southern Sahara, so-called Sangoan (more probably Lupemban) artifacts were found associated with tanged points typical of the Aterian culture.

It is essentially the picks, lanceheads, and *tranchets* that distinguish the Sangoan and Lupemban from other African cultures; apart from these distinctive artifacts, the Sangoan is very like the Fauresmith, while the Lupemban, with its laurel-leaf points, is very like the Stillbay. Further, the connections between the Lupemban of central Africa and the Aterian of the Sahara and North Africa are seen clearly at such sites as Lake Wanyanga, with its tanged points.

Characteristic Sangoan country, as we have seen, is the forested equatorial zone, which must have been one of the most favorable in Africa during the drier pre-Gamblian phase. The Sudan sites seem to be something of an anomaly, but they are all near the Nile and so a plentiful water supply was available throughout the drier period. Although much of central Africa was probably steppe country or scrub at that time, the distribution of Sangoan sites near the larger rivers leaves no doubt that the drainage pattern has remained essentially unchanged.

There can be little doubt that the Sangoan and Fauresmith cultures are closely related, though there is practically no overlap in their geographical distribution, except in southern Kavirondo, near Kericho, in Kenya. The same basic techniques were used in both: the hand-ax tradition is continued in the Fauresmith and eventually leads to the bifaced lanceheads of the Lupemban. At the same time, the faceted-platform technique becomes well controlled in both the Sangoan and Fauresmith, leading to a variety of flake implements.

Although the evolution of the Chelles-Acheul culture into the Sangoan is seen clearly in Uganda, this rather crude industry comes as something of an anticlimax after the perfect craftsmanship of Acheulian times. The nature of the raw material cannot be accepted as an excuse for the seemingly clumsy workmanship of the earliest Sangoan industries, for this hardly affected the hand-ax people. In Southern Rhodesia, Bond counted the numbers of different materials used by Stone Age peoples; plotted on a graph against time, the curve rises sharply from the pebble-culture stage to the Acheulian, after which it descends abruptly in Proto-Sangoan times and then rises again. If, however, the clumsy picks and heavy equipment be regarded simply as woodworking tools or perhaps as mining equipment for the extraction of raw material (such heavy equipment, incidentally, persisted right through the L. S. A.), Sangoan tools make sense; as a substitute for the earlier well-made cutting-edged tools or *bifaces* they would have no advantage.

"Acheulio-Levalloisian" of the Horn

Possibly some of the surface material collected by Seton-Kerr at Issatugan, southwest of Berbera, in the former British Somaliland, at the end of the last century may represent a Late Acheulian stage, but in the absence of stratigraphic evidence—and based on selective collecting—it would be rash to classify these implements on the basis of typology. Otherwise, the earliest industry of the Horn is the "Acheulio-Levalloisian," from the Older Tug Gravels of rivers in the northwestern part of the Somali Plateau.

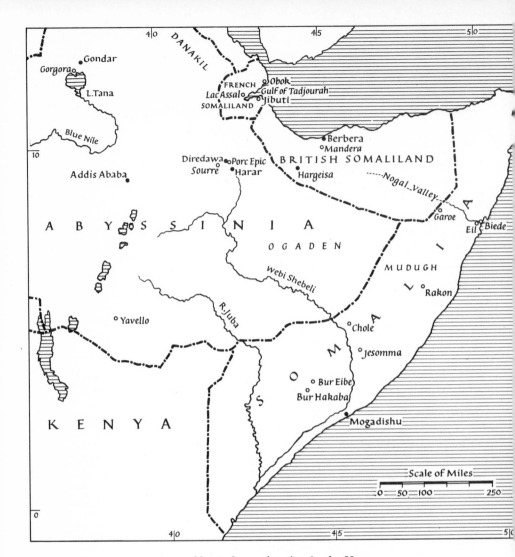

Map 9. Stone Age sites in the Horn.

In these industries, the hand-ax element made by the cylinder-hammer technique is stronger than the faceted-platform technique. The type site is Hargeisa, where implements were recovered from Older Tug Gravels I and II, with which they were apparently contemporary. These gravels were dated to a semi-arid period during the decline of the first peak of the Gamblian pluvial. Most of the hand axes were of Micoquian form (the latest stage of the Chelles-Acheul culture in Europe and Palestine); there were also cleavers made on end and side flakes, and cores and flake tools struck by the block-on-block and the faceted-platform techniques.

No "Acheulio-Levalloisian" industries have been found in central or southern Somalia, but this may be because the area has not been thoroughly searched. At coastal sites in the northeast, such as Obok, hand axes are poorly made and cleavers are lacking, while the faceted-platform technique is more in evidence. These industries are probably transitional between the "Acheulio-Levalloisian" of the Hargeisa area and the "Lower Levalloisian."

Apparently the "Levalloisian culture" lasted for a very long time (throughout the Later Pleistocene) and was widespread over the whole of the Horn. It developed very slowly, but more specialized tools and improved techniques appear in the Upper stage. The "Lower Levalloisian" is found *in situ* in the Lower Tug Gravels at many sites; some of the more important are Garoë, Eil, Hargeisa, and Jesomma (see Map 9). The industry is dated to the decline of the second Gamblian peak. Artifacts do not show much variety and comprise prepared cores, faceted flakes and flake blades, with a very few scrapers and points and some "trimming stones" or core scrapers.

The "Upper Levalloisian" is found in the Upper Tug Gravels, dated to the decline of the third Gamblian peak. Most of the tools are similar to those of the "Lower Levalloisian," but the prepared flakes are generally smaller. In addition, a few more specialized tools appear, including flakes converging toward the butt (but none with true tangs), some of them with the bulb and striking platform removed. Secondary retouch develops, and bifacial flaking results in points with thinner sections, heralding the succeeding Stillbay culture.

In the Sudan, Arkell found cores, scrapers, and flake tools with faceted platforms below the Fourth Cataract at Tangasi, 100 feet above high river level. The tools are made of indurated mudstone, a rock hardened by metamorphic contact; boulders of this material seemed to have been arranged at intervals and were presumably imported by makers of the "Levalloisian" industry as raw material for their tools. A "Developed Levalloisian" industry was found in desert country, between Nuri and Dongola, and also at Abu Tabari Well, showing that the desert was habitable during Gamblian times.

The question of raw material mentioned above may be of significance in determining the distribution of "Levalloisian" industries. Bordes attributed the fact that the faceted-platform technique is characteristic of northern France, but rare in the Dordogne, to the nature of the raw material. For this somewhat complicated technique, boulders of suitable size composed of homogeneous material are obviously of importance. Yet at Singa, on the Blue Nile, where the rock used for tools is particularly intractable, only one core was found, but this showed the faceted-platform technique; the resulting flake tools are very crude, and scrapers were made on cores as well as on flakes. Although the faceted-platform technique *can* be used where the material is unsuitable, there seems to be little point in employing it on these occasions; this technique reached its full development only in areas where good material could be obtained.

Proto-Stillbay Industries

There is considerable overlap in northeastern Africa of "Levalloisian" and Proto-Stillbay and Stillbay industries. If the term "Levalloisian" is abandoned in the future, perhaps Proto-Stillbay could be used to cover these industries in northeastern Africa, while the present Proto-Stillbay industries might be renamed Lower Stillbay. A similar re-shuffling has taken place in the Sangoan culture, and it is suggested here that some of the so-called "Levalloisian" industries of western Kenya—for example, at Muguruk—may in fact be part of the Sangoan. In the same way that bifacial lanceheads characterize the later (Lupemban) developments of the Sangoan, so bifacial spear points and arrow points characterize the later stages of the Stillbay. The Proto-Stillbay

Map 10. Distribution of (left) Sangoan-Lupemban-Tshitolian industries; (right) Stillbay-Magosian-Wilton industries.

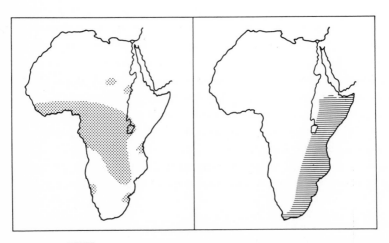

Sangoan-Lupemban-Tshitolian industries
Stillbay-Magosian-Wilton industries

and Stillbay sequence is dominant in the M.S.A. of the whole of eastern Africa from Ethiopia to the south of the continent, just as the Sangoan complex is dominant in the center and west, the two areas overlapping in the Rhodesias and in eastern Uganda (Map 10).

Proto-Stillbay and Stillbay industries are centered in South Africa (Natal) and in the Rhodesias. The most interesting occurrences of Proto-Stillbay industries are in association with Rhodesian Man at Broken Hill and in the painted Bambata Cave in the Matopos, Southern Rhodesia; similar industries are found at other stratified sites such as Lochard (where the industry is very similar to that of Singa, in the Sudan) and Sawmills, both in Southern Rhodesia. In Northern Rhodesia, the Proto-Stillbay is the most prolific culture of the Zambezi Valley. Here it is found on temporary living floors on the eroded slopes of Kalahari sands, overlying Sangoan industries, from which it is said to be a direct derivative. Its appearance was dated to the second half of the Gamblian pluvial by Clark. Thus the Proto-Stillbay may have developed independently from the Sangoan in the south and from the "Developed Levalloisian" in the north (Kenya and the Horn).

In Kenya, the Proto-Stillbay followed the "Developed Levalloisian" during the second peak of the Gamblian pluvial. In the meantime, a local industry had developed much earlier, contemporarily with the Early "Levalloisian" that Leakey has called the Pseudo-Stillbay. This industry is characterized by small points made from flakes with faceted platforms, with secondary retouch (not pressure flaking, as in the true Stillbay), generally on one face of the point only, very occasionally on both faces; there are also very small and rare hand axes. The industry is found at Wetherall's Site, in old swamp beds on the Kinangop Plateau, at about 8,000 feet. These swamp beds also contain Fauresmith industries, at the same horizon, though not at the same site. This Pseudo-Stillbay industry is unique so far as is at present known.

Whereas in the Pseudo-Stillbay, points showing retouch on both surfaces are very rare, in the Proto-Stillbay they are fairly common and are more carefully worked. In the Kenya Rift Valley, a Proto-Stillbay industry was first recognized near Old Government Farm, in the gorge of the Melawa River, near Naivasha. Here it was said to overlie "Developed Levalloisian" in the basal beds and is succeeded by a true Stillbay industry.

Chapter Seven

HUNTERS ANCIENT AND RECENT

In most parts of the world, Paleolithic hunters are succeeded by more settled Mesolithic folk, who are followed by—or who themselves turn into—Neolithic farmers. A Mesolithic economy is very often based on fishing, sometimes on some form of "vegeculture," or incipient agriculture. This may take the form of reaping wild grasses and eventually planting their seeds. Mesolithic people also kept dogs to help them in hunting and later, presumably, to round up young goats and sheep, which were added to man's domesticated stock. Hunting was by no means neglected while all this was going on, and the transition from Paleolithic to Mesolithic and thence to Neolithic was very gradual, an evolution rather than a revolution.

Often the territory of Paleolithic hunters was adjacent to that of Mesolithic and Neolithic groups, so that the various ways of life run parallel to one another rather than in succession. In general, however, this situation lasted for a relatively short time, and aboriginal hunters were soon converted to the more successful economy of their contemporaries. But in Africa the position was very different. A few groups of typically Mesolithic communities are known (described in Chapter Nine), but a Neolithic stage before the coming of iron seems to be generally absent. Stone Age hunters continued to roam parts of the country for a thousand years and more after iron-using peoples introduced food production, an event that took place in Africa south of the Sahara and south of the Nile only during the first millennium A.D., long after the Bronze Age had been succeeded by the Iron Age in the Middle East and Europe.

Some of these late hunters of Africa were directly ancestral to the present Bushmen, and their way of life must have been essentially the same as that of these fascinating Stone Age survivals. Bushman hunting bands generally consist of up to a hundred individuals, each group having its own rights over a particular stretch of territory and its water supplies. They have few possessions other than bows and arrows, throwing sticks and spears, digging sticks for grubbing up roots, ostrich eggshells, and gourds for use as containers. Their shelters are simple affairs made of branches and grass, and frequent house moving presents no problems.

Apart from the fact that the tools of the Later Stone Age people

Figure 23. Tranchet, *Nsongezi.*

Figure 24. Tanged arrowheads of quartz, Nsongezi.

were generally much smaller—more microlithic—their equipment and
no doubt their habits differed very little from that of their Middle
Stone Age predecessors, from about 40,000 B.C. to 10,000 B.C. In this
chapter, therefore, liberties are taken with chronology, and the hunters
of the M. S. A. and L. S. A. are discussed together.

In East Africa, there were two main traditions during this long
period: the Sangoan-Lupemban-Tshitolian of the wetter forested country; and the Stillbay-Magosian-Wilton of the drier savanna country
farther east (Map 10). Although there is no certain evidence, it is
tempting to suppose that the former industries were made by early
Negroids, while the latter were the work of Bushmanoid peoples. Very
recently, C. Gabel has excavated a hot-spring site on Lochinvar Ranch,
on the edge of the Kafue Flats, Northern Rhodesia, which yielded a
fine series of Wilton skeletons showing Bushmanoid features. The
Sangoan-Lupemban-Tshitolian group, which in its later stages has rather
sophisticated equipment, including efficient woodworking tools, is
known mainly from the Congo but occurs also in parts of Uganda and
western Kenya. The second tradition is ubiquitous from the Horn to
South Africa, and the Stillbay is very similar to the contemporary
Aterian culture of the Sahara and northern Africa—apart from the absence of tanged points so typical of the Aterian—while its beautifully
pressure-flaked points also recall those of the Solutrean of Europe. In
addition, the Nachikufan, which precedes the Wilton and is known
mainly from Northern Rhodesia, is found also in parts of Tanganyika
and may be associated with the earliest rock paintings, discussed in the
next chapter.

The Lupemban

THE LUPEMBAN OF UGANDA

After the end of the drier period represented by the MN horizon at
Nsongezi, the rain in Gamblian times started to erode the overlying
sands and gravels and up to 25 feet of finer sediments were deposited
on the eroded slopes. Man returned to the Kagera Valley and camped
around the swamps represented by the O horizon. This horizon is much
less pronounced than the MN horizon; it consists of a yellowish band of
ferruginized clays, which are found about 12 feet below the present
surface of the terrace.

Lupemban and Tshitolian artifacts occur in erosion gullies of the

Orichinga Valley, a tributary of the Kagera. In gray swamp deposits overlying the MN horizon are hand axes, flake tools, lanceheads, and a great many *tranchets* (Fig. 23). The smaller of these, less than three inches in length, are made of quartz, and the larger ones, presumably used as adzes, are of quartzite. Tanged arrowheads made of quartz (Fig. 24), representing a Lupembo-Tshitolian or Tshitolian stage, were found near the surface.[89]

In the true *tranchet* technique, well known in Europe, the cutting edge is produced by the intersection of two or more flake surfaces, and a special blow was struck at one corner of the extremity in a transverse direction; the edge could be resharpened when it became blunted by slicing off another flake. The transverse blow, however, was apparently not used in the manufacture of Lupemban *tranchets*, though their appearance is similar. As early as 1925 Menghin pointed out the resemblance between *tranchets* from Tumba in the Congo and those of the Campignian culture of northern Europe. A particularly fine collection of these implements was made by Colette at Kalina.

With African tools of this kind, it seems possible to trace an evolutionary sequence from Acheulian cleavers through "cleaver flakes" to Lupemban *tranchets* and finally to Neolithic axes with ground and polished edges. *Tranchets* are almost certainly woodworking tools, and there are also gougelike and chisel-like implements in the Lupemban of the Congo.

THE LUPEMBAN OF WESTERN KENYA

In Kenya, Sangoan-Lupemban and Lupembo-Tshitolian industries are confined to Nyanza Province, bordering Lake Victoria, where there are innumerable sites. This area of western Kenya is one of great importance; few sites in it have been properly excavated, but if this were done, the results would certainly increase our knowledge of East African prehistory very considerably. The area seems to have been one of mixture in later Paleolithic times; it lies on the eastern borders of Sangoan country and near the western limits of Stillbay penetration. During the L. S. A. there is, as well as Wilton industries, an interesting local industry similar to the Smithfield of South Africa. The country on the eastern side of Lake Victoria was apparently linked more with Uganda than with the rest of Kenya in the Stone Age, just as it is culturally today.

Sangoan, Lupemban, and Tshitolian industries discovered by the late Archdeacon Owen in western Kenya are essentially similar to those of Uganda. They have been found near Sotik and Kericho, but are best known from sites on the eastern border of Alego location and north of the Yala River. Five beds were distinguished in this area:

> *Bed 5* Stratified sands.
> Land surface with Lupembo-Tshitolian ("Upper Sangoan"), etc.
> *Bed 4* Red brick-earth with Magosian at the base.
> Land surface with Lupembo-Tshitolian ("Upper Sangoan") *in situ*.
> *Bed 3* Stony loam and clay with Lupemban ("Middle Sangoan").
> *Bed 2* Stony rubble with Sangoan ("Lower Sangoan").
> *Bed 1* Decomposed rock.

The only published site in Kenya where the Sangoan has been found *in situ* is at Yala Alego in Bed 2, though a number of other sites are known where this early stage is present. The assemblage at Yala Alego includes clumsy hand axes and picks, prepared cores and flakes with faceted platforms, and large, circular, and horse-hoof-shaped scrapers.

The Lupemban is found *in situ* at Muguruk, Ober Awach, and in Bed 3 at Yala Alego. Besides the persistence of earlier forms, lanceheads

appear for the first time, and the picks are less clumsy. Large side scrapers are characteristic of the lower part of Bed 3 at Muguruk and do not appear in later stages. The lanceheads are flaked by the cylinder-hammer technique, and some of them are very long and well made (Fig. 25).

At both Ober Awach and Muguruk the Lupemban is overlain in the upper part of Bed 3 by what Leakey called a "pure Levalloisian" industry. The interpretation could be either that an in-

Figure 25. Lupemban lancehead, Yala Alego (length: 28.5 cm.)

vading people ousted the Lupembans from their home, or, more likely, that the latter confined themselves to "Levalloisian" elements at this stage, omitting for some reason to make weapons such as lanceheads. Fluctuations of climate or of food supplies could lead to modifications in the type of tools needed. Stone Age equipment often varies according to seasonal needs; on the equator, although the contrast between summer and winter is not very great, alternating periods of drought and torrential rain profoundly affect the movements of game and hence of hunters. Perhaps the "Levalloisian" elements represent mainly woodworking and mining tools, domestic equipment rather than hunting weapons. This may not be the true explanation, but considerations along these lines seem more probable than the arrival of a different people with a different culture.

The "Levalloisian" industry at Muguruk is very similar to that of Red Hillock near Elmenteita, which is in the middle of Stillbay country. It was dated to the pause between the first and second Gamblian maximum; if the industries are contemporary, the underlying Lupemban industry at Muguruk is not later than the second Gamblian maximum.

A Lupembo-Tshitolian stage is found at Mbeji and Mur in central Kavirondo, the former being apparently a living site and the latter, a mile away, a "factory site," where many waste flakes were found; many of these were very small and flat, showing the use of the cylinder-hammer technique. In addition to the persistence of hand axes, crude picks, scrapers, prepared cores, and flakes, the lanceheads that first appeared in the preceding stage now become common and are highly developed. They are often very long, made from flat flakes and carefully retouched over both surfaces. A few large *tranchets* were also found, as in Uganda.

Tshitolian-like implements are known only from surface finds in western Kenya; they include diminutive lanceheads, small *bifaces* and *tranchets*, and laurel-leaf points that are indistinguishable on typological grounds from those of the Stillbay culture.

The East African Stillbay

The Stillbay culture is characterized by pressure flaking on bifacial points, which are generally made from flakes prepared by the faceted-

Figure 26. Stillbay point, Melawa Gorge.

platform technique. The points, which were presumably used as spear-heads or lanceheads, were leaf-shaped, or, more often, subtriangular (Fig. 26). In the later Stillbay of the Kenya Rift Valley, backed blades, lunates, and burins are found; these, Leakey believed, were introduced by the contemporary Upper Kenya Capsian people. Reasons are given later (p. 260) for suggesting that the latter lived in Post-Pleistocene times, perhaps about 8,000 B.C. Evolved Stillbay artifacts from the Kenya Rift Valley are said to have been dated by the new obsidian method (described in Chapter One) to about 33,000 years[90] which, on the archaeological evidence, seems rather early.

The most easterly finds of Stillbay artifacts in East Africa come from Nsongezi and from Káramoja, in eastern Uganda, where they were accompanied by Lupemban lanceheads and a *tranchet*. Backed blades and burins of the kind typical of the Upper Kenya Capsian (pp. 260–261) were also found with Stillbay tools in Karamoja, as well as in Turkana, northwestern Kenya.[91]

In Somalia, the Stillbay is the most widely spread of all the Stone Age cultures; its distribution follows closely that of the "Leval-loisïan," from which it seems to be derived. It is best represented in the plateau country around Hargeisa, where it is divided into Lower and Upper phases. In the Lower Stillbay, unifaced points predominate and are usually subtriangular in shape, with the butts left untrimmed. There are also bifacial points, both subtriangular and leaf-shaped, which become commoner in the Upper Stillbay. In the latter industry, striking platforms and bulbs of points are generally removed and the butts are carefully rounded and trimmed; pressure flaking is now perfected. Along with many beautifully finished points, poorly made backed blades are found in the Upper Stillbay. Most of the implements are made of chert, but those of quartzite are equally well finished (in Kenya, the tools are neary all of obsidian).

At Hargeisa, the Lower Stillbay is found at the base of Younger Tug Alluvium II, and is overlain by the Upper Stillbay. At three other strati-fied sites (Bur Eibe, Chole, and Jesomma) the Stillbay has been dated to the dry period between the end of Gamblian times and the begin-ning of the Makalian wet phase, which would bring it in line with the age suggested here for the later Stillbay of the Kenya Rift Valley. At

Biede, near the mouth of the Nogal River, the Stillbay is dated immediately after the 12-meter raised beach.

At a rock shelter at Gorgora, on the northern side of Lake Tana in Ethiopia, Stillbay industries were also divided into Lower, Middle, and Upper stages. They developed into a Magosian industry which was followed, not by the Wilton as is usual in similar sequences in East Africa, but by a local microlithic industry with pottery.

The rock shelter is in the side of a volcanic hill that rises from an alluvial plain stretching toward Gondar. The top 4 feet in the shelter consisted of black soil with humus; beneath this was gray volcanic ash down to 8 feet. Below the ash were concretions down to 12 feet, after which they become so consolidated that further excavation was impossible. From the bottom three feet of the excavation came Early Stillbay points and many flakes showing the faceted-platform technique. In the Middle Stillbay level, the points show better workmanship. Upper Stillbay implements above this were more varied, including scrapers and a few burins and backed blades. Three feet from the top was a Magosian industry, containing degenerate points, crude backed blades, lunates, scrapers, and a few potsherds. Finally there was a microlithic industry with poorly made lunates, small backed blades and scrapers, as well as undecorated potsherds. Throughout the layers, coloring materials were found, though no paintings were to be seen on the rock face.

Since the Stillbay underlies the Magosian at a number of sites, its distribution is considered further in the next section.

The East African Magosian

The Magosian of the Second Intermediate Period (between the M. S. A. and the L. S. A.) is found in the Horn and in parts of Uganda, Kenya, and Tanganyika, as well as in the eastern part of the Congo and the Rhodesias, where it is particularly well known at Sawmills and at Khami, Southern Rhodesia. In South Africa, the most important site is Rose Cottage Cave, Ladybrand, on the borders of the Orange Free State and Basutoland. Its distribution, in fact, coincides with that of the Stillbay, from which it is derived, although it is not nearly so widespread as the Stillbay.

Although perhaps starting during the Gamblian-Makalian dry inter-

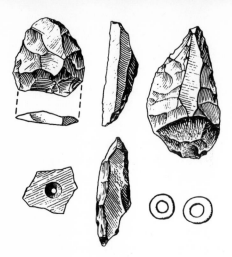

Figure 27. Magosian tools and ostrich eggshell beads, Apis Rock.

val, the Magosian continues into Makalian times and into the post-Makalian drier phase in some areas. A Magosian industry at Kalambo Falls has been dated by carbon-14 to about 7550 B.C. The culture is characterized by many microlithic implements (Fig. 27) and beads of ostrich eggshell, while pottery appears in the later stages. Magosian industries are not unlike the later stages of the Stillbay, though the triangular points are generally smaller, lozenge-shaped bifacial points are common, and there are far more end scrapers, burins, and microliths, including tiny blades and lunates. The cores are usually very small and are either disk or blade cores. The Magosian is also distinguished from the Stillbay by the appearance of fabricators known as *lames écaillées,** characteristic of the Elmenteitan culture of the Kenya Rift Valley.

THE MAGOSIAN OF UGANDA

The type site of the Magosian (now considered to be a late Magosian) is a water hole known as Magosi in Karamoja, 160 miles north of Mt. Elgon and less than 5 miles west of the rift escarpment forming the boundary between Uganda and the Turkana District of western Kenya. The site is at the foot of a huge overhanging rock of granite and was excavated by Wayland in 1926. This country is waterless for several months of the year, but a rock "cistern" or pit under the granite provides water during part of the dry season. Noticing microliths in the deposits, which had been removed from the cistern by natives in search of water, Wayland decided to excavate under the overhanging rock face. Here he found no stratification and realized that he was digging into another silted-up "cistern."

Wayland's explanation of the formation of these cisterns is as fol-
* Tools used for the manufacture of other implements.

lows. Rain water standing on the surface of the granite rots the rock, which crumbles and is removed during the ensuing dry season by wind or animals, resulting in small, saucer-like depressions. When this process has been repeated during alternate wet and dry seasons for some time, and the hollow becomes deeper than a few feet, wind can no longer remove the decomposed rock but will add to it by deposition of sands or brick earth. The depth of the archaeological deposits in this case was 11 feet, so that evidently man was responsible for deepening the hollow in order to improve his water supply.

Since there was no stratification, the deposits were removed in 2-foot layers down to 10 feet. Only one industry, in fact, is present, though the implements showed some sorting, largely as a result of rolling down the slope of the cistern, so that at the bottom there were rather larger artifacts than in the layers above. The 4- to 6-foot level was richest both in the number of tools and in the variety of forms: there were many backed blades, crescents, triangles, awls, small scrapers, and two types of burins. The top two feet contained mainly pygmy cores, geometric microliths, thumbnail scrapers, and burins.

Most of the collection from Magosi is housed at the Museum of Archaelogy at Cambridge, England, and in 1951 Clark re-examined the material and made a complete inventory of the tools and waste products.[92] By far the most numerous were microliths of various kinds (total, 1,040), particularly tiny blades. Some had been snapped off or blunted at one or both ends, presumably to facilitate hafting several together in sequence. Clark also found some large artifacts that had inadvertently been left out of the original publication on Magosi by Wayland and Burkitt in 1932. These include two stone balls, a muller or rubbing stone, and two bored stones characteristic of the L. S. A. but known from only one other Magosian site, Khami, in Southern Rhodesia. Bored stones served as weights for digging sticks, and rock paintings in South Africa show them being used in this way. A number have been found in Uganda, some lightweight and others heavy, often broken and abraded around the edges.[93]

Clark was struck by the fine, controlled pressure flaking on many of the bladelets, a technique normally found in late industries such as those of the Sahara Neolithic. He was also reminded of the Magosio-Doian and Doian industries of southern Somalia, which are attributed to the post-Makalian drier phase. He considers, therefore, that the Magosian from the type site may also date from this period rather than from the Gamblian-Makalian drier interval, as Wayland and Burkitt had suggested.

THE MAGOSIAN OF KENYA AND TANGANYIKA

The Magosian is found at many sites in western Kenya, including Muguruk, where, as we have seen, a so-called "pure Levalloisian" industry is found between two "Sangoan" industries (probably Lupemban and Lupembo-Tshitolian). Overlying the Lupembo-Tshitolian is a Magosian assemblage almost identical with one from the red bed of Deighton's Cliff, near Elmenteita in the rift valley. At this site, the Magosian rests on a land surface overlying Upper Gamblian lake beds; above it is volcanic ash which is cut into by the Makalian beach. Therefore this land surface with the Magosian industry was taken to represent the drier interval between the last Gamblian maximum and the first Makalian maximum.

At a shelter known as Apis Rock in northern Tanganyika, Leakey excavated, in 1932, a series of occupation layers in which there is an evolution from "Developed Levalloisian" at the bottom, through Proto-Stillbay, Stillbay, Magosian and finally Wilton. In the Magosian level there were *lames écaillées*, rough backed blades, burins, microlithic points, small flakes with faceted platforms, roughly made lunates, thumbnail scrapers similar to those of the Wilton, beads of ostrich eggshell (Fig. 27), and also pottery. Leakey thought that the Magosian of Apis Rock was of the time of the Makalian wet phase (that is, later than the industries of Deighton's Cliff, Muguruk, and so forth), since this rock shelter is in very dry country that would not have been habitable at all during arid periods. In view of Clark's comparisons of the industry at Magosi with the Doian of the Horn, attributed to post-Makalian times, the Apis Rock industry may also be later than was supposed. The site has recently been re-excavated by S. West, but the results have not yet been published.

THE MAGOSIAN OF THE HORN

The "Levalloisian"-Stillbay-Magosian sequence has long been recognized from surface finds in the Horn, but several stratified sites have also been excavated. The Magosian seems to be distributed in three main areas:

(1) In the Danakil Rift area in the northwest, where the most important sites are the Porc Epic Cave at Dire Dawa and at Obok, on the coast of Somaliland.

(2) In Ogaden, best represented by sites on the Webi Shebeli (collections from this area were made by the de Bourg de Bozas expedition in 1901–02).

(3) In southern Somalia, with Bur Eibe as the type site.

It is clear that the Magosian is derived from the Stillbay, which underlies it at a number of sites. Clark believes, however, that some of the new cultural elements that appear in the Magosian in southern Somalia may be the result of contact with the Hargeisan culture farther north. In southern Somalia, Magosian industries are succeeded by those of the Doian culture, while in Ogaden and the Danakil Rift area they are followed by Wilton industries.

In the Danakil area, the Gorgora Rock Shelter containing Stillbay, Magosian, and Wilton industries has already been described. The cave of Porc Epic, a few miles south of Dire Dawa, was discovered by Teilhard de Chardin in 1928. It yielded the "Rhodesioid" jaw, which has been compared with the Kanam mandible (p. 177) as well as Stillbay and Magosian industries. The cave is situated at the top of a limestone cliff, 200 meters above the right bank of the Dire Dawa River. The walls of the cave are painted, and the floor was filled with 1.70 meters of ash containing implements and fragmentary animal bones, while the jaw came from an intrusion in the floor. There is no way of associating it with the industries, but its character suggests that it was of the earlier Stillbay age rather than Magosian.

In the lowest part of the ash was a hematite crayon that apparently had been used for decorating the walls of the cave. The Stillbay implements of this lowest level were on the whole larger than those of the middle and upper parts of the deposit. The main industry of the cave, however, is Magosian, characterized by small bifaced or unifaced points, a few large thumbnail scrapers, scrapers made on flakes, and rare backed blades and microliths.

Other industries discovered by Teilhard de Chardin on the coast of French Somaliland are of considerable interest, as they can be linked with evidence of two periods of marine transgression. Bordering the sea near Obok and the Gulf of Tadjourah is a coral platform; the coral nearest the coast is the most ancient, followed by younger coral, and, farther inland still, lagoon coral. From the massif of Mt. Mabla to the west descend gravels of two distinct ages; the higher (at 60 meters) is correlated with the younger coral, and the lower (at 30 meters) is correlated with the lagoon coral. Industries associated with these gravels begin with "Acheulio-Levalloisian" and "Levalloisian" in the upper levels, with "Levalloisian" continuing in the lower levels. Stillbay and Magosian industries were found overlying the lagoon coral. On the grounds of typology and the amount of patination on the implements (it is now recognized that patination is a most unreliable guide to the age of surface finds), Breuil distinguished eight evolutionary stages ranging from "Acheulio-Levalloisian" to Magosian and finally Wilton. Most of the tools were made of local rhyolite, more rarely of chalcedony or obsidian. To the northeast of the Gulf of Tadjourah is a salt lake, Assal, lying in a depression 130 meters below sea level. On a hill between the lake and the gulf, Wernert found a series of long picks made of basalt. They are triangular in cross section, and the three faces have been retouched all over, with the extremities carefully worked, one ending in a sharp point. Breuil assigned these picks to the most recent stage, probably Wilton, and suggested that they may have been used to extract salt from the crust of the lake.

We turn now to the southern part of the Horn. The first excavations undertaken in Somalia were made by P. Graziosi in 1935 at Bur Eibe, a granite hill on the eastern side of which are several smaller "burs" (tors or inselbergs). Stone Age sites were found to be grouped around the western and southwestern sides of these hills, probably in order to obtain protection from the northeast monsoon. Above a layer of decomposed granite was a consolidated ironcrete deposit one to three feet thick containing a Stillbay industry at the base and Magosian above. The nature of this deposit points to a climate somewhat wetter than that prevailing in southern Somalia today. Above the ironcrete was a layer of compact sand five feet thick, indicating drier conditions. The sand contained an industry transitional between the Magosian and its derivative, the Doian, with true Doian in the upper levels.

Magosian-Doian Transitional Industries

Implements of the Magosian-Doian transitional industries are generally typical of the Magosian, though they include also new forms that lead to the Doian. These transitional industries have been found

Figure 28. Magosian-Doian transitional industry, Jesomma: (a & b) hollow-based arrowheads; (c) bifaced foliate point; (d) blade or "rod."

(a)   (b)   (c)   (d)

  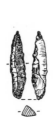 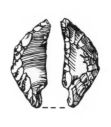

Figure 29. Doian industry, Bur Eibe and Bur Hakaba: (a) lanceolate bifaced point; (b) trihedral rod; (c) limace point; (d) blade with Heluan retouch.

(a)   (b)   (c)   (d)

at several sites in southern Somalia, including Jesomma, where one occurs both in and on the surface of a ferruginous deposit. A few hollow-based arrowheads were recovered (Fig. 28) and are the earliest known in the Horn, where they are very rare. Hollow-based arrowheads are typical of the Fayum Neolithic, the "Bedouin microlithic" of Kharga, and the Saharan Neolithic. Their presence in Somalia may indicate contact with the Sahara rather than with Egypt, since none have been found in the Sudan. Other new forms include leaf-shaped and lanceolate points, some with serrated edges, and rare pressure-flaked rods also make their appearance (Fig. 29). Blades with "Heluan retouch" in the Magosian-Doian and Doian industries of Gure Warbei, a shelter at the foot of Bur Eibe, are interesting, as they have not otherwise been found outside Egypt and Palestine; the "Heluan retouch" typical of a microlithic industry at Heluan, in Upper Egypt, consists of backing worked to a blunt edge by flaking directed from both sides of the tool (Fig. 29).

It will be remembered that Clark was struck by the similarity of some of the techniques and forms of the Magosian from the type site in Uganda with those of the transitional Magosian-Doian industries of the Horn, which he dates to the Makalian-Nakuran dry interval. The environment, too, is very similar, since Magosian-Doian and Doian sites are generally grouped around granite inselbergs, and, as at Magosi,

there are often rock cisterns still used by the Somali to obtain water
at the present time.

The Doian Culture

The Doian culture, which is apparently peculiar to southern Somalia,
was so called by Clark since it is widespread over the orange sand that
covers large areas of this country, known to the Somali as *doi* (Map
11). Graziosi first described this industry as the Eibian, but the assemblage from Bur Eibe has certain local specialties, so that a name with a
more generalized significance was chosen.

Graziosi distinguished 14 levels at Gure Makeke, Bur Eibe. The
fourth level from the top was the richest and included many very
well-made microliths, lunates, points, and *limaces*. These latter tools
are made on flakes, the upper side of which is carefully pressure-flaked
over the whole surface, while the underside is unworked and represents
the original flake surface. These implements are pointed at both ends
and were presumably used as knife blades. Unifaced lanceolate points,
which are also found, are distinguished from *limaces* by being pointed
at one end only, and were probably arrowheads (see Fig. 29).

Clark found a similar sequence in the shelter known as Gure Warbei,

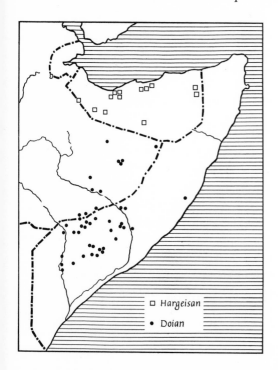

*Map 11. Distribution of Hargeisan and
Doian industries in the Horn. After
Clark.*

already mentioned in connection with the "Heluan retouch." Gure Warbei he translates as "The Cave of the Arrow Poison"; it is said to have been occupied by the traditional hero of the Eile, a Negroid people living in the area today who may perhaps be the descendants of the makers of the Doian industries. The Eile brought their arrows to this hero for him to apply poison, obtained from *Acokanthera*, an evergreen bush, which was also used by other tribes in East Africa for obtaining poison.

From sections excavated in three weeks in 1944, Clark obtained the following sequence. Layer D, at the bottom, contained a Magosian industry; this was overlain by Layer C, where kunkar deposits indicate drier conditions than those prevailing at the time of formation of the underlying layer (which is dated to the Makalian wet phase). Layer C contained a Magosian-Doian transitional industry; this was followed by the main Doian horizon in Layer B, subdivided into an earlier and a later phase. Wetter conditions apparently prevailed at this time, and Layer B is correlated with the Nakuran wet phase. In the earlier Doian industry, unifaced *limace* points and backed blades predominate, while in the later industry pressure-flaked bifaced and unifaced points are the main types of tool. The top layer, A, represents a long dry period during which the shelter was occupied sporadically, probably by the Eile (judging by the pottery, which is similar to that made by the modern Eile). There were, however, a few small sherds of fine, thin ware which are rather like the Wilton B pottery of Kenya and southern Ethiopia. The top three layers of Graziosi's excavation also contained a degenerate industry with pottery.

The development of the Doian culture from the Magosian can be seen most clearly at Gure Warbei. In the transitional stage between the two, Magosian-type points and scrapers persist, though they are rare. A considerable decrease in the prepared-core technique is noticeable in the transitional stage, with emphasis on the production of blades. Subtriangular points are replaced by *limaces*, culminating in beautiful pressure-flaked lanceolate and foliate points (Fig. 29) in which alternate flaking from either side of the tool is very well controlled and approaches Neolithic pressure-flaked implements of the Fayum or the Sahara.

A few ostrich eggshell beads were found in the Doian level, some showing polish on one side and a rough surface on the other, similar to those of the Upper Kenya Capsian of Gamble's Cave, which, Leakey suggested, were sewn onto leather garments as ornaments. Rubbers of limestone with one or more grinding surfaces suggest that grass seed may have been ground. (During the 1870s Dunn noticed that Bushmen ground grass seed that had been conveniently collected for them in ants' nests!)

Clark also excavated a rock shelter at the "Rifle Range" Site at Bur Hakaba (see Map 9), where, as well as human remains, he found Magosian and Doian industries, though the transitional stage between them was absent. Other than the jaw from Dire Dawa, the only other prehistoric human remains found so far in the Horn are from this site. During their administration, the Italians made a rifle range here, and in so doing, they uncovered a human burial. During the war, Clark collected the fragmentary bones, which included no less than 79 pieces of skull, some isolated teeth, and various other parts of the skeletons of two individuals. Judging by the degree of fossilization of the human remains, they seem to be contemporary with associated animal bones, though such comparisons can be most unreliable. With the animal bones was a Doian industry, and it seems probable that the human remains represent the makers of this culture, though they were too fragmentary to be useful in determining the racial type.

Although the makers of the Doian culture used pottery, they apparently had no domesticated animals or cultivation. Pottery with a Doian industry was found in Layer B at Gure Warbei; sherds in the upper part of this layer could conceivably have got into it from the overlying deposit, but one sherd at the base of Layer B was almost certainly *in situ*, as no artificial disturbance of the bottom part of this bed could be seen. This thin sherd had a plain tapered rim, rounded on both sides, with a faint line of decoration beneath it. Graziosi also found pottery in the upper layers of Gure Makeke, at Bur Eibe, that was associated with Doian implements.

Two other variants of the Doian culture were found in the Horn— one a strand-looping variant on the coast, the other a "Neolithic" variant, so called because of the excellence of the pressure flaking and not because of any pastoral or agricultural implications. This industry was discovered at Mirsale Wells in the eastern Mudugh; it differs from the ordinary Doian by the presence of rather large foliate points, which would have been too clumsy for arrowheads. Clark suggests that they may have been used for keeping water holes (bored through the gypsum pan) clear of silt.

The Hargeisan Culture

A blade-and-burin culture confined to the northern part of the Somali Plateau and the Gulf of Aden Rift has been named after the type site, Hargeisa. It is distinguished from the Kenya Capsian (see p. 258) by the presence of certain additional forms, such as disk cores and Magosian-type points. It was dated to the dry period between the Gamblian and the Makalian wet phase, and is therefore considerably later than the time claimed for the first appearance of blades and burins in the Kenya Capsian, though perhaps contemporary with the Upper Kenya Capsian. Clark believes that the Hargeisan culture originated on the Ethiopian Plateau, where similar industries have been found.

At Hargeisa itself this culture overlies a Lower Stillbay industry, but stratified sites are rare. When Hargeisan industries do occur in stratified sites, they are found in a sandy alluvium 2 to 3 feet thick, overlying land rubble containing Stillbay industries.

Characteristic implements are blade cores, microlithic blades with straight (or more rarely curved) blunted backs (Fig. 30), angle- or *bec-de-flute* burins, end scrapers, and small subtriangular unifaced points, similar to those of the Magosian.

At two sites, industries have been found that are later than the typical Hargeisan; they are transitional between this culture and the Wilton, and are dated to the end of the Makalian wet phase, contemporary with the Magosian-Doian transitional industries. In these Hargeisan derivative industries, small unifaced points are more common, and hollow-based arrowheads are worked over both faces. No tanged arrowheads, by the way, have been found farther east than western Uganda, where they are common, as they are in the Congo and in North Africa.

Figure 30. Hargeisan industry, Hargeisa: (a & b) backed blades; (c) double end scraper; (d) hollow-based arrowhead; (e) unifaced point; (f) bec-de-flute burin.

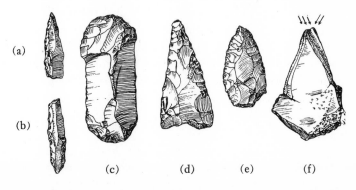

Figure 31. Wilton thumbnail scrapers.

The Wilton Industries

Following the Magosian at many sites in East Africa is the still more microlithic Wilton, which may start during the Makalian wet phase, perhaps around 3000 B.C., and certainly continues until the coming of iron, and much later in places. Wilton industries are far better known in southern Africa than in East Africa, and almost everywhere the great difference in the nature of the deposits containing Magosian and Wilton shows that an appreciable time must have elapsed between occupations by the two peoples. Carbon-14 dates for a Wilton layer in the Matjes River Cave range from 5758 B.C. ± 150 to 3443 B.C. ±250, but these unexpectedly early dates suggest that the deposit may have been contaminated. At Lochinvar Ranch on the edge of the Kafue Flats in Northern Rhodesia, a Wilton industry associated with skeletons has been dated to 2268 ± 100 B.C., and a Late Wilton hearth at Lusu Rapids near Mambova dates from 186 ± 150 B.C., according to unpublished information supplied by the archaeologist Brian Fagan of the Rhodes Livingstone Museum, Livingstone. Unfortunately East Africa is sadly lacking in carbon-14 dates, and at present we must depend on other areas to supply them.

According to Leakey, the three phases of the East African Wilton, which he calls A, B, and C, may all have started during the Makalian wet phase. Wilton A may be confined to this phase; Wilton B continues at least into Nakuran times and probably much later, while Wilton C lasted until—and long after—the coming of iron to East Africa. In South Africa, artifacts of the Wilton C type were still being made during the last century.

These three phases were distinguished, not because of any very marked differences in the tools, but because they are associated with different environments: open sites, rock shelters, and shell mounds on lake shores. Wilton A is found in widely scattered open sites in Kenya and northern Tanganyika, as well as in Ethiopia. The most characteristic tools are small double-ended scrapers the size of a thumbnail (Fig. 31). Wilton A industries also include larger scrapers, lunates, burins, and *lames écaillées*, perhaps showing the influence of the Elmenteitan culture of the Kenya Rift Valley. The pottery has a single incised wavy-line decoration in some instances, or is plain.

The supposed uses of the most characteristic implements, thumbnail scrapers, are of interest. They could have been effective only for rather fine woodwork, or perhaps for preparing skins of smaller animals such as hares. These scrapers may have been much larger originally and were constantly reflaked as they became blunted through use. Long ago it was stated in connection with Eskimos that, "The leather-worker is constantly touching up his scraper edge with the chipper [of bone] and in time he wears it out to a mere stub. This constant sharpening accounts for the fact that few specimens show signs of great wear.[94]

Turning from Eskimos to people much nearer at hand, the Bushmen, an observer, writing in 1905, had some interesting comments. "The stone scrapers were of two kinds, one employed in cleaning and rounding not only their bows, but also the handles and shafts of their kerries, darts and harpoons, which was generally a thin and nearly flat flake of stone, with a deep semicircular notch in one side, with a sharp edge, and varying in size according to the required thickness of the shaft to be manufactured. This was used as a primitive spokeshave. The other was also a tolerably flat, but thicker stone than the last, about two and a half to three inches across the broadest part, and of a rudely circular shape, but such as could be conveniently gripped by its outer edge between the forefinger and the thumb. It was used in the preparation of their skin mantles and bags, in scraping and clearing away any extraneous matter adhering to the skin under manipulation."[95]

It sounds, therefore, as if smaller scrapers were used for fine wood-working and larger ones for leather dressing.

It has also been suggested that some of the so-called scrapers may in fact have served as boxes of matches—that is to say, they were used as flints in the percussion or strike-a-light method of firemaking. Lumps of iron pyrites associated with flints have been found in Magdalenian deposits in Western Europe, but pyrites is not essential. Tobias saw Bushmen striking two tiny firestones together with great dexterity, though the drill method with two sticks is also used, and many Bushmen have also acquired metal flint rings from traders. The fine, irregular trimming marking the edges of the firestones reminded him strongly of the appearance of some of the L.S.A. microliths.[96]

Wilton B, found mainly in rock shelters, seems to be a direct derivative of the Magosian; this is well seen at such sites as Apis Rock in Tanganyika and at many rock shelters in the Horn. The Wilton industries of Uganda, described by van Riet Lowe as Wilton C, are comparable with the Wilton B of Kenya and Tanganyika. In Kenya, Wilton B is known from shelters at Kabete, near Nairobi, and at Lukenia Hill, on the road from Nairobi to Machakos; here burnished pottery was found similar to that of Njoro River Cave (described in Chapter Ten). The tools are like those of Wilton A, including thumbnail scrapers and lunates, but in addition there are small, degenerate points of the Stillbay-Magosian type.

Wilton C is found associated with large shell mounds along the shores of Lake Victoria and other East African lakes. Stone tools of any kind are rare, though occasional thumbnail scrapers are found; a diet almost exclusively of shellfish apparently made tools unnecessary. The pottery is coarse and quite different from that of Wilton A or B. Beads are common. Human remains were found buried near a series of shell mounds by the Kavirondo Gulf, near Kanam. Six skeletons were excavated from old lake deposits a little way away from one of the shell mounds. Such "kitchen middens" are well known along the coast of South Africa, where they are also accompanied by Wilton industries. The large size of the skulls, associated with small faces, also suggests connections between the strand-looping people of the two areas.

The skeletons were buried in various positions, some being fully contracted, others semi-contracted, lying either on the left or right side and with the faces turned in different directions. The graves are very shallow, but this may have been due to subsequent erosion. The skulls are dolichocephalic; the brow ridges are very poorly developed and the foreheads strongly arched. The mandibles are massive, with pronounced chins. The walls of the cranium are very thick; this feature, along with the large size of the skulls and the nature of the fragments of femora recovered, indicate that the people were very massively built. Even in the case of very old individuals, the teeth are hardly worn at all, doubtless owing to a monotonous diet of shellfish.

WILTON INDUSTRIES OF THE HORN

In common with most of East Africa, no evidence of a true Neolithic stage has ever been found in the Horn, though some industries have been referred to as "Neolithic" because of tool technology. L.S.A. industries such as the Wilton lingered on until they were very gradually superseded by iron.

The typical Wilton of Somalia is mainly confined to the northern plateau and coastal plain, but it is also known in the Danakil Rift and in eastern Mudugh. The type site is a small rock shelter at Mandera, where the Wilton industry was dated to the second or Nakuran post-pluvial wet phase. The tools are mostly microlithic, comprising crescents, short end scrapers and thumbnail scrapers (which are generally fan-shaped), utilized blades, and a few burins. A few sherds of pottery associated with it had no burnish or decoration. The industry is derived from the Hargeisan blade-and-burin culture, and its distribution is essentially the same.

In Ogaden, a Wilton industry was found differing slightly from the Wilton of the north. There were no burins or thumbnail scrapers, and the technique used was based on diminutive prepared cores. Clark thought this might be a survival of "Levalloisian" influence, which, in this part of the country, did not develop into the Stillbay-Magosian sequence, nor into the blade-and-burin industries of the north.

The industries of eastern Mudugh were described as a "Neolithic" variant of the Wilton, owing to the addition of pressure-flaked points and hollow-based arrowheads, probably borrowed from the Doian of southern Somalia. At Mirsale Wells a "Neolithic" variant of the Doian is characterized by crude foliate points. An industry at Rakon Wells, 10 miles farther north, seems to represent a mixture between the Doian and the Wilton complexes, and foliate points are very rare at this site.

A strand-looping variant was found in a midden at Biede Rock Shelter at the mouth of the Nogal River. The implements were degenerate and were associated with a piece of iron slag, perhaps obtained from other people who were already using iron.

Between intervals of soldiering, Clark made a rapid excavation of two rock shelters in granite outcrops at Yavello, southern Ethiopia, 500 miles south of Addis Ababa and 70 miles north of the Kenya frontier. The central part of the deposits in the main shelter had already been dug to form a gun pit, with the debris thrown around the perimeter as a parapet. Gray dust down to one foot from the surface yielded a microlithic industry with potsherds which may be a degenerate form of Wilton B; with it were two pieces of beaten copper, which is of interest since this metal has not been found elsewhere with a Wilton B industry. Below this layer was 5 feet of red to buff-colored earth, ending in a layer of granite boulders. In this deposit was a Stillbay industry with implements made of chert, quartz, and quartzite.

In the second shelter, the top 4 inches contained some coarse pottery; with this, and down to 6 inches from the surface, were thin sherds made from well-fired clays derived from shallow bowls and round-based pots; many of them were burnished and all but one sherd were undecorated. A fragment of a sandstone ring, with the edges ground and polished, also came from this layer. From the 6-inch level down to 1½ feet was a microlithic industry that may represent a degenerate Wilton. There were roughly made microlithic backed blades, but no true crescents or diminutive points. *Lames écaillées* showing scars made by battering had obviously been used to back the microliths. There were also some badly made thumbnail scrapers and two hollow scrapers.

On the walls of the shelter some schematic paintings were faintly visible, but had been badly destroyed by weathering. Pieces of ground hematite found with the Wilton B industry suggest that the paintings were the work of these people.

WILTON INDUSTRIES OF UGANDA

Wilton industries are found on the surface over most of Uganda and are probably of the Wilton B branch. Of the 600-odd caves noted by Wayland, only a handful have been excavated so far; several of these, including a rock shelter at Nsongezi and Aerodrome Cave Number 1 at Entebbe, yielded Wilton industries.

The Nsongezi Rock Shelter is situated 100 yards away from the Kagera River, on the left bank, where it emerges from a gorge. In places within the rock shelter, the accumulation of bone, shell, and implement-bearing layers with hearths and potsherds reaches a depth of over 9 feet. The implements are mostly microlithic, made of vein quartz; most numerous are lunates, often less than an inch long, and tiny awls or borers were also common. There were also some microlithic scrapers and a few burins and many cores and waste flakes.

The potsherds found by van Riet Lowe were coarse, with the exception of two elaborately decorated sherds of finely finished black burnished ware, found at a depth of 6 feet. O'Brien, writing in 1939, reported: "Pottery is abundant in the top 4 feet, below which it ceases. This pottery is, on the whole, well made and decorated with various incised designs, though some very rough sherds were also present." O'Brien found two metal objects in the top 2 feet; there were also rock crystals, sometimes worked into tiny awls, and two beads, a round one of ostrich eggshell and a square one of oyster shell.

Three feet above the two decorated sherds found by van Riet Lowe, a wrought-iron needle was recovered; it is of a type still used today for making baskets and fish traps. This was taken to mean either that the makers of the Wilton industry occupied the area at a time when skilled potters and ironworkers were in the vicinity, or that the industry of the occupants of the rock shelter is Iron Age and not Stone Age. Van Riet Lowe preferred the first explanation, since the contrast between the elaborate potsherds and the coarse ones is so marked. It now seems that the more sophisticated pottery is of the dimple-based variety (see Chapter Eleven) which is associated with the introduction of ironworking during the first millennium A.D. This culture may be connected with the spread of Bantu tribes into territory occupied by Wilton hunters.

Aerodrome Cave Number 1 at Entebbe was partially excavated by Wayland in 1934; it is one of a series of rock shelters in a thick band of laterite on which Entebbe is built. There was an accumulation of midden material in Cave Number 1 to a depth of 10 feet, but industries were richest between 3 and 4 feet from the surface and again between 7 and 8 feet. Typical Wilton tools were found at both these levels, but decorated pottery was confined to the 3–4-foot level. One sherd of well-baked pale coral-colored ware had herringbone decoration below the everted and narrow lip, while another was entirely covered by an impressed zigzag corded design, with black slip on the outer surface.

Chapter Eight

PRIMITIVE ARTISTS

Nearly everyone nowadays is familiar with the cave art of Western Europe, which has been well documented and illustrated by enthusiastic workers such as the late Abbé Breuil. South African rock paintings and engravings, first laboriously copied by the late G. W. Stow a hundred years ago (before Altamira had been discovered), are hardly less well known. More recently, remarkable works of art have been discovered in the central Sahara and in North Africa. The latest chapter in the history of primitive art has revealed a wealth of material in Tanganyika, linking the many cave paintings of Southern Rhodesia on the one hand with those of Ethiopia and the Sahara to the north on the other.

The problem of whether the paintings of eastern Spain and those of South Africa (to which they bear a striking resemblance) are connected has long occupied the minds of prehistorians. The art of the Aurignacians and Magdalenians of France is so different that it need not be taken into account; it must have evolved and flowered locally and

222

independently. But there seems little doubt that the art of eastern Spain, with its stylized human figures actively engaged in hunting with bows and arrows, is connected with that of the Capsians of North Africa. It is tempting to imagine that hunter-artists with essentially the same equipment and philosophy once extended from the Mediterranean to the Cape, ranging over the Sahara and the open plains of East Africa, but avoiding the dense forests of the Congo.

Because the Bushmen were found to be painting rocks when Europeans first arrived in South Africa, it was assumed that they were responsible for all the art found there. Burkitt was the first to point out that the South African paintings and engravings are not all of the same age and that some of them antedated the present Bushmen. The discovery of various ancient human remains with "Bushmanoid" traits in South Africa, associated with M.S.A. and L.S.A cultures, suggested that the artists found at work by the first Europeans were carrying on traditions handed down to them by their ancestors over thousands of years. For several reasons the dating of rock paintings is much more difficult in Africa than it is in Europe. Owing to intense climatic fluctuations in Europe, much of the fauna died out with dramatic suddenness; the mammoth and the woolly rhinoceros, equipped to withstand the rigors of the Würm Glaciation, could not compete with conditions after the end of glacial times and became extinct. Therefore, when we find a picture of one of these beasts in a French cave, we know it was painted during the Pleistocene, certainly more than ten thousand years ago. In Africa, extinct animals are rarely depicted, though sometimes types are shown that do not live in the area today—for example, most of the animals shown in the Saharan engravings, such as elephants, rhinos, and ostriches, have now retreated southward because of increasing desiccation.

In northern Spain and in France, the finest paintings are found in the deep recesses of caves, where they have been well preserved. The warmer climate of Africa and the rarity of limestone (and hence of caves) made man a nomad of the open plains or the rocky hills; his canvas was more often a slab of rock or an overhanging shelter, as it was in eastern Spain, than a cave wall; so his art has been exposed to the elements, which it has often withstood in a remarkable fashion. Excavations in the caves of Western Europe have revealed stratified industries associated with fragments of coloring material and artists' utensils (palettes, stones for grinding pigments, and so forth) which have made the dating of the paintings certain. In Africa, however, caves such as Bambata in Southern Rhodesia that have yielded comparable dating material are extremely rare. European artists, too, often decorated small objects (engraved bone or ivory tools, stones, or painted pebbles) that were sometimes incorporated in cave deposits and could be correlated by their styles with wall paintings; in Africa, such decorated objects are very scarce.

Although the absolute ages of African rock paintings are difficult to determine, the relative ages of different styles can be worked out by a study of the superposition of styles and colors. Perhaps because suitable rocks with smooth surfaces were not easily found, perhaps because certain sites were frequented over long periods and acquired magical or religious significance, generations of artists used the same canvas and, with complete lack of respect, painted over the masterpieces of their predecessors. If we find in a certain rock shelter that, say, stylized human figures in brown paint overlie well-painted, naturalistic claret-colored animals, which in turn are superimposed over crude outlines of animals done in an entirely different style in yellow paint, it is easy enough to say that the yellow animals are earliest, followed by the claret and lastly the brown figures. But we do not know whether the difference in time was a matter of a few months or several thousand years. When, however, we find similar styles and colors in the same order over a wide area in many scattered sites, it is assumed that the fashion of the time is reflected rather than the whim of individual artists, and it is fairly certain that a considerable length of time between the various styles is involved.

A. L. Armstrong's excavations at Bambata Cave in 1928 revealed for the first time in Africa an apparent connection between paintings and prehistoric cultures. Not only were coloring materials found in stratified deposits corresponding to the order of superposition of the paintings, but it seemed at that time that the earliest paintings were the work of the makers of the Bambata culture, as it was then called (now included in the Stillbay). In Europe, the earliest paintings that have survived are Aurignacian, almost certainly much older than any paintings known in Africa. The earliest paintings in eastern Africa have been attributed to the Nachikufans of Northern Rhodesia and Tanganyika; the first phase of their culture has been dated to 4300 B.C. by carbon-14, but the second and third phases are much later. In South Africa many paintings are associated with the Wilton culture, which survived

in places up till a few centuries ago, and some of the Tanganyika paintings are probably similarly connected with the Wilton. Only systematic
excavation of the hundreds of rock shelters where paintings have been
found will enable the art to be linked with cultures. Dr. and Mrs.
Leakey made a start at this formidable task, and in 1956 R. Inskeep
carried out a small excavation in one of the painted shelters, Kisese II,
about 40 miles north of Kondoa.

While most of the Tanganyika shelters that have been tested show
no great depth of deposit, at Kisese there is up to 14 feet of cultural
material and bedrock was reached at a depth of 20 feet. At one side
of the shelter is a large piece of rock in the process of breaking away
from the wall, part of which has already done so. In the area once
covered by the fallen rock are some red paintings, overlain by recent
white ones. Two feet below the floor were found two slabs that were
too heavy to lift back into place, but plaster casts left little doubt that
at least one of the slabs fitted the break in the wall of the shelter.
Clearly the slab must have fallen before the scar left on the rock face
was painted and, from its position near the top of the sequence, it
must have broken away during the latest part of the L.S.A. It is
probably contemporary with ironworking, since slag and a broken
tuyère were found in the top levels. The L.S.A. seems to start about
a third of the way down the deposits, where there is a sudden decrease
in larger scrapers and other tools and an increase of microliths.

Although pieces of ocher occurred throughout the deposit, more
came from the level of the slab than anywhere else, supporting the
conclusion that the paintings must be associated with this period.
Inskeep concluded that the age of some at least of the Kondoa paintings
should be measured in centuries rather than millennia, though whether
this applies to all of them is not yet known.[97]

The Nature and Purpose of Rock Paintings

Man was, of course, dependent on his environment for his painting
materials; he used mainly mineral pigments mixed with animal fats or
marrow. Iron oxide, heated to various temperatures, gives colors
ranging from yellow through dark red and brown; the best material
for black pigment is manganese, though charcoal was probably used as
well. Many of the later paintings are done in white, obtainable from

kaolin or even bird droppings. Blues and greens rarely survive; it seems
likely that they were used, but were probably made from vegetable
dyes that have disappeared. The earliest observer of an old Bushman
actually engaged in painting a rock reported that he sharpened a bird
bone to form a flexible spatula to apply the paint; presumably feathers
and fur were also used as brushes, while the fingertips are the most
elementary "brushes" of all. Modern natives in Tanganyika have been
seen to beat the end of a stick to make a brush for daubing for ritual
purposes.

This brings up the question of the incentive to paint rocks at all.
There are many reasons why a man would want to decorate the wall of
his shelter—as a means of self-expression, to beautify his home, or
merely to "doodle," to pass an idle hour. Dr. Julian Huxley has
described how he watched a young gorilla in the zoo trace the outline
of his shadow on the wall with his finger. An observer reported
seeing rhesus monkeys near Bombay trace the outlines of their hands
in the dust, using a twig held like a pencil. Recently, chimpanzee "art"
has become celebrated and fetches high prices.

It is unnecessary to speculate over the significance of many of the
paintings, but some, on the other hand, obviously have a deeper meaning. Two of the motives have been described as "wishful thinking" and
"sympathetic magic."[98] In the first case you draw what you would like
to have, whether it is a successful hunt, fat cattle, or a lovely girl. In the
second case, the artist is convinced that an object can be made to suffer
or act in a certain way in sympathy with the model. The custom of
sticking pins into an effigy of an enemy in the hope that he will meet
the same fate survives to the present day in many parts of the world.
Similarly, it does not require much imagination to suppose that an
artist who painted a buck stuck full of arrows hoped that he would
succeed with a real animal in the same way.

Some paintings probably commemorate an outstanding event. Just
as we like to record a wedding or a holiday with our cameras, so the
primitive artist would paint the scene of a successful hunt, or an initiation ceremony, or perhaps a masked witch doctor praying for rain. The
later Bushman paintings of South Africa often represent battles between
themselves and tall, black figures armed with shields, who are obviously
Bantu.

Almost invariably (except sometimes in the case of the recent "Late
White" paintings) the modern inhabitants of Tanganyika are ignorant

of the artists responsible for the rock paintings, saying that they were done before they arrived in the country. Often painted rock shelters are treated with considerable awe and respect. The Wagogo, for example, say that the paintings near Bahi were done by the Wamia who preceded them; there is a tradition that these people sacrificed cattle at the shelters and painted the signs with pigment mixed with fat from the slaughtered animals. The Wagogo carry on this custom when they pray for rain, painting over the old signs, following the same lines, using fat from a sacrificed beast and a beaten stick as a brush. Although they have no idea what the signs mean, they fully believe in their magic properties. The present Wamia, who live in a different area, have elaborate funeral rites. When an important personage dies, the senior elder paints a portrait of the deceased along with his personal property such as cattle, gourds, pestles and mortars, ornaments, and so forth. It seems not unlikely that similar ceremonies took place in prehistoric times and that some of the weird symbols that we are unable to interpret may be conventional signs for household goods, weapons, and ornaments that accompanied a man to his grave.

The Art of Tanganyika

One of the first discoveries of rock paintings in Tanganyika was made by missionaries in 1908, near Bukoba, on the western shores of Lake Victoria, where stylized human figures in red paint were depicted on the walls of several shelters. No further reports of paintings came until 1923, when F. B. Bagshawe discovered paintings at Kolo, near Kondoa, and described those of the Kangeju Bushmen west of Lake Eyasi. In 1929, T. A. M. Nash discovered others near Kondoa, which has since proved to be the center of an incredible number of painted rock shelters (Map 12). A. T. Culwick described paintings near Dodoma in 1931; R. D. H. Arundell studied the Bukoba shelters in more detail; and Leakey discovered many more sites near Kondoa, to mention but a few.

Some of the paintings discovered by Bagshawe were at Kisana, on the eastern edge of the Iramba Plateau. One rock showed the heads and necks of two ostriches; a second had a faint representation of a giraffe and other animals, including antelopes and perhaps a dog. The best painting, on a third rock, was of an eland cow and calf. All were badly

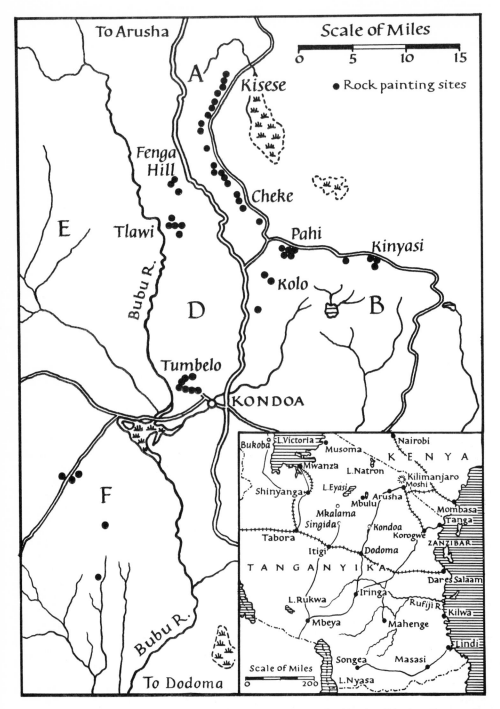

*Map 12. Distribution of rock-painting sites in the Kondoa District, Tanganyika.
(Inset: other rock-painting sites in Tanganyika.)*

preserved, as they are exposed to the sun and rain and to the destructive habits of the local children.

In dense bush country near Kondoa Irangi, Nash discovered a small hill composed of slabs of metamorphic rock, many of which were painted, but again the state of preservation was bad. Some of the figures were drawn in outline only, others were filled in, and superposition could be seen in many cases. Nash copied an amusing picture of an elephant followed by a stylized human figure who seems to be driving it along with a stick; the man is not actually holding the stick, which is depicted by itself between him and the elephant, and it may, in fact, represent a spear. A second painting shows two giraffes, one of which is well finished. Of a third design, Nash wrote as follows: "This fragment might represent anything, but it gave me the impression of a

Plate 15. Paintings at Cheke rock shelter.

rhinoceros round whose fore-limb a device comparable to the South American bolas had been flung. I admit this is highly fanciful.[99] From the illustration, it is impossible to make out the rhinoceros, or its leg, but the balls attached to strings certainly look like a bolas; this is very interesting indeed, as it might conceivably mean that this weapon had survived in use since the times of Olorgesailie.

Culwick described two sites 60 miles apart, one on the Iramba Plateau in Mkalama District, the other at Ilongero, 16 miles north-east of Singida Station.[100] Near Ilongero was a hill that the local natives were afraid to climb, as it was reputed to be the residence of the devil. With considerable reluctance, the chief accompanied Culwick up it, followed at a respectful distance by the other inhabitants. Culwick was acting in an official capacity and remarked that the chief probably thought that the government would be a match for the devil! Halfway up the hill was an overhanging rock 70 feet long by 9 feet wide, ab-solutely covered with paintings. The natives showed such astonishment at seeing these that Culwick was convinced that they did not know of their existence. The paintings were all in red, both line drawings and plain color and also combined (figures filled in, but with a darker out-line). The line drawings were evidently the oldest, since they were overlain by those in color with dark outlines; the plain color paintings are the latest of all. Only fragments of the earliest line drawings remain. Most of the figures are animals, with a great many giraffes. There is a feline that may be a leopard and also a possible hyena jumping. Carnivores are rather rare in rock paintings (though magnificent lions appear on the Saharan engravings), presumably because they were not good to eat and therefore neither the "wishful-thinking" nor the "sympathetic-magic" aspects applied. By far the most commonly represented are antelopes of all kinds, with giraffe a good second. On this shelter was an elephant upside down, obviously drawn with con-siderable difficulty; it is supposed that this may be a convention for a dead animal (again perhaps "wishful thinking" or possibly commemora-tive). There is also an extraordinary picture of a tree with very long roots and also what appears to be a game trap with a block suspended from the top.

At Singida, 12 miles away, paintings were found on large boulders around a spring. On one of them the shape of an elephant was faintly discernible; the artist showed originality by making use of pink granite coming to the surface of the gray-covered rock; this he had chipped away to form the rough outline of the beast, filling in the gaps with red pigment. Another curious feature of this site was piles of curiously shaped pieces of granite, obviously collected by man, though it was impossible to tell whether he shaped them or whether he amassed natural blocks of particular shapes and colors for some obscure purpose. At Ilongero similar piles were found, sorted into gray slabs, red slabs, and a collection of pieces with sharp edges. It is difficult to speculate on the purpose of such collections, which may in fact be nothing more subtle than the equivalent of our children's hoards of seashells, picked up and sorted simply because they have pretty shapes or colors.

Several shelters at Bwanjai, in the Kiziba chieftainship, discovered by Arundell, are painted with conventional figures (probably human), mostly red, but some black or white. These are obviously fairly modern, and similar signs are painted today. In the Ihangiro chieftainship, 45 miles south of Bukoba, however, the designs are different and brighter in color. Superposition of claret on red is seen, and there are also paintings in yellow. The present inhabitants are unaware of the origin of these designs, which are therefore presumably at least a hundred years old or more.

The Kondoa-Irangi District is apparently the main art center of Tanganyika. In 1935, no less than 14 different styles had been distinguished, of which the last 3 are very recent. Several other styles had been noted, but there was no evidence of their position in the sequence. Since that time, five earlier styles have been discovered. The area was divided up into six parts, lettered from A to F (Map 12) and each site was numbered within those divisions—for example, A 1-18, B 1-19, and so forth. The best-known sites are Kisese and Cheke in A division, north of Kondoa township and east of the Cape-to-Cairo road (this sounds impressive, but the illusion is quickly dispelled when one actually motors along this particular section, especially in the rainy season).

In 1951, Dr. and Mrs. Leakey started to intensify their previous work on the Kondoa paintings. Seventy-four sites were known at that time, of which 17 had been found in the southwestern corner of A. Concentrating on this section, within the year 186 sites had been mapped in A, only 67 of which were sufficiently well preserved for study. Although some of the visible art is old, most of it is probably relatively recent; the oldest styles of all could not be seen when the Leakeys started work, but they devised a means for bringing them out. In many cases the paintings are covered by a thin film of silica; it was found that by spraying with water this film becomes temporarily transparent, so that the paintings beneath it can be deciphered and traced before the water dries. If more paintings have been added on top of the silica film at a later date, the spraying has to be done very carefully so as not to damage them. In other cases, the paintings are obscured by thick deposits of the excreta of hyraxes or "rock rabbits"; this sticky black substance looks and feels like tar and is difficult to dislodge.

Most people would not think the country particularly pleasant to work in, though it has undoubted fascination. To reach the shelters, one has to struggle up steep slopes through dense and often very prickly bush, where at any moment a snake or a rhino may be disturbed. Exploration is a lengthy and exhausting business, for the paintings are often completely obscured by bush; they occur on walls of granite and metamorphic rocks, which sometimes overhang in the form of

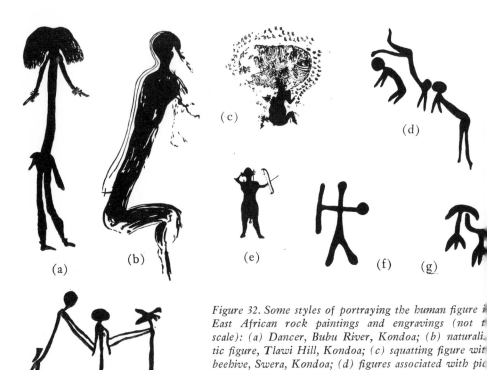

(c)

(d)

(a)

(b)

(e)

(f)

(g)

(h)

Figure 32. Some styles of portraying the human figure i East African rock paintings and engravings (not t scale): (a) Dancer, Bubu River, Kondoa; (b) naturali tic figure, Tlawi Hill, Kondoa; (c) squatting figure wit beehive, Swera, Kondoa; (d) figures associated with pic ture of elephant, Cheke, Kondoa; (e) archer with com in the hair, Sourre, Ethiopia; (f) man armed with shiel and spear, Bur Dahir, Somalia (engraving); (g) conver tionalized human figures, Bwanjai, Tanganyika; (h) "Th Abduction," Kolo, Kondoa.

shelters. They are found both in high country and on the edge of the plains. Parts of the area have not yet been cleared of "fly," so that when leaving for "clean" areas, you and your car are sprayed with insecticide by workers of the Tsetse Control, who also whisk around the wheels with a butterfly net in an ineffective and rather absurd way.

Some of the paintings may be the work of the ancestors of Sandawe and Hadza (sometimes known as Tindiga) tribes who live in northern Tanganyika today and have affinities with the Hottentots and Bushmen. Paintings in the Hadza area include naturalistic animals in red, or in outline filled with stripes; some of the paintings also depict men with very long bows, which is a characteristic of the present Hadza (some of their bows measure more than six feet along the curve). The modern Hadza, however, deny any knowledge of the authorship of the paintings.

In some cases an industry was found in the shelters which was thought at first to be a Tanganyika variant of the Wilton culture, but was later recognized to be connected with the Nachikufan culture of Northern Rhodesia. In some of the Tanganyika shelters, coloring pencils, palettes, flexible bone spatulas, and knives have been recovered; these are said to be occasionally lower (that is, earlier) than the Nachikufan level.

The 19 superimposed styles (including the 5 oldest, which were revealed by spraying over the silica film that concealed them) fall into four or five major groups. All these styles are not continuous in any one area, and there is no sequence of the major groups, only of the subsidiary styles within the main divisions. Each main group has a distinct conception of the human figure, which may be naturalistic, or stylized in various ways (Fig. 32). True portraits are practically never made, presumably because of the dangers of "sympathetic magic" from an ill-wisher. Many of the animals, however, are so well painted that there can be little doubt that the artists were capable of producing good likenesses if they had wished to.

No true polychromes have been found as in South Africa and Europe, though a variety of colors were used for both outline and filled-in paintings. In some cases it was possible to compare the pigments found in the deposits with the actual paintings. Often it is a matter of great difficulty to decide the order of superposition, which can be determined only with a high-powered lens. In the most comprehensive publication on the subject, which does not include the new styles recognized since 1951, Leakey differentiated two main groups: (A) in the Kisese and Cheke area; (B) in the Kolo area.[101] The styles noted in (A) are briefly as follows:

(1) The earliest are animals in red; the whole figure is colored except for the face (which may have been painted in a pigment that has faded?); this is drawn in outline only.

(2) Curious human figures in purple, and rather badly drawn animals, also in purple; there are also concentric rings of dots, apparently applied with the fingertips.

(3) Outline drawings of animals, mostly ostriches and giraffes, in purplish-red.

(4) A few indistinct outline figures in black, better drawn than in (3).

(5) The art is at its best in this style; animals are naturalistic, with details shown in many cases, delicately outlined. The color is claret-red.

(6) Rather badly drawn human and animal figures in yellow and orange.

(7) Animals with the whole body colored in claret-red. The details are often not well shown.

(8) Animals drawn in a thick red outline, less naturalistic than those of style (5). The commonest representations are of elephants, with the wrinkles on the trunks carefully shown, though less attention is paid to other details.

(9) Animals outlined in brick-red color, stiff and conventionalized.

(10) Peculiar human figures and badly drawn animals in solid orange color.

The last three groups are apparently very recent and need not concern us here.

The sequence in the second group at Mungomi wa Kolo (B1) is as follows:

(1) Dark red filled-in human figures.

(2) Animals drawn in outline, filled in with red color.

(3) Thick, dark claret tectiforms (equivalent to style 2 in A, above).

(4) Animals drawn in irregular outline (equivalent to style 3, above).

(5) Thin outline drawings, well drawn except for the feet (equivalent to style 5, above).

(6) Animals in thick outline, including elephants with well-defined ears (equivalent to style 8, above).

(7) Human figures with filled-in heads and streaky bodies.

(8) Crude animals in this outline and also rectangular euphorbia trees, colored in various shades of red (equivalent to style 9, above).

(9) Rust-colored and orange outline drawings, somewhat stylized.

There are also crude recent white paintings that sometimes depict humped Zebu cattle. In addition, eight earlier styles have been recognized, but these do not fit into the scheme of superpositioning mentioned above.

(a) Human figures with tails and headdresses.
(b) Yellow-white thin outline figures that are underneath style 8.
(c) Elephants with thin, narrow heads, without ears, and with streaky filling to the body; these appear over style 3.
(d) Well-drawn outline animals with bodies filled in with bold brush marks in purple.
(e) Roundheaded human figures probably equivalent to style A, 7; there are also some masked figures that may belong to this style.
(f) Bright red animals and trees, overlying style 3.
(g) Outline animals filled in with parallel lines, overlying style 7.
(h) Animals in thick outline with the center of the body left blank.

No domestic articles or domestic animals are portrayed except in the very late styles; the majority of the animals are antelopes, buffalo, elephant, rhino, and ostrich, all of which were presumably used for food. Bows and arrows are represented, and at Fenga Hill and also at Cheke there is a scene that may portray an elephant caught in a trap. Clothing is sometimes represented by knee-length garments; belts with clubs or other weapons attached to them seem to have been worn, as well as ornaments on wrists, knees, and ankles, and elaborate headdresses.

While most of the paintings show no signs of a planned composition, and consist of single figures often superimposed one on top of the other, occasionally an effective frieze or scene has been depicted. The Cheke elephant in the trap, for example, is surrounded by a group of human figures (Fig. 32d), one of which may have been tossed by the elephant, or perhaps the man is doing a handstand for joy at having caught him. A pair of rhinos (beautifully outlined in style 5) at Kisese shows an acute observance of natural history, for the female is pursuing the male, which is the rhino's normal method of courtship! At Bubu, site D 5, a pregnant giraffe is prancing most actively. "The Dancers" (one of whom is shown in Fig. 32a), also from a rock near the Bubu River, though completely stylized, makes a delightful composition; anyone who has watched African dances cannot fail to be impressed by the action in the outstretched arms; one can readily imagine the head slightly thrust back, the eyes half closed, the elaborate headdress or

plaited hair shaken over the face. An amusing scene is painted at Kolo
—"The Abduction"(h)—in which a central female figure is restrained
by two males to the left, while to the right two masked figures attempt
to drag her away. A squatting human figure at Tlawi seems to have
thrust his head into a beehive and is being attacked by the angry
swarm (c). One could go on almost indefinitely describing similar
delightful scenes.

One of the most interesting of the painted rock shelters is Cheke,
where a frieze of elands and giraffes may be seen (Plate 15). Some of the
different styles distinguished at Cheke are illustrated in the frontispiece
to Leakey's *Stone Age Africa*. The earlier styles, and animals in outline
only, do not show up in photographs. The animals in Plate 15 as well as
a human figure with what appears to be a comb in his hair, are in full
color (claret-red) and represent style 7. The elephant surrounded by a
ring of parallel lines with human figures above (Fig. 32[d]) are also
in style 7.

At the Kisese rock shelters there are a number of different kinds of
animals, including giraffes and an ostrich in style 3 (with purplish outline), and the naturalistic male and female rhinos in style 5 (outlined in
claret color). An impala (in style 5) has part of the body of an animal
in style 3 beneath it, which is overlaid by a rhino's head in style 8.
There is also an extraordinary animal with large body and small head;
the body is filled in with patterns of irregular shapes. In addition, there
are conventionalized human figures in purple (style 2), some with
elaborate headdresses, either basketwork or plaits.

The following notes on some of the sites are taken from Mrs.
Fosbrooke's account,[102] as unfortunately I have not had the opportunity
personally to visit any other than the Kisese and Cheke sites.

TUMBELO DISTRICT (WEST OF KONDOA)

Three rocks close to a native smithy are painted, one covered with
patterns, the others showing indistinct figures in red. Behind these
rocks and over a hill are two small shelters, in one of which is a
delicate picture of a grasshopper (or mantis) in red, less than 6 inches
long. In the other shelter is a red figure with a basket-like headdress,
resembling the squatting figure of Tlawi Hill (Swera) (Fig. 32c).
Below the human figure is an antelope that has been shaded to give the
impression that it is wearing a saddle cloth.

PAHI AND KINYASI (EAST OF KOLO)

At Pahi is a giraffe over two feet high outlined in orange, with mane and tail shown in detail; a large rhino is outlined in the same style. Under the giraffe is a creature with a thick neck and absurdly small head, outlined in red and filled in with yellowish-white, similar to one of the earliest styles at Cheke (of which only a few examples are known). Close to the main shelter are a number of rocks covered with "Late White" patterns. At Kinyasi, some seven miles away, is a fine naturalistic panel of graceful antelopes in various attitudes, some sitting down, some standing, others grazing. Here also is what appears to be a flat-roofed hut (or possibly a trap) and various other designs.

MUNGONI WA KOLO

Two "caves" or rock shelters on a wooded hillside near Kolo were first visited by Bagshawe in 1923; the Africans call them "the caves of spirits." Mrs. Fosbrooke says the upper cave (B1) is still used by local rainmakers, and the first time she visited it she saw the remains of a sacrifice. Three elongated human figures about 2 feet long wear very striking headdresses; "The Abduction" also comes from this site. A tectiform resembling a Celtic cross is one of the earliest paintings, and the same symbol is found on other rocks in the area.

TLAWI (SWERA) (WEST OF KOLO)

There are a great many interesting paintings in this area, including the "trapped elephants" of Fenga Hill; bushy objects in and around the "trap" have been interpreted as branches that originally concealed the pit, or perhaps they are men camouflaged in branches. On Tlawi Hill is a rock face with pictures of a buffalo or wildebeest head, a giraffe straining forward, and a small human figure. In another shelter are human figures sitting with crossed legs, and objects that look like pegged-out skins. Nearby is one of the rare pictures of a carnivore— a red lion outlined in black. Toward the Bubu River is "The Hunter," who stands with bow in hand, having shot an arrow into the chest of an antelope. In this area too is the scene of an antelope hunt, a large panel 7 feet, 6 inches, by 5 feet, in which more than a dozen animals are fleeing from faintly discernible human figures with bows.

A very fine rhino and a prancing giraffe are also to be seen here. Another shelter contains "The Dancers"; there are many other painted rocks in this area, including a sketch of a figure vigorously throwing a stick at someone. Another shelter is covered with very large animals, so large that they are difficult to trace. There are in fact so many paintings in this area that it is probable that many more await discovery.

A word on the method of copying devised by the Leakeys may be of interest. To get at the more inaccessible paintings, they erected light aluminium alloy scaffolding that is easily carried and is put together on the spot. The rock surface is often rough and far from easy to trace on, but they fixed large sheets of cellophane on to the wall with adhesive tape. Glass ink (made in many different colors) is used to trace on to the cellophane, since it sticks well and dries quickly. Later the tracing is transferred from the cellophane to paper and then taken back to the rock face for comparison with the original. The slow process of matching colors then begins; often it is necessary to mix natural raw ochers (in powder form) with powdered crayon colors to get the exact tones. The whole process, from the first tracing to the finished colored reproduction, is done on the spot, instead of guessing at the colors afterward with the aid of notes, as is done so often with the copying of rock paintings.

So far we have spoken only of paintings; there are also engravings in East Africa, not naturalistic, as in South and North Africa, but consisting of schematic lines, designs, and cup marks. Their occurrence in East Africa is not common, but farther south this schematic art is characteristic of a vast region stretching from Northern Rhodesia through Katanga in the Congo to northeastern Angola. Breuil and Mortelmans attributed this art to "Mesolithic" peoples and believed that only the most advanced paintings (which postdate the engravings) are contemporary with an intrusive "Neolithic" culture that reached this area from the north, penetrating down the shores of Lakes Tanganyika and Mweru. The engravings consist of deeply and lightly incised lines and also a series of dots. The symmetry of these holes, which are very common, led Breuil to assume that they were executed with a rotary drill, worked with a bow. This device almost certainly did not reach South Africa until late in Later Stone Age times. In some cases there is a deep patina over the engravings, comparable with that of the original rock surface, but this evidence is not at all reliable as a means of dating, since under certain circumstances patina can form comparatively rapidly.

The schematic engravings in East Africa are probably mostly quite modern, but some may be several hundred years old; they may be compared with the "Late White" schematic paintings found on so many rock shelters. They are, nevertheless, important, since in some cases they are linked with oral tradition, which gives the meaning of ceremonies with which they were connected.

On a steep rock face near the Kagera River at Nsongezi, Wayland discovered a great number of cup marks; the whole design reminded him of a star map. He also found a quartzite drill, over 5 inches long, which was most probably used for punching the cup marks. A cup-marked stone is also reported from the village of Samunge in the Tanganyika Rift Valley; its irregular markings make it clear that this was not a *bau* game (commonly played in Africa and consisting of a number of regular depressions in a rock or board to hold little stones or balls).

Four large stones on the lower slopes of Kilimanjaro, in the densely populated country of the Chagga tribe, are covered with long, meandering lines and, in some cases, pock-marked depressions. They are associated with the final stage of initiation ceremonies held in the past in this part of the country. The initiates camped in the bush, without shelter or clothes, and were taught tribal lore and the duties of their age group. A few selected youths were also instructed in the meaning of the engravings on the stones, which were secret and in no circumstances to be divulged. Each age group engraved a line on the rock, so that the numbers of lines represent the work of a great many generations.

Comparisons with Northern Rhodesia

In view of the fact that industries found in some of the Kondoa rock shelters are similar to the Nachikufan of Northern Rhodesia, a summary may be given of some of the features of this culture.

The rock shelter of Nachikufu is situated some 30 miles south of Mpika, in the Muchinga Hills. The walls of the cave are decorated with seminaturalistic paintings, and those of the small shelter have schematic figures which are thought to be later. Excavations in the cave revealed three Later Stone Age industries, which have been called Nachikufan I, II, and III; they were overlain by traces of Bantu occupation, and beneath Nachikufan I were Middle Stone Age artifacts.

The Nachikufan industries differ from the Rhodesian Wilton in the type of microliths, the quantity of bored stones, the number of polished axes, the number and form of pestles, and the Smithfield "N" type of scrapers and other implements, which resemble those of Natal. The sequence at Nachikufu was supported by evidence from other excavations made at two rock shelters farther south.

A connection was established between the paintings and industries, for pencils and faceted lumps of pigment, grindstones, and pestles were associated with Nachikufan I, II, and III. The earliest paintings are seminaturalistic and black, and some of them were found only one inch above floor level, suggesting that when they were painted the floor was considerably lower. (An amusing drawing appeared in *Punch* some years ago. One cave man is drawing on the rock, standing on another's shoulders; he says, "They will think either that the floor has sunk or that we had ladders.") At another shelter 15 feet above a stream are painted engravings the lower half of which is covered by 7 feet of sand that was blown or washed into the shelter. Beneath the sand was an occupation layer containing quantities of pigment and a microlithic industry, which is Nachikufan I; this proves that the paintings must be contemporary with (or, less probably, earlier than) the Nachikufan I industry. Clark was worried at first by the earliness of the radiocarbon date of charcoal from the Nachikufan I level in the Chifubwa Stream Shelter on the Solwezi River: 6310 ± 250 years or about 4350 B.C. In 1950, in his presidential address to the South African Archaeological Society he had hazarded a guess of 850 B.C. for Nachikufan I.[103] If the radiocarbon date is correct, and it is now generally accepted, East African rock paintings may be much earlier than had been imagined.

The roots of the Nachikufan culture (particularly those of industries II and III) are believed to lie farther to the northwest in the equatorial region of the Congo basin, while Wilton industries occupy the area to the east. The Nachikufan resembles in several ways the Mesolithic industry of Khartoum and the later industry of Jebel Moya; to the west, similarities are noticed with Congo and Angola sites, while the "Kavirondo Smithfield" of Nyarindi, western Kenya (see p. 201), may also be connected. With these cultural resemblances in mind, it would be tempting to suppose that the Nachikufans were Negroids. Unfortunately, the skeletal evidence, such as it is, is rather ambiguous. At Hora Mountain in Nyasaland, Clark found two skeletons associated with a Nachikufan II industry. One is that of a young woman, the other that of a young man who was short and muscular. The young woman had long forearm and leg bones characteristic of both Negroes and Bushmen, and her face is essentially that of a Bushwoman, though the skull is moderately long and the braincase high. The young man, on the other hand, had very short forearms, a high but longer braincase, large mastoid processes, and no Bushman features at all. He could have passed as a Negro if it were not for the lower jaw, which is slender, with a well-developed chin and essentially Mediterranean Caucasoid in character. The face region is missing, but from the articulation of the jaw it was deduced that the face must have been long and orthognathous.[104]

These Nachikufans, then, appear to be a blend of Caucasoid, Bushman, and Negro, a nice problem for the physical anthropologist. But such an admixture must have been quite common and need occasion no surprise. Nor should we be worried if it turns out that not all the rock paintings of East Africa were the work of Bushman-like people; the urge to decorate rocks, after all, occurred to men in countries as far apart as the Scandinavian nations, Spain, and Australia.

Paintings and Engravings in the Horn and the Sudan

No rock paintings of very great antiquity have yet been found in Ethiopia or Somaliland. The earliest series, from the Dire Dawa area (unknown from Somaliland) represents pastoral scenes in a naturalistic style that are very similar to the later Neolithic paintings of the Sahara, both in technique and in the garments and weapons of the human figures. Both dress and weapons, however, also resemble those of the present Hamitic inhabitants of the Horn. The cattle are depicted with long horns and no humps and must therefore antedate the introduction of the humped Zebu cattle from Asia.

A later series is painted in schematic or conventionalized style; humped cattle now appear, together with the camel. This series Clark considers to be not earlier than the fourth century A.D., and is probably much later.

The earliest groups of paintings are those painted on a limestone cliff at Genda Biftou, Sourre, about 40 miles southwest of Dire Dawa. Both the early naturalistic series and the later schematic series are represented, and 8 different styles were recognized by Breuil.

The colors are yellow (earliest), black, pale red, red-brown (the most numerous), yellow again, red, and black, in that order. All human figures painted later than the red-brown group of style 4 are schematic, represented in the form of an H. The early naturalistic figures, however, are shown full face; one man carries a bow and wears a comb in his hair (Fig. 32). Apart from this one hunting scene in the later series, and one showing a bullfight, the others are all pastoral.

As well as cattle with long horns, there are a number of other individual animals; antelopes and a cheetah (?) are painted in black (style 2), a large bounding cheetah (?) in light red (style 3), antelopes and buffaloes (style 4).

At Lago Oda, about 14 miles from Sourre, a French priest, P. Azais discovered two more painted shelters. Near the top of one of them was a series of nearly a thousand figures, stretching for over 45 yards. Pastoral scenes were again depicted, including the defense of the flock against wild beasts. Among the animals represented are cattle, elephants, rhinos, giraffes, antelopes, buffaloes, lions, cheetahs, and hyenas. As at Genda Biftou, there is an earlier naturalistic series and a later schematic series. A Wilton industry was found on the surface of the shelter; whenever rock paintings in Ethiopia or Somaliland have been associated with an industry, it has always been Wilton.

The first rock paintings to be discovered in Ethiopia were in the cave of Porc Epic. They are later than those of Genda Biftou and Lago Oda, and the earlier naturalistic style is not represented. Excavations in this cave have already been described (a Wilton industry overlays the Magosian). The paintings have been covered over by stalagmitic formations and are therefore, according to Breuil, earlier than the most recent stalagmitic formations in the floor of the cave. No domestic animals are represented, but there are two carnivores with pointed ears, elephants, lion, antelopes, and buffalo. A picture of an unmistakable stag is most interesting; deer in Africa are now confined to Tunisia, but they were depicted in protodynastic Egypt, and Breuil figured one from a church in Ethiopia (Fig. 33). He also said that the natives report them to be still living in forests around Lake Tana. Dunn, in his account of the Bushmen in the last century, said that they portray and talk about a legendary antlered deer or Tak-horn (which Dunn took to be evidence of the southward migration of these animals from the Mediterranean). A possible—but rather improbable—"deer" has recently been discovered among the cave paintings of Mt. Elgon (see p. 244). Among 20 human figures represented at Porc Epic, some have steatopygia, but this feature is fairly common in Somali women, so that it should not necessarily be taken as evidence of Bushman occupation of Ethiopia.

Another group of painted granite shelters north of Harar was discovered by Count Björn von Rosen. Figures include long-horned cattle, humans with outstretched arms (an attitude which Clark compares with that adopted by Somali and Galla herdsmen of today, who rest their arms over a stick lying across the shoulders), a hunter with a bow aiming at an ostrich, a naturalistic painting of a jackal, and line drawings of cattle with the heads left blank; one of the beasts has a branding mark. At a second shelter, paired "soles of feet" are depicted; at a third, there is superposition of three styles and colors. A Wilton industry was found in one of the shelters.

The sites described above were all in the Harar region. Another group of paintings is found on the edge of the Gulf of Aden rift. Those of the Tug Gerbakele are the most interesting, for here pecked engravings were found between two styles of the later-painted (schematic) series. The earliest paintings are in black; over these came the engravings of cattle or camels, and on top of these are red paintings of animals and finger marks.

Polychrome paintings in red, white, and black are described from a shelter at the eastern end of the fault scarp. Here the cows are horn-less, but bulls, twice the size of cows, have long, back-sweeping horns. Paintings in a shelter southwest of Bur Eibe show the conventionalized style in its extreme form with caricatures of cattle; these, however, are not very recent, as the modern Eile do not know anything about them. Engravings in two small shelters in a gypsum hill rising from the edge of the Webi Shebeli were divided into three series; the earliest, on fallen rocks, had assumed a deep brown patina with the rock itself, and the engravings were difficult to distinguish. They were pecked all over, but some had been outlined with a sharp incision made, perhaps, with a metal knife. All are domestic animals, and all conventionalized.

The Sudan

Rock paintings are known in several places in the Sudan, including northern Darfur, but some of the most interesting sites are in the Dajo Hills of southern Darfur. Only a few years ago, hundreds of black and red paintings were discovered at rock shelters in these hills. Some represent wild animals, including elephants, giraffes, and antelopes; others show horses with riders and armed foot soldiers. Domesticated horses arrived in the Sudan toward the end of the first millennium B.C., but there is no means of knowing whether the pictures of wild animals are contemporary or earlier.

The horses are depicted in various styles, and many of them show lively movement. Their riders are generally armed with swords, while the foot soldiers carry shields and spears. One horse has padded armor, a characteristic of many parts of western Africa and the Sudan up to recent times.

A Painted Cave in Kenya

Apart from very recent daubings, some of which are believed to be the work of the Masai, no rock paintings had ever been found in Kenya until 1960, when they were discovered by Mrs. D. R. Tweedie in a shelter at 8,000 feet in the forests of Mt. Elgon, about 15 miles northwest of Kitale. This elderly lady, a keen amateur archaeologist and geologist, has been braving elephants and buffaloes for some 40 years in her explorations of Mt. Elgon.

Fortunately the paintings have been preserved from weathering by a deep overhang and by trees growing immediately in front of the shelter; equally important, they have been saved from vandalism by the extreme difficulty of finding the site. Most of the paintings form a

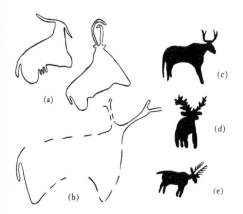

Figure 33. Paintings of cattle and deer illustrating the different treatment of forked horns and antlers: (a) cattle, Tweedie's Shelter, Mt. Elgon; (b) supposed "deer," Tweedie's Shelter; (c) ox with forked horn, Wadi Zirmei, Tibesti; (d) deer, church of Zara Brouk, Ethiopia; (e) deer, cave of Porc Epic, Ethiopia.

frieze on the best-protected wall of the shelter; others are visible on a more weathered surface in the center; and more occur 15 feet above the floor in an alcove. Since the floor of the shelter is bare rock, there is no chance of relating the paintings with an occupational level. Twenty-five can be interpreted with reasonable certainty; of these 15 are in white, 8 in red, and 2 are bichromes in white and red.

Most of the figures represent cattle, almost certainly domesticated, since in some cases there is emphasis on the udders and in nearly all, the horns are peculiarly shaped, twisted and irregular, and sometimes downturned. None are humped like the Zebu, the only cattle known south of the Sahara in modern times apart from recent imports. There are a few crudely drawn human figures, one of whom may be armed with a bow and arrow. The most interesting painting, however, is of an animal with a distinct fork in one horn, which Wright interprets as the antler of a deer (Fig. 33).[105] If this is correct, it must imply connections with the north, since there is no fossil evidence of deer having existed as far south as Kenya in Pleistocene or recent times. Deer did, however, survive in Egypt until at least 2000 B.C., for they are depicted on Middle Kingdom tombs at Beni Hasan, as well as on the late predynastic "lion-hunt" slate palette now in the British Museum. Paintings from Ethiopia suggest that deer lived even farther south later still.

Connections with engraved elks from Wadi Zirmei in northeastern Tibesti can be ruled out, for the "antler" is entirely different. The Tibesti elk has an unmistakable thick, heavy-branched antler and it has been interpreted as depicting *Megaceroides algericus*, whose fossil remains are known from Upper Pleistocene cave deposits in the Atlas. Apparently it migrated to North Africa from Europe, with bears and "Merck's rhinoceros," but its presence south of the Atlas had been completely unsuspected. Its picture at Tibesti is the most convincing evidence possible of a very much colder and wetter climate at that time (there is no way of telling the date of these engravings).

Paintings of stags at the cave of Porc Epic near Dire Dawa and from the church of Zara Brouk (see Fig. 33), both in Ethiopia, have been illustrated by Breuil as already mentioned.[106] They bear no resemblance at all to the crude drawing from Tweedie's Shelter.

It is always disappointing to have to throw cold water on interesting theories, but it must be admitted that the most likely explanation of the Mt. Elgon "deer" is that it is a cow or an ox with deformed horns.

Artificial deformation of cattle horns is quite a common practice in Africa, either as a mark of ownership or in connection with ritual. Arkell found engravings of cattle with double or forked horns at Wadi Zirmei, and others are known from Upper Egypt.[107] The variety of horns shown in the Mt. Elgon paintings, each obviously the most essential feature in the portrait of individual animals well known to the artist, makes it seem very likely that the "deer" is one of the same group. Forked horns can be produced by a binding applied to the calf when quite young. Crude though the drawing is, the fact that only one branch is shown seems to rule out the possibility that it was meant to represent an antler. The Egyptian deer from Beni Hasan, and the Ethiopian paintings, have a great number of tines—so many, in fact, that the antlers look like a toothbrush. If the Mt. Elgon artist had been drawing a deer, he too would surely have exaggerated rather than minimized such a striking feature.

Paintings in Uganda

Most of the rock paintings discovered so far in Uganda are schematic or geometric designs in white paint, probably done within the past few centuries, though a few are naturalistic, in red paint. At Nyiro, in Teso District, geometric designs are superimposed over more naturalistic paintings in red. Some of the latter represent human figures, acacia pods, and canoes, the largest of which is seven feet in length. A small excavation in the shelter revealed a Late Wilton industry in quartz, with some pottery and a bone engraved with three concentric circles similar to the designs on the rock walls. The Iteso regard the Nyiro rock as a magic place and they perform rainmaking ceremonies at it; they have a tradition that the paintings were the work of light-skinned people, presumably Bushmen.[108]

In 1953, police officers searching for Mau Mau refugees from Kenya discovered paintings on Lolui Island in Lake Victoria, 20 miles from the eastern shore. The designs are on the underside of a large boulder and on some of its supporting boulders, which form a small shelter. Only one is naturalistic, a canoe with a sail; the others are mostly concentric circles and dumbbell shapes, in two shades of red. Pottery was found below the site.[109]

Chapter Nine

FISHERMEN AND POTTERS

In this chapter we shall look at three groups of fishermen living beside lakes in the Kenya Rift Valley, on the shores of Lake Edward in the Congo, and beside the Nile at Khartoum. The Khartoum fishermen may well have invented pottery, and all three groups lived in settled communities, implying a "Mesolithic" stage. Unfortunately there are no very reliable dates for these people, so we do not know whether they were roughly contemporary with Mesolithic peoples like the Natufians of Palestine, about 8000 B.C., which seems quite likely on the available evidence.

For the first time in the prehistory of East Africa whole skeletons have been preserved, so we know well what some of these people looked like. The Upper Kenya Capsians of the rift valley were typical Mediterranean Caucasoids; the Khartoum fishermen were among the earliest-known Negroids; and the Lake Edward people from Ishango —whose remains are more fragmentary—have been described as Proto-Bushmanoid with some Negroid affinities.

Ishango

Ishango lies at the source of the Semliki River on the northwestern shore of Lake Edward (see Map 8). Since it is in the Congo, strictly speaking it should not come into a book on East Africa, but it has been included for several very good reasons. First is the extreme interest of the Ishangian bone industry, composed very largely of a great number of points, harpoons, and possibly arrowheads, which has an important bearing on the problem of the Upper Kenya Capsian. If other excuses are required, one is that the site is close to the border of western Uganda and that the deposits on either side of Lake Edward are continuous; another is that the report on Ishango has been published in French in a monograph not easily obtained by English and American readers.[110]

At Ishango the fossiliferous Kaiso series, of Villafranchian age in its upper part but extending down to an unknown depth and period, is overlain unconformably by the Semliki series, which contains Acheulian industries and fauna comparable with Olduvai, Bed IV. An Upper Terrace of the Semliki series lies at 25-30 meters above the river. Lower Terraces consist of the Ishango Terrace at 10-12 meters, contemporary with tuffs ejected from Katwe Volcano in Uganda, to the east; a terrace at about the same height posterior to the tuffs; and a modern low terrace. There is evidence that the climate at the time of the Upper Terrace was wetter than at present, and the terrace is attributed to the Gamblian pluvial. Wetter conditions also seem to have prevailed at the time of the Ishango Terrace and ejection of the tuffs, and this period was attributed to the Makalian Post-Pleistocene wet phase.

In 1950, de Heinzelin excavated a site in the Ishango Terrace, which is about 4 meters thick. It was subdivided into many different levels, but the main artifact horizons are as follows:

(1) Bantu occupation.
(2) Level containing undecorated non-Bantu pottery with flat bases.
(3) A horizon postdating the emersion of the terrace with a stone industry and fragmentary human remains.
(4) Tuffs and sands containing harpoons with one row of barbs, Ishangian C.
(5) Main fossiliferous level with animal bones and human remains, midden refuse, harpoons with two rows of barbs, Ishangian B.
(6) Gravels with less evolved harpoons with two rows of barbs, Ishangian A.

Here we are concerned with the three lower levels containing Ishangian industries. The stone industry is practically the same throughout these levels and needs little description, as it is crude and indeterminate, with M. S. A. techniques allied to the production of microliths, vaguely resembling certain elements of the Nachikufan, Wilton, and Smithfield. It is above all the hundreds of bone harpoons and similar weapons that distinguish the Ishangian.

We can pass over Ishangian A, which contains similar material to that of Ishangian B; improvements in the "harpoons" of the two levels are mentioned later. The main fossiliferous level with Ishangian B contains much kitchen refuse, including innumerable bone splinters and broken human remains, suggesting cannibalistic habits. Skull bones and mandibles are very thick; the large molars are much abraded; and the limb bones are rather slender. These people seem to have been rather similar to the Wilton C "strand-loopers" of Lake Victoria, and de Heinzelin describes them as Proto-Bushmanoid with some Negroid affinities (Fig. 34). The mammal remains are all of modern species, but include several forest or wooded savanna types not found in the region today and which suggest a wetter climate. Among the fish are a few Nilotic species that have now disappeared from Lake Edward. Large accumulations of mollusks, which are also different from those living in the lake today, seem to be almost in their living positions, and, as they are unbroken, were presumably not collected or eaten by man.

Figure 34. Mesolithic fishermen at Ishango, Lake Edward, Congo.

Stone artifacts include grindstones and mullers, some of which must have been used for rubbing and polishing the bone tools. These include numerous points, awls, and needles, but above all a wealth of biserial "harpoons," well polished to help their powers of penetration. Evolution of the "harpoons" from Ishangian A to C shows, not only a change from two rows of barbs to one, but also a gradual reduction in the number of barbs (see Fig. 40). The numbers vary from a maximum of 26 to a minimum of 2, but are mostly between 4 and 10 in each row; presumably different kinds were used for various sorts and sizes of game and fish. Most were true harpoons with detachable heads, notched to hold the line, but some heads must have been fixed. Arkell considers that the smaller biserial "harpoons," particularly those of Ishangian A, were very probably arrowheads. The enormous numbers of unbroken specimens found at Ishango suggests that they had been shot into the muddy water and lost; eventually someone had the brilliant idea of attaching a line to a notch in the bone head, and harpoons were invented (Fig. 34). He points out that fish are still shot with bow and arrow along the Upper Nile and Congo and that nesting *Tilapia* in Lake Edward would have provided an easy sitting target.

De Heinzelin describes how Lake Edward today is often covered with clouds of insects (*Corethra*) that are devoured by shoals of small fish. As they rise, they in turn are attacked by the larger carnivorous fish, *Clarias*, *Protopterus*, and, in Ishangian times, presumably also by the Nilotic *Lates*, whose bones occur in the midden. At such times, the fish would have been very easy to harpoon. The Ishangians may also have hunted hippopotamuses in the way still practiced on the Niger, where sometimes over a hundred hunters pelt the animals with harpoons. The beast becomes entangled in the lines and vegetation and eventually sinks. Ishangian lines may have been made from strips of hide rather than vegetable fibers, and it is suggested that the heavy abrasion of the human teeth found at Ishango may be the result of chewing leather, just as the modern Eskimos wear down their teeth in the same way. Presumably the Ishangians must have had boats of some kind, probably rafts.

A most intriguing object from one of the Ishangian C levels is a carved "baton" made from a long bone, which had a quartz flake wedged into one end, presumably for use as an engraving tool. It is decorated with about 168 transverse lines, arranged in groups and in three columns, which might conceivably have arithmetical implications.

Shells from the main fossiliferous level were dated by carbon-14 to 21,000 ± 500 years, which de Heinzelin dismissed as an impossibly early age for such an apparently "Mesolithic" and thus presumably Post-Pleistocene industry. Confirmation that something was wrong is given by results from modern shells from Ishango: 3000 ± 200 years. The error is attributed to contamination due to the high carbon-dioxide content of the water in which the shells lived, due to volcanic activity. On archaeological grounds, de Heinzelin adopted a conservative estimate of 6500 B.C. ± 2000 for the Ishangian. The bone harpoons of Mesolithic Khartoum, described below, seem to be rather more evolved and hence perhaps somewhat later, though the occupation has generally been attributed to about 7000 B.C. Arkell is now inclined to think that it is more likely to date from before 8000 B.C., and that the Ishangian may be even earlier. He suggests that bone harpoons were invented in the Ishango area. The known distribution of ancient bone harpoons follows two lines, one down the Nile Valley, the other westward across the southern Sahara, with Ishango more or less at the apex of the two branches. Bone harpoons have also been found in the Lake Rudolf area. Technologically the method of attachment of the line evolves from a notch (Ishango) to grooves (Mesolithic Khartoum) and finally to a perforation (Neolithic Shaheinab).

Arkell considers that bone harpoons may have been diffused over the Sahara, which was not desert at that time, to the Mediterranean; and that they were subsequently adopted by the Magdalenians of Europe, whose culture begins *circa* 15,000 B.C. Since the modern shells of Ishango gave a carbon-14 result that is too early by 3,000 years, it may be legitimate to deduct 3,000 years from the age obtained for the Ishangian shells (21,000 years), which would give a result of 18,000 years, or about 16,000 B.C. If this is correct, the Ishangian would date from the latter part of the Gamblian pluvial rather than the Makalian wet phase. It seems far more likely, however, that if bone harpoons were diffused rather than invented in two areas independently, the movement would have been in the opposite direction; from the Magdalenians of Europe to North Africa and thence southward across the Sahara.

The Khartoum Mesolithic

A site near the railway station at Khartoum (see Map 13), excavated by Arkell in 1944-45, contained a Mesolithic industry with the earliest

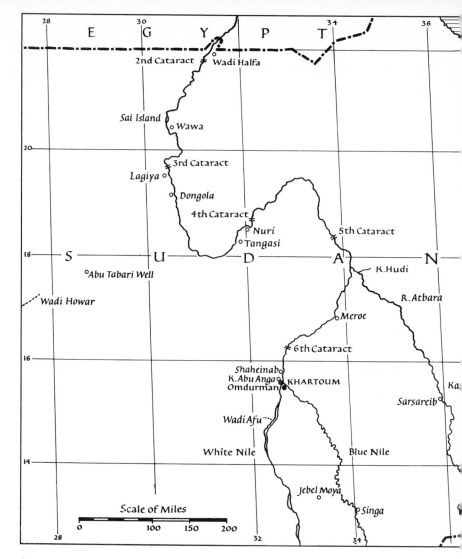

Map 13. Stone Age sites in the Sudan.

pottery known so far in Africa and which may even be the earliest in the world. The stone industry has many microlithic tools, including quartz lunates and larger crescents, along with a few trapezoids or transverse (chisel-ended) arrowheads that were widely used in Mesolithic Europe and in Neolithic and Dynastic Egypt (it is not known for certain whether the transverse arrowheads came from the Mesolithic level at Khartoum). There are long, narrow backed blades merging into crescents, borers, and crude scrapers, but burins are rare and atypical.

Pebbles and pieces of sandstone were found with a keel around part of the circumference, left standing after the top and bottom had been worn away by grinding; some of these grinders were stained with ocher. There are also disk grinders, with a circular depression on each face that in some cases met to form a hole through the middle; these may have been used for grinding ocher in the initial stages, but after the hole through the middle had formed, they could have been used as clubheads. No complete rings were found; they were always broken, and no two pieces fitted together. Sandstone rubbers were probably used for working bone and wood. Other small sandstone pebbles had a groove around the middle, which may have been fishing-line sinkers (Fig. 35). No fish hooks were found at Khartoum, though there were many at Neolithic Shaheinab. *Ampullaria* shell was, however, abundant in the occupation layers. This snail is never eaten by modern Nilotes, but is used as bait for fishing. This fact, along with bone harpoons and grooved "sinkers," supports the obvious inference that the people living on the banks of the Nile in Mesolithic times were fishermen.

Impressions on pottery show that fiber had been plaited into cord, which might have been used for fishing nets as well as for bowstrings. Wattle was made from reeds laid parallel and held together by cross-strands and then daubed with clay.

Some of the harpoon heads or spearheads have at least four barbs on one side of the shaft. Of the 270 or so fragments recovered, all except three are barbed on only one side. Many of the butts of these broken harpoon heads have from four to eight grooves to hold the cord to bind them to the shaft, while a very few others are bored through the base of a barb. Fragments of bone arrowheads, too small to have been spearheads, were also recovered.

Numerous small clay balls and other objects may have been toys, and some were perhaps parts of figurines (one suggests the head of a crocodile or a hippo). No complete pots were found, but there were many sherds with a wavy-line decoration, which Arkell found could be produced by combing with the spine of a catfish; prepared combs made from such spines were found on the site (Fig. 35). A later version of the pottery combined wavy-line decoration and dots impressed afterward by the rocker technique (Fig. 36). A few sherds had a red slip made from ocher. Some of the bowls had more or less conical bases and had been built up by the coil technique.

The most easterly site where pottery with wavy-line decoration has

Figure 35. Fishing equipment and "comb" for decorating pottery, Khartoum Mesolithic: (a) fishing-line sinker; (b) barbed bone spearhead; (c) spine of modern catfish; (d) potter's comb made from spine of catfish.

been found is at Kassala, directly east of Khartoum, on the main route through the hills to the Red Sea. West of Khartoum, similar sites are known in northern Darfur, and dotted wavy-line pottery was found near Wadi Howar; recently it has also been discovered at Lake Wanyanga, Ounianga Kebir, in Chad, a thousand miles west of Khartoum. It has also been reported from the Hoggar, another thousand miles farther west, where it has been dated by carbon-14 to about 5400 B.C. The simpler wavy-line pottery without dots is apparently confined to the Nile Valley near Khartoum; it seems very likely that it was invented in this area, perhaps as the result of accidental burning of mud-lined baskets. Most of the pots of Mesolithic Khartoum imitate baskets, and Arkell has pointed out that the Shilluk—who, a few centuries ago, lived as far north as Khartoum—still line baskets with mud to prevent seeds from falling through the holes. He suggests that pottery was invented before 8000 B.C. along the Upper Nile, from where it spread northwestward across the Sahara and thence to the Mediterranean, following the same route as he envisages being taken by bone harpoons from equatorial Africa.[111]

The Sahara, of course, was relatively well watered at that time. Animal remains from Mesolithic Khartoum such as the extinct reed rat *Thryonomys* indicate that the climate was then considerably wetter than it is today. Reed rats live only where there is a thick covering of reeds, conditions which certainly do not exist near Khartoum at the present time. Remains of the Nile lechwe and a water mongoose also imply swamps in the vicinity. It has been estimated that the Nile at high flood was then 10 meters higher than today (rather than 4 meters higher, as originally published). At Lake Wanyanga, too, the climate at the time of the settlements associated with dotted wavy-line pottery must have been much wetter. Bones of large fish and crocodiles, as well as remains of antelopes and elephants, imply that there was a fresh-water lake or river nearby, whereas today the lake is salt. Communication between the Tibesti area and the Nile was

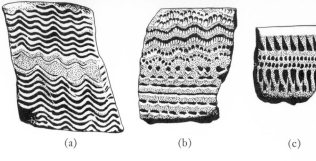

Figure 36. Sherds of (a) wavy-line; (b) dotted wavy-line pottery, Khartoum Mesolithic; (c) sherd with cuneiform impressions, Shaheinab/ Neolithic.

(a)   (b)   (c)

probably fairly easy at that time, and pottery traditions were apparently diffused over long distances.

Probably the oldest-known representatives of the Negroid stock in East Africa come from Mesolithic Khartoum. Here Arkell discovered some tightly contracted burials that had been much disturbed and their bones badly broken. The bones were heavily coated with kunkar after the disturbance had taken place (kunkar is a concretion of calcium carbonate, believed to form only when the annual rainfall is less than 20 inches). It is practically certain that these bones are contemporary with the Mesolithic culture, since one skull was resting on a pillow of wavy-line pottery.

Only one skull was sufficiently well preserved to permit restoration. It is long and narrow, with a long and very wide face. The nose is wide and flat at the bridge, though the nasal bones are narrow. In Derry's report of this skull, he points out that the arrangement of the teeth shows parallelism, often seen in Negroids and associated with subnasal prognathism, contrasting with the horseshoe-shaped dental arch of other races. The mandible is massive and the ascending ramus is wide and low, another well-recognized Negro feature. Along with a skull from Asselar, 200 miles northeast of Timbuktu, which may date from approximately the same period, the Khartoum skull is thought to be the earliest recognizable Negro in Africa.

The Kenya Capsian

The Kenya Capsian has been one of the most controversial of all cultures in East Africa. This was due to the fact that Leakey dated the whole of it to the time of the Gamblian pluvial and it is thus presumably Pleistocene in age. It now seems almost certain that, while the Lower Kenya Capsian appears during the Gamblian and may have begun as early as about 30,000 B.C., the Upper Kenya Capsian is either very late Pleistocene or more probably Post-Pleistocene and contemporary with typical Mesolithic industries elsewhere.

The lower stages of this blade-and-burin culture are comparable with the earliest Upper Paleolithic recognized recently in the Middle East, such as the Baradostian of Iran and the Antelian of Iraq. The former has been dated to about 34,000 B.C. by carbon-14. Even more recently, a surprisingly early carbon-14 date of 35,000 B.C. has been obtained for the Upper Paleolithic Dabba culture of Libya, named after Hagfet ed Dabba, or the "Cave of the Hyena," in the Gebel Akhdar Hills of Cyrenaica. In France, the earliest Upper Paleolithic of the Dordogne, Perigordian I, appears about 30,000 B.C. and the Aurignacian somewhat later.

At first the Kenya Capsian was called the Kenya Aurignacian, but later it was renamed, since its affinities were thought to be closer to the Capsian of North Africa. This should have given a clue to the true age of the Upper Kenya Capsian. The Capsian, named after Gafsa (Latin: *Capsa*) in Tunisia, is essentially a culture of the high plateaus, characterized by the use of blades, burins, microliths, and bone tools. Its "Mesolithic" aspects have long been recognized, and carbon-14 dated the "*Capsien typique*" to 6450 B.C. ± 400 years.

Miss Caton-Thompson believed that the North African Capsian and the Kenya Capsian are unrelated, their resemblances being attributed to convergent evolution.[112] Leakey, on the other hand, thought that the Kenya Capsian reached East Africa from Palestine, via Arabia and land connections over the Bab-el-Mandeb Strait at the southern end of the Red Sea; and that from East Africa it spread northwestward across the Sahara to Tunisia. With the new evidence from carbon-14, it appears that the problem resolves into two separate parts: one, the origin of the Lower Kenya Capsian; two, the connections, if any, between the Upper Kenya Capsian and the Capsian of North Africa. In fact, it might be less confusing to refer to the Lower stage as "Kenya Aurignacian," as originally proposed, and to restrict the term "Kenya Capsian" to its much later Upper stage.

Leakey's theory that the Lower Kenya Capsian arrived from Palestine was, of course, the result of Professor Garrod's discovery in 1937 of backed blades and burins among Late Acheulian levels at the cave of Et Tabun, Mt. Carmel. This "Pre-Aurignacian," or Amudian, as it is now called, dates from the time of the Last Interglacial and hence is earlier than 70,000 B.C. Later, Rust also found a roughly contemporary blade-and-burin industry between Late Acheulian horizons at Jabrud in Syria. It therefore seemed logical to suppose that the Upper

Paleolithic originated somewhere in this region and that the efficient tools associated with it should spread rapidly. More recently still, McBurney has discovered a Libyan "Pre-Aurignacian," dating from the Last Interglacial, probably at least from 100,000 B.C., in the cave of Haua Fteah in Cyrenaica. It is thought that this industry was derived from southwestern Asia. So, if the Kenya Capsian is derived rather than autochonous, it might have come either directly from southwestern Asia, or from a secondary source in North Africa.

The Kenya Capsian is known mainly in the Kenya Rift Valley and northern Tanganyika and so occupies a very limited area. It is intimately associated with Stillbay industries, a situation that seems somewhat similar to the *Blattspitzenkultur* of central Europe, where there

Map 14. Sites in the Kenya Rift Valley (detail from Map 7).

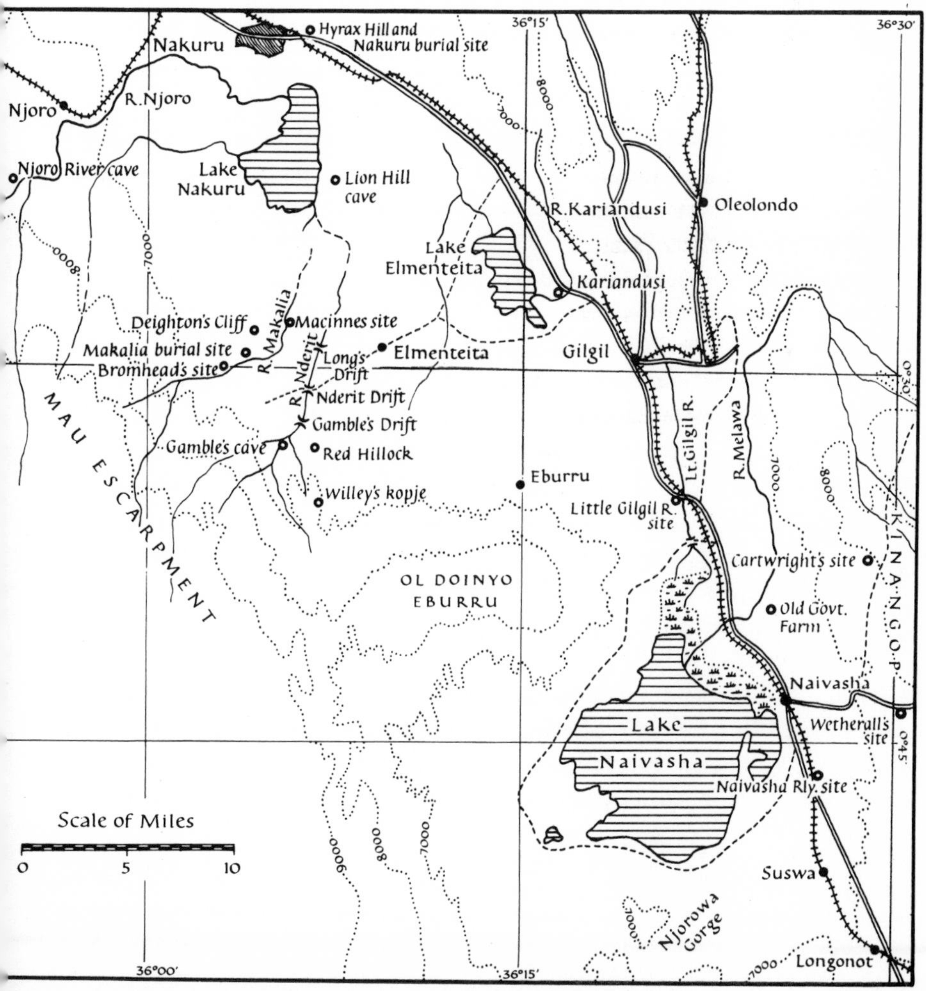

is an association of bifacial tools and blade tools. There is at least a possibility that some of the Stillbay and Kenya Capsian industries of the rift valley may be part and parcel of the same culture, rather than separate industries made by contemporary but different peoples.

Whether movements from southwestern Asia or from North Africa did take place can only be proved by discoveries of Lower Kenya Capsian-like industries in the intervening areas, which so far have not been found. In northwestern Somaliland the Hargeisan blade-and-burin industry with microliths also contains elements adopted from the underlying Stillbay industries. The Hargeisan is apparently contemporary with the Magosian of the central and southern parts of the plateau, and is therefore too late in time to have any bearing on possible southward movements of Lower Kenya Capsian people from southwest Asia to Kenya. Evidence from the coast of Somaliland indicates that there was a fall in sea level in early Gamblian times, and it seems quite likely that there was a land connection with Arabia at this period (it is estimated that a fall in sea level of 180 meters would be necessary for there to have been land connections between Arabia and Somaliland over the Bab-el-Mandeb Strait area). It is unlikely, however, that such a connection would have existed later than early Gamblian times. From collections made by Moysey in Ethiopia, Clark concluded that the blade-and-burin influence was greater, and probably earlier, there than in Somaliland.

At Cartwright's Site on the Kinangop Plateau, above the Kenya Rift Valley, there is an industry in deposits dating from the very end of the Kanjeran pluvial, which was called Basal Kenya Capsian since it includes crude backed blades. After this rather doubtful industry comes the Lower Kenya Capsian *in situ* in deposits attributed to the first Gamblian maximum at 'Nderit Drift and in Melawa Gorge, with large backed blades, burins, and end scrapers, but without other tool types such as lunates which are characteristic of the Upper Kenya Capsian.

Four phases of the Upper Kenya Capsian were distinguished: phases A and B were dated by Leakey to the second Gamblian maximum, phase C to the third maximum; while phase D alone he considered to be post-Gamblian. The Gamblian pluvial is now generally estimated to have begun about 40,000 years ago and continued until about 8000 B.C. By the time of the North African Capsian, 6500 B.C., the Kenya Capsian may well have reached phase D; but evidence discussed below suggests that phases A, B, and C may have preceded it

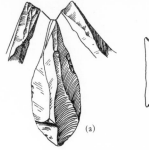

Figure 37. (a) Burin, probably used for grooving arrow shafts to hold; (b) lunate, used as a barb. Views of each side of the chisel-ended top of the burin are also shown. Upper Kenya Capsian, Gamble's Cave.

by not more than two thousand years, rather than tens of thousands of years, as Leakey supposed.

The Upper Kenya Capsian is one of the most widespread and best known of all the Stone Age cultures of the Kenya rift. It was divided into four phases, not because there is any marked difference in the typology of the implements, nor in their numerical proportions, but because of a gradual improvement in workmanship between phases A and B, followed by a slight degeneration in phase C, while in phase D there is more evolved pottery. The industries are found on the surface of Gamblian lake terraces and also in stratified rock shelters such as the type site, Gamble's Cave II (Map 14). Other sites include Little Gilgil River Site (where Upper Kenya Capsian and Stillbay artifacts exist side by side), 'Nderit Drift, Melawa Gorge, Kabete, and Naivasha Railway Rock Shelter (phase D). Upper Kenya Capsian industries have also been found near Kisumu in western Kenya and in northern Tanganyika—for example, at Olduvai.

Leakey's excavations at Gamble's Cave II between 1926 and 1929 revealed four main prehistoric occupation levels, as well as two modern ones. The cave—actually a rock shelter—is reached after a fairly steep climb on land formerly belonging to a Mr. Gamble, a few miles past 'Nderit Drift, where the road from Elementeita Station (no longer in use) to Mau Narok crosses the 'Nderit River. The shelter was cut into thick Kanjeran deposits by the waters of the Gamblian lake. At the present time, Lake Nakuru is 12 miles distant and 510 feet below Gamble's Cave.

The total thickness of deposits excavated was 28 feet. The prehistoric occupation levels were divided from each other by rock debris fallen from the roof of the shelter. Between the Elmenteitan and "Stillbay" levels was red, wind-blown sand, said to represent the Gamblian-Makalian dry interval, and above the Elmenteitan level was another layer of aeolian sand, said to represent the Makalian-Nakuran interval. If a Post-Pleistocene date for the underlying Upper Kenya Capsian occupations is accepted, the lower sand might be taken to represent a drier period between the two Makalian maxima rather than the Gamblian-Makalian dry interval.

Artifacts in the "Stillbay" level, layer 10, consisted only of "a few flakes and broken tools of Kenya Stillbay type,"[113] which might perhaps have been made or even collected by the Upper Kenya Capsians rather than representing a true Stillbay occupation of the shelter. Upper Kenya Capsian phase C was associated with burials in layer 11. The fourth prehistoric occupation, Upper Kenya Capsian phases A and B, occurs in layer 14. This had a thickness of 10 feet, consisting of ash, dust, bones, and obsidian fragments, as well as numerous fish remains. Evidently the edge of the lake must have been fairly close at that time, but it could have been some 150 feet below the shelter rather than at the actual level of the shelter; in this case, the lake would have been at 375 feet above its present level rather than 510 feet. Leakey has stated that the lake was at 375 feet both at the time of the third Gamblian maximum and during the Makalian wet phase. Hence the Upper Kenya Capsian occupation might well date from either of these periods rather than from the time of the second Gamblian maximum, when Lake Nakuru stood at 510 feet.

Although the line dividing the lower layers containing Upper Kenya Capsian phases A and B is purely arbitrary, there was said to be a gradual evolution of workmanship of the tools from bottom to top. As in the very much earlier Lower Perigordian of the Dordogne, the characteristic implements are backed blades, burins or gravers, and end scrapers. Lunates, which are lacking in the Perigordian but present in the Capsian of North Africa, are very common. Nearly all the tools at Gamble's Cave are made of obsidian, which gives a very sharp cutting edge (a thin blade of obsidian will shave a man as closely as a razor). Blades are made on long, narrow flakes with one edge left sharp and the other "backed" by removing small flakes to form a blunt surface on which the fingers can be pressed without getting injured (see Fig. 42). These blades were probably put to as many uses as our own penknives—for example, for woodworking, for skinning game, and for cutting off pieces of meat. Most of the blades are of Lower Perigordian ("Châtelperronian") type, with one edge straight and the other curved; narrow, pointed blades are much rarer.

Burins (see Fig. 37) are common and exist in many forms, such as angle burins, single- and double-blow burins, and so on. These tools are very common in the Upper Paleolithic of Western Europe, where their main use must have been for woodworking, though no doubt they also served for engraving designs on bone and rock faces. These tools are produced by striking a special blow on the side of a blade held obliquely, resulting in the removal of a flake from the side of the blade and leaving the tool with a chisel end.

Some crescent-shaped tools are fairly large and may be variations of the backed blade, but the majority are quite small, ranging from an inch to less than half an inch in length. These are known as lunates (Fig. 37) and have the straight edge untrimmed, while the thicker, rounded edge is backed. There can be little doubt as to what these lunates were; they must have served as barbs for harpoons, spears, or arrows, set into grooves in a wooden shaft. The grooves must have been made by hollowing out the wood with the aid of burins.

On two occasions, once at Gamble's Cave and again on a hill near

Figure 38. Upper Kenya Capsian man shooting an arrow barbed with lunates.

Kikuyu Station, Leakey found lunates lying in such a position that there could be no doubt that they had been hafted in this way. Lunates have been found actually in position in bone points in Denmark, and at Stellmoor, in Germany, they were hafted into pinewood shafts.

At Capsian sites in North Africa they have occasionally been found inserted into bone shafts. Very likely one of their main uses was to impale fish at Gamble's Cave, though they may possibly have been used also as arrowheads for hunting land animals. The introduction of the bow and arrow, of course, marked a tremendous step in man's progress, but the time when this weapon was first invented is most uncertain. It has been suggested that the smaller tanged points of the Aterians of the Sahara and North Africa may have been arrowheads, though most of them are far too heavy and clumsy to have been used in this way and were more likely spearheads. Giving the Upper Kenya Capsians the benefit of the doubt, one of them is shown shooting an arrow made from six lunates set on opposite sides of the shaft in Fig. 38.

Artifacts with one, two, or sometimes three edges showing signs of wear or battering are known as "fabricators." These were used for

Figure 39. Tools for leather dressing: (a) end scraper; (b) sinew frayer; (c) bone awls. Upper Kenya Capsian, Gamble's Cave.

(b)

(c)

(a)

pressing off small flakes in the manufacture of the various tools. Cores are always very small, probably because obsidian had to be fetched from some distance and as much as possible of the material was used to avoid wastage; the only two obsidian mines known in this part of the rift valley are on Eburru Mountain and in the side of Njorowa Gorge, and a steep climb is involved in order to reach either of them. Large flakes first removed from the cores produced bigger tools, such as scrapers; afterward, small, narrow flakes were detached to form the smaller blades, lunates, and so on, leaving typical "blade cores."

Scrapers are of various kinds, the commonest being round-ended ones made on blades, the ends trimmed by the removal of tiny flakes. Stone scrapers are ubiquitous from Paleolithic times right through the Neolithic and continued even into the metal ages in many parts of the world. Some were almost certainly used mainly for dressing hides, even as the Eskimo continue to use them today, generally hafted into handles of various kinds. Tools have been found which Leakey calls "sinew frayers" (Fig. 39); they are blades with the working edge rough and irregular. They could have been used to fray animal sinews or vegetable fibers to make into thread for sewing leather garments or bags (alternatively, they might have been used as saws for.wood-working; Bushmen used flakes with serrated edges in this way in the past). A number of bone awls were found at Gamble's Cave that were probably used for punching holes in leather prior to sewing. They are mostly made from small bird bones, with one end polished to a point, but others are made from splinters of mammal bone (Fig. 39).

In Europe, finds of stone tools are often supplemented by imple-ments of bone and sometimes of wood, but, while it is inconceivable that Stone Age man would not have made great use of these materials

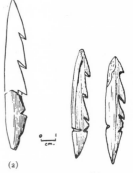

Figure 40. Bone harpoons from Upper Kenya Capsian and Ishan-gian industries; (a) butt-end of bone harpoon from Upper Kenya Capsian level 13, Gamble's Cave; (b) uniserial bone harpoons from tufaceous level, Ishango C.

in Africa too, a tropical climate is not favorable to their preservation. Bone tools would survive only if, for example, they chanced to fall into a lake, as at Ishango, or become buried by a fall from a cave roof. Very few bone tools have been found in East Africa as compared with Europe, where they are often preserved in peat bogs or under similar favorable conditions. In Africa, bones are quickly crunched up by hyenas or nibbled by porcupines unless they are instantly and deeply buried. Wood stands still less chance of preservation since it is com-monly eaten by termites.

Oakley has described the butt end of a bone harpoon from level 13 in Gamble's Cave II, which, according to Leakey, separates phase C from phase B. It is remarkably similar to bone harpoons from the late phase (C) of the Ishangian culture from the western shore of Lake

Edward. Both the Ishangian harpoons and the Gamble's Cave specimen have a V-shaped notch below the basal barb, which presumably served for the attachment of the line (Fig. 40). The bone harpoon, with the presence of pottery and ostrich eggshell beads, strongly suggests that the Upper Kenya Capsian is Post-Pleistocene in age, comparable with the Khartoum Mesolithic, which also includes bone harpoons and rather similar pottery.[114]

Many fragments of red ocher were interspersed all through the deposits; one large pebble had an impression worn by constant rubbing with another pebble (which was also recovered), both of them stained with red ocher. The stones had obviously been used for pulverizing the ocher, which was used extensively in connection with burial ceremonies and presumably also for decorating the body and face and perhaps the hair, as Masai warriors use it today. Ocher in the hair is not only considered chic but is said to prevent infestation by vermin.

Other decorative articles include beads made of perforated disks of ostrich eggshell and occasionally hippo ivory. They are of irregular shape, sometimes drilled from one side only, sometimes from both sides. Many had obviously been threaded, as there are signs of rubbing on both sides. Others (always of shell stained a dark color) are rough and unpolished on one side, but highly rubbed on the other surface; possibly they were sewn on leather clothing as ornaments. Bored pendants made from fresh-water mollusk shells are sometimes decorated with little rows of dots. The Turkana of the Northern Province of Kenya still wear beads of ostrich eggshell, which are also common among Bushmen. The latter used to rub beads of ostrich eggshell along a groove in a stone slab to reduce them all to the same size.

One of the most unexpected discoveries made at Gamble's Cave was sherds of pottery; at the time of the excavations, pottery had not been found in sites earlier than the Neolithic, though since then it has turned up at numerous Mesolithic sites. Two of the sherds were found *in situ* in the fourth prehistoric occupation level, and several others,

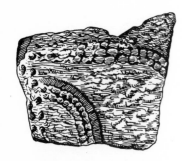

Figure 41. Potsherd of Upper Kenya Capsian, Gamble's Cave.

which might possibly have dropped from higher levels, turned up in the riddles. One of the pieces was considered by Leakey to show unmistakable signs of having been made by smearing clay on the inside of a basket, which got baked, perhaps accidentally; the basketwork impression can be clearly seen (Fig. 41). Arkell informs me, however, that he does not believe that the clay was smeared on a basket, but that the pottery was decorated to simulate basketwork. He considers that the Gamble's Cave pottery belongs to the Mesolithic Khartoum pottery group, tentatively dated to about 7000 B.C. A second piece of pottery is thicker and very rough; when cleaned in water it started to disintegrate, which explains why so few pieces were found. The sherds are quite unlike those of the higher levels in Gamble's Cave.

Phase C of the Upper Kenya Capsian is represented in the third occupation level in Gamble's Cave by comparatively few implements; these appear to be of a lower standard of workmanship than those of phase B, though the types of tool are similar. In the phase-C level were found the human remains described on pp. 266–269.

A fourth phase (D) of the Upper Kenya Capsian has been recognized from the Naivasha Railway Site, associated with a human skeleton; here the tools are more microlithic, including a high proportion of micro-burins, and fragments of more evolved pottery were also found. This phase was dated to the Makalian wet period and was perhaps contemporary with the Elmenteitan culture, described later.

The Makalian wet phase is estimated to have lasted from about 5500 to 2500 B.C., though its first stage may possibly have begun earlier; such a period is comparable with carbon-14 dates for Capsian industries in North Africa. In the North African Capsian, as in phase D of the Upper Kenya Capsian, there is a microlithic phase—that is, the majority of tools become very small. A microlith may be defined as a thin flake, blunted on one or both edges by secondary working, but devoid of secondary working on either of the flat faces. In Africa these diminutive implements have a wide distribution during the L. S. A., and in Europe they are common in Mesolithic industries; their remarkable spread is one of the most striking features of this period.

Microliths must always have been hafted to form composite tools, held in place in the shaft by some natural gum or resin. Fishermen with barbed harpoons and hunters in possession of bows and arrows would have such an immense superiority over their contemporaries that it can well be imagined that the revolutionary idea would not take long to spread in Africa south of the Sahara, though the Natufians of Palestine may have had composite tools earlier.

Skeletons of the Upper Kenya Capsians

Gamble's Cave II yielded parts of five skeletons of the makers of the Upper Kenya Capsian, phase C. The skeletons were buried 14 feet beneath the present surface of the ground. The top occupation layer, it will be remembered, contained implements of the Elmenteitan culture; the second was associated with the Kenya Stillbay. It was at the base of this layer that the first three fragmentary skeletons were found in 1927, but the subsequent discovery of two better-preserved skeletons made it apparent that all the burials were the makers of Upper Kenya Capsian phase C, which occurred in the third occupation layer. The burials were found in level 11, overlying and clearly later than level 13, which contained the bone harpoon. One of the skeletons was taken to England for study, still embedded in the hard matrix in which it was found.

The bodies were laid on the right side (with one exception) and the knees were drawn up to the chin in the ultracontracted position, with the face turned toward the opening of the rock shelter. The back of the corpse had been pushed up against the wall, and big stones had been placed over and around the body. Traces of red ocher were found in the surrounding earth and had evidently been used to decorate the bodies. This custom was prevalent in the Upper Paleolithic, Mesolithic, and Neolithic in many areas, even as far as eastern Siberia.

The Upper Kenya Capsian people were very tall, over 5 feet, 10 inches, and had long, narrow skulls with prominent chins and noses (see Fig. 44[a]). They are apparently of Mediterranean Caucasoid type, and have been called "Proto-Hamites" to emphasize their resemblance to the present inhabitants of North Africa and the Horn (it will be remembered that the term "Hamite," often used to describe North and northeast African people with marked racial characteristics, should, strictly speaking, apply to a language group only).

Skeleton No. 4 from Gamble's Cave was an individual of about twenty-five years of age, probably male (Fig. 44[a]). The greater part of the skull and face is preserved, though they are slightly warped and suffered from crushing; the mandible is intact and very well preserved. The superciliary ridges are poorly developed and the occipital region projects markedly. The face is of medium length and great width, and there is no subnasal prognathism, as is usual in Negro skulls, but instead a marked orthognathism. The nose is very long and fairly wide. The mandible is lightly built, with a slight chin, and the palate is very deep.

The body of skeleton No. 5 lay on the left side instead of the right and was not in an ultracontracted position. The individual is thought to have been a young man of about twenty. The greater part of the skull and face is intact and the mandible is in good condition. The cranial index is about 73 (that of skeleton No. 4 is about 71 and the occipital region does not project, as in No. 4. The top of the skull is comparatively flat, and the forehead is well developed. The face is, again, long and orthognathous, and the nose is very long. The palate is wide, though not very long, and is shallow, unlike that of No. 4. The chin is well developed but the mandible is not very massive.

In 1940 Mrs. Leakey excavated a prehistoric living site, which was about to be destroyed by a new alignment of the railway, at the base of a cliff a few miles from Naivasha. In one of the pits dug out by the railway contractors, some human bones were noticed, and excavations determined the exact position of the skeleton in relation to the known sequence of deposits containing implements. Further parts of the skull and skeleton were recovered *in situ* in lake silts; there was no sign of a grave, and if one had existed it must have been a shallow one by the lake shore; or possibly the individual was drowned, since the bones were widely dispersed.

Although reasons have been given for considering Upper Kenya Capsian phases A to C to be Post-Pleistocene, and D as later still, the dating evidence according to the excavator is as follows. The skeleton was attributed to the end of Gamblian times, both on stratigraphical evidence and because of the associated culture. The 200-foot beach of Lake Naivasha, which is banked against the cliff behind the site, was dated to the second peak of the Gamblian pluvial, since rolled tools of so-called "Developed Levalloisian" type were found in the beach. The silts containing the skeleton were 33.5 feet below the highest point of the beach; since the highest beach of the succeeding Makalian wet phase does not go above 120 feet in this area, the skeleton was dated to between the second Gamblian peak and the end of that period.[115]

The skeleton is that of a male, about fifty years of age. Of the skull, the left half of the face is missing and the right half is incomplete, with the nasal bones and the upper part of the maxilla lacking, and only part of the mandible is present. The right maxilla has only one tooth, a very worn first molar, all the others having been lost in life; many of the teeth in the lower jaw were also lost before death. The mandible is small, but thick and strongly built, and the chin is well developed, though not large. The cranium is very long and narrow, with a cranial index of 64.5.

Both the Gamble's Cave skeletons and the Naivasha skeleton show marked resemblances to one found at Olduvai that is apparently contemporary with them. This skeleton was the first Paleolithic human remains to be found in Africa south of the Sahara. As a result of the accidental discovery of Olduvai Gorge in 1911 by a German scientist, an expedition was sent there in 1913 under the leadership of the late Dr. Hans Reck. Not only did he bring back to Berlin a large number of fossil mammals from Olduvai, but he also discovered a nearly complete human skeleton embedded in the top of what is now known as Bed II. Dr. Reck was convinced that the skeleton, which is obviously *Homo sapiens*, was contemporary with the fossil fauna from Bed II, which included many extinct forms.

The outbreak of the First World War prevented the matter from being settled for many years. During Leakey's third archaeological expedition in 1931–32, however, he visited Olduvai accompanied by Reck to try to determine whether the skeleton was in fact contemporary with the extinct fauna of Bed II, or whether it represented an intrusive burial into the deposit. It was finally established that the skeleton had been buried in the top of Bed II after erosion had removed the whole of Beds III and IV in that particular locality. It was, however, beneath deposits laid down just before the formation of Bed V, which consists of redeposited material from Bed III. An industry belonging to Upper Kenya Capsian Phase C was found at several places in this same horizon, indicating that the Olduvai skeleton is contemporaneous with those from Gamble's Cave.

While the skull and face resemble the Upper Kenya Capsian people from Gamble's Cave, the mandible is more like the later Elmenteitan people from Bromhead's Site, so that Olduvai Man seems to form a link between the two. The burial was again in the contracted position;

again, too, the man was tall (over 5 feet, 10½ inches) and had a very long head and particularly long face, while the nose must have been very prominent. The lower jaw and chin are massive and the palate has a high arch.

Comparisons with Upper Paleolithic Man in Europe

Before leaving the Upper Kenya Capsians we should glance briefly at their rather similar predecessors living in Europe during the last glacial period. Some of the Upper Paleolithic people who invaded Western Europe during the early phase of Middle Würm, about 30,000 B.C., may have come from the direction of southwestern Asia. First are the Combe Capelle people, makers of the earliest Upper Paleolithic culture, formerly known as "Châtelperronian" but now included in the Perigordian. Movius recognized five stages of the Aurignacian, developing in parallel with the Perigordian industries of the Dordogne, Perigordian I being earlier than Aurignacian I; the terms "Châtelperronian" and "Gravettian" have generally been abandoned in the Dordogne. The Combe Capelle people are the earliest known representatives of modern *Homo sapiens* in Europe, apart from the Swanscombe, Steinheim, and Fontéchevade fossils, which are thought to be ancestral both to *Homo sapiens* and to the Neanderthalers (see Table 3). They were followed by the Aurignacians of Grimaldi and by the robust Cro-Magnons, associated with Aurignacian and "Gravettian" industries. The Cro-Magnons are divisible into a dolichocephalic eastern, or Prêdmost, type (which is very close to Combe Capelle), and a broadheaded western type, the Cro-Magnons proper. After them came the Magdalenians, known from Chancelade. All these people may have appeared in Western Europe within a period of about fifteen thousand years.

The skulls from Gamble's Cave, the Naivasha Rock Shelter, and Olduvai are rather similar to the much earlier large-brained Combe Capelle type, who are more "modern" in appearance than the later Cro-Magnons. The Cro-Magnons resemble the type represented at sites in Algeria, notably at Mechta el Arbi and Afalou Bou Rhummel, where they are associated with the early blade culture known as the Oranian. This well-known type, of which numerous skeletons have been found, probably dates from about 15,000 B.C., and is thus presumably intermediate in age between the Cro-Magnons and the Gamble's Cave people. The Mechta skulls are characterized by a strong development of the supraorbital ridges and in general by rugged muscularity. They are very similar to those of the extinct Guanches of the Canaries, who were probably a late survival of the same physical type.

The Elmenteitan Culture

The Elmenteitan culture seems to be unique to the Kenya Rift Valley and has therefore been given a local name. It probably develops directly out of the Upper Kenya Capsian during the Makalian wet phase and the type site is also Gamble's Cave.

There are lunates, end scrapers, and bone awls in the Elmenteitan as in the Kenya Capsian, as well as a few burins. The lunates are more symmetrical and better made, though the rarity of burins is remarkable. Although a few degenerate backed blades are found in the Elmenteitan, the commonest and most typical tools are long, two-edged blades (Fig. 42). In some cases the thick butt or bulb of percussion had been trimmed away, presumably to facilitate hafting into handles, so that the blades could conveniently be used as knives. They vary from about 3 to 6 inches in length and from 1½ to less than ½ inch wide. The material is obsidian and the edges are very sharp indeed.

Another difference between the Upper Kenya Capsian and the Elmenteitan is in the type of fabricator. Whereas those of the earlier culture are made from long, narrow blades, triangular in cross section (with a broad back and the opposite edge thin), those of the Elmen-

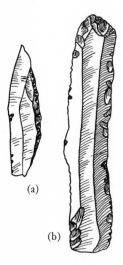

(a)

(b)

Figure 42. (a) Backed-blade, Upper Kenya Capsian and (b) two-edged blade, Elmenteitan Gamble's Cave.

teitan culture are square-shaped with a rectangular cross section. This same type occurs in the "Gravettian" of France, where the implements are known as *lames écaillées*. The edges have a typical *écrasé*, or abraded appearance, and Leakey proved experimentally that by using such flakes to make other implements he produced just such a scaling of the edges.

In the type site of the Elmenteitan, the top occupation level of Gamble's Cave, a great many potsherds were found. The size ranges from small bowls with a diameter of 4½ inches to huge jars with an estimated diameter of over a foot at the neck. The shape of the pots and the type of rims vary considerably; some pots have pointed bases, others are rounded, and still others are nearly flat. Pointed bases were presumably made so that the pots could be stood between three large stones over a fire, as is done by some modern African tribes. Some pots have holes drilled through either side for attaching cords or sinews as handles. At Bromhead's Site, a few miles from Gamble's Cave, one complete pot was recovered (Fig. 43) that had a simple line of decoration under the rim. At this site the industry was identical with that of Gamble's Cave and was accompanied by human burials described below. An Elmenteitan industry was also found above the Upper Kenya Capsian in Lion Hill Cave on the eastern side of Lake Nakuru. At that time, Lion Hill may have been an island, owing to the rise of the lake; this is suggested by the animal bones, which are all hyrax; presumably they got trapped on the island.

Remains of more than 28 of the makers of the Elmenteitan culture were found at Bromhead's Site (see Map 14). As in the case of the earlier skeletons from Gamble's Cave, most of the Elmenteitan people were tall and dolichocephalic, but they had extremely long faces and were distinctive enough to be spoken of as the "Elmenteitan type." A few of the individuals from Bromhead's Site, however, were much shorter, with mesocephalic or brachycephalic skulls and broader faces, somewhat reminiscent of late M. S. A. skulls from South Africa, especially one from Tuinplaats (Springbok Flats).

Figure 43. Elmenteitan pot, Bromhead's Site.

The geological history of Bromhead's Site is an interesting one. At the beginning of the Makalian wet phase, when the waters of the lake were rising, but before they reached their maximum, big eruptions in the neighborhood caused thick beds of volcanic ash to be laid down; these filled up an existing valley at the spot where Bromhead's Site now stands. As the climate became wetter, moisture caused the volcanic ash to become consolidated and through it the Makalia River cut a gorge. Along the edge of this gorge the Elmenteitan people buried their dead;

Figure 44. (a) Upper Kenya Capsian male, Gamble's Cave; (b) Elmenteita A male, Bromhead's Site; (c) Elmenteita Fl female, Bromhead's Site; (d) Gumban A male, Willey's Kopje.

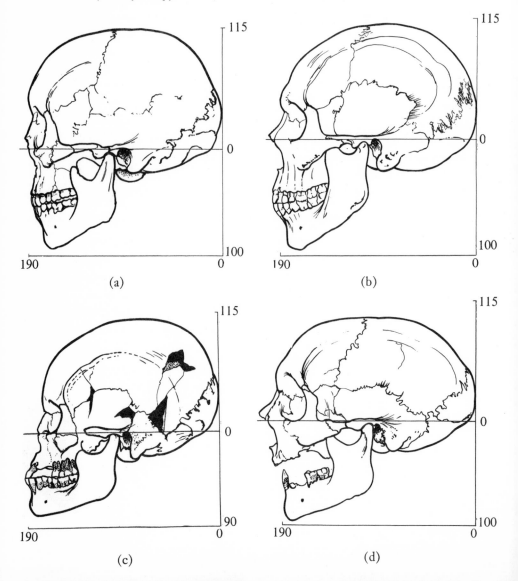

the bodies were put into crevices in the rock face and a few large stones were piled up in front. The site of the burials is 30 feet below the maximum level reached by the lake during the Makalian wet phase; as the waters rose, they filled the gorge and covered the bottom of it with stratified silts. The water washed out the bones and redeposited them in the silts; in many cases the skeletons were broken up and scattered, though in others they were held in position by rock slabs. During the decline of the Makalian wet phase and after, the river again scoured out the gorge, washing away most of the lake silts. At certain points, however, masses of rock from the cliff face accumulated over the silts and protected them from further erosion.

Seven of the skulls could be reconstructed, some of which had associated mandibles. In addition, there were 11 fragmentary crania, some of them of infants, and 24 isolated mandibles, some very fragmentary. The individual known as Elmenteita A (see Fig. 44[b]) was a male of about twenty-five to thirty-five years of age; the cranium is long and narrow, with a somewhat receding forehead and strongly marked superciliary ridges. The face is long and wide and the nose must have been very long and broad. The orbits are small and somewhat rectangular. The mandible is very large and massive, with the chin strongly developed, and the palate is large. Elmenteita D is a female of the same type as A. The skull of Elmenteita B is larger and broader than that of A, and the mastoids are larger; the face is very similar to A and they represent essentially the same type. Two females, F and F_1 (see Fig. 44[c]), are very like the male B. The skull F_1 shows traces of having been burned, possibly in a ceremony before the slab was placed over it. Although none of the other more complete skulls show traces of burning, among the many other skull fragments are several which are heavily calcined. Elmenteita F_1 is a brachycephalic skull with bulging parietal bosses. The mandible is small but stockily built, with a well-pronounced chin.

Chapter Ten

FOOD PRODUCTION

The change from a hunting economy to one of food production is the essential difference between Paleolithic and Mesolithic stages and the Neolithic. Such a change implies a settled mode of life, in villages or even towns (as at Jericho), although of course the life of pastoral peoples, while "Neolithic" in the sense that they keep stock, is anything but settled. The change must have been a very gradual one, and hunting continued to be important not only for meat but also as a source of supply of raw materials such as hides and bone for making clothing and implements. In its early stages, primitive agriculture, first by reaping wild grasses and afterward by planting their seeds and harvesting them, could not have revolutionized man's diet to any great extent.

The domestication of animals, also, must have been a gradual process, and at first they were probably too precious to have been killed for food except on ceremonial occasions. East African pastoralists today regard their stock with esteem and affection, and many tribes— the Masai, for example—use their cattle mainly for the milk and blood;

their reluctance to eat the flesh except for ritual purposes may have its roots in the time when domestic animals were a novelty. Just as the shifting methods of slash-and-burn cultivation are unlikely to leave any traces for posterity, so pastoral nomadism may have been practiced over wide areas and over long periods without our knowing anything about it. Sometimes rock paintings or engravings, notably in the Sahara, reveal the presence of pastoralists; but stratified settlement sites of agriculturalists and stock-keepers, while common in the Middle East, are extremely rare in Africa. Only after the introduction of ironworking do we find evidence of food production, except at a very few sites such as Shaheinab in the Sudan.

This does not mean that some form of vegeculture did not exist—perhaps based mainly on plants with edible roots or tubers—but merely that there is no way of knowing whether such plants were cultivated rather than gathered wild. Probably the earliest agriculturalists in the continent were those of West Africa, perhaps as early as the fifth millennium B.C. As far as cereals are concerned, probably the only ones indigenous to Africa are the millets—sorghum and pearl millet in West Africa; eleusine or finger millet in Ethiopia. The other staple foods of agricultural peoples today were all introduced: the banana and Asian yam from southeastern Asia perhaps two thousand years ago (another kind of yam is indigenous in West Africa); and maize, cassava, and sweet potatoes from America. After the introduction of the banana and the yam, and with the simultaneous production of iron tools, agriculturalists were able to spread into the wetter, more forested areas. It has been suggested that this was the period of Bantu expansion, from a source area in West Africa, according to linguistic studies (see Map 15).[116]

Apart from evidence of agriculture and domesticated animals, two other criteria of the Neolithic were once thought to be the invention of pottery and the grinding and polishing of stone axes and adzes. It is now clear that both these techniques had already been achieved before a true Neolithic economy. Thus in northern Europe, Mesolithic forest dwellers started to grind the edges of their axes, made crude pottery, and domesticated the dog, though they were still in the food-gathering stage of economy. The Mesolithic Natufians of Palestine had sickles, which they may have used to glean wild grasses. Recent excavations at many sites in the Middle East, particularly at Jericho, have shown that there was a long "prepottery" period during which people lived in sizable towns, kept domesticated goats and sheep, cultivated wheat and barley, but did not make pottery. The pottery of Mesolithic Khartoum may be older than any yet known from the Middle East. The earliest pottery at Jericho, for example, is already relatively elaborate; it is burnished, sometimes with a cream slip and red design and with lug handles. In the Sudan, pottery was first burnished at the time of the Neolithic of Shaheinab, whereas the pottery of Mesolithic Khartoum was never burnished. Pottery is already known in the Upper Kenya Capsian and was fairly elaborate by Elmenteitan times, but polished axes do not appear until later.

The food-gathering stage is sometimes spoken of with contempt, but one writer has championed the pre-Neolithic peoples rather delightfully. "Personally, I have always found 'Food Gatherers' to be more intelligent and versatile than most people in the so-called higher stages of civilization. Food-gatherers for one thing are independent persons who have to think for themselves. . . . There is a lightheartedness about food-gatherers which is not so much in evidence in those who live entirely by agriculture. . . . Day after day he [the farmer] was tied to the same small patch of soil, while the food-gatherer could range the hills, or sail the seas in any direction. Of course the term 'food-gatherer' is absurd when applied to hunters and fishermen and should be confined to people living on winkles and crab-apples."[117] While such people as the East African Wilton C shellfish eaters made little contribution toward the progress of mankind, others, such as the Ishangians, the Upper Kenya Capsians, and the Mesolithic people of Khartoum, with their composite tools and fishing equipment, their basketry and pottery, their love of personal adornment, must be considered as inventive pioneers; it is from their cultures that the Neolithic of the Sudan was directly evolved.

Food growing and animal keeping started somewhere in the uplands of the Middle East before 7500 B.C. in the region where wheat and barley grows wild and where wild goats and sheep are found; recent evidence from Zawi Chemi Shanidar in northern Iraq suggests that domesticated sheep may have been kept as early as 9000 B.C. There is, of course, a tremendous difference in the way of life of pastoral nomads with their flocks and herds and that of settled peasant farmers, and the domestication of plants and animals need not necessarily occur together. In Africa south of the Sahara it is extremely difficult to recognize an agricultural stage, first, because grain cereals were probably rarely cultivated; and, second, because, even if they had been, their chances of preservation are remote. Stone bowls, pestles and mortars probably imply the grinding of vegetable food of some kind; but the possibility that they were used for pulverizing coloring material such as ocher cannot always be ruled out. In Egypt the earliest Neolithic of the Fayum is about 4500 B.C. Arkell's discoveries in the Sudan show that the Neolithic site of Esh Shaheinab existed at least by 3300 B.C. He has suggested that both the Fayum and the Khartoum area received influences from a dispersal area somewhere west of the Nile, an area that probably included Tibesti and Lake Wanyanga. On archaeological grounds he considers that the carbon-14 date of Shaheinab may be too young, as the result of contamination by recent carbon, and that an age of about 4500 B.C., comparable with that of Neolithic Fayum, is more likely. In East Africa the earliest suggestions of a Neolithic way of life (and it must be admitted that the evidence is not very strong) come from the Hyrax Hill variant of the Stone Bowl culture, which is probably considerably later than the Shaheinab Neolithic. In general, however, food production in Africa south of the Nile seems to have started only with ironworking.

The Sudan Neolithic

Esh Shaheinab, which was excavated in 1949, is situated on the west bank of the Nile 30 miles north of Khartoum. The site lies four and a half meters above present high flood level and extends for about 100 yards along a gravel ridge that represents a bank of the Nile in Neolithic times; at that time the river lay half a mile west of the modern bank. Shaheinab was also used as a cemetery during Protodynastic, Meroitic, medieval Christian, and Moslem times, but the Neolithic people were evidently not buried at the settlement, for no human remains of this period were found.

The Neolithic occupation level is characterized by stone gouges, which are also typical of the Fayum Neolithic, and by burnished and incised pottery. Similar gouges and pottery have been found at a number of sites between Jebel Aulia and the Sixth Cataract, and sherds of typical "Shaheinab" pottery have been discovered recently as far west as Lake Wanyanga and Ennedi in the Sahara.

The most characteristic tool, the gouge (Fig. 46), was probably

Figure 45. Stages in making of shell fish hooks, Shaheinab.

used as an adze for woodworking, perhaps mainly for such things as containers rather than for canoes, since reed rafts are more likely to have been used on the Nile. Possibly these gouges may be derived from prototypes in the Late Lupemban and Tshitolian of equatorial Africa, though these are not partially ground like the ones from Shaheinab. Partially ground gouges have also been found at Ténéré, north of Lake Chad, and as far north as Tummo, 250 miles west of Eghei.

As well as stone gouges, there were a number of remarkable partly polished ax heads or adze heads made from the long bones of animals (Fig. 46). They are narrowed at the butt end, presumably for insertion into a wooden handle, while the broad end has a sharp cutting edge made by rubbing on sandstone or other abrasive material. These bone tools may perhaps be the prototypes of polished stone axes and adzes. The people evidently hunted large animals such as hippos, rhinos, and elephants. Having invented bone axes for chopping meat, they went on to produce stone gouges, adzes, and axes for woodworking (in Scandinavia too, bone axes and adzes seem to have been used before stone ones and Eskimos sometimes use bone blades with gougelike edges, bound to wooden handles with sinews, as beaming tools in leather dressing). Other carpenters' tools at Shaheinab include "chisels," planes, and borers; similar types were found in Neolithic Fayum.

Links with early predynastic Egypt are found not only in the pottery

Figure 46. Typical implements of the Shaheinab Neolithic: (a) stone gouge; (b) bone ax head.

(a)   (b)

but also in stone mace heads. A few fragments of disk mace heads were recovered, as well as a flat-topped granite mace head evidently made from an ocher grinder. Most of the ocher grinders were made of sandstone, as in Mesolithic Khartoum. There were also cylindrical stone rubbers, tapering at one or both ends, used for working bone and ivory, as well as fish hooks made from the shell of the Nile oyster. A number of complete hooks were found and many partly finished hooks that showed the various stages of their manufacture (Fig. 45). Several fragments of bone spearheads and harpoons have at least three barbs on one side, with a hole through which the line was passed, while one complete one has two barbs on either side of a cylindrical shaft, with a bulge behind the barbs for the attachment of the line (Fig. 47). Many thousands of lunates made of quartz, chert, and other materials may have been used for arrowheads, but there were no tanged or hollow-based arrowheads as in the Fayum.

In spite of connections with the Fayum and Badari (suggested by stone gouges, mace heads, and pottery), Arkell believes the Shaheinab culture was more closely connected with the west than with Egypt. This theory he bases on the presence of beads made of green Amazon stone (microcline felspar), the source of which is most likely to have been in the Eghei Mountains, north of Tibesti. Amazon-stone beads are also known in the Fayum, the material again apparently having been brought from Tibesti. Incised potsherds and gouges have also been found near Tibesti, and excavations in a painted rock shelter at Delibo in that area revealed dotted wavy-line pottery as in the oldest levels of Mesolithic Khartoum, followed by burnished dotted wavy-line pottery exactly like that of Shaheinab. Arkell believes that this area was one of dispersal, and that with increasing desiccation in the western desert, people would tend to move eastward toward the Nile Valley, probably along the Ennedi route (Map 15).

Although importation of Amazon stone to Shaheinab necessarily implies a movement toward the east, hunter-traders probably wandered

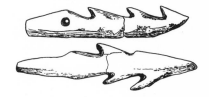

Figure 47. Fishing equipment from the Shaheinab. Neolithic: (top) bone harpoon; (bottom) bone spearhead.

between the two areas in both directions. The Ishangians may have traded their bone harpoons; and the Upper Kenya Capsians might have spread the idea of spearheads or arrowheads barbed with lunates northward into the Sudan, from whence the invention might have been carried westward toward Tibesti and then north to the Constantine Plateau.

No complete pots were found at Shaheinab, but there were many sherds. A very few were of the dotted wavy-line variety, as in Mesolithic Khartoum, and all the pottery of the Neolithic "gouge-culture" sites in the Sudan is burnished. Some sherds are plain black, or blackish-gray; others have a red slip; while still others are red burnished ware with a blackened rim. The rims are thicker than the rest of the pot, whereas rims of Mesolithic pots are always thinner. The smaller bowls have a decoration of fine incised lines, or sometimes rows of fine dots, derived from the thin brown ware of Mesolithic Khartoum. The characteristic Neolithic ware (Fig. 36) has a pattern of bands of small cuneiform impressions, alternating with several rows of impressed dots on the larger pots. Some sherds with a finely incised pattern on the black rim are coated with red slip, which ends just below the rim in a dogtooth pattern of alternate red and black triangles. This was presumably an early stage of the black-topped red ware characteristic of Badarian and early predynastic pottery in Egypt.

Although there are no signs of cultivation at Shaheinab, the late Miss D. M. A. Bate believed that the domestication of animals may have taken place in Africa independently of the Near East, since a dwarf goat at Shaheinab may have been derived from Algeria, where a similar type is found at Neolithic sites. Only two per cent of the bones found at Shaheinab were those of domestic animals (goats and possibly sheep). The wild fauna included forest-living types such as the bush duiker and grivet monkey but was mainly typical of steppe conditions (lion, oryx, hare, and ground squirrel). This suggests that patches of forests existed in predominantly steppe country during Neolithic times. The reed rat and Nile lechwe found at Mesolithic Khartoum, implying swamps, had disappeared, and the climate of Neolithic times was probably intermediate between that of the Mesolithic and the semi-desert conditions of today. This evidence of declining rainfall is borne out by flood levels of the Nile, which stood 10 meters and 5 meters higher than at present during Mesolithic and Neolithic times, respectively.

According to carbon-14, the Neolithic occupation dates from about

3300 ± 415 B.C. Owing to the new half-life of carbon-14, calculated since these results were obtained, the age would be a few hundred years older. Arkell considers that the samples of charcoal and shell may well have been contaminated with modern carbon, since they came from loose gravel at a depth of only 6 to 18 inches. The site is on a track much used by cattle watering in the Nile, and the material from the Neolithic level is probably contaminated by their urine, as well as by the roots of the vegetation that grows here during wet seasons. The obvious connections with Neolithic Fayum, particularly in the gouges and Amazon-stone beads, make it seem possible that the date of Shaheinab may be at least a thousand years earlier than the one obtained by carbon-14.

Considerably later than the Neolithic of Shaheinab was the occupation and cemeteries of Jebel Moya, a site 170 miles south of Khartoum between the Blue and White Niles, at one of the few places between the two rivers where permanent water is obtainable. Here Sir Henry (then Mr.) Wellcome started excavations in 1910 that were interrupted by the start of the First World War and unfortunately never continued. Supported by unlimited funds, Wellcome's excavations were on an unprecedented scale; hundreds of workmen were employed, huge sifting machines were installed, and some of the first archaeological air photographs ever taken were obtained by the use of a camera carried by a large kite. Famous archaeologists came and went, seldom remaining for more than one season; the original excavators are now dead and many of the records have been lost. From a mass of incomplete and often conflicting field notes and from vast cases of material brought back to England, F. Addison undertook the formidable task of compiling an account of excavations made twenty-five years earlier, in which he had taken part. This eagerly awaited publication appeared in 1949. Unfortunately, owing to the methods of excavation and the disturbed condition of the burials, no stratified series of artifacts was obtained to throw light on the dating and cultural succession of a site that would have been expected to solve many problems of African archaeology. As Arkell has commented, "A few cubic metres of occupation debris, undisturbed since it was laid down . . . and excavated with knife and brush, will tell more of the history of a village than tons of debris put through sifting machines."

Addison concluded that the site was occupied first about 1000 B.C., continuing through the Napatan Period, when iron was a novelty, and was abandoned before the beginning of the Meroitic Period in the fifth century B.C. (see p. 301). Both Caton-Thompson and Arkell have suggested that material earlier than 1000 B.C. is present, while the latter also believes that burials continued into the Meroitic age and very likely later. The population of Jebel Moya was probably at its maximum during the time of the Kingdom of Kush, when the Sudan was an important power.

Evidence of the earliest occupation is provided by potsherds with impressed decoration made of clay containing mica similar to that found in Mesolithic Khartoum, but the rims are thickened and more sophisticated. Links with Neolithic Shaheinab appear in lip plugs found with many of the burials, as well as in some of the pottery. The lip plugs of Shaheinab are made of zeolite and quartz, but at Jebel Moya they were made of pottery and ivory as well as these materials. Other connections with Shaheinab can be seen in rare bone and ivory celts and flat-topped mace heads. At Jebel Moya, however, there were no stone gouges, Amazon-stone beads, or black-topped red pottery; this supports the evidence that it is later than Shaheinab. The absence of bone harpoons and fish hooks is accounted for by the distance of Jebel Moya from the Nile. Microlithic implements such as trapezoidal arrowheads are fairly common; they do not help much with the dating, since they are already known from Mesolithic Khartoum and continue into dynastic times in Egypt. The same applies to hollow-based arrowheads, found also at many sites in the Nile Valley and over the southern Sahara.

The skeletons from Jebel Moya show that the people were rugged, heavily built Negroes, with enormous mastoid processes and massive jaws. The lower central incisors had been removed, unlike the individual from Mesolithic Khartoum who had had the upper central incisors extracted. Although all the burials show a great diversity of attitudes, most of the earlier ones were oriented in a westerly direction, while the majority of the Napatan graves face toward the east.

The Hyrax Hill Variant of Kenya

In Kenya, the earliest so-called "Neolithic" is represented at Hyrax Hill, a rocky spur half a mile long which rises to 160 feet above the floor of the rift valley south of Nakuru. It is known as the "Hyrax Hill variant," one of several which together comprise the Stone Bowl culture. The other variants, which include Gumban A and Gumban B, are almost certainly Iron Age and are described in the next chapter. There is no certain evidence of food production in the Hyrax Hill variant, apart from the presence of stone platters which might have been used to grind vegetable food, either wild or cultivated, but which may equally well have served for grinding ocher. Nor are there any bones of animals that were certainly domesticated. But the evidence of a settled way of life was taken to indicate a "Neolithic" economy, although many Mesolithic folk were also fairly settled.

The site was excavated by Mrs. Leakey in 1937–38. It consists of a "Neolithic" (Hyrax Hill variant) occupation and cemetery; a Gumban B settlement known as the Northeast Village; and a later collection of stone-walled enclosures. The Gumban B village does contain bones of domesticated animals, but, although no iron has been preserved, analogies with similar sites makes it seem likely that this phase is contemporary with iron-using peoples.

The early Hyrax Hill layer lies directly on the 325-foot beach assigned to the recession of the Makalian lake after its first maximum. The occupation was therefore thought to date from the period between about 5500 b.c. and the beginning of the drier Makalian-Nakuran phase, about 2500 b.c.; but it may well be later than this. Stony structures contained 18 contracted burials, and the females were invariably accompanied by characteristic flat stone bowls or platters (Fig. 48), much shallower than those of the Gumban variants. The dead were buried on the actual living site, a custom that still prevails among certain East African tribes, who bury their dead beneath the floors of their huts; it was also the case with the Upper Kenya Capsians of Gamble's Cave, so the tradition has a long history. In the center of the site, water-worn pebbles were leveled to form a roughly cobbled floor. Large numbers of potsherds and stone tools were found, and sometimes there were concentrations of pottery and of certain tools within restricted areas. This practice also occurred at Gamble's Cave, and Mrs. Leakey suggested that specialization of crafts may have taken place in different areas. Perhaps, on the other hand, it might mean simply that these people were tidy and kept things together so that they could be found easily, in the way that we try to arrange our closets or our filing systems.

The Hyrax Hill industry was apparently derived from the Upper

Kenya Capsian, and the difference in age between them cannot be very great. Apart from the pottery and stone bowls, it might be described as a more microlithic Capsian. The commonest tools were crescents, some of them "beveled-edged," having fine retouch along the edge opposite to the blunted back. There were also burins, micro-burins, scrapers, non-crescentic backed blades, *lames écaillées,* and fabricators of Capsian type, obliquely trimmed points and sinew frayers. Altogether 229 micro-burins were found, and none of them showed any trace of utilization; evidently they were by-products of the manufacture of crescents. Nine types of full-sized burins were distinguished, most of them being angle burins. The scrapers, too, were of various kinds, including end scrapers, discoidal, double-ended scrapers, and square-ended forms made on narrow blades.

The most common form of pottery is the ovoid beaker (Fig. 49), which is characteristic of the Hyrax Hill variant. The pottery is very simple, and the coil technique was used for its manufacture. The rims

Figure 48. Stone platters, Hyrax Hill.

are straight or slightly incurved, with a few sherds showing beveled rims. The bases are sometimes flat or "knobbed," but a blunt conical base is most frequent. Conical bases were presumably made, as is customary among certain modern African tribes, so that the pot could stand upright between three stones. The color ranges from black and gray-brown to light buff, with smooth texture, moderately well fired. The decoration shows a wide range of different incised or impressed patterns, including combed and incised lines both straight and curved, impressed dots and triangles, or a ridged "all-over" decoration formed by parallel lines of tooth impressions. Bushman pottery made in the last century was decorated with parallel lines of "tooth" impressions made by pressing with a stick with a flat end like a chisel, about ¼ inch wide, with a notch in the middle. Decoration of the ovoid Hyrax Hill beakers, however, is confined to a horizontal band immediately beneath the rim.

Nine complete stone platters were found with female burials; two of them have traces of burning, possibly related to food offerings at

the funerary ceremonies. Apart from Hyrax Hill, only 5 other shallow bowls are known out of 160 stone vessels found in Kenya and
Tanganyika; the concentration of platters at Hyrax Hill is typical only
of this variant. One unfinished platter shows how they were manufactured: the central area, on which there are tool marks, has been
hollowed out to a depth of ½ inch, but there are no tool marks on
the rim or on the exterior of the platter. In the middle the pecking has
evidently been made by a pointed implement, while the marks on the
sloping edge consist of overlapping flat chiselings. Pestles from
Hyrax Hill may perhaps have been used for crushing roots, since they
are not stained with ocher. Similar pestles have been found at many
other sites in Kenya, always made from hard rocks such as quartz or
gneiss. One flat disk bead made of chalcedony and two beads made

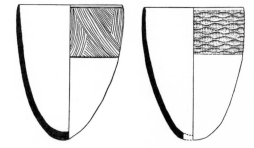

Figure 49. Ovoid beakers, Hyrax Hill.

from sedge seeds are exactly like those from Njoro River Cave, described below.

The low, stone-covered mounds with central graves containing contracted burials resemble those of the later Gumban A people, whose
culture was probably derived from the Hyrax Hill variant. Two distinct types are distinguished among the skeletons: one is ultra-
dolichocephalic and the other mesocephalic, resembling the two types
present in the Elmenteitan burials at Bromhead's Site.

Few of the skulls were sufficiently well preserved for reconstruction,
though there were seven from which it was possible to take measurements. Unfortunately none have the faces intact, so that nasal and
orbital indices and facial heights and breadths are completely unknown.
Among the ultra-dolichocephalic group is an old male with a massive
skull but small mastoids; the one superciliary ridge preserved is very
strongly developed. In three other cases the cranial index was found to

be 68: two of these (both female) have well-developed chins and show marked subnasal prognathism, a Negroid characteristic. Included in the mesocephalic group is a female of twenty to twenty-five years, whose skull is small, with bulging parietal bosses. The area of the superciliary and supraorbital arches is smooth and infantile in character; the mandible is weak, and the chin only slightly developed. The palate is deep, and a good deal of subnasal prognathism is present.

Njoro River Cave

The Njoro River Cave crematorium is not to be confused with the "Njoroan culture" mentioned by Leakey in his *Stone Age Cultures of Kenya Colony*. (On a farm near Njoro, full-length burials were found accompanied by a polished stone ax, but since no further discoveries of a similar nature were made, the term "Njoroan culture" was abandoned.) The site, excavated by Dr. and Mrs. Leakey in 1938, consists of a large rock shelter from which a low cave extends in a westerly direction roughly parallel with the Njoro River (see Map 14). The cave is cut into volcanic ash laid down at the time of the Gamblian-Makalian dry interval and was itself presumably cut during the Makalian wet phase. Since the rock floor of the shelter lies only 5 feet above the present level of the river and the overlying deposits are less than 4 feet thick, it must have been flooded during the Nakuran wet phase and was therefore not used at this time. A carbon-14 date of 2920 ± 80 years, or about 960 B.C., was obtained for the Njoro River Cave crematorium—the first carbon-14 date ever obtained in Kenya— that suggests that occupation was immediately before the Nakuran wet phase.

The cremated human remains from this rock shelter consist of about 80 individuals. The number of adults correspond almost exactly with the number of stone bowls (78), pestles (78), and lower grindstones (77); these were apparently grave goods accompanying both males and females, unlike the custom prevailing at Hyrax Hill, where only the females were provided with platters to accompany them to the next world.

The pestles and lower grindstones were, presumably, used for preparing vegetable foods, though it is possible that they served also for

Plate 16. Carbonized wooden vessel from Njoro River Cave. (Height: c. 5½ in.)

grinding ocher. Bowls of local lava are often well made, but others made from volcanic tuffs are soft and friable and crudely finished. A number of different-shaped vessels were found, including shallow basins or platters with round bases, deeper bowls with round or flat bases, bowls with convex sides and narrow, sharp rims, and oblong or oval varieties of these forms. There were also some indeterminate vessels of poor workmanship made from water-worn boulders, which were left in their natural shape on the exterior but had been hollowed out to form crude basins. With these exceptions, the outsides are always better finished than the insides, and the bases had been rubbed smooth. In some cases, pecked tool marks can be seen inside the bowls on the base. Stone bowls are very rare elsewhere in Africa, but some have been found in southwest Africa, and a deep bowl similar to those of Njoro River Cave has been reported from Bechuanaland.

Many of the bowls are charred *inside*, a feature that occurs also at other East African sites. Mrs. Leakey suggested that they may have

been used for cooking, the bowls having been heated by placing charcoal or hot embers inside (the bases and sides of the bowls are so thick
that heat would not penetrate if they were used for cooking over a
fire). Alternatively, she suggested that they were braziers, either for
household purposes or in connection with funerary rites, or possibly
some may have been lamps. Stone lamps, such as are used by Eskimos,
have been found in many painted caves in France; presumably they
were used with a wick of moss floating in fat.

The stone bowls from Njoro (Fig. 50) resemble the Gumban B
types from the Nakuru Burial Site described in the next chapter,
though here there are no shallow platters or sharp-rimmed types,
while the deep, straight-sided bowls with flat bases and the "pudding-
basin" type characteristic of Gumban B are not represented at Njoro.
Only two really flat platters like those of the Hyrax Hill variant were
found at Njoro.

While the bowls are all made of volcanic rocks found locally, the
pestles and lower grindstones were hewn out of various kinds of very
hard rocks of the ancient formation known as the "Basement System";
these must have been imported, as there are no outcrops in the neighborhood of Njoro. Some of the pestles were stained with ocher; the
bodies and grave goods had in many cases been smeared with this
coloring matter, and a layer of it was found on the floor of the
shelter. The pestles are cylindrical, pear-shaped, triangular, discoidal,
ovoid, and other shapes. One of these stones had five hollows on different faces (a similar type has been found at other sites) and may have
been a form of anvil. The lower grindstones consist of thin flat slabs
of rock, generally with one face hollowed out by wear. Although
those found in the ocherous layers of the deposit were stained red,
others from carbonized levels are unstained, so it seems that they
at least were used for grinding vegetable foods rather than ocher.

The obsidian industry is very like the Elmenteitan. The most numerous implements are crescents, which were mostly fresh and showed
no signs of use. Were they made especially for the purpose of burying
with the dead? Or perhaps each man's store of unused weapons was
placed with him to insure good hunting in the next world, just as he

*Figure 50. Stone platter and
bowls, Njoro River Cave.*

was provided with a bowl, pestle, and grindstone for domestic use. The lunates were broad and had no dorsal ridge, characteristics that are seen in Elmenteitan types but not in the Upper Kenya Capsian and its later derivatives.

The next most numerous tools were two-edged blades, also essentially characteristic of the Elmenteitan culture. Many of these show signs of much use on both edges, and often both faces of the butt end have been trimmed to reduce the thickness for hafting. Other tools were scarce, but included *lames écaillées* of Elmenteitan type, some crude backed blades, a few burins and scrapers. Only three cores and one hammerstone were found, and there was little waste material, suggesting that most of the implements were not made on the spot.

The pottery, which includes globular pots with pointed bases (Fig. 51) and shallow flat-bottomed bowls, also resembles Elmenteitan forms. Among about 500 sherds it was possible to distinguish 12 vessels, only 2 of which were sufficiently complete for reconstruction. All were made by the coil technique. A feature that is unknown elsewhere is seen in three examples of pierced lugs, two of them on a small vessel of burnished ware. The lugs were not large enough to have served anything other than a decorative purpose (true handles are first found in Gumban B pots).

Some of the sherds are very thick and poorly fired, containing coarse grits; the finer wares, however, have an even texture and are well fired. The secondary firing that took place with cremation of the bodies has often masked the original color of the pottery, which seems to have been reddish-brown or buff on the outside, gray or black inside. One large vessel has three holes drilled after firing, two close together below the rim, and another near the base. The decoration shows little variety and includes rows of dotted or incised lines.

The Njoro River Cave is undoubtedly the most interesting Late Stone Age site discovered in East Africa; as well as its uniqueness as a

Figure 51. Pot with pointed base, Njoro River Cave.

crematorium, it has provided the finest series of stone bowls, pestles, and grindstones and a most interesting collection of over 800 beads and some pendants. Beads from other East African sites are very rare and are generally thought to have been imported; but the large number found at Njoro, and the fact that all the materials used for their manufacture exist in Kenya, makes it probable that they were made locally. The majority of beads were scattered through the deposit, but some were found in groups forming necklaces (Plate 17). The work-manship is skillful and the beads made of chalcedony, agate, and Amazon stone were highly polished; probably they were bored with the aid of corundum or emery.

Chalcedony and agate were almost certainly obtained from shallow workings and mine shafts known in volcanic tuffs of the Mau Escarp-ment nearby. The origin of Amazon stone is uncertain; it probably comes from near the Mara River, Sotik, some sixty miles away from Njoro. It will be remembered that beads of this material were found at Shaheinab—brought, it is thought, from Tibesti. Arkell pointed out the similarity between the Njoro stone beads and some from Egypt. "There are other points that suggest a cultural connexion with the Nile valley in Dynastic times. The C group people of Nubia also wore leather, used bone awls, made stone pendants, stone beads and beads of bird bone similar to those of Njoro and sometimes buried with their dead thick, shallow stone bowls."[118]

Plate 17. Reconstructed necklaces from Njoro River Cave. (Length of pendant: c. 2½ in.)

The beads are of various shapes, the most common being flat disks of chalcedony. Most of the drill holes are of "hourglass" form, the perforations from either side meeting in the middle. Two beads of obsidian have natural bubble holes which had been used instead of perforations; they had been shaped merely by chipping and were not polished or ground like those made of other materials. Mrs. Leakey suggested that naturally perforated pieces of obsidian were worn as amulets; possibly because obsidian was so commonly used for tools, it was little valued and considered not worth the trouble of polishing or grinding.

Five necklaces were found, four of which had stone beads interspaced with beads made from sedge seeds, while in the fifth, black steatite disks replace the seed beads. One necklace was 27½ inches long and was presumably worn as a double string; near it was a bone pendant, which was possibly worn with it; another may perhaps have been a headband, since a double row of seed beads on either side of the string could have been looped over the ears; still another was a very short necklet or perhaps an armlet. The beads had been badly burned and had lost their color, except in the case of one necklace from an ocherous layer.

The beads from Njoro appear to be similar to those found by Reck in 1915–16 during the excavation of burial mounds in the Ngorongoro Crater, Tanganyika, and again in 1941 when Mrs. Leakey and Dr. J. Trevor opened another mound in Ngorongoro. Cylindrical bone beads

Figure 52. Bone artifacts from Njoro River Cave: (a-d) bone pendants; (e, f) bone beads; (g) bone awl.

(a)

(b)   (d)   (c)   (e)   (f)   (g) also seem to be unique to these two sites. It is interesting that, whereas seeds of various kinds are commonly used as beads by modern East African tribes, the only other known case of sedge seeds' being made into beads is by the Bagishu, a primitive tribe living on the north-eastern slopes of Mt. Elgon.

Bone pendants were decorated with notches, lines, or dots (Fig. 52); a few were well made, but the majority, especially the undecorated ones, were crude splinters of bone, drilled and partly polished. From their position in association with immature skeletons, it seems that they were worn only by young people. Bone pendants have been found only at one other site, a fairly late Iron Age settlement at Hyrax Hill. Four bone awls from Njoro are highly polished and have particularly sharp points; and there were also two tips of elephants' tusks with the broad ends cut and rounded off.

A number of perishable objects had been preserved by carbonization (that is, they were turned into charcoal instead of ash) during the cremations; these include a carved wooden vessel (Plate 16), gourds, basketwork, plaited cord, and leather. The wooden vessel, probably a drinking cup, is carved all over the outside with an elaborate honey-comb pattern, the base being ornamented with concentric circles. The basketwork is made from vegetable fibers, hand-woven into string bags; quantities of cord were also found, used for binding the bodies into contracted positions before they were cremated. These perishable materials were immediately treated with "Durofix" dissolved in amyl acetate, so that the charcoal dust was transformed into a fairly hard substance before it had time to disintegrate.

Two remarkable facts have emerged from a study of this site: one is that the method of cremation practiced at Njoro seems to be unique in East Africa; the other apparently rather surprising feature is that the people appear to be still essentially non-Negroid at this late date. Links with the present-day tribes of East Africa are in fact very few. The only people reported sometimes partially to burn their dead are the Bagishu, of whom it has been recorded (though denied by later investi-gators) that the flesh of dead persons was eaten in ritual cannibalism, some of the bones then being burned and the rest of the body thrown out into the bush. This practice is therefore not at all comparable with the true cremation found at Njoro. At Bromhead's Site there was some trace of burning on human bones, but, again, the firing was only partial.

Before cremation, the bodies were bound into a contracted or ultra-contracted position with a cord; charred substance surrounding them shows that they were either buried in their clothes or wrapped in skins. In some cases, as we have seen, necklaces and other ornaments were left on the bodies, and each adult was accompanied by a stone bowl, pestle, and grindstone. The bodies were covered with red ocher and placed in shallow graves that were covered with soil; a fire was then lit on top so that they were baked rather than burned.

Two distinct physical types were present, and the skulls range from ultra-dolichocephalic to brachycephalic, but both the occipital and the nasal indices show marked uniformity. In these latter characters the Njoro people are said to differ markedly from present-day Negroids. The lower central incisors were removed, and in many ways these individuals are similar to other Late Stone Age peoples of Kenya. At least 78 adults were present, although the bones were in such a disturbed condition that it was difficult to estimate the exact numbers.

A site similar to Njoro River Cave has been excavated recently by R. Wright, who has kindly allowed me to mention his unpublished finds.

The site is a rock shelter near Molo, and, apart from the lack of carbonized wooden objects, the culture is almost identical with that of the Njoro River Cave. Beneath the Stone Bowl level was an occupation horizon containing an obsidian industry; this is the first time that stone bowls have been found in a stratified context.

Having come to an end of the rather meager evidence for a Neolithic way of life before the advent of ironworking, described in the next chapter, it may be useful to say something about East African pottery and finally to describe some scattered finds of polished stone axes of uncertain date.

Notes on Pottery

A description of pot making in Bugufi, Tanganyika, gives a very good idea of a craft that has probably been handed down more or less unchanged for thousands of years. River clay is sometimes mixed with sand, but usually with rotten quartzite ground down in a mortar, since the sand is too fine. New pots are molded on the broken bases of old ones. They are made by the coil technique—that is to say, strips

of clay about 18 inches long are rolled between the hands and built up
in a spiral. After the pot is shaped, the inside is smoothed with pieces
of gourd, each shaped according to the size of the pot.

Cords woven from grass and knotted at the ends are used for
ornamentation, which is generally confined to a band beneath the neck.
The usual decoration consists of a diagonal series of string impressions,
sometimes with the addition of incised lines.

After being molded, the pot is left for a day to dry. Next the outside
is smoothed, with a bent spearhead used as a scraper and with the
aid of water. The pot is then left to dry for a further three or four days.

Baking is done in a shallow pit 8 feet long, 4 feet broad, and only 9
inches deep. The bottom of this pit is lined with wood, overlaid with
grass; on the grass is placed the first layer of pots, closely packed,
followed by more grass and a second layer of pots. More grass is laid
over these, and finally wood. Breakages in firing amount to 1 in 4
or 5, but when the pots crack in drying only in a horizontal direction,
a fresh top is built on. When the pots emerge from the furnace they are
not fully baked and the process is completed on the home fire before
they are strong enough for use. The potters, both men and women, are
always specialists, and the completion of 8 pots of the usual dimensions
(10 inches in diameter, 12 inches high) is considered an ordinary day's
work.[119]

Pottery is the favorite artifact of many archaeologists; from a handful
of sherds they work out zones of contact, spheres of influence, migration routes over half a continent, and many other things besides. All
this could not be plotted on a map if individual pot makers departed
from the accepted pattern of their culture; since they did not, to any
great extent—for potters are notoriously conservative—one can only
deplore their lack of imagination. But this conservatism is the greatest
boon to the archaeologist; the fact that he seldom allows for the
possibility of itinerant potters' wandering from site to site and mixing
things up is not really a serious complication, and one should not be
disrespectful about pots, nor about those who study them.

The distribution of dotted wavy-line pottery from the Nile Valley
westward for about 2,000 miles over the southern part of the Sahara
suggests that this tradition, though not even the earliest, was near the
beginning of pottery in Africa. "Only when pottery was newly invented," said Arkell, "is the same pattern likely to have prevailed over
such a great distance. Once potters realised the possibilities of their

material, each area tended to develop its own patterns and the distribution of any one ware seldom exceeded 100 miles."[120]

Preceding the dotted wavy line is the plain wavy line. Even this is well made—too well made to represent the first experiment in pot making—the clay having been carefully prepared with the addition of quartz sand and very well fired. The earliest pottery of all would be unlikely to survive, since it would not have been well fired during the initial experimental stage.

A brief summary of some of the main shapes and patterns, textures, and techniques of East African pottery up to and including the Iron Age may be helpful.

Sudan
  (1) *Khartoum-Mesolithic* Perhaps because somebody dropped a mud-lined basket into a fire, or because a hut got burned, pottery is invented. Date at least 7000 B.C., perhaps earlier. Wavy-line decoration later elaborated into dotted wavy line.
  (2) *Shaheinab-Neolithic* Date at least 3300 B.C., perhaps about 4500 B.C. Burnished dotted wavy line with thick rims. Other ware decorated with cuneiform impressions.

Kenya, Tanganyika, Uganda
  (3) *Upper Kenya Capsian* Perhaps roughly contemporary with Mesolithic Khartoum. Pottery decorated to imitate basketwork in phase B; more variety in phase D.
  (4) *Elmenteitan* Globular pots with conical bases; shallow, flat bowls and other forms. Notched rims; smooth surface. Decoration of holes punched with reeds or grass stems, rows of incised lines, lozenge impressions.
  (5) *Hyrax Hill variant* Ovoid beakers with blunt, conical bases. Notched rims; smooth surface. Incised or impressed decoration, often in a horizontal band just beneath the rim, with lines, dots, triangles, ridged all-over patterns.
  (6) *Njoro River Cave* As in Elmenteitan, but with the addition of lugs in some cases. 950 B.C.
  (7) *Wilton Phase A* Rims thick and straight; smooth surface; single incised wavy-line decoration occasionally, but usually plain. Phase B: similar, but usually burnished. Phase C: very coarse pottery.
  (8) *Gumban A* Conical bases; beveled rims; smooth surface. Internal scoring characteristic only of this variant; basketwork decoration on exterior. Probably Iron Age.
  (9) *Gumban B* Round or conical bases; straight rims; smooth or "sandpaper" surface. Impressed cord decoration. Spouts and handles common. Iron Age.
  (10) *Dimple-based* Sophisticated decorations of channeling, crosshatch-

ing, etc. The hollow on the base may be in imitation of baskets. Associated with the earliest spread of ironworking in eastern and central Africa.

(11) *Bigo culture* Roulette decoration; applied paint; square rims. Associated with Uganda earthworks, fifteenth century A.D.

(12) *Entebbe ware* Rims with bulge on inner surface. Inner surface decorated with grooves, outer surface with herringbone decoration beneath rim. Later Iron Age.

Notes on Polished Stone Axes

The polished stone axes found in East Africa—all from Kenya, with the exception of two from Tanganyika and five made of hematite found subsequently in Uganda—were classified by Mrs. Leakey into five types (Fig. 53). Four of these types are pecked, and the fifth, represented by two specimens from Mombasa, is ground. Except for this last category, no one type seems to be confined to any particular region. Most of the specimens were found in the rift valley near Njoro, Molo, and Naivasha, where the ax heads were discovered during plowing on European-owned farms. Ten out of twenty-two complete ax heads are made of dolerite, probably imported from the Kavirondo District; others are made of various kinds of lava obtained in the rift valley, while the Mombasa specimens are made of local sandstone pebbles.

Type A, represented by eight examples, includes ax heads with narrow butts and variable types of cutting edges and sides; some are polished all over, while others are polished only near the cutting edges; traces of pecking can be seen on all of them, especially near the butt end. This type is well known in the Sudan and in the former territory of Eritrea.

Type B is represented by a horned or lugged ax from Molo, the only one of its kind known in East Africa. The butt is convex and the sides are greatly expanded to form lugs on either side; the cutting edge is curved and sharp, and the surface is polished all over. A similar type has been found at Wadi Halfa and also in Eritrea; they are undoubtedly copied from Egyptian two-lugged metal axes.

Type C, bossed or knobbed axes, have knobs on either side of the butt, which is concave in the center; the sides are almost parallel. Seven complete axes of this type have been found, including two from near Lake Eyasi in northern Tanganyika, which were reported to be associated with stone-covered burial mounds, and internally scored pottery of Gumban A type. Two others came from the Kinangop Plateau, in one case associated with stone bowls, pestles, and a lower grindstone; all were turned up on the surface during plowing.

Type D (*haches à gorges*) has grooves running around the butt end; in one case the groove runs obliquely (an ax from Kisumu) and in another (from Njoro) the groove is straight.

Type E, the two specimens found near the coast, have central grooves; one has a single groove running around the middle, while the other has three parallel grooves. Natural pebbles of sandstone were used to make these axes, which are of cruder workmanship than the up-country types. The presence of striae indicates that they were ground, though the grooves had been pecked out.

Although there are no known equivalents elsewhere in Africa to the centrally grooved type, Type D with grooves around the butt is common all over the Sahara and Sudan between the 17th and 21st parallels. The Kenya specimens are particularly like those of Ténéré (where they were associated with pottery and querns), and like many found in the Libyan Desert. Polished hematite celts from the Azande country in the Sudan may date from the dynastic period or the early Iron Age.

Polished axes have been reported from only two sites in Ethiopia. Fifty-seven were found on the Tuli Kapi Plateau and 20 came from Iubdo in the Uollege District, west of Addis Ababa. These had all been flaked and chipped into shape before polishing, not pecked as in Kenya. Pecked axes are, however, common in Northern Rhodesia, where they are associated with Wilton industries. In Southern Rhodesia, Neville Jones believed that all polished axes were the work of Wilton people. Polished axes are very rare in South Africa.

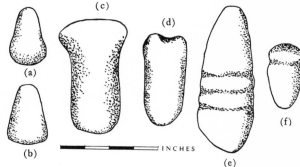
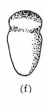

Figure 53. Types of polished stone ax heads: Type A (*a*) Molo (*b*) Naivasha; Type B, *lugged or horned ax* (*c*) Molo; Type C, *bossed or knobbed ax* (*d*) Kinangop; Type D, *haches-á-gorges* (*e*) Mombasa, (*f*) Njoro.

These implements reach a high summit of excellence in the Congo, where they are characteristic of the high plateaus from the Uele River to Katanga. According to a classification and distribution map of polished axes from the Congo, they are especially large and finely made in the Uele region, where many of them are of hematite. An ax head and an adze head of this material, almost certainly imported from the Congo, were until recently the only examples known from Uganda (three more have been found since); they come from Arua, Gulu, in the northwestern part of the country, and are of Type A, with narrow butts.[121] In the northern and eastern parts of the Congo, polished axes are sometimes found with bored stones and are evidently the work of people concerned with forest clearance and the collection of vegetable foods. The Late Stone Age of the central and western parts of the Congo is quite different: here arrowheads and daggers indicate a hunting people, perhaps the pygmies, who were driven further into the forests by invaders from the north and east. Polished axes in the Congo include pear-shaped and subtriangular celts, as well as rectangular and hexagonal forms. An excellent history of the evolution of the ax, with many illustrations to show the methods of hafting, has been written.[122]

Chapter Eleven

THE COMING OF IRON

Ironworking in the Sudan

It is remarkable that Egyptian influence seems to have been so slight within the African continent—so slight, in fact, that this one great early civilization of Africa impinges on our story only because it was through Egypt that the knowledge of ironworking reached the Sudan and, eventually, East Africa. In order to see this momentous event in perspective we must look briefly at the background leading up to Meroë and its industry in iron.

The Egyptians were sufficient unto themselves and had no desire to diffuse their civilization among their barbaric neighbors. They were not enterprising explorers, and confined their activities to the "land of Punt" along the Red Sea coast and to parts of Ethiopia, collecting ivory, incense, and slaves. Although their influence penetrated through Nubia into the Sudan, it seems to have been slight south of Khartoum, where there has been progressive desiccation for the past 6,000 years, at least.

Further progress southward by the Nile was barred to the Egyptians and other travelers by the sudd swamps.

The greatest barrier in Africa today is the Sahara, but, as we have seen frequently in the course of this book, this was not always so. After the temporarily more favorable climate of the Saharan Neolithic, however, desiccation set in. At the time when Egyptian civilization was at its height (Old Kingdom, 3100 B.C.; Middle Kingdom, 2000 B.C.; New Kingdom, 1577–1050 B.C.) the southern part of the continent was cut off from practically all contact with the north.

Even in the southern Sudan, traces of Egyptian influence are few. Protodynastic graves have been found at Omdurman and at Qoz Regab, 200 miles to the east. Very little is known of the dynastic period in this area, though stone celts with lugs, imitating the Egyptian two-lugged copper ax, have been discovered along the Wadi Howar, 500 miles west of Khartoum. Far more, of course, is known about the northern Sudan, or Nubia, which was visited frequently by explorers and traders from earliest Old Kingdom times, though the area was not occupied until the Middle Kingdom.

Contemporary with the First Dynasty, from about 3100 B.C., were the "A group" people of Nubia. Skeletally they were of Mediterranean type, and copper tools from their graves are the earliest metal objects known in the Sudan. The "B group" people who succeeded them have much poorer grave goods. The "C group" (about 2500–2150 B.C.) were probably related to the "A group" and were also of Mediterranean type; their pottery has been found as far west as the Wadi Howar and also to the east, at Agordat, in what was formerly Eritrea; very similar pottery is still made today in the Nuba Hills. These pastoral people, who kept many cattle, may have come from the west, owing to increasing desiccation, and most of them migrated again later toward the southwest.

During the time of the Twenty-fifth Dynasty (751–664 B.C.) the Kingdom of Kush ruled Egypt, and thus the Sudan came into contact with the Mediterranean world. Egyptian objects of this period have come to light as far south as Sennar, on the Blue Nile, Kosti, on the White Nile, and Jebel Moya, between the two rivers.

Egypt had been brought suddenly and unpleasantly in contact with iron weapons for the first time during the Assyrian invasions of the seventh century B.C. The Assyrians, of course, guarded their secret very closely. But when the Kushites retired back to the Sudan as a result of pressure from these iron-using people, the Saites (who then came into power and formed the Twenty-sixth Dynasty) sent expeditions to the Sudan that included Greek mercenaries. Napata was sacked and the capital of Kush moved to Meroë. This was a very important event in the history of East Africa because it was from Meroë that the knowledge of ironworking was gradually diffused. It may have been Greek craftsmen among the mercenaries who taught the art of ironworking to the inhabitants of Meroë, during the fifth century B.C.

In the neighborhood there was plenty of wood for fuel, and iron was obtained from the hills of Nubian sandstone. Meroë has been called the Birmingham of Africa, and 12 immense slag heaps are still visible there today, though there is no means of telling their date. Little progress has been made in deciphering the Meroitic language, since no multilingual texts have been discovered; inscriptions that might tell us much remain unread. Soon after 300 A.D., Meroë was destroyed by the king of Axum. Strangely enough, few iron objects have been found in Meroitic graves, though they are plentiful in the succeeding "X group" graves of the fourth to the sixth centuries A.D. It seems, then, that ironworking in Meroitic times may not have been on a very large scale.

Meroitic pottery has been found along the Blue Nile as far as Roseires and along the White Nile as far as the Sobat mouth, but, presumably, influences from Meroë did not penetrate farther south, owing to the sudd. Knowledge of ironworking may have traveled westward to Lake Chad and then southeastward toward East Africa; or it may have reached this region by diffusion east of the *sudd* and along the foothills of Ethiopia. It also reached the coasts of the Red Sea and the Indian Ocean from India before the first century A.D., as mentioned in the *Periplus of the Erythraean Sea.**

According to traditions of the Baganda, ironworking did not begin in their country before 1000 A.D., having been introduced probably from Bunyoro. It seems to have started in Uganda some time during the second half of the first millennium A.D., according to a carbon-14 date from Nsongezi. Surprisingly, the earliest carbon-14 dates for Iron Age industries south of Meroë itself come not from East Africa but from much farther south, in Northern Rhodesia, during the first century A.D. This may be due to the fact that very few carbon-14 dates

* A pilot's guide to the Indian Ocean and the east coast of Africa, written by an unknown Greek in the first century A.D.

for the Early Iron Age have been obtained in East Africa, but industries of this period can be linked with those of Northern Rhodesia by means of those distinctive and useful artifacts, sherds of pottery.

Dimple-Based Pottery

Only within the last few years has it become apparent that the earliest evidence of ironworking in eastern and central Africa is associated with very characteristic pottery. It was called dimple-based, since the first pots of this type to be discovered—in western Kenya— have a clearly defined hollow in the base (Plate 18). It has been suggested that the reason for the dimple is conservatism, a long tradition of imitating basketwork that began with the Khartoum Mesolithic. Baskets from Neolithic Fayum have been preserved and show the "dimple" well. But a natural "dimple" also occurs on the base of a calabash. Bases of pots art not always to be found, nor do they invariably have dimples; but there is no mistaking the sophisticated and attractive decoration on pottery of this type, which seems to be unrelated to basketry prototypes.

It was Hiernaux in Ruanda who first pointed out that the dimple-based is invariably the oldest form of pottery associated with iron, and that wherever it has been found it directly follows the Wilton and similar microlithic industries or is contemporary with them.[123] Iron objects themselves are seldom preserved in the acid soils of Africa for more than a few hundred years, though sometimes the rust remains. Iron slag, on the other hand, is virtually indestructible, and other evidence of ironworking is often provided by *tuyères* (the bowl bellows of wood or terracotta, with a skin diaphragm, have a nozzle leading into a clay funnel, which is known as a *tuyère*). It seems very probable that once the knowledge of ironworking was "released" from Meroë, it would be diffused very rapidly, probably among the early Bantu, who are known to have expanded enormously early in the first millennium A.D. Very likely they were responsible for the spread of both ironworking and food production simultaneously, and they also made the dimple-based pottery. The indigenous Stone Age Wiltons, presumably Bushmanoid, would have retreated before this invasion of a far superior culture; and at the same time many of their women may have interbred with the invaders, to produce new racial types. This tremendous radiation of the Bantu, associated with iron using and

Plate 18. Pottery bowl from Urewe, western Kenya; the dimple base is shown at right. (Height: c. 4¾ in.)

food production, meant that many areas that had previously been occupied only by scattered hunting tribes now became quite densely populated. It is most unfortunate that no skeletal remains have yet been found with dimple-based pottery, so its association with the Bantu is still speculative.

The first dimple-based pottery was discovered in country around the Yala River, in western Kenya, particularly at Urewe, by that great collector, the late Archdeacon Owen. Numerous sherds on the surface were found to be derived from red silty clays, described as Bed 4 in his paper on the "Tumbian" (Lupemban) culture in western Kenya that has been mentioned earlier. The presence of pottery in the top of Bed 4 (which antedates the hill wash of Bed 5, referred to the time of the Nakuran wet phase) does not mean that it was contemporary with the deposition of that bed; on the contrary, the pottery was evidently much later, since it was associated with iron objects and slag.

The decoration is most elaborate and shows great variety, including parallel grooves or "channeling," either straight or curved, scrolls and circles, triangles, crosshatching, and dots. The rims generally have two or three bevels. The pots consist of a number of different forms: wide- and narrow-mouthed bowls, bowls with flared rims, globular pots with flared rims, and beakers.

The pottery of Bed 5 is far less elaborate; the pots have round bases without dimples, plain rims, coarse comb decoration in deeply incised lines, and deep prick marks. Above this bed, modern pottery appears, characterized by impressed cord decoration applied by means of a roulette.

Parallels with the dimple-based pottery of western Kenya have now been recognized from many parts of Uganda; from surface sites in the Sandawe country of central Tanganyika; in Ruanda; in Kivu and Kasai provinces of the Congo; in Barotseland, at Kalambo Falls, and at other sites in Northern Rhodesia (Map 15). Dimple bases have been found in Darfur and Kordofan in the Sudan, but not the characteristic decoration of the ware, which therefore may be quite unrelated. It is conceivable, though, that the dimple bases of the Sudan may be another link in the chain of evidence associating dimple-based pottery with the spread of ironworking from Meroë; possibly the decorative features might have been evolved later, by the Bantu, in equatorial Africa. Hollow-based pots have also been found at Zimbabwe and other sites in Southern Rhodesia, but their age is unknown and they too lack the characteristic decoration. The present Makaranga tribe of the Chibi Reserve sometimes make pots with depressions in the base that serve a

Map 15. Distribution of dimple-based and channeled-ware sites.

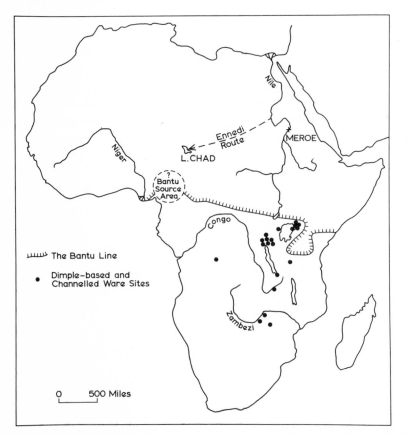

Figure 54. Sherds of dimple-based pottery with characteristic decoration, from Sandaweland, Tanganyika.

most useful purpose—for carrying on the head.[124]

In Uganda, the Nsongezi Rock Shelter contained a Wilton industry that van Riet Lowe believed to be associated with coarse, undecorated pottery; there were also a few iron objects, notably a needle, which he suggested were associated with finer, decorated sherds—now recognized to be of the dimple-based type. Reinvestigations of the shelter by Posnansky convinced him that none of the pottery belongs with the lowest (Wilton) level. Between the Wilton layer and the overlying one containing dimple-based sherds was a hearth that was dated by carbon-14 to about 924 ± 150 A.D. Above the dimple-based level were sherds with roulette decoration similar to that of the Bigo culture (p. 323). Other finds of dimple-based pottery in Uganda have been made on an island in the Kagera River at Nsongezi; on islands in Lake Victoria; in Mubende; at Mwiri Hill, near Jinja; and in the neighborhood of Entebbe and Kampala.[125]

In Ruanda, dimple-based pottery is accompanied by *tuyères* and the remains of furnaces, and sometimes by baked clay bricks marked by the builders' fingers. Following it comes a cruder kind of pottery associated with skeletons like those of the present Hutu, a caste of Bantu agriculturalists who are serfs to the Tutsi aristocracy.

Sherds with characteristic "dimple-based" decoration were found at a number of surface sites in the Sandawe country of central Tanganyika, about 75 miles southwest of Kondoa, by Kohl-Larsen during his expeditions in the 1930s. They have been described and illustrated recently by Smolla, and typical decorations are shown in Fig. 54.

In Southern Rhodesia, the earliest Iron Age industries are associated with Gokomere ware, which is similar to dimple-based pottery and to the "channeled ware" of Northern Rhodesia, which is now known as

Plate 19. Pots from Mubende Hill, Uganda: (left) height: c. 25 in.; (center) height: c. 8½ in.; (right) height: c. 15 in.

Kalambo ware at Kalambo Falls and Situmpa ware in the Zambezi valley. The distribution of Gokomere ware is at present known only very incompletely, but it has recently been found on the "Acropolis" at Zimbabwe, underlying the main occupation level of about 350 A.D. It is also found in Mashonaland, and Matabeleland. Both Gokomere ware and the Situmpa ware of the Zambezi valley are sometimes associated with Wilton microliths and bone tools. This presumably implies that the Bushman-like makers of the Wilton industries lived peacefully alongside Iron Age immigrants, perhaps from East Africa and the Sudan. The Situmpa ware of the middle Zambezi has been dated by carbon-14 to as early as 100 A.D. in Barotseland; and at Kalambo Falls, similar pottery is found about halfway up a long strati-fied sequence where carbon-14 dates range around 1080 A.D. These and other dates show that the tradition survived for a long period of time.

The Stone Bowl Culture

In Kenya, dimple-based pottery has been found only in the western part of the country. Almost certainly dating from later in the Iron Age, however, are several variants of the Stone Bowl culture, of which the first phase is the possible "Neolithic" Hyrax Hill variant, described in Chapter Ten.

The Gumban A and B variants are named after the "Gumba," the traditional inhabitants of those parts of Kenya that were occupied by the Kikuyu when they arrived some time before the sixteenth century (see p. 316). These variants seem to be contemporary with ironworking, although iron objects are very seldom preserved.

Figure 55. Sherds of Gumban A pottery, Stable's Drift: (left) exterior; (right) interior, showing scoring.

THE GUMBAN A VARIANT

This is apparently a direct derivative of the Hyrax Hill variant; both the low, stone-covered burial mounds with central graves containing contracted interments and most of the pottery is very similar, though the internally scored bowls of Gumban A are not found with the Hyrax Hill variant. The Gumban A variant was associated with human burials at Willey's Kopje on Eburru Mountain and at the Makalia Burial Site on a flat-topped hill overlooking the Makalia Valley.

At Willey's Kopje no stone tools were found within the burial mounds, though a few flakes and potsherds were found scattered on the surface, but the method of burial leaves little doubt that these people were the makers of the Gumban A variant. At the Makalia Burial Site, too, the finds were fragmentary; there were a few lunates and crude scrapers, some pieces of stone bowls and pottery. The potsherds are, however, most unusual and exactly like those recovered at Stable's Drift on the 'Nderit River, found in a bank of stratified mud. Over the exterior surface of the pottery was an all-over decoration suggesting basketwork, while the whole of the inside of the pots had been scratched with deep, irregular lines while the clay was still wet (Fig. 55). The pottery of Gumban A, apart from the internal scoring, is rather similar to that of the "Neolithic" Hyrax Hill variant. The outside decoration includes close-set triangular impressions and dotted herringbone patterns; both the pottery of Hyrax Hill and the Gumban A have combed decoration, and both include red slip wares, though these are rarer at Hyrax Hill.

One fragmentary skeleton was recovered from the surface at Willey's Kopje and excavation under cairns of stones yielded two more complete skeletons. Unfortunately these were not associated with artifacts, although stone tools and potsherds were found on the surface. A corroded iron ring was found near the foot of one of the skeletons, suggesting that the burials must date from the Iron Age. The bodies were in shallow, circular graves, with limbs drawn up so that they were in a semiflexed position, lying on their right sides. The skulls are all ultra-dolichocephalic, with indices of from 65 to 67. Many years ago it was found that cephalic indices among living races of Africa ranged from about 69 to 83—in other words, none of the individuals measured had heads as long and narrow as those of the Later Stone Age and early Iron Age inhabitants of East Africa.[126]

All three skeletons from Willey's Kopje are those of very old males. They had lost nearly all their teeth before death, but the state of the bone showed that the two lower central incisors had been removed in early youth in each case. The face of the skeleton found on the surface was missing, but in the other two cases the nose was long and must have been hooked (see Fig. 44[d]). The nose of No. II is narrow, while that of No. III is considerably broader. The orbits or eye sockets of No. 2 are unusually large, but those of No. III are low and rectangular.

At the Makalia Burial Site, the same type of burial mound and the practice of extracting the two lower central incisors link the burials with those of Willey's Kopje. One skull shows marked resemblances to Elmenteita A; this is not surprising, since the makers of the Gumban variants are probably descended from the Elmenteitans.

One of the Makalia skeletons shows signs of bone disease, which to a certain extent affected the skull as well. The cranium is long, but broader than those of Willey's Kopje, with a cephalic index of 73; the index of the second Makalia skull, however, is only 67 and is more like those from Willey's Kopje. The forehead of Makalia I slopes back as in Elmenteita A, whereas that of Willey's Kopje II is prominent. The mastoid processes are massive and the temporal crests very strongly developed. The face is long and very broad and the nose is long and rather wide. The palate and mandible are large, and the chin is prominent.

In 1957 and 1961, Mrs. Jean Brown excavated two of the three low cairns near Ilkek Station, close to the Little Gilgil River Site, where

Plate 20. Finished and unfinished Gumban B stone bowls from Nakuru Burial Site (c. 7½ in. and 11 in. in diameter).

she discovered burials accompanied by stone bowls. She has kindly given me permission to mention these finds, which have not yet been published. The cairns are about 22 to 24 feet in diameter, situated on the slopes of a rocky kopje. Cairn A was built of loose rocks covering a circle of larger rocks on the old ground surface. Beneath this was a shallow grave surrounded by more stones. It contained a male skeleton in the contracted position, surrounded by obsidian flakes and some peculiar-shaped lumps of diatomite. Cairn B is bigger and built of larger rocks; in the center were massive boulders packed tightly over a flat-topped rock. The shallow grave was cut into the slope of the hill. It contained a skull and 34 teeth apparently "planted" into the jaws, as some of the lower teeth were set into the upper jaw. Two feet away was the skull of an older person and two leg bones. On the edge of the grave was a stone platter with signs of burning on the inside edge—also large cores of obsidian, a crescent, and some pieces of red ocher.

THE GUMBAN B VARIANT

This has been found near Nanyuki; at the Nakuru Burial Site (associated with a peculiar form of burial); and at the Northeast Village

Figure 56. Mortar and pestle, Gumban B, Nakuru Burial Site (⅛ size).

Plate 21. Three stages in the excavation of a Gumban B burial site, near Nakuru: (top) the top of the broken skull is seen at the center bottom of the picture; (center) during excavation; (bottom) the contracted skeleton of a Gumban B youth after excavation.

at Hyrax Hill. There are certain points of dissimilarity between these last two sites; stone bowls are plentiful at the Nakuru Burial Site, but there are none at the Northeast Village, while fish bones are found at Nakuru and not at Hyrax Hill. Beads found at the Northeast Village, resembling those of Zanzibar and Pemba, imply trade with the coast, probably as late as the seventeenth or eighteenth century A.D. Although there is no actual proof of coastal trade before this time, surely contact with the coast had been established long before; implements of obsidian from Mombasa, for example, imply up-country trading. Although no metal tools were found in the Northeast Village, Mrs. Leakey suggested that they may have been known, since stone tools of any kind were very rare.

The Nakuru Burial Site, a quarter of a mile from Hyrax Hill, was excavated in 1926. Many obsidian tools, bones, broken stone bowls, mortars, and querns were found in the soil filling gaps between rocks piled up against the cliff face; in a crevice in the cliff, near the top of the mound, was one complete stone bowl and a smaller stone dish. An unfinished stone bowl, and a triangular tool with which it was apparently made, had been left near the complete skeleton at the bottom of the mound, along with two beads, one of faïence and the other of agate.

The method of manufacture of the deep bowls and basins of the Gumban B variant is quite different from the simple hollowing out of the shallow platters associated with the Hyrax Hill variant. From the unfinished bowl, it was seen that the soft pumiceous lava had been picked out, leaving a circular trench around a central core (Plate 20). When the trench was deep enough, the central core would have been detached by a sharp blow. This unfinished stone bowl can be seen at the Museum of Archaeology and Ethnology, Cambridge, England; here too are a stone bowl with rounded base, a mortar with a flat base (Fig. 56), a pestle, and a quern, along with a stone rubber stained with red ocher, all from the Nakuru Burial Site. The most characteristic bowls are of "pudding-basin" type, or very deep bowls with straight sides and flat bases.

At the Nakuru Burial Site, parts of eight broken-up skeletons were found against a rock face thrown in among scree. At the lowest level of one of these piles, one complete skeleton was found carefully buried in the ultracontracted position, covered with red ocher. This was evidently an important personage, perhaps a chief, while the fragmentary skeletons may represent unfortunate wives or slaves sacrificed beside the grave and thrown into the pile of rocks and debris during the process of building it up.

This custom of sacrifice at the grave of an important personage, known in India as suttee, is fairly widespread both in its distribution and in time. It is found, for example, at Ur in Sumeria, in the Neolithic of eastern Siberia, and in quite recent times among the Banyoro of Uganda, who buried their king in a grave lined with the living bodies of his wives and retainers, whose arms and legs were broken to prevent them from escaping.

The remains of the skeletons thrown into the mound at Nakuru were in such a bad state of preservation that they were useless for purposes of study, but the "chief's" skeleton was well preserved. A break in the right femur shows no sign of having healed, and was evidently caused immediately before or just after death, perhaps during the process of forcing a partly stiffened corpse into the ultracontracted position. The femora, incidentally, are long and slender and remarkably straight. The skull is long and narrow, with a cephalic index of 69. The forehead is prominent, but the supraorbital ridges are poorly developed. The face is both long and wide; the facial length is due to the great development of the premaxillary region, and not, as in the case of Elmenteita A, to great nasal length. The nasal bones of the Nakuru skeleton are long, with a well-developed bridge, and the orbits are large and somewhat rectangular. The palate is very deep indeed. The mandible is not massive, but the chin is prominent.

The singular method of burial observed at Nakuru seems to be characteristic only of the Gumban B people in East Africa. A similar burial was excavated in 1949 a few miles from the Nakuru Burial Site, on the opposite side of the Gilgil-Nakuru Road (Plate 21). In this case, the only complete burial was that of a youth of about fifteen years of age. Why he should have been accorded such honor is hard to see, since chieftainship is more likely to have been achieved by merit or strength than by heredity. He was trussed up like a chicken, with his knee (only one was present) right up to his forehead, the whole length from the top of the head to the foot being compressed into 1 foot, 10 inches.

In ancient times it was not uncommon for bodies to be buried in the ultracontracted position. A number of theories have been put forward to account for this practice, such as the idea that a body after death should revert to the prenatal position it occupied in the mother's womb. The most practical explanation seems to be that a contracted body takes up less room and saves digging a large hole or carrying many stones to cover it. Presumably some reverence for the dead must have been felt or they would not have been buried at all, for in Africa vultures and hyenas make formal disposal quite unnecessary. A Greek writer in the second century B.C. tells us that at that time no sacred rites accompanied Hamitic burials in northeast Africa. "The troglodytes bind the neck of the dead to the feet with cords of paliurus fibre; then, placing the body on a mound, they cover it with stones of a size convenient to carry, talking and laughing all the time . . . they depart, still laughing, and without any display of emotion."

But we must return to our Gumban B burials. As well as in the Kenya Rift Valley, similar customs prevailed in the Ngorongoro Crater in northern Tanganyika. In 1913 and 1915, Reck found human skeletons and associated artifacts, including beads, which were unfortunately lost during the First World War. From his description of the method of interment and of the culture, these people were clearly of the same type as those of Nakuru, though at Ngorongoro the burial places were true mounds, since there was no rock face against which to pile the scree. Other burials at Ngorongoro were excavated in 1941.

At the Northeast Village at Hyrax Hill were 13 pit dwellings, 2 of which were excavated. Their entrances faced away from the hill, and outside them low mounds of rubbish had been piled up; in these were found bones of domestic sheep and cattle, potsherds, and a few obsidian implements. Pit dwellings in Kenya are assigned traditionally to the "Gumba," but thousands of hollows, always dug into the slopes of hills, are found over a very wide area. Their dating is discussed in connection with the Lanet culture (p. 315).

The Iraqiw tribe in northern Tanganyika still live in hollows, with square, flat-roofed huts; nothing is known of the origins of these people, but recent studies of their language showed no evidence of their having come from the north, as had sometimes been suggested.

Gumban B pottery with cord decoration and fragmentary spouts and handles has been found with various middens near Nakuru, including Lanet; at Molo, north of Nakuru; at Nanyuki and other sites near the slopes of Mt. Kenya, and in northern Tanganyika. Pots from the Northeast Village at Hyrax Hill are globular, with round bases and straight or slightly everted rims, with impressed cord decoration. On two of the four more complete vessels, a spout is combined with a small handle on the opposite side, making a kind of jug. A third has a spout but no handle, while the fourth, a very large jar, has two handles but no spout (Fig. 57). This pottery is similar to that of the Nakuru Burial Site, where the texture and hardness of the ware are identical. The pottery is hard and well fired, with fine grits, though the surface is imperfectly smoothed and feels rough and gritty to touch. In many cases the impressed cord decoration has been carelessly applied, in bands of uneven width. The colors include black, buff, gray, and red, sometimes with a very superficial blackening of the surfaces; the ware is never burnished. At the southeastern side of Hyrax Hill, in the same area as that of the earlier Hyrax Hill variant described in the last chapter, Mrs. Leakey excavated a site which can be ascribed to the Iron Age with not even a shadow of doubt. All that can be said of its date is that coastal trade had been established and that it preceded the arrival of the Masai, a period that could cover at least a thousand years; but it may well belong to the early part of the second millennium A.D.

Two horseshoe-shaped enclosures, or kraals, 40 and 60 feet across, respectively, and considerably more in length, were divided by a common wall. Against the outer walls, both inside and outside the enclosures, were small hut circles loosely built of small boulders, which were possiby only the foundations for a wooden superstructure. About 19 individuals had been thrown into nine shallow burial pits, all of them males and mostly young adults, with the exception of 1 child; some had been decapitated and a few had been dismembered.

A large midden at the entrance of the larger of the two kraals was excavated. It contained bones of domestic animals, potsherds, bone

Figure 57. Pots with spouts and handles, Northeast Village, Hyrax Hill.

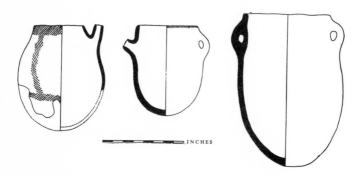

INCHES

pendants, beads, cowrie shells, water-pipe bowls, and iron objects. The cowrie shells and pipe bowls show that coastal trade had been established (water pipes were introduced by Arab hemp smokers). The iron objects included rings, bracelets, triangular razor blades, an ax, and part of a multiple barbed arrow, or javelin head.

The sherds were all very small, and it was impossible to reconstruct a complete pot. The ware was well fired, with fine grit and evenly finished surfaces, though in cases where it was not burnished it was slightly rough, like fine sandpaper. Most of the vessels seem to have had necks and handles. Some of the decoration is elaborate, with bands of impressed cord decoration below the rim; a few sherds show an all-over pattern apparently applied by the impression of some coarse fiber.

THE LANET CULTURE

In 1957, Posnansky excavated one of the 60 or so hollows dug into the slope of a rise facing Lake Nakuru, a few miles south of Hyrax Hill. As a result, he described the "Lanet culture" and considers that finds from the Northeast Village at Hyrax Hill belong to the same culture. Both the pottery and the very scarce stone tools are similar to those of Gumban B. One very rusted iron hoe was found, and at Sotik similar pottery from the same kind of hollow was also said to be associated with iron. The decoration on the potsherds, applied with a roulette of twisted grass, as well as the square rims, bear some resemblance to the Iron Age pottery of Uganda and Ruanda that follows on after the dimple-based ware.

The hollows surround an irregular, triangular-shaped enclosure that probably served as a cattle kraal. A 15-foot bank, breached by several gaps, and a broad, shallow ditch enclose 6 acres of land. Vast quantities of animal bones were found, as well as several hearths and bone tools for working leather. Charcoal from beneath the bank gave a carbon-14 date of 375 ± 175 years before the present, or 1585 ± 175 A.D., thus fully confirming Posnansky's impression that the occupation was quite late.[127]

The Lanet hollows are paralleled in many parts of western Kenya and northern Tanganyika, where they are traditionally linked with the "Sirikwa," an iron-using people who preceded the Nandi and Masai. A survey of hut circles in Nandi showed that the population at the time must have been much larger than it is today, since there are about ten times as many ancient hut circles as there are modern dwellings in the area. Stone-walled enclosures and fortifications were also built in this part of the country, evidently up until quite recent times; on islands south of Jinja they are said to have been made for defense against the Baganda, Luo, and Masai.

Posnansky has suggested an evolution of the Lanet-type hollows, or "Sirikwa holes," which have also been found recently on the slopes of Mt. Elgon, to hollows lined with stone walling and eventually to well-built stone enclosures up to three feet thick.

In the area of Mt. Kenya, too, there are many saucer-shaped depressions from 8 to 20 feet in diameter similar to the "Sirikwa holes" farthest west. These are attributed to the "Gumba," "a people of small stature and hideous features,"[128] who were said to have been a group of hunters occupying the country when the Kikuyu arrived, probably less than six centuries ago. The "Gumbans," of course, have given their name to the two variants of the Stone Bowl culture already described. On the moorlands of Mt. Kenya above 10,0,00 feet, pots with handles similar to those from the Northeast Village of Hyrax Hill have been found; presumably the "Gumbans" fled to these inhospitable altitudes to escape from the Kikuyu.

The "Hamitic" Influence in East Africa

People presumed to have come from the Horn of Africa and hence of Hamitic origin, the "Kushites," may perhaps have occupied areas of Kenya, Tanganyika, and Uganda during the first fifteen centuries A.D. They were essentially pastoralists and introduced several new elements apparently unknown to the Bantu tribes, who preceded and followed them, apparently being skilled builders in stone, road makers, and irrigators. There are no traditions of contact between these people and the modern Bantu, who refer to them vaguely as "the tall ones," "the bearded ones," or "the enemies."

Such people erected megalithic monuments in many parts of the Horn; Huntingford refers to the "hagiolithic culture" of East Africa (Greek: *hagios*, sacred; *lithos*, stone), and has traced modern survivals of this cult both in sacred stones and in sacred wooden objects.[129] In the Harar highlands of Ethiopia and in the lake region, "dolmens" consisting of two or three uprights capped with a large slab, menhirs or standing stones, and cairns are common. Some of these may go back to Axumite times, including sculptured obelisks at Axum itself, as well as crude human figures and swords carved in stones at Gurage, in the lake region. Many of these stones are associated with fertility cults, and some of the menhirs are phallic. In the Sudan, too, there are a number of sacred stones, including the Soba stone of Jebel Gule in Darfung. Although only 18 inches in diameter, it is said to have been the throne of the Queen of Soba; she may have been a ruler of the Sembritae, the ancient inhabitants of Meroë, or possibly she was the Queen of "Sheba," queen of the Sabeans of Axum.

Huntingford considers that the influence of this "hagiolithic" cult is to be traced far beyond Sabea, perhaps in Indonesia. Parallels have been noticed between the sacred stones of Ethiopia and those of Assam. Madagascar was undoubtedly colonized from Indonesia, probably during the first to third centuries A.D., and on this island, too, there are stone tombs and monoliths. Indonesian influence must certainly have reached the East African coast at this time, and the spread of the banana and the Asian yam from southeastern Asia via the coast must have had profound effects on the subsistence of peoples in central Africa. The sewn boats still used on Lake Victoria, as well as certain musical instruments and their methods of tuning, are also believed to have been introduced from Indonesia.

Cairns and other kinds of graves built with stone are widely distributed in East Africa and are still made by the Galla today. Some, in the region of Lake Zwai, have a circumference of over 100 feet and are 45 feet high. They are also found in parts of Tanganyika and in Kenya, particularly in Nandi and on the Uasin Gisu Plateau in the west, in Masailand, and near Wajir and Mandera, in the Northern Province. Two miles south of Mandera is a cairn 36 feet in diameter, which the Somali say was built by giants. A skeleton with a copper bracelet was buried in a wooden chamber in this cairn. An earthenware bowl with little feet was also found, which was presumably a stand for food; it was very fragile and would have been quite unsuited to a nomadic tribe. "Giants" or supermen are also said to have been responsible for the deep wells of Wajir, El Wak, Marsabit, and other places in the Northern Province. It is fascinating to watch the natives descend into these wells and swing buckets of water up hand to hand to the accompaniment of a rhythmic part song, while cattle and goats patiently wait their turn to drink, and often an outer circle of baboons sit around to finish off any drops that remain.

In western Kenya, as well as in northern and southern Tanganyika, there are extensive systems of graded roads, cultivation terraces, and irrigation ditches. At Engaruka, northeast of Ngorongoro Crater, there is a dam 100 feet long faced with stone and associated with stone-built settlements and terraces. These are rather similar to the Inyanga terracing of the northeastern part of Southern Rhodesia. The Inyanga terraces and stone-walled enclosures cover a huge area and are believed to date from the sixteenth century A.D. in the highlands, later still in the lowlands. Associated skeletons are said to be of Bushmanoid type with some Negroid admixture. In parts of Tanganyika there are roads 10-12 feet wide, and rocks on hillsides have been cut away with tools. There was apparently a system of communication from north to south (on the eastern side of the great lakes), rather than with the coast.

Some of the best-preserved terracing is found near Lake Eyasi in northern Tanganyika and from Iringa in the south down to Lake Nyasa. Parallel terraces follow the contours of hills; their width today is about 1 foot, but was probably greater originally, and the depth between the terraces is 3 feet. There are modern tribes who practice terracing near Kilimanjaro and Mt. Meru, while the Wabena in the south are experts on hill cultivation—but these are exceptions, and most tribes seem to have had no knowledge of contour terracing until instructed by Europeans.

Near the Ndembera River, Iringa, an extensive system of dikes was laid out. The *mtutas* (banked-up earth upon which are grown crops such as potatoes, whose roots need to be protected by drainage) are arranged in rectangles, with the dividing dikes running toward the river. It is thought that these were intended primarily for drainage rather than irrigation.

At Mufundi in Iringa Province, secondary forest is growing on top of the ancient terraces; some of the hardwood trees have trunks over 2 feet in diameter, which shows that the terracing was abandoned a considerable time ago. Terracing in northern Darfur, at Ain Farah, is attributed by Arkell to Christian monks from Nubia (700–1000 A.D.), and it seems possible that the origins of some at least of the East African terracing should be sought in the Sudan rather than in Ethiopia —in other words, with the Nilotes as well as the Hamites.

Tantalizingly little is known of the early Hamitic invaders in East Africa, since their movements and the relics of their culture have been obscured by subsequent migrations of the Bantu peoples. Referring to the situation in Uganda in 1950, a writer drew attention to the problem of which cultural traits were brought by the Hamites into the lake region from western Ethiopia and which were brought by the Nilotic Luo from the west. He summed up as follows: "What is now required is an analysis of language, custom and ritual of the Lake kingdoms in the light of (a) the published archaeological material dealing with the language, custom and ritual of Napata and Meroe . . . (b) the published material, some of it only available in very rare books, dealing with the later medieval and renaissance culture of western Abyssinia . . . including also records of the early visits of Portuguese priests to western Ethiopia and the work of more recent Catholic students such as the Fathers D'Abbadia, Azais and Chambard."[130]

Since these words were written, a good deal of progress has been made, and experts from many different fields of study meet regularly at the conferences on African History and Archaeology organized by the School of Oriental and African Studies in London to communicate their discoveries. Oral traditions are gradually being collected, and some have been verified by excavation, notably in Uganda, where earthworks and other relics connected with earlier Hamitic and later Nilotic invasions have been distinguished.

It should be borne in mind that the extent of the "Hamitic" influence in East Africa may have been exaggerated and that these people were almost certainly not responsible for all the features at one time attributed to them. In other cases they may have been responsible only indirectly, the features in question having been produced by Bantu tribes or indigenous hunters as a result of imitation.

Ancient Earthworks of Uganda

In Uganda, there is little doubt about the presence of Hamitic peoples during the early part of the second millennium A.D. who left substantial relics of their occupation in Bunyoro, Buganda, and parts of Ankole. These were the lengendary Bacwezi, described to Stanley in 1889 by a chief as "tall, big men with long noses and a pale color." They were an iron-using, cattle-keeping people who presumably ar-

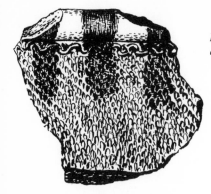

Figure 58. Sherd of characteristic Bigo ware with roulette decoration and smears of paint.

rived from the north and who are regarded with awe and respect in the traditions of the present inhabitants of Bunyoro and Buganda. Possibly they were a ruling clan of the Hima, a pastoral aristocracy comparable with the Tutsi of Ruanda; and several oral traditions insist that the Hima were already occupying the country when the Bacwezi arrived. Their power came to an end with the establishment of the present Bantu kingdoms during the fifteenth century.

The Bacwezi are alleged to have been responsible for huge systems of earthworks stretching from the Bugoma Forest east of Lake Albert to the south bank of the Katonga River (see Map 8), and perhaps also south of the Kagera in Tanganyika and also in Ruanda. These earthworks are usually situated near the banks of a river and often consist of a series of perimeter trenches encircling a hill or other strategic point. Some of them undoubtedly served as cattle kraals, and presumably one of their purposes was defense, though sometimes one or more of the sides is vulnerable.

The most extensive of these earthworks is Bigo, on the south bank of the Katonga River, which has given its name to the Bigo culture. This Iron Age culture is associated with characteristic pottery decorated by means of the roulette and often ornamented with smears of red, brown, blue, or black paint applied with the fingertips. Roulettes consist of rolls of knotted grass that were pressed into the wet clay and rolled around the pot, an easy way of making an attractive all-over pattern (Fig. 58).

The Bigo earthworks consist of an outer and an inner ring of trenches (Plate 22), the outer one running parallel to the river for over 2½ miles; the total length of all the trenches amounts to about 6½ miles. The inner system forms 4 enclosures, and the trenches are crossed by causeways at intervals. At the highest point of the hill and within the largest of the enclosures are 2 mounds 12 feet high, with a smaller mound outside this enclosure. The ditches are from 7 to 15 feet in depth and are often cut into the solid rock, no mean achievement. The first Europeans—elephant hunters—to visit Bigo were warned of the disaster that overcame anyone who cut down a tree or bush in the trenches. The Hima avoid the fortifications as a place connected with the supernatural, but they cross the river with their cattle at an ancient ford connecting Bigo with the north bank; at this point the Katonga is some 500 yards wide and is choked with papyrus. Fifteen miles from Bigo is a rock gong which is beaten during rainmaking ceremonies; the Hima connect the site with one Mugenyi, who is supposed to have been a leader of the Bacwezi and whose name is closely associated with Bigo.

Excavations done in 1957 and 1960 showed that there were two periods of occupation at Bigo. The first, Bigo A, is believed to have been a capital of the Hima ("Bacwezi"); there was a royal enclosure in the center with at least one large building, as shown by postholes. During the period of Bigo B, at the time of the Nilotic-influenced Babito Dynasty in the sixteenth century, a flat-topped mound was

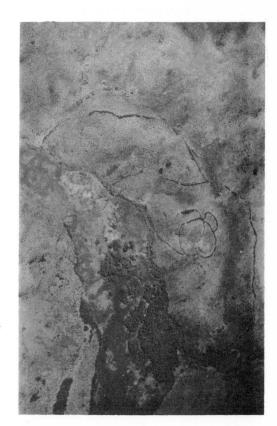

Plate 22. Air photograph of earthworks at Bigo, Uganda.

erected across the central ditch, the royal enclosure was probably destroyed, and rubbish was thrown into the trenches hewn out by the
former occupants. Finds include numerous bones of cattle and other
animals, potsherds, iron objects, a copper bracelet, and beads.[131]

On the north bank of the Katonga, eleven miles upstream from
Bigo, is Masaka Hill, which for centuries has been a place of pilgrimage
and worship. It is surrounded by two concentric ramparts with 6
openings in the outer circle. It is said that when the Bacwezi left the
area, they gave their sacred drum to a Muhima (singular of Bahima,
or Hima) of the Bushbuck clan, and his descendants guarded it and
other ritual objects at Masaka until about 1888, when the place was
looted and the big drum may have been taken to Mubende Hill (p.
324).[132]

Other earthworks of the Bigo type, though on a much smaller scale,
exist at Munsa, on the Katerere River, and at Kibengo, a few miles
from Lake Albert. This fortified hilltop encampment covers some
160 acres, with trenches forming 4 enclosures. A number of causeways span the trenches, presumably for the use of cattle. The camp
is a few miles from a natural crossing place of the Nkusi River, known
locally as "the crossing of the Bacwezi." Excavations produced iron
objects and pottery typical of the Bigo culture. Kibengo was first occupied before the foundation of the kingdom of Bunyoro-Kitara in the
second half of the fifteenth century, and oral tradition says it was then
deserted; after a time it was reoccupied. Local hunters maintain that
their grandparents lived in the outer enclosures up to the beginning
of the present century; at this time, animals were apparently trapped
in pits cut across the deep ditches dug by the original inhabitants of
Kibengo.

In Lunyoro (the language of Bunyoro), Kibengo means "the place of
grindstones," and querns as well as bottle-shaped grain pits were found
during the excavations.[133] Storage pits have been found recently at
Khami and at Leopard's Kopje in Southern Rhodesia and at the Isamu
Pati mound near Kalomo in Northern Rhodesia, about 80 miles north
of Livingstone, though the associated culture is quite different. The
nearby Kalundu mound at Kalomo contained much pottery, metal
objects, shell beads, and clay figurines of cattle.[134] These mounds have
been dated by carbon-14 to between 900 and 1300 A.D., and the people
who made them were very likely Bantu from the Lower Congo, according to Brian Fagan of the Rhodes Livingstone Museum, who has been

excavating many Iron Age sites in Northern Rhodesia within the past few years. If this is so, there is presumably no connection between the iron-using, cattle-keeping agriculturalists of Northern Rhodesia and Uganda during the first half of the second millennium A.D. After the establishment of the Nilotic-influenced Bantu kingdoms in Uganda, it is now generally assumed that the Bacwezi were absorbed rather than that they moved south, as was suggested at one time. Their presumed movements were once taken to be yet another link in the slender chain of evidence connecting the Horn of Africa, Uganda, Tanganyika, and the Rhodesias, possibly connecting Hamites with Hottentots. Along this route Hamitic people may have driven their cattle and fat-tailed

Figure 59. The Ntusi cylinder.

⌐⊤⌐ cm.

sheep, mixing with Bantu peoples on the way to produce new genetic combinations. Eventually their identity was lost, but the present Bantu and Hottentots may have adopted part of their culture, and some of them may carry their genes. Whether or not this was so—and there is no certain evidence—it seems unlikely that the Bacwezi themselves played any part in these hypothetical Hamitic migrations.

But we must leave these fascinating speculations and return to Uganda. Eight miles to the southwest of Bigo is Ntusi, in Masaka District, where there are dams, huge mounds, and deposits containing innumerable animal bones and potsherds. The site is a mile long and half a mile wide and is the largest settlement known in this part of Africa. There are traces of efficient systems of irrigation, and the earth dams may have served for impounding water by river diversion. The embankments were constructed with reference to the direction of the valley and the slope of the hills.

Some of the vessels from Ntusi were inverted over animal bones and iron objects, suggesting some kind of ritual, and part of a child's skull was found. Three main classes of pottery are distinguished, the most common being typical Bigo culture ware, brown and coarse and usually decorated with roulette patterns. In some cases triangular impressions are superimposed over the string roller patterns, a type that has been compared with Zimbabwe Class A. As at other sites of the Bigo culture, some of the sherds are decorated with red paint on the inside and some have smears of paint applied with the fingers on the outside of the rim and just below it (see Fig. 58).

An interesting object found at Ntusi was a cylinder of fired clay (Fig. 59), which may have been a cult object associated with divination, or possibly a mace head. The cylinder is shaped like a cotton reel, with flat ends and a hole through the center; eleven small holes penetrate the sides at an angle and one narrow hole pierces the cylinder from side to side. The most striking features are the numerous projections, or bosses, with traces of roulette patterns between them. Pottery objects rather like the cylinder were made in Ruanda for ritual purposes; the oracle placed a ball of fat in the depression in the top of the cylinder, which was then put inside a large pot tilted to one side, and the fat was then lit. From the position of the flame in relation to marks on the top of the cylinder, the medicine man drew his conclusions. The Ntusi cylinder has also been compared with one found at Zimbabwe in 1889, but this is believed to have been a support of some kind rather than for use in divination.

At Mubende Hill, 50 miles northeast of Bigo, is an occupation site covering 12 acres. In the center is a giant tree known locally as the witch tree, which is at least 350 years old. It is said that long before the tree was there, and before the arrival of the "Bacwezi," this place was the residence of a Hima woman who was the priestess of the spirit of smallpox. She was succeeded by many other priestesses, who received offerings from pilgrims; the last of these priestesses died in 1907, and her regalia was found only in 1953.

Noticing potsherds on the surface, Lanning made some trial excavations and was rewarded by finding several nearly complete and unusual pots (Plate 19) at a depth of about 3 feet. Some are very large—two are over two feet high—and may have been used for storing grain or beer; they are globular in shape, with rows of indentations in a band below the rim. Forty yards away, two flat-bottomed beakers were found with a decoration of crossed, incised lines in a band four inches wide. On a much smaller scale, they are like a large burial urn from Nkongora in Toro that was associated with the skeletons of an adult and an infant. Very few ancient human remains from Uganda are known, though a child's frontal bone was discovered at Ntusi and a burial ground with about 20 skeletons was found recently at Mweya, on Lake Edward. The skeletons were associated with pottery, and one sherd has a rim like those of the Mubende Hill beakers. Other objects from Mubende include typical Bigo pottery with smears of red, brown, and black paint, iron knives, scrapers, cowrie shells, and beads.[135]

In about 1930, part of the top of Luzira Hill near Port Bell on Lake Victoria was removed by prisoners during building operations; during this work, they uncovered the head of a pottery figure. Human representations being almost unknown among modern Uganda tribes, the prisoners were filled with apprehension, and operations were stopped until Wayland arrived to investigate. He discovered three channels filled with topsoil intruding through the underlying red earth and into a rubble beneath; they probably represent ancient rubbish pits. All three were carefully excavated. The head was found in one of these pits, as well as a pottery body with limbs and other fragments of human figures. There were also many potsherds.[136]

The head is conventionalized, with prominent chin and nose, and the coiffure reminded Wayland of a judge's wig (probably it is meant to represent ringlets plastered with mud or ocher). The more complete body, which does not fit well with the head (Fig. 60, left), is still more conventionalized; the trunk consists of a column, and no attempt has been made to shape the arms and legs, which are quite straight, with the arms resting on the knees. Around the arms, legs, and neck are bracelets or necklaces, and there is some sort of pad on the top of the head. It is thought that a more fragmentary body with female breasts fits better with the head (Fig. 60, right),[137] though the head itself certainly does not look like that of a woman. The Luzira figures have been compared with a Djenne one from the river Niger and with five from Mopti, as well as with others from Sao in the Chad region.

The fragments of pottery are too small for reconstruction, but some appear to have come from large vessels. The ornamentation differs

from modern Baganda pottery, with the exception of three small fragments (one from each pit) marked with plaited roulette decoration
like the local modern pottery. This seems to indicate that the finds
may not be more than a few centuries old.

A quarter of a mile from the pits was a modern "shrine," with a
four-legged pot containing recent coins surrounded by peculiar pottery objects (pestles), rings, and so forth, and iron spearheads, some
of which are unlike modern Baganda forms. There is probably no
connection between the shrine and the pits, which are certainly very
much older. The local people did not know of the existence of the pits
until they were opened up. But perhaps this spot had long been sacred,
like the Mubende witch tree, and the tradition handed down to the
modern inhabitants, who refused to divulge the purpose of the shrine.

At Kibiro, on the eastern shore of Lake Albert, is a deposit containing an astonishing number of potsherds (referred to by Wayland
as a "pottery conglomerate"). In 1959, Hiernaux excavated a 12-foot
mound and discovered wide, flat dishes used for evaporation in salt-
working. Halfway up the sequence were graphite wares of Bunyoro
type which must have been traded quite extensively and are believed
to have been mainly for royal use.

At Bweyorere Hill in Ankole, Oliver and Posnansky were able to

Figure 60. (Left) pottery head from Luzira as reconstructed originally with more complete body; (right) reconstruction with more
fragmentary female body.

date two periods of occupation by connecting them with local traditions. The first smaller village is probably seventeenth century; apart from graphite ware, there is pottery that seems to be derived from the Bigo culture and a few white glass beads, which it may be possible to link with coastal imports; tobacco pipes were also found, implying trade with the coast. The much larger eighteenth-century village at Bweyorere is represented by earthwork enclosures, including a large "royal" enclosure surrounded by banks. Nine cisterns had been dug out of the rock, but evidently they did not hold enough water to support the population, and the settlement was soon abandoned.

Later Iron Age pottery, known as Entebbe ware, has been discovered at several sites near Entebbe, notably at the Hippo Bay Rock Shelter, where it occurs in great quantities. It is characterized by rims with a bulge on the inner surface, which is decorated with grooves; the outer surface of the pots generally has a herringbone decoration below the rims. Other pottery from the shelter includes large water jars; sherds decorated with festoons; embossed pottery with a series of small lumps near the rim; and some with lattice decoration applied with a roller. There were also a few sherds of polished black ware, not the same as the fine Bunyoro graphite ware but probably imitating it. Other finds from the Hippo Bay Shelter consist of polished stone pestles; carbonized coffee beans, nuts, and vegetable fibers; and a few iron objects, including two arrowheads. The shelter was apparently occupied for only a short time, probably during the last two centuries, by people who lived by hunting, fishing, and strand-looping. They may well have been Bushman-like people, though no skeletal material has been found.[138]

Chapter Twelve

THE BEGINNINGS OF HISTORY

"History," said an eminent archaeologist, "is only prehistory encumbered with documents." Strictly speaking, the historic period with full written records started in East Africa only with the arrival of Europeans during the last century. This, obviously, is stretching the bounds of prehistory too far. We can use terms such as the "proto-historic" period or the Iron Age to bridge the gap between the Later Stone Age and the nineteenth century, but there is little point in trying to create artificial boundaries in the early history of Africa. Places on the coast mentioned in the *Periplus of the Erythraean Sea*, or in Arab manuscripts during the first millennium A.D. might qualify as "proto-historic," but we know practically nothing of the interior of darkest East Africa during this period. Similarly, while ironworking was practiced in some areas during the first millennium A.D., its advantages were neglected by a great many contemporary Stone Age hunters.

Ethiopia is, in fact, the only East African country with a history in the accepted sense of the word, though very little is known of it. This

328

is indeed tantalizing, since this area might well prove to be one of the most interesting of the whole of Africa; it is on the route from Asia and the Red Sea, and must certainly have been the scene of many migrations. It was the first country in East Africa to adopt Christianity by about 1,500 years, having been converted by Frumentius in 350 A.D. It is identified with the legendary kingdom of Prester John, and the Emperor himself is said to be a descendant of Solomon and the Queen of Sheba!

Apart from early civilizations in Ethiopia and the Sudan, East Africa had no real civilization until recent times, though Hamitic and Nilotic peoples carried some of the traditions of these early kingdoms southward. After Stone Age times, the cultural stagnation of most of Africa south of the Sahara set in. Here there was no Bronze Age, and the Iron Age penetrated southward and into the interior of the continent very slowly and gradually.

Building in stone is often attributed to the Hamites, as we have seen, though it is now certain that the great stone-walled structures of Southern Rhodesia of the fifteenth century onward were the work of Bantu tribes; this period includes the walling of the famous elliptical building at Zimbabwe, dating from 1450 ± 150 A.D., though the first rougher stone walls were built about 1100 A.D. East Africa can boast of no such architectural glories, nor of sculpture comparable with that of the West, which started during late Neolithic or Early Iron Age times (500 B.C.–200 A.D.), with the amazing figurines of Nok in Nigeria, and culminated more than a thousand years later in the beautiful naturalistic heads of Ife and Benin; almost the only works of art in East Africa are painted rock shelters, but these too are surpassed in the Rhodesias, in South Africa, and in the Sahara.

We know little about the origins of most present East African tribes, whence they came and when, nor why they were so uninterested in material comforts, labor-saving inventions, and cultural and artistic productions. A combination of isolation and disease seems the most likely explanation. Although the Egyptians were as debilitated by hookworm, bilharzia, and other parasites as the inhabitants of East Africa, they had the stimulus of contact with the Mediterranean world. West Africa was influenced from across the non-desiccated Sahara. But East Africa was hemmed in by forests to the west, the sudd to the north, and desolate scrub between the interior and the ocean to the east.

Apart from archaeology, we are entirely dependent on oral tradition for the interpretation of the past history of East Africa; much has been collected, but unfortunately much has been irretrievably lost, since it was not collected early enough. Traditions are easily forgotten under the impact of sudden contact with European civilization. Nevertheless, a few notable landmarks and scattered clues here and there have helped to solve the mystery of the past two thousand years.

The Coast

The sea in early days was by far the safest and quickest medium for travel, since currents and winds sped the voyager on his way, while on land deserts, forests, and mountains hindered his progress, and navigable rivers in Africa are few. Although we know something about the history of the East African coast for the past 2,500 years, our knowledge of events inland is very limited indeed. Early seafarers had little inclination to brave the unknown terrors of the interior. Pliny wrote: "It is said in the parts interior from the east coast there are people whose whole face is flat without a nose; and that some have no upper lip, others no tongue. We hear also of people who have no nostril nor any opening in the face beyond a single hole through which they breathe and through which they drink by means of an oaten straw, the grain of which, growing wild, they eat. Some tribes use nods and gestures instead of speech, and before the time of Ptolemy Lathyrus King of Egypt were ignorant of the use of fire." Small wonder that Arab traders stuck to the coastal plain!

We know that before 700 B.C. (when her independence came to an end) the Arab state of Ausan traded with, or perhaps held, the East African coast. Eight hundred years later, when the *Periplus of the Erythraean Sea* was written by an unknown Greek, southwestern Arabia was still apparently in control of the coast about Rhapta, which was the "very last market town of the continent of Azania." Azania signified the "dry country" of the coastal plain, while the interior was known to the Greeks as Barbaria. Certain connections were established with Barbaria through ports such as Prasum, situated where the Ruvuma River enters the sea.

The Sabeans of western Arabia founded the kingdom of Axum in northern Ethiopia, which first appears in history during the first century A.D., though it was probably founded earlier. It was Ezana, King of Axum, who sacked Meroë in 350 A.D. and the royal family who had ruled Kush for more than a thousand years then moved to Kordofan and Darfur, after which the name of Kush was no longer used and the Christian Kingdom of Dongola replaced Meroë. This civilization was skilled in the construction of stone buildings, and, as we have seen, its traditions were carried southward. Through the kingdom of Axum, trading contacts extended from Adulis on the Red Sea as far as Cyenium on the Blue Nile, which was said to be eight days' journey from the coast. Eastward, these people traded as far as the Persian Gulf, where they collected cargo brought from India.

The Hegira, the starting point of Moslem chronology, dates from 622 A.D. with the flight of Mohammad from Mecca. From this time on, Arabs overran North Africa and the Horn, converting the local inhabitants to the faith and customs of Islam. Owing to the Arab occupation of Egypt, Christian Nubia and Ethiopia were cut off from Rome. Arabs founded the empire of Zeila between the Ethiopian highlands and the sea and controlled the port of Adulis; but farther south, along the coasts of Kenya and Tanganyika, their sphere of influence was largely restricted to the coastal strip, from where they collected most of their slaves. Probably they ventured into the interior only rarely before the nineteenth century, when the great demand for ivory provided the incentive; slaves were then captured in the interior to carry the tusks, and the shameful depredations on the inhabitants of East Africa caused Arabs and Europeans alike to be regarded with suspicion and hatred.

Since 1947, an archaeological survey has been made of the East African coast and islands between Somaliland and the frontiers of Portuguese East Africa. Excavations have been made at the formerly important Arab town of Gedi, near Malindi, in Kenya, and on the island of Kilwa Kisiwani, off the Tanganyika coast, both dating from the fifteenth century. Arab settlements belong to the realm of history and do not come into this book; but mention must be made of some recent excavations that have provided the earliest material evidence of civilization on the East African coast. Near the site of the city of Kilwa, a huge structure covering two acres has been found. It was probably a ruler's residence, dating from about 1000 A.D., and is the largest pre-European building in equatorial Africa after Zimbabwe. It is known as Husuni Kubwa ("big Husuni"), while a smaller structure nearby is called Husuni Ndogo ("little Husuni").

A few settlements without mosques have been discovered that at one time were thought to be non-Islamic. One of these is on Sanje ya Koto Island, south of Kilwa, where Mathew discovered small oblong houses of dressed masonry grouped around a citadel whose walls rise to 16 feet. Iron objects were found, as well as thin red pottery. A tower 4 miles from the settlement was built in tiers with dressed blocks of sandstone. It is now recognized, however, that none of the coastal settlements known so far antedates the Arabs.

Three deserted cities inland in the former British Somaliland were also investigated, the most interesting of which is Amud. Here there are from 250 to 300 houses and a temple, which had been converted roughly into a mosque at some later date. It was built of carefully dressed masonry, and the building techniques, pottery, and lamps seem to suggest a close connection with Axumite sites of the second to fifth centuries A.D.

The amazing wealth of imports found along the East African coast, particularly Chinese porcelain, provides an invaluable means of dating sites on the Indian Ocean. Hopes of finding such imports inland have not been fulfilled so far except in a few cases. At Nkudzi Bay, on the southwestern shore of Lake Nyasa, for example, a cemetery with particularly fine pottery of local make was associated also with Chinese porcelain, thousands of beads, and many iron objects. On the basis of the imports, it has been dated tentatively to the nineteenth century. Such sites provide dates for local pottery traditions, but unfortunately they are extremely rare.

Racial Origins

In Africa south of the Sahara today, the indigenous inhabitants fall into three groups: Negroid; Caucasoid (Erythriote or "Eastern Hamites"); and Khoisan (Bushmen and Hottentots). In our study of the prehistoric origins of these peoples, we are severely handicapped by the complete absence of information on such diagnostic features as skin color, hair form, and so on, and there is a good deal of overlap in characteristic skeletal features of the three groups. The application of statistical methods to human remains in Africa has so far been very limited, but there is no doubt that future work in this direction will supply the answers to many vexing problems.

Another line of approach lies in the study of serology and other genetical characters in living peoples. Until a few years ago, the blood groups were thought to have neither positive nor negative selective value; but it is now known that some (and very possibly all) are linked with resistance to certain diseases. The implications of this new knowledge are very wide and must certainly help future research into origins and movements of peoples.

Probably much enlightening work also remains to be done on the effects of environment or ecology on natural selection. Often in the course of this book we have seen how populations became culturally adapted to different environments, and certainly their biological adaptations were just as marked. The effects of temperature, humidity, and altitude on body size and proportions are fairly well known, and of course the effects of strong sunlight on skin color are obvious. Less is known about the results of a deficiency or an excess of chemical substances in the soil, such as fluorine or iodine or certain trace elements. Natural selection must also operate in connection with the occupations of the subjects—for example, pastoralists have an advantage in being tall and long-legged, hunters in being small and wiry. Rigorous selection in a forest environment, where there is a lack of protein, probably accounts for the production of pygmies; the tall, slender build of Nilotic Negroes, on the other hand, is an adaptation to dry heat.

We have seen that there were apparently two basic stocks in Africa during early Later Pleistocene times: the Rhodesioids; and the Boskopoids or Proto-Bushmanoids. In East Africa, there is a long gap in the skeletal record between the Rhodesioid from Eyasi, the Singa skull, and the enigmatic Kanam mandible and Kanjera skulls, until we come to Post-Pleistocene times, a period that probably covers at least 40,000 years. Then, perhaps about 8000 B.C., we find the first appearance of the Negroid in Mesolithic Khartoum and of Caucasoids at Gamble's Cave in Kenya. We shall discuss the Bushmanoid stock (the present Khoisan peoples), the Caucasoid stock (the "Eastern Hamites"), and the Negroid stock in an attempt to discover something about their origins, their distribution in the past, and their bearing on the present inhabitants of East Africa.

THE BUSHMANOID STOCK

Various skulls from South Africa dating from Middle and Later Stone Age times (for example, the Boskop, Skildersgat, and Matjes River crania) are assumed to be ancestral to the Bushman because of their pedomorphic or infantile characters, though they differ from present-day Bushmen in the greater size of the skull and the far larger braincase.

There is some evidence that the same stock was present in East Africa in early times. The brachycephalic type, represented by Elmenteita F_1, has been compared with the Tuinplaats skull from South Africa. Did perhaps the Caucasoid peoples of Kenya at this time mix with Bushmanoid hunters, makers of the Wilton industries, inhabiting the same region? Probably the Wilton C people associated with shell mounds on the shores of Lake Victoria were of Bushmanoid stock; they have very large skulls with small faces, and both their features and culture are similar to those of the strand-looping, kitchen-midden people of South Africa. Van Riebeeck, in the sixteenth century, distinguished between the superior class of Hottentots at the Cape and bands of strand-loopers or beachcombers, who were crosses between Hottentot men and Bushwomen. The Wilton C people of Lake Victoria led a similar strand-looping life, and the Ishangians of Lake Edward were also probably rather similar to the Wilton C people.

Two widely different views are held about the spread of Bushman types. Many South African workers regard the "Bushmanoid" stock as native to South Africa, from whence it spread northward. On the other hand, some investigators believe that the "Bushmanoid" type originated farther north and spread southward. There can be no doubt that the Bushmen once extended over a much wider area than they do today, when they have been pushed into the Kalahari by Hottentots, Bantu, and Europeans; but their place of origin remains obscure.

The Bushmen today are a race of generally light-skinned people, characterized by bulging forehead, prominent cheekbones, a flat and triangular-shaped face, pointed chin, eye folds, and peppercorn hair. Bushwomen, and especially Hottentot women, are notorious for steatopygia, which probably acts as a kind of camel's hump for storing food and water, a reserve that is particularly needed in pregnancy. The average height of male Bushmen is about 5 feet, 2 inches, rather taller than the Congo pygmies. They live by hunting with bows and arrows (generally poisoned) and gathering wild foodstuffs. As well as having been talented artists in the past, they have a copious oral folklore. Some of the rock paintings of Tanganyika are very similar to those of the ancient Bushmen of the Rhodesias and South Africa; they may also be connected with those of the Sahara and North Africa.

At the present time in Tanganyika there are tribes speaking languages with clicks, like those of the Bushmen and Hottentots, who also bear certain skeletal resemblances to these tribes. As early as 1895, Virchow described two skulls of the Sandawe tribe that showed distinct Hottentot affinities; and in 1947 Trevor also concluded that there were physical similarities between the two peoples. As long ago as 1916, it was recognized that the language of the Sandawe of Kondoa Irangi has three clicks, like that of the Nama Hottentots. The origin of the Hottentots themselves is far from clear, though blood-group and other biological evidence makes it clear that they must be closely related to the Bushmen. Their appearance is very similar, though they are generally slightly taller (average 5 feet, 4 inches) and have a longer, narrower head and a more prognathous face. They are more advanced than the Bushmen, being pastoralists and ironworkers. Strangely enough, E.O.J. Westphal of London University, who has specialized in Bantu and Khoisan languages, insists that there are three distinct Bushman linguistic families, none of which are at all closely related to the Hottentot languages. The latter include certain Hamitic grammatical peculiarities, and the long-horned cattle and fat-tailed sheep of the Hottentots must have originated in northeast Africa, as already mentioned. Some of the Hottentot-like skeletons of the K2 site at Bambandyanalo, Mapungubwe, dated to 1050 A.D., are very like those of the Elmenteitans. These Proto-Hottentots, who have been called the "Kakamas type," are also said to resemble the present Tonga of the Kariba area.

Another tribe in Tanganyika, the Hadza of the Lake Eyasi region, are both culturally and linguistically very like the Bushmen. The Hadza language has four clicks; their culture is less advanced than that of the cattle-keeping Sandawe, and is based on hunting and food collecting. Apart from the fact that some of the females have steatopygia, the Hadza do not resemble the Bushmen at all in appearance; their skin color is very dark and they are typically Negroid.

A skull taken from beneath a tomb of 30 tons of limestone at Nebarara, in the Masai steppe country of northern Tanganyika, was found to have measurements corresponding closely with those of modern Bushmen, though certain features, such as the massive zygomatic arch, approach the Boskop skull. It has been suggested that the type of grave indicates the burial of some important personage of a tribe dominant in the country, rather than one in the position of subject. There is no evidence of the age of the burial, which is probably not very old. It does, however, support cultural and linguistic indications that Bushmen once lived as far north as Tanganyika, perhaps even that they were dominant in this part of the country.

Certainly they must have been fairly widespread over Northern Rhodesia not so very long ago, and a few Hukwe Bushmen still live in the southwestern corner of this country today. As already mentioned, Bushman-like skeletons were found associated with a Wilton industry at Lochinvar, on the edge of the Kafue Flats. Skeletal remains from Chipongwe Cave near Lusaka are mostly of Bushmen and pygmy type, though some of the larger bones resemble those of Hottentots; this material is a particularly interesting illustration of the possible connections between the pygmies and Bush-Hottentots in the past. The industry associated with the human remains is similar to other degenerate industries of the very end of the L.S.A., and pottery shows resemblances with that made during the second half of the last century by the Soli-Lenje and Plateau Tonga.[139] Probably the cave formed a refuge for a surviving group of Bushman-like people surrounded by Bantu.

Blood-group evidence leaves little doubt that the Khoisan peoples must be regarded as a branch of the Negroid stock, rather than a distinct and separate stock, as has sometimes been suggested. They share with all Negroid groups a very high frequence of the Rhesus group cDe gene combination, which is almost if not entirely confined to Africa, as well as a number of other blood-group genes, such as Henshaw and Js, that are characteristic of Negroids.

Rather surprisingly there are a few significant differences between Bushmen and Hottentots in the distribution of the ABO groups; while Bushmen have an extremely low incidence of B (about 2 per cent), Hottentots have a rather high incidence (about 22 per cent). Although a high frequency of group B is particularly characteristic of Asia, this feature in the Hottentots should not be taken as support for the theory that suggested Mongoloid connections, based mainly on the similar eye folds and yellowish skin color. This theory has few serious supporters today. A relatively high incidence of blood-group B is also found among Congo pygmies, and early connections with central Africa are much more likely to account for the frequency of this gene among Hottentots than the alternative suggestion of recent contacts with Asian traders.

Another basic East African stock is Caucasoid, or Mediterranean. There are two alternative theories as to the origin of the present Hamites; one that they arose in North Africa, the other that they came across the Red Sea from Arabia. Hamitic languages today are spoken by people spread over about one-fifth of Africa. They are divided into two groups: the Northern Hamites, including the Berbers and Tuareg, and the Eastern Hamites, or Erythriotes, including the Egyptians and the inhabitants of the Horn, such as the Galla and Somali.

Crossing between the Eastern Hamites and Negroids has happened very frequently, with the result that every grade of skin color from light brown to black is found among them, as well as every kind of hair from slightly wavy to frizzy. Traces of Negroid admixture are generally least apparent in the Somali, who are very like the lightly built Arabs, typical members of the Mediterranean race. Although there is such tremendous variation of surface features among the Eastern Hamites, their skeletal measurements nearly always show Mediterranean rather than Negroid proportions.

Those who fear the deleterious effects of miscegenation—and there are very few among serious anthropologists—would do well to remember that a combination of Negroid and Caucasoid genes has produced some of the handsomest people of Africa. The Nilo-Hamites, who include the Iteso and Karamojong of eastern Uganda, the Turkana of northern Kenya, the Nandi group of western Kenya, the Masai of Kenya and northern Tanganyika, are the result of crosses between Nilotic Negroes and Hamites. Their fine features and graceful build, their pride and independence, has won the admiration of many a pioneer traveler and devoted administrator. Only comparatively recently, as the result of disease, change of diet, and perhaps boredom in the absence of warfare, have some of these fierce warriors begun to fight a losing battle with civilization.

Until quite recently, it was thought that the Caucasoid stock was present in East Africa long before any other modern race could be recognized. Now that it seems more likely that the Upper Kenya Capsians lived in Post-Pleistocene times, there is no evidence of Caucasoids in East Africa before the appearance of the first Negroids in the Sudan. The earliest of these Caucasoids are the tall, dolicho-cephalic people of Gamble's Cave, Naivasha, and Olduvai. Perhaps a few thousand years later, two distinct types can be distinguished: the "Elmenteitan type," represented by the skull Elmenteita A from Bromhead's Site (Fig. 44[b]) which is ultra-dolichocephalic, with long face and narrow nose; and the brachycephalic type, with shorter face, represented by Elmenteita F 1 (Fig. 44[c]) which is more "Bushmanoid" in appearance and has been compared with the Proto-Hottentots of Mapungubwe. These two types persist into the Early Iron Age, but now a third variation appears in the ultra-dolichocephalic skulls from Willey's Kopje (Fig. 44[d]), which differ from the "El-menteitan type" in having a shorter face, a more prominent nose, and a robuster mandible. This third type is also known from Hyrax Hill and from Njoro River Cave.

Surprise has sometimes been expressed at the fact that as late as 950 B.C., the time of Njoro River Cave, there is still no trace of Negroid features. But apart from the Nilotic Luo of western Kenya, the present Negroid inhabitants are mostly Bantu, who certainly did not arrive before the latter part of the first millennium A.D. There is no reason why we should expect the pre-Bantu inhabitants of Kenya to have been Negroids, whose home is farther west and northwest.

Before the Upper Kenya Capsians, there is simply no evidence to suggest the presence of Caucasoids in East Africa. The Kanjera skulls, whose dating is most uncertain, are too fragmentary for a proper assessment of racial affinities to be made. Comparisons have been drawn between them and Bushmanoid skulls, mainly because of the ex-ceptionally smooth brows, though this feature occurs also in the Upper Kenya Capsians and often in Negroids. The ultra-dolichocephaly of the Kanjera fragments recalls the Upper Kenya Capsians, but, again, a long, narrow skull is a typically Negroid feature.

THE NEGROID STOCK

Although Negroes are most typical of Africa today, the problem of their origin is even more obscure than that of the other two stocks, since no skeletal remains with recognizable Negroid traits have yet been found anywhere dating from the Pleistocene. As we have seen, the earliest known representatives come from Mesolithic Khartoum, and, perhaps roughly contemporaneously, from Asselar, north of

Timbuktu. In the Sudan, the next evidence is provided by the rugged, heavily built Negroes of Jebel Moya. In Kenya, the first unmistakable Negroids appear during the Iron Age, though possibly some of the skulls with the Hyrax Hill variant of the Stone Bowl culture may be Negroid.

Among the features that distinguish present Negroes are a very dark skin, frizzy hair, broad nose, thick and everted lips. Their blood groups, too, are very distinctive: particularly characteristic are the rhesus combination cDe, the V gene, the Hunter and Henshaw genes, and the independent system Js. Fortunately Negroes also have certain characteristics that can be studied in skeletal remains—for example, subnasal prognathism (a protruding upper jaw), rounded forehead, rather poorly developed chin, narrow skull, very broad nasal aperture, long, slender forearm and shin, narrow pelvis.

There are, of course, various subdivisions within the Negroid stock. Most "Negroid" of all is the West African Negro, who does not concern us in this book. The huge group of Bantu-speakers is very variable, being more typically "Negroid" in the west, less so in the east and south. The Nilotic Negroes are distinguished by their tall stature—they are the tallest people in the world—and the Negrillos or pygmies, of course, are the shortest people in the world. Some people believe that the pygmies represent a very ancient basic stock, from which the full-sized Negro was derived; a more likely theory is that they are reduced survivors of the Negroid stock who have been subjected to intensive selection in a refuge area. Ancient skeletons are unlikely to survive in a forest environment, and even if the ancestors of the present pygmies were larger, we would be unable to recognize connections, so that the question may never be settled. There may well be some basic relationship between Negrillos and the Khoisan peoples, both of whom have probably developed their particular characteristics comparatively recently as a result of isolation and natural selection in two very different but equally specialized environments.

Blood-group evidence gives little or no support for theories of connections between African Negrillos and Asiatic Negritos, nor for suggested connections between full-sized African Negroes and the dark-skinned, frizzy-haired Melanesians of Papua and Fiji. A most intriguing problem is presented by the Andaman Islanders, whose peppercorn hair and very pronounced steatopygia makes them look so strikingly like Bushmen and Bushwomen. Most authorities today accept the explanation of independent natural selection, operating on a fundamentally rather similar aboriginal substratum in Africa and Asia. In their blood groups, the Andaman Islanders seem to be connected with the Oceanic Negritos and not at all with African peoples.

Apart from the pygmies, there are various aboriginal Negroid tribes scattered over East Africa and other parts of the continent about whom very little is known. Many of these primitive hunters must have been dispersed by Bantu invasions and survive only in oral traditions, though a few still exist, such as the Ndorobo of Kenya. There is a certain amount of archaeological evidence for non-Bantu ironworkers, though whether they learned this art from the Bantu or direct from travelers from the north is not at all clear. In Kenya, there are the "Gumbans" who preceded the Kikuyu. In Ruanda, there are the "Renge," who are said to have occupied the country before the arrival of the Hamitic Tutsi and the Bantu Hutu. Right down in southwest Africa there are small, heavily built people with a very dark skin—the Bergdama—who live by hunting and food collecting but who are believed to have acquired the knowledge of ironworking before they reached their present home; although they have adopted the language of the Nama Hottentots, they are quite unlike them in appearance.

In the Horn, there is very interesting evidence of direct connections between Stone Age, Iron Age, and people who still survive today. The triangular, hollow-based arrowheads of the L.S.A. Doian culture were copied in iron in the upper levels of sites such as Gure Warbei, Bur Eibe, and Bur Hakaba; these levels contain pottery similar to that made by the modern Eile, who are said to be descended from small aboriginal Negroid hunters.

As more data is collected, serology and the study of other genetical characters such as hemoglobins and other blood proteins may be expected to solve many problems concerning the origins of the Khoisan peoples and Negroids. A feature once thought to be diagnostic only of Negroes, the sickle-cell trait, has been found also among Veddoids of southern India and among some Mediterranean peoples. This abnormal hemoglobin, while resulting in lethal anemia in the homozygous state, gives resistance to malaria in the heterozygous state, and for this reason it has been encouraged by natural selection in malarial areas.

In Uganda, Lehmann and Raper examined 5,000 natives for the sickle-cell trait. The lowest incidence was in the Hamitic tribes and the highest was found in the Baamba, a pygmoid tribe living west of Ruwenzori, and in the Bagishu, who live on the slopes of Mt. Elgon. It

is interesting that Mrs. Leakey drew comparisons between the sedge-
seed beads found with the industry of Njoro River Cave (p. 291) and
those made by the Bagishu; probably this tribe has retained its identity
for a very long time. The Nilotic tribes of Uganda were found to be
very homogeneous with regard to sicklemia, but a wide variation was
found among the Bantu, the incidence being apparently inversely pro-
portional to the contact the tribes have had with Hamitic invaders.[140]

How far can we link up the present inhabitants of East Africa with
their prehistoric forebears? Not very far, it must be admitted, but a
little speculation may be attempted. In Europe, we find a generalized
Homo—represented, for example, by the Steinheim and Swanscombe
remains—preceding the Neanderthalers; these generalized forms presumably gave rise to modern *Homo sapiens* as well as to the
Neanderthal side branch. The same situation may well have occurred
in Africa, although there is little proof. A generalized *Homo* may have
followed the Pithecanthropine of Bed II, Olduvai, giving rise to the
type represented by the Florisbad skull and to "Boskopoid" or "Bushmanoid" forms on the one hand; and to a side branch represented by
the Rhodesioids. The latter made early M.S.A. industries such as the
Proto-Stillbay and the Fauresmith. The only clue as to the appearance
of the makers of the succeeding Stillbay culture is the Dire Dawa jaw,
which may be "Rhodesioid," but there are no jaws of these people with
which to compare it other than a fragment found with the Saldanha
cranium.

We can imagine that by the end of the long period covered by the
Stillbay, the descendants of our hypothetical ancestral *Homo* had
evolved into men of modern appearance, probably "Bushmanoid." In
South Africa, many skeletal remains of this type have been associated
with later M.S.A. industries. In East Africa, there is a gradual transition
from Stillbay to Magosian and finally to Wilton, a culture that seems to
be associated with Bushmanoid people.

The Sangoans, Lupembans, and Tshitolians are equally enigmatic,
though we might guess that they were ancestral to the Negroids in
general, and perhaps to the pygmies in particular, since they occupied
the same forested environment (they need not, of course, have been
of pygmy stature; in fact it is more likely that they were not). In-
dulging in still more speculation, we could suppose that the Stillbay
Bushmanoids crossed with the Negroid Lupembans—or that their
respective descendants did so—to produce as end products the Khoisan

peoples on the one hand and the pygmies and various aboriginal hunting tribes on the other.

Farther north, in the Sudan, the oldest human remains consist of the Singa skull. Recent studies suggest that its so-called "Bushmanoid" affinities are fortuitous and that this individual was aberrant (see pp. 176–177), in which case no useful deductions can be drawn from it. Two alternative theories seem possible. The first is that the Singa community may have been ancestral to the Negroids of Mesolithic Khartoum and thence to the modern Nilotes. The second is that its descendants may have been Bushmanoid, and that the Negroids of Mesolithic Khartoum were derived from Sangoan-Lupemban ancestry.

Perhaps only after the end of the Pleistocene, Caucasoids from the Mediterranean moved down into the Horn and East Africa to complicate the picture still further. Presumably they crossed with indigenous Bushmanoids and Negroids, and also perhaps with the products of Bushmanoid-Negroid crosses such as the Ishangians of Lake Edward. These Caucasoids gave rise to the present Hamitic-speakers, while Hamitic-Nilotic admixture produced Nilo-Hamites such as the Masai. It has even been suggested that the eastern Bantu may be the result of Hamitic-Negroid crosses, though clearly they are mainly Negroid.

There is, as we have seen, a certain amount of evidence to suggest that Hamitic peoples may have moved as far south as the Rhodesias and that the Hottentots adopted elements of their culture, though whether they also assimilated their genes is less certain.

From the scraps of information given in this and the previous chapter, it will be apparent that our knowledge of the history of East Africa during the past two thousand years is rudimentary and largely conjectural. The artifacts are there, but seldom the bones of the people who made them. Very often, too, the means of dating the artifacts is lacking, and radiocarbon laboratories cannot keep pace with such samples as are submitted to them. Oral tradition, though useful, is generally very vague as to dates, and the occasions when an event can be fixed by such phenomena as a solar eclipse—as in Kabaka Juko of Buganda's reign, 1680 A.D.—are almost as rare as an eclipse itself.

The first need is for many more detailed excavations of Early Iron Age sites, supported by a whole series of carbon-14 dates. Linguistic studies may be expected to give much new information about tribal origins and connections; but perhaps above all we can hope for a great deal of new knowledge from genetical work on blood groups and blood proteins.

REFERENCES • GLOSSARY

BIBLIOGRAPHY • INDEX

References in the Text

All sources cited are listed in the Bibliography alphabetically by author. Where an author has published more than one work in the same year, each is distinguished in the References by the addition of the letters a, b, c, and so forth, referring to the first, second, and third work listed for that year.

1. Clark, D. L., 1961
2. Matthews, L. H., 1962
3. Hoyle, F., 1952
4. Goodwin, A. J. H., 1953
5. Flint, R. F., 1947
6. Cooke, H. B. S., 1957
7. Toit, A. L., du, 1947
8. Bernard, E. A., 1962
9. Simpson, G. C., 1957
10. Bakker, E. M. van Z., 1962
11. Caswell, P. V., 1953
12. Chittick, N., 1962
13. Biberson, P., 1961 (a), (b)
14. Cooke, H. B. S., 1958
15. Flint, R. F., 1959 (a), (b)
16. Bishop, W. W., 1962 (b)
17. Clark, J. D., 1961
18. Pickering, R., 1960
19. Oakley, K. P., 1962 (a)
20. Bishop, W. W., and Posnansky, M., 1960
21. Howell, F. C., et al, 1962
22. Clark, J. D., 1954 (a)
23. Butzer, K. W., 1962
24. Butzer, K. W., 1962
25. Higgs, E. S., 1961
26. Martin, H., 1957
27. Bishop, W. W., 1962 (c)
28. Napier, J., 1959
29. Leakey, L. S. B., 1962 (a)
30. Simons, E. L., 1961
31. Leakey, L. S. B., 1951
32. Leakey, L. S. B., 1962 et al
33. Cooke, H. B. S., 1960
34. Montagu, M. F. A., 1950
35. Mayr, E., 1950
36. Higgs, E. S., 1961
37. Wells, L. H., 1957 (a)
    Weiner, J. S., 1958
38. Napier, J., 1961
39. Oakley, K. P., 1962 (b)
40. Pickering, R., 1960
41. Leakey, L. S. B., 1959
42. Leakey, L. S. B., 1960 (b)
43. Leakey, L. S. B., 1961
44. Clark, W. E., Le Gros, 1961
45. Leakey, L. S. B., Evernden, J. S., and Curtis, G. H., 1961

46. Koenigswald, G. H. R. von, Gentner, W., and Lippolt, H. J., 1961
47. Curtis, G. H., and Evernden, J. F., 1962
48. Straus, W. L., and Hunt, C. B., 1962
49. Napier, J., 1961
50. Leakey, L. S. B., 1951
51. Mason, R. J., 1961
52. Bishop, W. W., 1959
53. Kleindienst, M. R., 1962
54. Leakey, L. S. B., 1957 (a)
55. Robinson, J. T., 1960
56. Dahlberg, A. A., 1960
57. Leakey, L. S. B., 1951
58. Biberson, P., 1961 (b)
59. Leakey, L. S. B., Evernden, J. F., and Curtis, G. H., 1961
60. Mason, R. J., 1961
61. Leakey, L. S. B., 1951
62. Leakey, L. S. B., 1951
63. Oakley, K. P., 1958 (a)
64. Posnansky, M., 1959 (a)
65. Kleindienst, M. R., 1962
66. Clark, J. D., 1953
67. Clark, J. D., 1960
68. Bishop, W. W., 1962 (a)
69. Howell, F. C., et al, 1962
70. Clark, J. D., 1954 (b) and 1962 (a)
71. Howell, F. C., et al, 1962
72. Clark, J. D., 1959 (a)
73. Tobias, P. V., 1959
74. Clark, J. D., 1959 (b)
75. Tobias, P. V., 1960 and 1962
76. Lowe, C. van Riet, 1945
77. Movius, H. L., 1953
78. Shackleton, R. M., 1955
79. Clark, J. D., 1945 (a)
80. Leakey, L. S. B. and Owen, W. E., 1945
81. Breuil, H., and Lowe, C. van Riet, 1944
82. Lowe, C. van Riet, 1944
83. Caton-Thompson, G., 1947
84. Leakey, L. S. B., 1949
85. Janmart, J., 1953
86. Lowe, C. van Riet, 1952
87. Bishop, W. W., and Posnansky, M., 1960
88. Lowe, C. van Riet, 1952
89. Posnansky, M., 1962 (a)
90. Leakey, L. S. B., 1962 (b)
91. Posnansky, M., 1962 (a)
92. Clark, J. D., 1957 (b)
93. Posnansky, M., and Sekibengo, J. W., 1959
94. Mason, O. T., 1895
95. Stow, G. W., 1905
96. Tobias, P. V., 1959
97. Inskeep, R., 1962 (a)
98. Goodwin, A. J. H., 1946
99. Nash, T. A. M., 1929
100. Culwick, A. T., 1931
101. Fosbrooke, H. A., et al, 1950
102. Fosbrooke, H. A., et al, 1950
103. Clark, J. D., 1950
104. Wells, L. H., 1956 (b)
105. Wright, R., 1961
106. Breuil, H., 1934
107. Arkell, A. J., 1962 (c)
108. Lawrence, J. C. D., 1953
109. Posnansky, M., 1961 (c)
110. Heinzelin, J. de, 1957
111. Arkell, A. J., 1962 (b)
112. Caton-Thompson, G., 1946
113. Leakey, L. S. B., 1931
114. Oakley, K. P., 1961
115. Leakey, L. S. B., 1942
116. Greenberg, J. H., 1955 Posnansky, M., 1961 (b)
117. Lethbridge, T. C., 1952
118. Arkell, A. J., 1951
119. Hall, R. de Z., 1939
120. Arkell, A. J., 1962 (b)
121. Posnansky, M., and Sekibengo, J. W., 1959
122. Coghlan, H. H., 1943
123. Hiernaux, J., 1959
124. Robinson, K. R., 1961
125. Posnansky, M., 1961

126. Struck, I. B., 1922
127. Posnansky, M., 1962 (b)
128. Leakey, L. S. B., 1952 (b)
129. Huntingford, G. W. B., 1950
130. Wright, A. C., 1950
131. Shinnie, P. L., 1960
    Posnansky, M., 1962 (c)
132. Lanning, E. C., 1958 (a)
133. Lanning, E. C., 1960
134. Inskeep, R., 1962 (b)
135. Lanning, E. C., 1958 (b)
136. Wayland, E. J., Burkitt, M. C., and Braunholtz, H. J., 1933
137. Braunholtz, H. J., 1936
138. Posnansky, M., 1962 (c)
    Brachi, M., 1960
139. Clark, J. D., and Toerien, M. J., 1955
140. Lehmann, H., and Raper, A. B., 1949

Glossary

Acheulian Later and more evolved of the two stages of the Chelles-Acheul culture, characterized by hand axes; named after St. Acheul, France.

Acheulio-Levalloisian Culture recognized mainly in Somalia, which includes Acheulian-type hand axes and flake tools made by the Levalloisian or faceted-platform technique.

Alveolar arch Curve of the jaw containing the teeth, also known as dental arch.

Amazon stone Green microcline felspar.

Aritifact Any manmade object.

"Atlanthropus mauritanicus" Probably the same species as *Pithecanthropus erectus;* represented by jaws from Ternifine, Algeria, and Casablanca, Morocco.

Aurignacian Early Upper Paleolithic culture of Europe associated with Cro-Magnon Man and cave paintings.

Australopithecinae Subfamily of the family Hominidae; the earliest upright-walking, tool-making hominids, known mainly from South and East Africa.

Australopithecines Members of the subfamily Australopithecinae.

Australopithecus Genus of the subfamily Australopithecinae, represented by two species, *A. africanus* and *A. robustus.*

349

Axumite Period Period of the kingdom of Axum in Ethiopia, founded at least by the first century A.D.

Backed blade Blade blunted or backed on the side opposite the sharp edge by the removal of small flakes.

"Bacwezi" Legendary rulers of parts of Uganda before the establishment of present Bantu kingdoms in the fifteenth century A.D.

Bantu Negroids speaking Bantu languages spread over a large area of Africa (see Map 4).

Basalt A fine-grained, dark gray igneous rock representing a lava flow.

Biface Tool such as a hand ax or a point flaked on two surfaces.

Bigo culture An Iron Age culture associated with extensive earthworks in Uganda, named after Bigo, on the Katonga River.

Biotite Dark-colored mica.

Block-on-block technique Employed in manufacturing tools by swinging a lump of rock against a stone anvil; used extensively in the Clactonian culture of England but also in many early African cultures.

Bolas stones Stone balls in groups of three enclosed in skin bags attached together by thongs and used by Patagonian Indians to entwine in the legs of running animals; sometimes used to describe smooth-surfaced stone balls found with Acheulian and later African cultures, though there is no certain evidence that they were used as bolas.

Boskopoid Term applied to ancestral Bushman skulls of the type first recognized in a skull from Boskop, South Africa.

Brachycephalic A short, broad skull with cranial index greater than 81 per cent.

Burin Tool with a chisel end prepared by a special blow; probably used mainly for cutting grooves in wood and bone.

Burnish Smooth surface on pottery produced by smoothing the clay with a rounded object.

Capsian Mesolithic culture of North Africa characterized by blades, burins, and microliths; named after Gafsa (Latin: *Capsa*) in Tunisia.

Capsian, Kenya Culture known mainly from the Kenya Rift Valley and similar to the Capsian of North Africa.

Carbon–14 dating Method of absolute dating of material containing carbon of not more than 70,000 years old; based on the rate of radioactive decay of the isotope carbon–14.

Caucasoid Major division of mankind represented by "whites" or Europeans, but also by many peoples in Western Asia and India and by Hamitic-speaking and Semitic-speaking peoples in North and Northeast Africa; named after people in the Caucasus region.

Cephalic index Ratio of length to breadth of the head on a living subject, obtained by dividing breadth into length and expressing this as a percentage.

Channeled ware Earliest Iron Age pottery of the Rhodesias, decorated with grooves or channeling.

Chellean Earlier and less evolved stage of the Chelles-Acheul culture, characterized by crude hand axes; named after Chelles, France.

Chellean Man Represented by a skull from Bed II, Olduvai Gorge, Tanganyika, which was accompanied by Chellean hand axes; probably a species of *Pithecanthropus*.

Chelles-Acheul Lower Paleolithic hand-ax culture of Europe, Africa, and parts of Asia; named after Chelles and St. Acheul, France.

Cleaver Tool with one straight edge, shaped like an ax head, particularly characteristic of the Acheulian and probably used for chopping meat and skinning.

Coil technique Used in building up a pot with strips or coils of clay.

Condyles Bony projections joining the lower jaw with the upper jaw.

Cranial capacity Volume occupied by the brain expressed in cubic centimeters.

Cranial index Ratio of length to breadth on the skull, obtained by dividing breadth into length and expressing this as a percentage.

Cro-Magnon Man Tall, large-brained people associated with the Aurignacian culture of Europe, named after a site in the Dordogne, France.

Cromerian Interglacial First (Günz-Mindel) Interglacial of Europe, equivalent to the Aftonian Interglacial of North America, named after Cromer, Norfolk, England.

Culture Assemblage of artifacts occurring frequently together.

Cylinder-hammer technique Used in the Acheulian culture for removing shallow flakes in the manufacture of hand axes and other tools, which are believed to have been shaped with the side of a cylindrical "hammer" of bone or hard wood.

Diatomite White deposit composed of almost pure silica and made up of the skeletons of diatoms, microscopic, lake-living organisms.

Dimple-based pottery Associated with the earliest Iron Age culture of eastern and central Africa, so-called because the base often has a hollow; characterized by elaborate decoration of grooves, crosshatching, etc.

Doian Culture of southern Somalia characterized by microliths and pottery, named after the Somali word "*doi*," used to describe orange-colored sand.

Dolerite An igneous rock, coarser-grained than basalt.

Dolichocephalic Long, narrow skull with cranial index less than 75 per cent.

Dotted wavy-line pottery Pottery decorated with wavy lines and impressed dots characteristic of the Khartoum Mesolithic and of the Shaheinab Neolithic.

Earlier Stone Age Usually abbreviated to E.S.A., including cultures up to the end of the Chelles-Acheul and the African equivalent of the Lower Paleolithic of Europe.

Eemian Interglacial Third (Riss-Würm) Interglacial of Europe, equivalent to the Sangamon Interglacial of North America, named after River Eem, in the Netherlands.

Elmenteitan Culture known mainly from the Kenya Rift Valley; follows the Upper Kenya Capsian and is characterized by long, two-edged blades.

Elmenteitan type Represented by a skull from Bromhead's Site in the Kenya Rift Valley, ultra-dolichocephalic with a long face and narrow nose, a type common in Later Stone Age cultures of East Africa.

End scraper Scraper with small flakes removed at one end to form a jagged edge.

Eyasi Man Represented by fragmentary skulls from Lake Eyasi, Tanganyika, similar to that of Rhodesian Man.

Fabricator Tool used for manufacturing other implements.

Faceted-platform technique Based on the striking of flakes from a core previously prepared by making a platform with facets, used in many Middle Stone Age cultures.

Fault Fracture line along which rocks on one side are displaced relatively to those on the other.

Fauresmith· culture Culture of the First Intermediate Period following the Chelles-Acheul in South and East Africa, named after a site in South Africa.

Felspar or *feldspar* Minerals common in many rocks, composed largely of aluminum silicates.

Ferricrete Soil crust resulting from decomposition of rocks by weathering, composed of hydrated oxides of aluminium and iron; alternative name: laterite.

First Intermediate Period Period between the Earlier Stone Age and the Middle Stone Age in Africa, about 40,000 years ago.

Flake tool Any kind of tool made on a flake rather than a core.

Fluorine test Method of relative dating of bone based on the amount of fluorine contained in it.

Foramen magnum Hole at the base of the skull through which the spinal column passes into the brain.

Frankfurt plane Horizontal line passing through the lower margin of the eye socket and the upper margin of the ear passage, used for orientating skulls in measuring or drawing.

Frontal bone Bone forming the front of the skull or forehead.

Gamblian Fourth pluvial period distinguished in East Africa, dating from the Upper Pleistocene and named after deposits on the farm of a Mr. Gamble in the Kenya Rift Valley.

Gerontomorphic Exaggerated or "masculine" features of a skull, such as heavy brow ridges—as seen, for example, in the Rhodesioids.

Glabella Central and most forward point between the eyebrow ridges.

Göttweig Interstadial Warmer interval following the early part of the Würm Glaciation of Europe, about 45,000 B.C.

Great Interglacial Second (Mindel-Riss) Interglacial of Europe, also known as Hoxnian Interglacial, equivalent to Yarmouth Interglacial of North America.

Gumban A and B Variants of the Stone Bowl culture of the Kenya Rift Valley, named after the "Gumba," traditional inhabitants of the area before the arrival of the Kikuyu.

Günz Glaciation First main Pleistocene glaciation of the Alps, equivalent to the Nebraskan Glaciation of North America.

Hamites Inhabitants of northeastern Africa speaking Hamitic languages, members of the Caucasoid stock, though generally mixed with Negroids.

Hammerstone Stone used as a hammer in shaping a lump of rock in tool-making.

Hand ax Pear-shaped stone tool, pointed at one end, characteristic of the Chelles-Acheul culture.

Hargeisan Culture of northern Somalia characterized by blades and burins and named after the town of Hargeisa.

Hematite A reddish iron-oxide ore.

Hollow scraper Scraper with the jagged working edge in a concavity at the side.

Hominidae Family that includes the Australopithecines and extinct and modern forms of man.

Hominids Upright-walking, toolmaking members of the family Hominidae.

Homininae Subfamily of the family Hominidae, including extinct and modern forms of man but excluding the Australopithecines.

Hominoidea Superfamily of the suborder Anthropoidea, which includes apes and hominids.

Homo erectus Alternative name for *Pithecanthropus erectus* ("Java Man" and similar forms).

Homo neanderthalensis Neanderthal Man of the early Upper Pleistocene of Europe, Asia, and North Africa.

Homo rhodesiensis Rhodesian Man of the early Upper Pleistocene of

Africa, represented by a skull from Broken Hill, Northern Rhodesia, and similar forms.

Homo sapiens.   Modern man.

Homo soloensis   Solo Man of the early Upper Pleistocene of Java, rather similar to Rhodesian Man.

Hope Fountain   Formerly used to denote a culture, but now recognized to be a variant or occupation phase in various cultures, named after a site in Southern Rhodesia.

Hoxnian Interglacial   Second (Mindel-Riss) Interglacial of Europe, also known as the Great Interglacial, equivalent to Yarmouth Interglacial of North America, named after Hoxne, Suffolk, England.

Hyrax Hill   Earliest variant of the Stone Bowl culture, probably Neolithic, named after a site in the Kenya Rift Valley near Nakuru.

Igneous rocks   Rocks produced by consolidation of deep-seated molten fluids or magma.

Industry   Assemblage of artifacts at a particular site which may differ slightly from those of other sites, yet all such assemblages are sufficiently similar to be included in the same culture.

Interpluvial   Period when the rainfall was less than it is at present over a considerable time.

Ishangian   Mesolithic culture based on fishing named after Ishango, on the western shore of Lake Edward in the Congo; characterized by bone harpoons.

Kageran pluvial   First pluvial period distinguished in East Africa dated to the Lower Pleistocene, named after the Kagera River of Uganda; term now largely abandoned for lack of evidence of the existence of this pluvial.

Kaiso series   Lake deposits in the western rift in the Congo and Uganda containing fossil fauna, base of unknown age but deposits extend into the Lower Pleistocene; named after a village on Lake Albert.

Kamasian pluvial   Second pluvial period distinguished in East Africa and dated to the Middle Pleistocene; evidence of its existence has been disputed. Named after deposits of a former "Lake Kamasia" near the Kamasian escarpment of the Kenya Rift Valley.

Kanam stage   First Pleistocene faunal stage of East Africa, dated to the Lower Pleistocene; named after a site on the Kavirondo Gulf of Lake Victoria, western Kenya.

Kanjeran pluvial   Third pluvial period distinguished in East Africa and dated to the later part of the Middle Pleistocene (but is more probably early Upper Pleistocene); named after a site on the Kavirondo Gulf of Lake Victoria, western Kenya.

Kenya Capsian   See *Capsian, Kenya.*

Khartoum Mesolithic Culture based on fishing on the banks of the Nile at Khartoum, characterized by bone harpoons and "wavy-line" pottery.

Khoisan people Bushmen and Hottentots speaking languages with clicks and distinguished from other Negroids by yellowish skin, eye folds, peppercorn hair, and distinctive blood-group frequencies.

Kunkar Concretion of calcium carbonate formed under dry conditions.

Kush Kingdom of the Sudan which ruled Egypt as the Twenty-fifth Dynasty and which ceased to exist after 350 A.D. (alternative spelling: Cush).

Lacustrine Deposits formed in lakes.

Lame écaillée Tool showing signs of abrasion, used for the manufacture of other implements.

Lanet culture Associated with ironworking and dated to the sixteenth century A.D., named after a site in the Kenya Rift Valley near Nakuru.

Laterite Alternative name for *Ferricrete*, q.v.

Later Stone Age Usually abbreviated to L.S.A., stage following the Second Intermediate Period in Africa, beginning about 8000 B.C. (equivalent in time to the Mesolithic of Europe), and characterized by microlithic cultures.

Levalloisian A term sometimes used to describe a culture based on tools made from flakes with faceted platforms; also used to describe a technique known more properly as the *Faceted-platform technique*, q.v.

Limace Small implement pointed at both ends and flaked over one surface.

Lunate Small, crescent-shaped implement used for arrow barbs.

Lupemban Middle Stone Age culture following the Sangoan in the forested and steppe country of central Africa, characterized by lanceheads and *tranchets*.

Magosian Culture of the Second Intermediate Period, characterized by microliths, named after Magosi, a water hole in eastern Uganda.

Makalian First postpluvial wet phase lasting from about 5500 B.C. to 2500 B.C., named after the Makalia River in the Kenya Rift Valley.

Malar Cheekbone.

Mandible Lower jaw.

Mastoid process Bony knob situated behind the ear hole.

Maxilla One side of upper jaw.

"*Meganthropus africanus*" Name given to a jaw fragment from Laetolil, Lake Eyasi, Tanganyika, now generally considered to belong to the species *Australopithecus robustus*.

"*Meganthropus paleojavanicus*" Name given to a specimen from the Djetis beds, Java, which may be a species of *Australopithecus robustus*.

Meroitic Period of the kingdom of Meroë on the Nile, about 400 B.C. to 300 A.D., associated with ironworking.

Mesocephalic Skull of medium length with cranial index between 76 and 80.9 per cent.

Mesolithic Stage following the Paleolithic and implying a more settled way of life often based on fishing; the name means Middle Stone Age, but is not the equivalent of the M.S.A. of Africa.

Metamorphic Pre-existing rocks altered by heat and pressure into new forms.

Microliths Small tools of various kinds characteristic of Later Stone Age cultures.

Midden Heap of refuse.

Middle Stone Age Usually abbreviated to M.S.A., stage following the First Intermediate Period in Africa and beginning about 40,000 B.C., characterized by cultures which include many flake tools.

Mindel Glaciation Second main Pleistocene Glaciation of the Alps, equivalent to the Kansan Glaciation of North America.

Miocene Fourth period of the Tertiary era, lasting from about 25 to 14 million years ago.

Nachikufan Later Stone Age culture first recognized at the Nachikufu caves, Northern Rhodesia, where it is associated with rock paintings.

Nakuran Second postpluvial wet phase beginning about 850 B.C., named after Nakuru in the Kenya Rift Valley.

Nasion Central point at the top of the nasal bones.

Neolithic Stage based on food production, with the growing of vegetable or cereal crops and the keeping of domesticated animals; the name means "New Stone Age."

Obsidian Black or dark-colored volcanic glass common in the Kenya Rift Valley and used extensively for toolmaking.

Obsidian dating Method of absolute dating of obsidian artifacts depending on the thickness of an outer hydrated layer containing more water than the interior of the rock; effective range from about 50,000 to 2000 B.C.

Occipital Bone at the back of the skull.

Oldowan Earliest known culture, preceding the Chelles-Acheul, and probably made by the Australopithecines; characterized by simple choppers or "pebble tools" and named after Olduvai Gorge, Tanganyika.

Omo-Kanam stage First faunal stage formerly recognized in the Pleistocene of East Africa, dated to the Lower Pleistocene and named after sites in the Omo Valley, southern Ethiopia, and at Kanam in western Kenya.

Orbit Eye socket.

Paleolithic Stage of hunter-gatherers, lasting from the time of the first toolmaking hominids up to about 55,000 B.C. in Africa; the name means "Old Stone Age."

"Paranthropus" Genus of Australopithecines, now generally replaced by the name *Australopithecus robustus*.

Parietals Bones on either side of the skull, behind the frontal bone and above the temporal bones.

Pebble culture Equivalent to the Oldowan culture, preceding the Chelles-Acheul.

Pebble tool Crude chopping tool made by removing a few flakes to form a cutting edge at one end of a pebble or lump of rock.

Pedomorphic "Feminine" or infantile features retained by the adult, seen typically in skulls of Mongoloid peoples and Bushmen.

Perigordian Earliest Upper Paleolithic culture of France, named after the Perigord District.

Pithecanthropus Genus of extinct men which includes two species from Java, one from Peking, "Chellean Man" from Olduvai, and "*Atlanthropus*" of North Africa; alternative name: *Homo erectus*.

Pleistocene First period of the Quaternary era, beginning about 2 million years ago and ending about 8000 B.C.

Pliocene Last period of the Tertiary era, lasting from about 14 million to 2 million years ago.

Pluvial Period when the rainfall was greater than it is at present over a considerable time.

Pollen analysis Also known as palynology, the study of pollen grains to determine the nature of the vegetation at the time of formation of the deposits containing the pollen.

Polyhedral stones Stone spheres with facets, probably used mainly for pounding or as anvils, common in Acheulian and later cultures.

Pongidae Family that includes the apes or pongids.

Potassium-argon dating Method of absolute dating of rocks rich in potassium, based on the rate of disintegration of potassium-40 into calcium-40 and argon-40, applicable to rocks of more than about 400,000 years old.

Prepared-core technique Based on the preparation of a striking platform on a core from which flakes are removed, commonly used in Middle Stone Age cultures.

Pre-"Zinjanthropus" A hominid from a lower level of Bed I, Olduvai Gorge, than "*Zinjanthropus*."

Prognathism Protrusion of the upper jaw, particularly characteristic of Negroids.

Quartz Silica crystallized as a generally colorless mineral but sometimes colored by impurities.

Quartzite Metamorphic rock composed largely of quartz.

Radiocarbon dating See *Carbon-14 dating.*

Raised beach Strand line left above present sea level during an interglacial period when sea level was higher owing to increased volume of water contributed by melted ice.

Rhodesian Man *Homo rhodesiensis*, first named after a skull from Broken Hill, Northern Rhodesia, dating from the early part of the Upper Pleistocene; the African equivalent of Neanderthal Man.

Rhodesioids Type represented by Rhodesian Man, distinguished by heavy brow ridges and other gerontomorphic features.

Riss Glaciation Third main Pleistocene glaciation of the Alps, equivalent to the Illinoan Glaciation of North America.

Roulette decoration Decoration on pottery produced by rolling plaited grass over the wet clay.

Sabeans Inhabitants of western Arabia who founded the kingdom of Axum in Ethiopia before the first century A.D.

Saldanha Man One of the Rhodesioids, represented by a skull from Hopefield, near Saldanha Bay, Cape Province.

Sangoan Early Middle Stone Age culture of the forested and steppe country of central Africa, named after Sango Bay of Lake Victoria.

Scraper Stone tool with a jagged edge used for scraping skins and wood.

Second Intermediate Period Period between the Middle Stone Age and the Later Stone Age in Africa, from about 10,500 to 6500 B.C.

Sedimentary rocks Rocks composed of material originally laid down in water.

Semliki series Lake and river deposits of the western rift area in the Congo and Uganda containing Acheulian hand axes and attributed to the time of the Kanjeran pluvial.

Shaheinab Neolithic Earliest culture with evidence of domesticated animals in eastern Africa, characterized by stone gouges, bone axheads, and pottery with cuneiform impressions, named after a site on the Nile 30 miles north of Khartoum.

Sherd Fragment of pottery or potsherd.

Sickle-cell trait Abnormal hemoglobin resulting in the distortion of red blood cells into sickle-shaped forms when placed in a medium deficient of oxygen; particularly characteristic of Negroids living in malarial areas.

Side scraper Scraper with small flakes removed along one side to form a jagged edge.

Simian shelf Bony projection at the back of the symphysis of the lower jaw serving as a reinforcement; present in apes but not in hominids.

Steinheim skull Skull from Steinheim, Germany, with features reminiscent of *Homo sapiens* as well as Neanderthal Man, dating from the end of the Second (Mindel-Riss) Interglacial.

Stillbay Middle Stone Age culture of the eastern part of Africa characterized by leaf-shaped points.

Stone Bowl culture Culture of the Kenya Rift Valley characterized by stone bowls; the earliest variant is probably Neolithic, the later variants Iron Age.

Strand-loopers (or strand-lopers) People living along the seashore or lake shores, subsisting largely on shellfish.

S-twist ovate Oval-shaped hand ax with a sinuous cutting edge.

Sudd Swamps choked with papyrus on the Upper Nile.

Superciliary ridges Bony ridges above the eye sockets.

Supraorbital torus Heavy bar of bone forming a continuous ridge above the eye sockets; seen in many forms of early man and particularly marked in male gorillas.

Swanscombe skull Fragmentary skull from Swanscombe, Kent, England, rather similar to the Steinheim skull; associated with Acheulian hand axes and dated to the Second (Mindel-Riss) Interglacial.

Symphysis Area at the back of the chin where the two sides of the lower jaw meet.

"*Telanthropus*" Name given originally to a jaw fragment from Swartkrans, South Africa, but now considered to be a representative of *Homo erectus* (*Pithecanthropus*).

Temporal bones Bones on either side of the skull in the region of the temples.

Thumbnail scraper Small scraper the size of a thumbnail with a scraping edge at both ends, characteristic of the Wilton culture.

Torus Bony ridge for the attachment of muscles, as, for example, the supraorbital torus.

Tranchet Tool with a straight cutting edge produced by the intersection of two or more flake surfaces, probably used mainly for woodworking; characteristic of the Lupemban culture.

Tshitolian Later Stone Age culture of central Africa following the Lupemban and with similar tools, though generally smaller, and with the addition of tanged arrowheads.

Tuff Fine material ejected from a volcano into a lake and subsequently consolidated as a deposit.

Uranium test Method of establishing relative age of bones based on the amount of uranium they contain.

Victoria West Industry of the Acheulian culture characterized by side-struck flakes, named after a site in South Africa.

Villafranchian   Equivalent to the earlier part of the Lower Pleistocene and characterized by a particular fauna, named after Villafranca d'Asti, Italy.

Wavy-line pottery   Pottery decorated with wavy lines characteristic of the Khartoum Mesolithic.

Wilton   Later Stone Age culture of southern and eastern Africa beginning about 2000 B.C. and continuing up till recent times in some areas, often associated with cave paintings and probably made by ancestors of the Bushmen.

Würm Glaciation   Fourth and last main Pleistocene glaciation of the Alps, equivalent to Wisconsin Glaciation of North America.

Zeolite   Hydrated silicate of calcium and aluminium produced by alteration of other minerals and often occurring as a filling in cavities and fissures.

"*Zinjanthropus boisei*"   An Australopithecine from Bed I, Olduvai Gorge, Tanganyika, named after the ancient name for East Africa, Zinj, and after a Mr. Boise, who financed excavations; probably a representative of *Australopithecus robustus*.

Bibliography

Addison, F., *Jebel Moya*, Oxford, 1949.

Allison, A. C., "Blood Groups and African Prehistory," in Balout, L. (ed.), 1955, pp. 307–13.

Arambourg, C., "Contribution a l'étude géologique et paléontologique du Bassin du Lac Rodolphe et de la basse vallée de l'Omo," *Mission scientifique de l'Omo 1932–33*, fasc. 3, Paris, Mus. Hist. Nat., 1947.

—— "Les Mamminfères Pleistocène d'Afrique," *Bull. Soc. Geol. de France*, 17, 5 ser., 1947, p. 301.

—— "Récentes découvertes de paléontologie humaine réalisées en Afrique du Nord française," in Clark, J. D. (ed.), 1957, p. 186.

Arkell, A. J., "The Old Stone Age in the Anglo-Egyptian Sudan," *Sudan Antiquities Service Occ. Pap. No. 1*, 1949.

—— *Early Khartoum*, Oxford, 1949.

—— Review of "Excavations at Njoro River Cave," by M. D. and L. S. B. Leakey, *Antiquity*, 25, 1951, pp. 104–05.

—— *Shaheinab*, Oxford, 1953.

—— *A History of the Sudan to 1821*, London, 1955.

—— "Khartoum's part in the development of the Neolithic," *Kush*, 5, 1957, pp. 8–12.

—— "The Aterian and Great Wanyanga (Ounianga Kebir)," in Mortelmans, G. (ed.), 1962, pp. 233–42.

—— "The Distribution in Central Africa of One Early Neolithic Ware (Dotted Wavy-Line Pottery) and Its Possible Connection with the Beginning of Pottery," *ibid.*, pp. 283–88.

—— "The Petroglyphs of Wadi Zirmei in Northeastern Tibesti," *ibid.*, pp. 391–94.

—— Review of "The Prehistory of the Nile Valley and Its Connection with Surrounding Areas," on press.

Arundell, R. D. H., "Rock Paintings in Bukoba District," *Journ. Roy. Anthrop. Inst.*, 66, 1936, pp. 113–15.

Bagshawe, F. J., "Rock Paintings of the Kangeju Bushmen, Tanganyika." *Man*, 10, 1923.

Baker, B. H., "Geology of the Magadi Sheet," *Mem. Geol. Surv. Kenya*, Rpt. No. 42, 1958, pp. 1–81.

Bakker, E. M. van Z., "Carbon-14 Dates," *Current Anthropology*, 3, 1962, p. 218.

Balout, L. (ed.), *Congrès Panafricain de Préhistoire Actes de la IIᵉ Session, Alger, 1952*, Paris, 1955.

Bate, D. M. A., in *The Pleistocene Fauna of Two Blue Nile Sites*, London, British Museum Nat. Hist., 1951.

Bequaert, M., "Les fouilles de Jean Colette à Kalina," *Ann. du Mus. Congo Belge*, 1938.

—— "The Masaka Cylinder," *Uganda Journ.*, 13, 1949, pp. 23–30.

Bernard, E. A., "Les climats d'insolation des latitudes tropicales au Quaternaire," *Bull. de l'Acad. roy. des Sci. coloniales*, 5, 2, 1959, pp. 344–63.

—— "Interpretation astronomique des Pluviaux et Interpluviaux du Quaternaire africain," in Mortelmans, G. (ed.), 1962, pp. 67–93.

Biberson, P., *Le Cadre paléogéographique de la Préhistoire du Maroc Atlantique*, Service des Antiquités du Maroc, Rabat, 1961.

—— "Le Paléolithique Inférieur du Maroc Atlantique," *ibid.*

Bishop, W. W., "Miocene Mammalia from the Napak Volcanics, Karamoja, Uganda," *Nature*, 182, 1958, pp. 1480–82.

—— "Kafu Stratigraphy and Kafuan Artifacts," *S. Afr. Journ. Sci.*, 1959, pp. 117–21.

—— "A Review of the Pleistocene Stratigraphy of the Uganda Protectorate," *Proc. C.C.T.A. Joint Ctee. for Geol., Leopoldville 1958*, 1960, pp. 91–105.

—— "The Later Tertiary and Pleistocene in Eastern Equatorial Africa" (paper read at Wenner-Gren Foundation Symposium, Burg Wartenstein), on press.

—— "Pleistocene Correlation in the Uganda Section of the Albert-Edward Rift Valley," in Mortelmans, G. (ed.), 1962, pp. 245–52.

—— "A Summary of the Present Position Regarding Quaternary Stratigraphical Research in Uganda," *ibid*, pp. 209–14.

—— "The Mammalian Fauna and Geomorphological Relations of the Napak Volcanics, Karamoja," *Geol. Surv. Uganda*, Records 1957–58, 1962.

Bishop, W. W., and Posnansky, M., "Pleistocene Environments and Early Man in Uganda," *Uganda Journ.*, 24, 1960, pp. 44–61.

Bleek, D. F., "Traces of Former Bushman Occupation in Tanganyika," *S. Afr. Journ. Sci.*, 28, 1931, pp. 423–29.

Bond, G., "The Pleistocene Succession near Bulawayo," *Occ. Pap. Nat. Mus. S. Rhodesia*, 2, No. 12, 1946.

—— "Rhodesian Stone Age Man and His Raw Materials," *Bull. S. Afr. Arch. Soc.*, 3, 1948, pp. 55–60.

Brachi, M., "The Excavation of a Rock Shelter at Hippo Bay, Entebbe," *Uganda Journ.*, 24, 1960, pp. 62–71.

Brain, C. K., "New Evidence for the Correlation of the Transvaal Ape-Man-Bearing Cave Deposits," in Clark, J. D. (ed.), 1957, pp. 143–48.

Braunholtz, H. J., "The Luzira Head," *Man*, 92, 1936.

Breuil, H., "Peintures rupestres préhistoriques du Harar," *L'Anthropologie*, 44, 1934, pp. 473–83.

Breuil H. and Lowe, C. van Riet, "Le Paléolithique au Congo Belge, *Trans. Roy. Soc. S. Afr.*, 30, Pt. 2, 1944.

Brooks, C. E. P., *Climate through the Ages*, London, 1950.

Broom, R., and Schepers, G. W. H., *The South African Fossil Ape-Men: the Australopithecinae*, Transvaal Museum, Pretoria, Mem. No. 2, 1946.

Burkitt, M. C., *South Africa's Past in Stone and Paint*, Cambridge, 1928.

Burkitt, M. C., and Glover, P. E., "Prehistoric Investigations in British Somaliland, *Proc. Prehist. Soc.*, N.S. 12, 1946, pp. 49–56.

Butzer, K. W., "The Pleistocene sequence in Egypt and its implication for pluvial-glacial correlation in the Sahara," in Mortelmans, G. (ed.), 1962, pp. 133–39.

Caswell, P. V., "Geology of the Mombasa Kwale Area," *Geol. Surv. Kenya*, Rpt. No. 24, 1953.

Caton-Thompson, G., "The Levalloisian Industries of Egypt," *Proc. Prehist. Soc.*, N.S. 12, 1946, pp. 57–120.

—— "The Aterian Industry," *Roy. Anthrop. Inst.*, Huxley Memorial Lecture for 1946, 1947.

Caton-Thompson, G., and Gardner, E. W., *The Desert Fayum*, London, 1934.

—— *Kharga Oasis in Prehistory*, London, 1952.

Chittick, N., "Recent Discoveries in Tanganyika," in Mortelmans, G. (ed.), 1962, pp. 215–24.

Clark, D. L., "The Obsidian Dating Method," *Current Anthropology*, 2, 1961, pp. 111–14.

Clark, J. D., "A Kenya Fauresmith Factory and Home Site at Gondar, N. Abyssinia," *Trans. Roy. Soc. S. Afr.*, 31, 1945, pp. 19–27.

—— "Short Notes on Stone Age Sites at Yavello, S. Abyssinia," *Trans. Roy. Soc. S. Afr.*, 31, 1945, pp. 29–35.

—— *The Stone Age Cultures of Northern Rhodesia*, Claremont, Cape, 1950.

—— "New Light on Early Man in Africa," *Antiquity*, 27, 1953, pp. 242–43.

—— "A Provisional Correlation of Prehistoric Cultures North and South of the Sahara," *S. Afr. Arch. Bull.*, 9, 1954, pp. 3–15.

—— "An Early Upper Pleistocene Site at the Kalambo Falls on the Northern Rhodesia-Tanganyika Border," *S. Afr. Arch. Bull.*, 9, 1954, pp. 51–56.

—— *The Prehistoric Cultures of the Horn of Africa*, Cambridge, 1954.

—— (ed.), Third Pan-African Congress on Prehistory, Livingstone, 1955, London, 1957.

—— A Re-Examination of the Industry from the Type Site of Magosi, Uganda, *ibid.*, pp. 228–41.

—— "The Natural Fracture of Pebbles from the Batoka Gorge, Northern Rhodesia, and its Bearing on the Kafuan Industries of Africa," *Proc. Prehist. Soc.*, 24, 1958, pp. 64–77.

—— *The Prehistory of Southern Africa*, London, 1959.

—— "Further Excavations at Broken Hill, Northern Rhodesia," *Journ. Roy. Anthrop. Inst.*, 89, Pt. 2, 1959.

—— "Human Ecology During Pleistocene and Later Times in Africa South of the Sahara," *Current Anthropology*, 1, 1960, pp. 307–24.

—— "Sites Yielding Hominid Remains in Bed I, Olduvai Gorge," *Nature*, 189, 1961, pp. 903–04.

—— "The Kalambo Falls Prehistoric Site: An Interim Report," in Mortelmans, G. (ed.), 1962, pp. 195–202.

—— "Carbon-14 Chronology in Africa South of the Sahara," *ibid.*, pp. 303–14.

Clark, J. D., *et al*, "New Studies on Rhodesian Man," *Journ. Roy. Anthrop. Inst.*, 77, 1947, pp. 7–32.

Clark, J. D., and Toerien, M. J., "Human Skeletal and Cultural Material from a Deep Cave at Chipongwe, Northern Rhodesia," *S. Afr. Arch. Bull.*, 10, 1955, pp. 107–15.

Clark, W. E. Le Gros, "New Palaeontological Evidence Bearing on the Evolution of the Hominoidea," *Quart. Journ. Geol. Soc. London*, 105, 1950, pp. 225–64.

—— Letter to *New Scientist*, March 16, 1961.

Clark, W. E. Le Gros, and Leakey, L. S. B., *The Miocene Hominoidea of East Africa*, London, British Museum Nat. Hist., 1951.

Coghlan, H. H., "Evolution of the Axe from Prehistoric to Roman Times," *Journ. Roy. Anthrop. Inst.*, 73, 1943, pp. 27–56.

Cole, S., *An Outline of the Geology of Kenya*, London, 1950.

—— *The Prehistory of East Africa*, London, 1954.

—— "The Oldest Tool-Maker," *New Scientist*, 6, 1959, pp. 678–80.

—— "How Fast Did Man Evolve?" *New Scientist*, 11, 1961, pp. 208–10.

Cooke, H. B. S., "The Problem of Quaternary Glacio-Pluvial Correlation in East and Southern Africa," in Clark, J. D. (ed.), 1957, pp. 51–55.

—— "Observations relating to Quaternary environments in East and Southern Africa," *Geol. Soc. S. Afr. Bull.*, annexation to vol. 60, 1958.

—— "Further Revision of the Fossil Elephantidae of Southern Africa," *Palaeontologia Africana*, 7, 1960, pp. 46–57.

Coppens, Y., "Découverte d'un Australopithéciné dans le Villafranchien du Tchad," *C. R. Acad. Sci.*, Paris, 1961, pp. 3851–52.

Culwick, A. T., "Ritual use of rock paintings at Bahi," *Man*, 41, 1931.

Curle, A. T., "Prehistoric graves in the Northern Province of Kenya Colony," *Man*, 102, 1933.

Curtis, G. H., and Evernden, J. F., "Age of Basalt underlying Bed I, Olduvai," *Nature*, 194, 1962, p. 611.

Dahlberg, A. A., "The Olduvai Giant Hominid Tooth," *Nature*, 188, 1960, p. 962.

Davies, O., "African Pleistocene Pluvials and European Glaciations," *Nature*, 178, 1956, pp. 757–58.

Drennan, M. R., "A preliminary note on the Saldanha skull," *S. Afr. Journ. Sci.*, 50, 1953, pp. 7–11.

Ewer, R. F., "Faunal evidence on the dating of the Australopithecinae," in Clark, J. D. (ed.), 1957, pp. 135–42.

——— In Kurten, B., "The Dating of the Earliest Hominids," *Adv. Sci.*, 18, 1962, p. 490.

Flint, R. F., *Glacial Geology and the Pleistocene Epoch*, London, 1947.

——— "Pleistocene Climates in Eastern and Southern Africa," *Bull. Geol. Soc. Amer.*, 70, 1959, pp. 343–74.

——— "On the Basis of Pleistocene Correlation in East Africa," *Geol. Mag.*, 96, 1959, pp. 265–84.

Fock, G. J., "Stone Bowls from South West Africa," *S. Afr. Journ. Sci.*, 52, 1956, p. 165.

——— "Steinöpfe im Südliche Afrika," *Journ. der S. W. A. Wissenschaftlichen Gesellschaft*, Windhoek, 15, 1961, pp. 41–46.

Fosbrooke, H. A., "The engraved rocks of Kilimanjaro," *Man*, 244, 263, 1952.

——— "Early Iron Age Sites in Tanganyika Relative to Traditional History," in Clark, J. D. (ed.), 1957, pp. 318–25.

——— "Prehistoric Wells, Rainponds and Associated Burials in Northern Tanganyika," *ibid.*, 1957, pp. 326–35.

Fosbrooke, H. A., *et al*, "Tanganyika Rock Paintings: a Guide and Record," *Tanganykia Notes & Records*, Dar es Salaam, 1950.

Galloway, A., "The Nebarara skull," *S. Afr. Journ. Sci.*, 30, 1933, pp. 585–96.

Gardner, G. A., "Mapungubwe 1935–1940," *S. Afr. Arch. Bull.*, 10, 1955, p. 73.

Gillman, C., "An annotated list of ancient and modern indigenous stone structures in East Africa," *Tanganyika Notes & Records*, 1944, pp. 44–45.

Goodwin, A. J. H., "Exhibition of Prehistoric Art in S. Africa," *S. Afr. Assoc. of Arts*, 1946.

——— "Man and Climates in Africa," *Man*, 46, 1953.

Greenberg, J. H., *Studies in African Linguistic Classification*, New Haven, Conn., 1955.

Hall, R. de Z., "Pottery in Bugufi, Tanganyika Territory," *Man*, 132, 1939.

Heinzelin, J. de, "Les Fouilles d'Ishango," *Exploration du Parc National Albert*," fasc. 2, Bruxelles, Inst. des Parcs Nationaux du Congo Belge, 1957.

——— "Le Paléolithique aux Abords d'Ishango," *ibid.*, fasc. 6, 1961.

Hiernaux, J., "Recent Research at Protohistoric Sites in Ruanda in the Belgian Congo (Katanga Province) and in Uganda (Kibiro), *Uganda Mus. Occ. Pap.*, No. 4, 1959, pp. 26–31.

―――― "Cultures préhistoriques de l'age des métaux au Ruanda Urundi et au Kivu," *Acad. Roy. des Sci. d'Outre-mer*, 10, 1960, pp. 5–102.

―――― "Le début de l'Age des Métaux dans la région des Grands Lacs Africains," in Mortelmans, G. (ed.), 1962, pp. 381–90.

Higgs, E. S., "Some Pleistocene Faunas of the Mediterranean Coastal Areas," *Proc. Prehist. Soc.*, 27, 1961, pp. 144–54.

Hooijer, D. A., "Palaeontology of Hominid Deposits in Asia," *Adv. Sci.*, 18, 1962, pp. 485–89.

Hopwood, A. T., "The Olduvai Fauna," in Leakey, L. S. B., 1951.

Howell, F. C., "A preliminary note on a historic donga (Maclennan's Donga) in central Tanganyika," *S. Afr. Arch. Bull.*, 10, 1955, pp. 43–51.

―――― "Excavations at the Acheulian occupation sites of Isimila, Iringa highlands, southern Tanganyika," *Year Bk. Amer. Phil. Soc.*, 1959, pp. 481–85.

Howell, F. C. *et al*, "Isimila an Acheulian occupation site in the Iringa highlands, Southern Highlands Province, Tanganyika," in Mortelmans, G. (ed.), 1962, pp. 43–80.

Hoyle, F., Review of "Sir James Jeans" by E. A. Milne, *Sunday Times*, Nov. 23, 1952.

Huntingford, G. W. B., "The Azanian Civilization of Kenya," *Antiquity*, 7, 1933, pp. 153–65.

―――― "The Hagiolithic Culture of East Africa," *Eastern Anthropologist*, 3, 1950, pp. 119–36.

Huntingford, G. W. B., and Bell, C. R. V., *East African Background*, London, 1950.

Inskeep, R., "The age of the Kondoa rock paintings in the light of recent excavations at Kisese II Rock Shelter," in Mortelmans, G (ed.), 1962, pp. 249–56.

―――― "Recent developments in Iron Age studies in Northern Rhodesia and Nyasaland, *ibid.*, 1962, 351–56.

Janmart, J., *The Kalahari Sands of the Lunda (N. E. Angola)*, Museu do Dundo, Lisboa, 1953.

Jeffreys, M. D. W., "What are they?" *S. Afr. Arch. Bull.*, 10, 1955, p. 26.

Jones, D. H. (ed.), "History and Archaeology in Africa," *Rpt. of 2nd Conf. on African History and Archaeology* at S. O. A. S., London, 1959.

Jones, N., *The Prehistory of Southern Rhodesia*, Cambridge, 1959.

Jungraithmayr, H., "Rock Paintings in the Sudan," *Current Anthropology*, 2, 1961, p. 388.

Keith, A., *The Antiquity of Man*, 2nd ed., London and New York, 1931.

―――― *New Discoveries Relating to the Antiquity of Man*, London and New York, 1931.

Kent, P. E., "Pleistocene deposits near Lake Manyara, Tanganyika," *Geol. Mag.*, 79, 1942, pp. 72–77.

―――― "The Pleistocene Beds of Kanam and Kanjera," *ibid.*, pp. 117–32.

—— "Pleistocene Climates in Kenya and Abyssinia," *Nature*, 149, 1942, p. 736.

Kleindienst, M. R., "Variability within the Late Acheulian Assemblage in East Africa," *S. Afr. Arch. Bull.*, 16, 1961, pp. 35–48.

—— "Components of the East African Acheulian Assemblage: an Analytical Approach," in Mortelmans, G. (ed.), 1962, pp. 81–112.

Koenigswald, G. H. R. von, Gentner, W., and Lippolt, H. J., "Age of the Basalt Flow at Olduvai, East Africa," *Nature*, 192, 1961, pp. 720–21.

Kohl-Larsen, L., *Die Bildersrasse Ostafrikas*, Kassel, 1958.

Kurten, B., "The Dating of the Earliest Hominids," *Adv. Sci.*, 18, 1962, pp. 489–90.

Lanning, E. C., "Ancient Earthworks in W. Uganda," *Uganda Journ.*, 17, 1953, pp. 51–61.

—— "Masaka Hill," *Uganda Journ.*, 18, 1954, pp. 24–29.

—— "Mubende Hill," *Man*, 54, 1954.

—— "The Munsa Earthworks," *Uganda Journ.*, 19, 1955, pp. 177–82.

—— "Protohistoric Pottery in Uganda," in Clark, J. D. (ed.), 1957, pp. 313–17.

—— "A Burial Site at Mweya, Toro," *Uganda Journ.*, 22, 1958, pp. 170–172.

—— "The Identity of the Bachwezi," *ibid.*, 1958, p. 188.

—— "The Earthworks at Kibengo, Mubende District," *Uganda Journ.*, 24, 1960, pp. 183–96.

Lawrence, J. C. D., "Rock paintings in Teso and Bukedi," *Uganda Journ.*, 17, 1953, pp. 8–13.

—— *Ibid.*, 19, 1955, p. 90.

—— *Ibid.*, 22, 1958, pp. 39–42.

Leakey, L. S. B., *The Stone Age Cultures of Kenya Colony*, Cambridge, 1931.

—— "The status of the Kanam mandible and the Kanjera skulls," *Man*, 210, 1933.

—— *The Stone Age Races of Kenya*, Oxford, 1935.

—— *Stone Age Africa*, Oxford, 1936.

—— "A New Fossil Skull from Eyasi," *Nature*, 138, 1936, p. 1082.

—— "The Naivasha fossil skull and skeleton," *Journ. E. Afr. Nat. Hist. Soc.*, 16, 1942, pp. 169–77.

—— "Skull of Proconsul from Rusinga Island," *Nature*, 162, 1948, p. 688.

—— *Tentative Study of the Pleistocene Climatic Changes and Stone Age Culture Sequence in N. E. Angola*, Museu do Dundo, Lisboa, 1949.

—— *Olduvai Gorge*, Cambridge, 1951.

—— (Ed.), *Proceedings of the 1947 Pan-African Congress on Prehistory, Nairobi*, Oxford, 1952.

—— *Mau Mau and the Kikuyu*, London, 1952.

—— "Results of recent research in Kenya," *3rd Internat. Congr. Prehist. and Protohist. Sci., Zurich, 1950*, 1953, pp. 169–70.

—— *Adam's Ancestors*, 4th ed., London, 1953.

—— "The climatic sequence of the Pleistocene in Africa," in Balout, L. (ed.), 1955, p. 293.

—— "Preliminary Notes on a Survey of Prehistoric Art in Tanganyika," *ibid.*, p. 723.

—— "Preliminary Report on a Chellean I Living Site at BK. II, Olduvai Gorge, Tanganyika Territory," in Clark, J. D. (ed.), 1957, p. 217.

—— "Techniques of Recording Prehistoric Art," *ibid.*, p. 304.

—— "Recent Discoveries at Olduvai Gorge, Tanganyika," *Nature*, 181, 1958, pp. 1099–1103.

—— "A new fossil skull from Olduvai," *Nature*, 184, 1959, pp. 491–93.

—— "An alternative interpretation of the supposed giant deciduous hominid tooth from Olduvai," *Nature*, 185, 1960, p. 408.

—— "Recent discoveries at Olduvai Gorge," *Nature*, 188, 1960, pp. 1050–1051.

—— "New finds at Olduvai Gorge," *Nature*, 189, 1961, pp. 649–50.

—— "A New Lower Pliocene Fossil Primate from Kenya," *Ann. and Mag. Nat. Hist.*, 4, 13th ser., 1962, pp. 689–96.

—— Discussion in Mortelmans, G. (ed.), 1962, p. 310.

Leakey, L. S. B., and Owen, W. E., "A contribution to the study of the Tumbian culture in East Africa," *Coryndon Mus. Occ. Pap.* No. 1, Nairobi, 1945.

Leakey, L. S. B., and Reeve, W. H., "Report on a visit to the site of the Eyasi skull," *Journ. E. Afr. Nat. Hist. Soc.*, 19, 1946, pp. 40–50.

Leakey, L. S. B., and Clark, W. E. le Gros, "British-Kenya Miocene Expeditions, *Nature*, 175, 1955, p. 234.

Leakey, L. S. B., Evernden, J. F., and Curtis, G. H., "The Age of Bed I, Olduvai Gorge, Tanganyika, *Nature*, 191, 1961, p. 478.

Leakey, L. S. B., *et al*, "Age of Basalt underlying Bed I, Olduvai," *Nature*, 194, 1962, pp. 610–12.

Leakey, M. D., "Notes on the Ground and Polished Stone Axes of East Africa," *Journ. E. Afr. Nat. Hist. Soc.*, 17, 1943.

Leakey, M. D., and Leakey, L. S. B., "Report on the excavations at Hyrax Hill, Nakuru, Kenya Colony," *Trans. Roy. Soc. S. Afr.*, 30, 1945, pp. 271–409.

—— *Excavations at the Njoro River Cave*, Oxford, 1950.

Leakey, M. D., Owen, W. E., and Leakey, L. S. B., "Dimple-based pottery from Central Kavirondo," *Coryndon Mus. Occ. Pap.* No. 2, Nairobi, 1948.

Lehmann, H., and Raper, A. B., "Distribution of the Sickle-cell Trait in Uganda," *Nature*, 164, 1949, p. 494.

Lethbridge, T. C., *Boats and Boatmen*, London, 1952.

Loncarevic, B. D., and Matthews, D. H., "Geophysical Reconnaissance of the Arabian Sea," *New Scientist*, 14, 1962, pp. 513–15.

Lowe, C., van Riet, "Notes on Dr. Francis Cabu's Collection of Stone Implements from the Belgian Congo," *Trans. Roy. Soc. S. Afr.*, 30, 1944, pp. 169–74.

—— "The Evolution of the Levallois Technique in South Africa," *Man*, 37, 1945.

—— "A new African Acheul stage IV site in Tanganyika," *S. Afr. Arch. Bull.*, 6, 1951, pp. 94–98.

—— "The Pleistocene Geology and Prehistory of Uganda—Part II (Prehistory)," *Geol. Surv. Uganda*, Mem. No. VI, 1952.

Martin, H., *The Sheltering Desert*, London, 1957.

Mason, O. T., *The Origins of Invention*, London, 1895.

Mason, R. J., "The Acheulian Culture in South Africa, *S. Afr. Arch. Bull.*, 16, 1961, pp. 107–10.

Matthews, L. H., "A new development in the conservation of African animals," *Adv. Sci.*, 18, 1962, p. 581.

Mayr, E., "Taxonomic categories in fossil hominids," in *Cold Spring Harbor Symposia on Quantitative Biology*, 15, 1950, p. 112.

McBurney, C. B. M., *The Stone Age of Northern Africa*, London, 1960.

—— "Absolute chronology of the Palaeolithic in Eastern Libya," *Adv. Sci.*, 18, 1962, pp. 494–97.

Menghin, O., "Die Tumbakultur an unteren Kongo," *Anthropos*, 20, 1925, pp. 516–57.

Montagu, M. F. A., "A Consideration of the Concept of Race," *Cold Spring Harbor Symposia on Quantitative Biology*, 15, 1950, p. 317.

Mortelmans, G., "Le Quaternaire de l'Afrique Sud-Equatoriale," *III*ᵉ *Congrès Nat. des Sci.*, Bruxelles, 1950.

Mortelmans, G., and Nenquin, J. (eds.), *Actes du IV*ᵉ *Congrès Panafricain de Préhistoire (Leopoldville 1959)*, Tervuren, 1962.

Mourant, A. E., *The Distribution of the Human Blood Groups*, Oxford, 1954.

Movius, H. L., "Old World Prehistory: Palaeolithic," in Kroeber, A. L. (ed.), *Anthropology Today*, Chicago, 1953, p. 170.

—— "Radiocarbon Dates and Upper Palaeolithic Archaeology in Central and Western Europe," *Current Anthropology*, 1, 1960, pp. 355–87.

Moysey, F., and Leakey, L. S. B., "Excavation of a rock shelter at Gorgora, Lake Tana, Ethiopia," *Journ. E. Afr. Nat. Hist. Soc.*, 17, 1943, pp. 196–203.

Napier, J., *Fossil metacarpals from Swartkrans*, British Museum Nat. Hist., London, 1959.

—— "Human Origins," *Lancet*, vol. II for 1961, pp. 767–68.

Napier, J., and Davis, P. R., *The Fore-limb Skeleton and Associated Remains of Proconsul Africanus*, British Museum Nat. Hist., London, 1959.

Napier, J., and Weiner, J. S., "Olduvai Gorge and Human Origins," *Antiquity*, 36, 1962, pp. 41–47.

Nash, T. A. M., "Note on the discovery of some rock paintings near Kondoa Irangi in Tanganyika Territory," *Journ. Roy. Anthrop. Inst.*, 59, 1929, pp. 199–206.

Nilsson, E., "Ancient changes of climate in British East Africa and Abyssinia," *Geol. Ann.* 1–2 (No. 50 *Medd. Stock. Hog. Geol. Inst.*), Stockholm, 1940.

—— "Pleistocene climatic changes in East Africa," in Leakey, L. S. B. (ed.), 1952, pp. 45–54.

Oakley, K. P., in Clark, J. D. *et al*, "New Studies on Rhodesian Man," *Journ. Roy. Anthrop. Inst.*, 77, 1947, pp. 7–10.

—— *Man the Tool-maker*, 3rd ed., British Museum Nat. Hist., London, 1956.

—— "The Dating of the Broken Hill, Florisbad and Saldanha skulls," in Clark, J. D. (ed.), 1957, pp. 76–79.

—— "Dating the Australopithecines, *ibid.*, pp. 155–57.

—— "Tools makyth Man," *Antiquity*, 31, 1957, pp. 199–208.

—— "Physical Anthropology in the British Museum," in Roberts, D. F., and Weiner, J. S. (eds.), "The Scope of Physical Anthropology and its place in Academic Studies," *Soc. for the Study of Human Biology & Wenner-Gren* Foundation, 1958, pp. 51–54.

—— "Dating the Stages of Hominoid Evolution," *The Leech*, 28, Nos. 3–5, 1958.

—— "The Kanam Jaw," *Nature*, 195, 1960, pp. 945–46.

—— "Bone Harpoon from Gamble's Cave, Kenya," *Antiquaries Journ.*, 41, 1961, pp. 86–87.

—— "Dating the Emergence of Man," *Adv. Sci.*, 18, 1962, pp. 415–25.

—— "The Earliest Tool-makers," in Kurth, G. (ed.), *Evolution and Hominisation*, Stuttgart, 1962, pp. 157–69.

O'Brien, T. P., *The Prehistory of Uganda Protectorate*, Cambridge, 1939.

Owen, W. E., "The Kombewa culture, Kenya Colony," *Man*, 218, 1938.

Pearce, S. V., (unpublished), "The Appearance of Iron and its use in Proto-historic Africa," *Thesis for M.A. Degree, Univ. of London*, 1960.

Pickering, R., A Preliminary Note on the Quaternary Geology of Tanganyika, *Proc. C. C. T. A. Joint Ctee. Geol., Leopoldville, 1958*, 1960, pp. 77–89.

Posnansky, M., "A Hope Fountain Site at Olorgesailie, Kenya Colony," *S. Afr. Arch. Bull.*, 14, 1959, pp. 83–89.

—— "Progress and Prospects in Historical Archaeology of Uganda," *Uganda Mus. Occ. Pap.* No. 4, 1959, pp. 31–38.

—— "Dimple-based Pottery from Uganda," *Man*, 168, 1961.

—— "Bantu Genesis," *Uganda Journ.*, 25, 1961, pp. 86-92.

—— "Rock Paintings on Lolui Island, Lake Victoria," *ibid.*, pp. 105–10.

—— "Recent Palaeolithic discoveries in Uganda," in Mortelmans, G. (ed.), 1962, pp. 207–12.

—— "The Neolithic Cultures of East Africa," *ibid.*, pp. 273–82.

—— "Some archaeological aspects of the Ethnohistory of Uganda," *ibid.*, pp. 375–80.

Posnansky, M., and Sekibengo, J. W., "Ground Stone Axes and Bored Stones in Uganda," *Uganda Journ.*, 23, 1959, pp. 179–81.

Rawoski, R. F., "On a collection of Neolithic axes and celts from the Welle Basin, Belgian Congo," *Journ. Roy. Anthrop. Inst.*, 51, 1921, p. 154.

Robinson, J. T., "An alternative interpretation of the supposed giant deciduous hominid tooth from Oldvuai," *Nature*, 185, 1960, pp. 407–8.

—— "The Australopithecines and their bearing on the origin of Man and of stone tool-making," *S. Afr. Journ. Sci.*, 57, 1961, pp. 3–13.

Robinson, J. T., and Mason, R. J., "Occurrence of Stone Artifacts with Australopithecines at Sterkfontein," *Nature*, 180, 1957, pp. 521–24.

Robinson, K. R., "A Note on Hollow-based Pottery from Southern Rhodesia," *Man*, 105, 1961.

Rubin, M., and Suess, H. E., "U. S. Geological Survey Radiocarbon Dates III," *Science*, 123, 1955, pp. 442–48.

Seligman, C. G., *The Races of Africa*, 3rd ed., London, 1957.

Shackleton, R. M., "Pleistocene Movements in the Gregory Rift Valley," *Geol. Rundschau*, 43, 1955, pp. 257–63.

Shinnie, P., "Excavations at Bigo, Uganda," *Antiquity*, 33, 1959, pp. 55–57.

—— "Excavations at Bigo 1957," *Uganda Journ.*, 24, 1960, p. 16.

Simons, E. L., "The Phyletic Position of Ramapithecus," *Postilla*, Yale Peabody Mus. No. 57, 1961.

Simpson, G. C., "Possible causes of change in climate and their limitations," *Proc. Linnaean Soc. London*, 152, 1940, pp. 190–219.

—— "Further studies in world climate," *Quart. Journ. Roy. Meteorol. Soc.*, 83, 1957, pp. 459–85.

—— "World temperatures during the Pleistocene," *ibid.*, 85, 1959, pp. 332–49.

Singer, R., "Investigations at the Hopefield site," in Clark, J. D. (ed.), 1957, pp. 175–82.

Smolla, G., "Prähistorische Keramik aus Ostafrika," *Tribus*, Linden Mus., Stuttgart, 6, 1957, pp. 35–59.

—— "Steingeräte vom Tendaguru," in Mortelmans, G. (ed.), 1962, pp. 243–48.

Stow, G. W., *The Native Races of South Africa*, London, 1905.

Straus, W. L., and Hunt, C. B., "Age of Zinjanthropus," *Science*, 136, 1962, pp. 293–95.

Struck, I. B., "Versuch einer Karte des Kopfindex im mittleren Afrika," *Zeitschrift für Ethnologie*, 45, 1922, pp. 51–113.

Threlfall, B. A., "Some Physical Features of the Dar es Salaam District," *Tanganyika Notes & Records* No. 29, 1950.

Tobias, P. V., "Some developments in South African Physical Anthropology 1938–1958," Epilogue in Galloway, A., *The Skeletal Remains of Bambandyanalo*, Johannesburg, 1959, pp. 129–54.

—— "The Kanam Jaw," *Nature*, 185, 1960, pp. 946–47.

—— "A Re-Examination of the Kanam Mandible," in Mortelmans, G. (ed.), 1962, pp. 341–58.

Toit, A. L., du, "Palaeolithic environments in Kenya and the Union—a contrast," *S. Afr. Arch. Bull.*, 2, 1947, p. 6.

Trevor, J. C., "The physical characters of the Sandawe," *Journ. Roy. Anthrop. Inst.*, 77, 1947, pp. 61–78.

Trowell, M., "A Rosette Cylinder of Clay from Uganda," *Man*, 100, 1945.

—— "The Rosette Cylinder from Ntusi," *Uganda Journ.*, 10, 1946, p. 151.

Wayland, E. J., "The Magosian Culture of Uganda," *Journ. Roy. Anthrop. Inst.*, 62, 1932, p. 369.

—— "Rifts, Rivers, Rains and Early Man in Uganda," *ibid.*, 64, 1934, pp. 333–52.

———— "Notes on the Biggo bya Mugenyi," *Uganda Journ.*, 2, 1934, pp. 21–32.

———— "Note on a prehistoric 'inscription' in Ankole, Uganda," *Uganda Journ.*, 5, 1938, p. 252.

———— "The study of past climates in tropical Africa," in Leakey, L. S. B. (ed.), 1952, pp. 59–65.

Wayland, E. J., *et al*, "Archaeological Discoveries at Luzira," *Man*, 29, 1933.

Weiner, J. S., "The Pattern of Evolutionary Development of the Genus Homo," *S. Afr. Journ. Med. Sci.*, 23, 1958, pp. 111–20.

———— "Blood-group investigations on Central Kalahari Bushmen," *Nature*, 183, 1959, p. 843.

———— "The East African fossil men," *New Scientist*, 10, 1961, pp. 534–36.

Wells, L. H., "The Fossil Human Skull from Singa, in *The Pleistocene Fauna of Two Blue Nile Sites*, British Museum Nat. Hist., London, 1951.

———— "Human crania of the M. S. A. in South Africa," in Leakey, L. S. B. (ed.), 1952, pp. 125–32.

———— "The Place of the Broken Hill Skull among Human Types," in Clark, J. D. (ed.), 1957, pp. 172–74.

———— "Late Stone Age human types in Central Africa," *ibid.*, pp. 183–85.

Whitworth, T., "A Contribution to the Geology of Rusinga Island, Kenya," *Quart. Journ. Geol. Soc. London*, 109, 1953, pp. 75–96.

Wilson, G. E. H., "The ancient civilization of the Rift Valley," *Man*, 298, 1932.

Wright, A. C., Review of "The Zimbabwe-Monomotopa Culture in S. E. Africa" by H. A. Wieschhoff, *Uganda Journ.*, 14, 1950, pp. 111–14.

Wright, R., "A Painted Rock Shelter on Mount Elgon, Kenya," *Proc. Prehist. Soc.*, 27, 1961, pp. 28–34.

Zeuner, F. E., "Climate and Early Man in Kenya," *Man*, 14, 1948.

———— *Dating the Past*, 3rd. ed., London, 1952.

Index of Individuals

Index of Localities

General Index

About The Author

Sonia Cole studied geology at University College in London. After joining the A. T. S. during World War II, she went to Kenya in 1945 with her husband and children. For the following five years Mrs. Cole traveled extensively in East Africa, joining Dr. L. S. B. Leakey on numerous geological and archaeological expeditions organized by the Coryndon Museum (in Nairobi), of which Dr. Leakey was the curator. She collected on Rusinga Island and worked also at Olorgesailie, an important living site of hand-ax man.

Mrs. Cole is a member of the Council of the Royal Anthropological Institute. Since her return to England in 1950, she has been engaged mostly in literary and editorial work and has written, among other books, *An Outline of the Geology of Kenya, Counterfeit, The Neolothic Revolution,* and *The Races of Man.*